D1525526

HARLEQUIN BRITAIN

Harlequin Britain

PANTOMIME AND ENTERTAINMENT, 1690–1760

John O'Brien

THE JOHNS HOPKINS UNIVERSITY PRESS
Baltimore and London

The Johns Hopkins University Press
2715 North Charles Street
Baltimore, Maryland 21218-4363
www.press.jhu.edu

LIBRARY OF CONGRESS CATALOGING-IN-PUBLICATION DATA

O'Brien, John, 1962–
   Harlequin Britain : pantomime and entertainment, 1690–1760 / John
O'Brien
      p. cm.
Includes bibliographical references and index.
   ISBN 0-8018-7910-8 (alk. paper)
   1. Pantomime—Great Britain—History—18th century.
2. Pantomime—Great Britain—History—17th century. I. Title.
   PN1987.G7O27 2004
   792.3′8′09033—dc22

                                                       2003021417

A catalog record for this book is available from the British Library.

For Vicki

CONTENTS

ILLUSTRATIONS

ACKNOWLEDGMENTS

*L*ike any performance, this book is in the end a collaboration, and has been shaped by the input and support of readers, friends, and institutions. The institutions first. The Interdisciplinary Group for Historical Literary Studies at Texas A & M University provided an unmatched environment for pursuing a project like this, and provided the forums in which I was able to present very early versions of the material in this book. Long may it prosper in its new institutional form as the Melbern G. Glasscock Center for Humanities Research.

This project gained its primary focus on eighteenth-century pantomime in the course of a summer spent at the Huntington Library in 1997, an excursion made possible by a Fletcher Jones Fellowship from the Huntington. The Office of the Vice-President for Research at the University of Virginia and the American Council of Learned Societies provided fellowship funds that enabled me to devote the entirety of the 2000–2001 academic year to thinking, writing, and rewriting. The Department of English and the Committee on Summer Grants at the University of Virginia provided funds that helped at crucial moments. My research assistant, Andy Jones, helped locate the archives where the images reproduced in this book were located.

The research for this book was done at many different libraries, and I want in particular to thank the librarians, curators, and staff at the Huntington Library, the British Library, the British Museum, the Newberry Library, the Ransom Center at the University of Texas, and the Alderman Library at the University of Virginia. Other archives have also provided illustrations for this book, including the Theatre Museum, London, the Harvard Theatre

Collection, the Houghton Library, and the Duke University Library; my thanks to the staffs at all of these archives for their prompt and professional help. Some components of chapters 1, 4, and 7 appeared, in a rather different form, in the December 1998 issue of *Theatre Journal;* I want to thank the journal for permission to reprint.

I owe special thanks to the many people who have generously read this book in whole or in part: Jeffrey Cox, Margaret Ezell, Howard Marchitello, Robert Markley, Patricia Spacks, Ralph Cohen, Jim Chandler, Paul Hunter, Cynthia Wall, David Vander Meulen, and Greg Colomb. Their advice, encouragement, and prodding have not only focused the book's argument but helped me find ways to frame and shape its object of study. The anonymous reader for the Johns Hopkins University Press gave excellent advice, enabling me to accomplish a final set of revisions that sharpened the book as a whole. Audiences at the American Society for Eighteenth-Century Studies annual meeting in New Orleans in 2001, the DeBartolo Conference in Tampa in 2003, and the colloquium on "Bodies, Voices, Performance" at the Center for Humanities and the Arts at the University of Colorado in Boulder in 2003 provided valuable feedback on earlier versions of several chapters. Friends like Maureen McLane, Lynne Vallone, Franny Nudelman, David Holton, Marion Rust, Lou Bograd, Eric Lott, and Lisa Freeman have provided intellectual advice and moral support. Many years ago, my parents endorsed my decision to pursue an academic career, and it gives me pleasure to thank them for their support, advice, and encouragement now that that pursuit has, at long last, taken material form in this book.

Finally, I owe a debt larger than I can put into words to Vicki Olwell, whose critical eye has improved every page of this book, and whose love has enriched the time during which it was composed. This book is dedicated, with love, to her.

Entertainments and Modernity

*D*iversion is a very old human activity, but entertainment in the way that we now understand it is comparatively new. The modern conception of entertainment as a form of diversion directed to a mass culture began in the first half of the eighteenth century in Britain. This book is about a discourse where that conception became most apparent: the extensive public debate over the theatrical form known as "pantomime." This mode of performance, which fused Continental commedia dell'arte characters, classical mythology, dance, opera, acrobatics, and farce, took its name from silent dance performances of the classical world but would come to be considered a characteristically British form. Harlequin, the commedia dell'arte character who became the central figure of eighteenth-century English pantomime, put a name and a face on the moment when entertainment in the modern sense became intelligible as such.[1]

That last claim puts a premium on the way this book defines both modernity and entertainment, neither of which is a straightforward or uncontested concept. My emphasis on the *modernity* of pantomime is intended to indicate the many things that the eighteenth-century discourse about pantomime and contemporary debates over the propriety of diversions—television, movies, the Internet—have in common. For example, both share a considerable level of anxiety about works and performances that seem to have no higher purpose than sensual gratification. And that anxiety frequently derives from a considerable concern about the effects of such entertainments on the audience, which since the eighteenth century has frequently been figured as a faceless, unpredictable, and ungovernable mass, a collectivity whose responses to what is placed before it can be neither predicted nor controlled. Eighteenth-century observers of the theater remembered (with the rose-tinted glasses of nostalgia) how the Restoration theater was dominated by a court coterie whose values and tastes, however questionable, were at least shared and knowable. These observers sometimes took the theater that developed after the turn of the eighteenth century to be a degraded institution because of the greater democratization of the audience. In so doing, they were also in effect mourning the passing of the more face-to-face world of the past, a world that was in the process of being replaced by an anonymous, urban society dominated by commerce. That society was not just like ours, to be sure, but it has important continuities with our own, continuities that make it a relevant object of study for anyone who wants to understand the geneal-ogy of contemporary debates about entertainment. Perhaps most important, early eighteenth-century Britons frequently described themselves as living in a "modern" period, a time that had decisively broken with what they some-times referred to as the "last age," frequently described as the period before the Interregnum and the English Civil War. Because the London theater, as everyone knew, had been closed during this period, it served as a potent sym-bol of the difference between the present and a past that was conceived *as* past, as a time existing on the other side of an historical breach that gave birth to a more modern culture. Britons experienced modernity as the product of political and cultural revolutions that led them to think that their own era was different in kind from a traditional, rural society.

Entertainment poses a still more complicated case. Then and now, enter-tainment had multiple meanings and implications; there is a sense in which entertainment does not so much specify a single entity as identify a set of ever-shifting relationships: between high and low culture, between the insti-tution of the theater and the audience, between performer and spectator. The word does not have a stable and singular definition; rather, it needs to be understood as the name we have come to give to certain kinds of inter-action between a performance and those present to see, hear, or read it. The eighteenth century frequently used entertainment in a sense still familiar to us, to identify cultural productions intended primarily as diversions—works or performances that seem to make no greater claim than to be gratifying current tastes. But the eighteenth-century use of the word *entertainment* was more complex than our own, with ramifications into broader areas of the culture and the psyche.

When printed on a theatrical program, for example, "entertainment" des-ignated a specific class of performances, most particularly afterpieces, which were in this way distinguished from the five-act mainpiece dramas that they followed. Thus pantomimes were typically referred to as "entertainments," and indeed, according to Henry Fielding, by the 1730s the two terms had in some contexts become synonymous owing to pantomime's enormous success.[2] By implication, such performances were understood to be intended for diversion rather than for moral uplift, to be less serious than the plays that constituted the mainpiece repertory; the adjective *mere* frequently seems implied. The word also was used in what was already a slightly archaic sense to designate a kind of meal, particularly one put on for guests. In his 1731 play *The London Merchant,* George Lillo deliberately uses this sense of the term as a way of marking the play's setting in the Elizabethan England of a century and a half earlier. Lillo's anachronism, as I will argue at greater length in chapter 5, counters the modern sense of entertainment as a diversion by reminding auditors of a residual understanding of the concept. The meaning of entertainment as a meal also had, by the early eighteenth century, broadened to encompass a relationship of internal sustenance as well, as it described a form of mentation, the engagement of the cognitive apparatus as it contemplates data drawn in by the senses. In the eighteenth century, entertainment was a keyword with several core meanings and numerous associations, the proliferation of which testifies to its significance to a culture that used the term to designate crucial relationships that were both hierarchical (between literature and mere entertainment, for example) and lateral (between the observer and the spectacle).

Because I am interested not only in pantomime but in the effect it had on the eighteenth century's habits for understanding its own culture, I will frequently call upon the concept that we have learned to call, following the lead of Jürgen Habermas, the "bourgeois public sphere."[3] Habermas's notion of the public sphere is protean in its own right, but he defines its most significant meaning as "a realm of our social life in which something approaching public opinion can be formed."[4] Habermas's construct is particularly germane to the early eighteenth-century British theater, in part because of his emphasis on the constitutive role of print. On the one hand, the lifting of prior censorship with the lapse of the Press Licensing Act in 1695 created new venues for theatrical criticism, and periodicals like the *Gentleman's Journal* (1692–94), *The Tatler,* and *The Spectator* made the theater into an object of discourse, critiquing texts, performances, and the institution as a whole. On the other hand, antitheatrical writers now had a means of disseminating their opinions more broadly than ever before, a fact that was made clear in the controversy over the London theater catalyzed by Jeremy Collier, whose

A Short View of the Immorality and Prophaneness of the English Stage initiated
a deluge of printed works attacking and defending the theater, constituting a
public controversy that could not have achieved the same scope and intensity
before 1695. Such transformations in media have a habit of altering the
objects that they purport merely to describe, and the London theater was no
different; subjected to the critical scrutiny and reformist impulses unleashed
by the expansion of print, the theater became a different institution than it
once had been. It was public in a new sense, subject to critique, debate, and
attack in a way that had not been possible before.

The early eighteenth-century British theater also offers an excellent case
study in how the ideal of the bourgeois public sphere is continually beset by
forces that seek to undermine it. In its ideal form, the bourgeois public
sphere emerged in the late seventeenth and early eighteenth centuries as a
counter to the court and the absolutist state, as it challenged the court's
monopoly over information and cultural authority. But in Habermas's
account, the bourgeois public sphere was also quickly threatened by the
emergence of the bureaucratic state apparatus, which could impose censorship, and by the growing power of the capitalist market system, which
seemed to wish to hijack the public sphere to its own interests. In many
respects, the history of the eighteenth-century British theater followed the
course that might have been predicted by this model. Nominally still linked
to the court (its legal authority derived from letters patent issued by Charles
II at the Restoration), the theater found its relationship to the monarchy to
be increasingly attenuated. But it was confronted with the power of the state
in a new form in 1737, when the government of Sir Robert Walpole imposed
prior censorship in the form of the Stage Licensing Act. Meanwhile, there
can be no doubt that the London theater was powerfully influenced by the
marketplace; the theaters were run as money-making ventures, and one of
the persistent complaints levied against their managers was that they were
putting the profit motive ahead of their responsibility to uplift the nation.
The theater is an exemplary public-sphere institution in its Janus-faced relationship to the very modernity that brought the public sphere into being;
liberated from dependence on the feudal state, it quickly found itself challenged by more subtle forms of power that threatened it with banalization
and irrelevance.[5]

To complement Habermas's framework, I have also drawn upon Michel
Foucault's account of the science that he called "governmentality." The concept has been most succinctly described by Mitchell Dean as the "conduct of
conduct," the effort on the part of the state to predict, assess, measure, guide,

and regulate the behavior of its citizens.[6] Here Foucault sees the state operating not just in a disciplinary, but in what he describes as a "pastoral" fashion, attempting to harness and maximize the contribution of all members of society.[7] Pastimes and other diversions were thus an important aspect of the monarch's role as in effect the shepherd of his people, providing for their amusement. As the power of the absolutist monarchy waned, the responsibility for assessing and then shaping the relationship between popular diversions and other domains of the culture was assumed by the bureaucratic state apparatus, which deployed a discourse known to the eighteenth century as "police." This definition of police was more comprehensive than it would become later, designating, not the body of men charged with preserving civil order by preventing and solving crimes, but the broader assemblage of techniques by which the government attempted to prevent criminal breaches in the civil order from appearing in the first place. In the writings of critics of pantomime like Samuel Richardson, Henry Fielding, and George Lillo, we can see how the science of governmentality and the discourse of police through which it was implemented were brought to bear on the new order and status of diversions that pantomime represented.

Richardson, Fielding, and Lillo were also, of course, contributors to the period's literary culture, and their animosity toward pantomime probably derives in part from their realization that its silent motion and extraordinary popularity might displace modes of performance centered on the word. Another central focus of this book will thus be the way that the controversy over pantomime entertainments was in part a public debate about the role and scope of the literary, which found itself doubly threatened by pantomime's success and its shape. Pantomime's enormous popularity in the 1720s and beyond, and not just with the lower classes but with fashionable theatergoers as well, scandalized and infuriated many observers, who saw it as the regrettable sign that performance genres that had originated in the fairground had now found a permanent place in the patent theaters. Pantomime's apparent lack of moral purpose and its seeming indulgence in sensual gratification made the London theater vulnerable to charges that it was shirking its responsibility to promote virtue by offering exemplary heroes in its tragedies and satirical foils in its comedies. Pantomime might be understood as an example of the class of activities that Susan Stewart has termed "crimes of writing," practices that seem to be "inversions or negations of cultural rules" that serve both to bring those rules into intelligibility and to expose their status as equally friable "written" practices.[8] Or, to specify the particular order of threat that pantomime posed, we might rather think of it as a "crime *against* writing," an action that undercut the theater's desire to define itself as a space of language, and therefore as a literary medium on a par with epic poetry. This desire, which has been felt by many participants in the theater throughout history, had its logical counterpart in a corresponding fear that the theater's materiality—its use of costumes, scenery, and the bodies of performers—interfered with the transparency of its language and compromised its claim to be a site whose rules were those of the word, in particular of the written word. Pantomime's reliance on dance, music, and spectacle allowed critics to accuse it of indulging the very *sensuality* that frequently has made the theater suspect to begin with, a hazard to those whose loyalties lie with what we might call a literary conception of culture, one that takes the written word to be the most significant means of embodying and transmitting its values and accomplishments. It seemed to prove the antitheatricalist's point that the theater's materiality could nullify the ability of words to convey an author's ideas to an audience.[9] With pantomime, the theater had done away with spoken language (although it retained song lyrics), and to many early eighteenth-century observers, that meant that it had eliminated meaning from performance altogether. At the extreme, such exploitation of the theater's sensual capacity threatened to overwhelm the spectator's critical abilities, hijacking the cognitive apparatus and installing passion over reason as the dominant faculty in the spectator's mind.

The theater and the pantomimes that would come to dominate it in the 1720s and 1730s were of course far from alone in being seen to offer gratification in the place of education and uplift, and William Warner has recently argued that the early "novel of amorous intrigue" was understood in much the same way in this period.[10] But Warner admits "that theater of various kinds would have been the dominant context for conceptualizing entertainment in the Restoration and the first half of the eighteenth century" (232); through at least the first half of the eighteenth century, drama was the form to which critics, trained largely in neo-Aristotelian principles, turned to exemplify their claims; the theater remained the destination to which ambitious writers like Joseph Addison, Henry Fielding, and Samuel Johnson directed their energies; and the stage was the institution that Britons used to assess the standing of their own national culture in relation to classical examples (the ancient Romans) and contemporary rivals (the French). The theater's continuing significance as a normative site for conceptualizing entertainment is partly indebted to the fact that the eighteenth century typically conceived of entertainment in material as much as it did in abstract terms. Eighteenth-century writers stressed the theater's sensual immediacy and its liveness, the fact that performers and spectators are in such close physical proximity as to interact with each other.[11] It is fair to say that the eighteenth-century British theater was notorious then, and is sometimes remembered now, for the moments when this interaction tipped over into abusive or riotous excess, with spectators mocking and even at times attacking the performers. But the live, embodied social interaction offered by the theater also contrasted favorably with the privatizing or solipsistic effects of reading, and the playhouse for this reason typically remained the first place that most eighteenth-century Londoners thought of when they imagined themselves being entertained.

This book's object of study, then, is not so much the history of eighteenth-century pantomime, or even of the London theater in this period, than it is of the relationship between these performances and the culture that produced them. It is for that reason less a book about or a history of eighteenth-century English pantomime than it is about what its emergence signaled to contemporary observers: a new kind of public performance, one that challenged existing assumptions about the relationship between high and low cultures, the word and the body, the theater and society. Because I take my object of study to be a relationship rather than a pregiven thing, this book will frequently go beyond the walls of the London playhouses themselves to consider the ways that performances referred to, reflected, or condensed in ways direct and indirect the events and conditions of their cultural moment.

Pantomime's rise to prominence in the early 1720s, for example, can be understood as a function of significant shifts in the nature and scope of political debate in early eighteenth-century Britain. Pantomime became among the first instances of an entertainment *fad,* a form whose seemingly sudden emergence and widespread popularity were so striking as to generate a second-order discourse about its own effects in the public sphere. But it was able to become such a focus of attention at this moment because the public sphere had been temporarily cleared of other objects of debate in the wake of the South Sea Bubble and the rise to power of Robert Walpole, whose one-party rule had the effect of greatly dampening the level and ferocity of public debate. To tell pantomime's story then, is to tell the story, not just of the eighteenth-century theater, but of British culture more broadly, of the way that the concept of entertainment seemed to claim an increasingly large share of the public sphere. One result of this phenomenon was that, as we shall see, issues of state—for example, ministerial politics, the system of justice— seemed to be modeling themselves on the theater rather than the other way around. Close attention to eighteenth-century pantomime, the theater, and the culture of entertainment that they defined will help us investigate important aspects of eighteenth-century British culture: the constitution and shape of the public sphere; the emergence within it of what Michael Warner has termed the "mass subject"; and the reconceptualization of temporality under the pressure of a commercial society's desire for more regularized calendars and workspaces.[12]

Pantomime is in many respects a difficult object of study, as the evidence of what these performances were like to eighteenth-century audiences is sketchy at best. But that same shortfall of primary evidence, frustrating as it is, also serves a useful purpose in reminding us how much of the past of any cultural practice—performance, reading, talking, thinking, feeling—is irretrievable. In particular, the challenge of re-creating and thinking about eighteenth-century British pantomime underscores how inadequate the printed word is as a means to capture the full texture of embodied performance. My attention to the theater, and particularly to largely ignored forms like pantomime, implicitly argues for a new literary history of eighteenth-century Britain, indeed, for a history that is less exclusively literary in that it considers theater as a site of performance rather than solely as a written or printed text. But if pantomime is elusive as an object of study, as an object of discourse, pantomime is ubiquitous from the 1720s until at least mid-century. That discourse touches on virtually every aspect of British culture in that period; once you go looking for Harlequin, he shows up in every imaginable context. In particular, the shockwave set off by the emergence of pantomime provoked a debate over the place and propriety of entertainment that has not ended. Recovering the terms of that debate will help provide an important genealogy of the entertainment culture that we still inhabit.

This book can essentially be divided into two parts. Chapters 1 through 4 describe the history and significance of pantomime itself. Chapters 5, 6, and 7 describe some of the broader implications of pantomime's emergence in the 1720s and 1730s, using the discourse that pantomime generated to interrogate issues about the pervasiveness of the logic of entertainment in eighteenth-century culture. The two sections are separated by an unnumbered chapter, that, in the spirit of my object of study, I have dubbed an entr'acte. More speculative than the other chapters, the entr'acte explores the extent to which eighteenth-century Britons might have been able to take Harlequin's black mask as a racial sign, a referent to Africans, and what that might have meant in performance. Throughout this book, I attempt to keep two different horizons in view. The first is the history of eighteenth-century British pantomime itself, which has only been told in fits and starts, and generally with a great deal of condescension and even hostility. The second horizon is defined by the cultural issues that pantomime, and particularly the enormous public debate it provoked, seem to bring into intelligibility: the nature of modernity, the purposes and propriety of entertainment, the desire to comprehend and manage the population. In a sense, the two halves of the book emphasize each of these horizons in order, but my hope is that both horizons or levels of inquiry are accessible to the reader's critical gaze at all times.

It makes sense to begin by giving the reader the fullest possible description of what an eighteenth-century pantomime was like. In chapter 1, I reconstruct a representative pantomime, the 1730 production at Lincoln's Inn Fields of *Perseus and Andromeda; or, the Spaniard Outwitted,* composed by Lewis Theobald and John Rich, who was also the most famous Harlequin of the eighteenth century in Britain. *Perseus and Andromeda* was enormously popular and successful—it continued to be revived up to the 1780s—but it also seems fairly typical of the genre as it was performed in the decades of its greatest impact and notoriety, the 1720s and 1730s. Moreover, *Perseus and Andromeda* has the added virtue of making spectatorship into its theme, fusing the Medusa myth, which is about the hazards of the male gaze, with an allegory about the change in the nature of political spectacle in the succession of the absolutist state.

Chapter 2 looks back to the origins of English pantomime in Continental commedia dell'arte, fairground performances, and Stuart court masques, among other sources, better to understand the originality and significance of its popularity on the eighteenth-century London stage. I argue that it was in the 1690s that observers began to realize that these older modes of theatrical performance were being appropriated for new uses, and that this made the theater a different kind of institution than it had been before, one that unsettled any easily made distinctions between elite and popular cultures. Tracing the emergence of discourse about the place of the theater in its culture through an archive of stage histories and critiques (in particular the critical dispute over the significance of the Roman *mimi* and *pantomimi,* the ritual dancers who gave modern pantomime a name and a classical pedigree), this chapter demonstrates how the 1690s can be considered to be the moment when the British stage first became intelligible as an entity in itself, a domain of the culture that was separate from the royal court, the traditional pastimes associated with rural culture, or a continuous performance tradition linked to the classical period.

Through its deployment of dance, movement, and spectacle, pantomime appealed to and in part created a new conception of the "spectator." Chapter 3 makes the case that the concept of spectatorship as articulated in the pages of Addison and Steele's *The Spectator* needs to be understood as a material relation, a corporeal engagement between the onstage performer and the viewer. In their writings of the 1710s, Addison and Steele prepare the way for a form of performance that could engage the attention of spectators who lacked the formal education that had traditionally been considered necessary. Pantomime's claim to be a form of universal language—an art whose silent mimeticism bypassed the distortions of speech and the vagaries of text—gave it a utopian dimension, as it expanded the possible scope of entertainment to include all orders of society.

Chapter 4 describes what has generally been taken to be the moment of pantomime's emergence as a dominant popular form, the fall of 1723, when afterpiece entertainments based on the Faust legend premiered at both of London's patent theaters, Drury Lane and Lincoln's Inn Fields. That it was entertainments based on the Faustus story that initiated the boom is particularly important for understanding the logic and appeal of eighteenth-century pantomime. To its first spectators, the Faust legend told not just the familiar story about power and ambition à la Marlowe and Goethe, but a story about the "magical" origins of printing, which was understood to be the mimetic art that most directly rivaled the theater. As an allegory about mimeticism and the transformation of an age of faith into an age of enlightenment, the Faustus pantomimes brought the theater's understanding of itself and the period's understanding of its own historical position together.

"Why is Harlequin's face black?" asks a young woman visiting from the country of her cousin William during a pantomime performance described in Samuel Richardson's *Familiar Letters on Important Occasions* (1741). The question remains unanswered because her cousin does not know why Harlequin wore a black mask. In the context of Richardson's letter collection, the cousin's ignorance serves as a mark of the way he has been so narcotized by the culture of urban entertainment as to miss the significance of so obvious a detail. Her question is a good question *because* it is a naïve one, resonating with the force of the knowledge that a culture takes for granted and therefore need not bring to the level of utterance. In this chapter, which I call an entr'acte to mark its place at the midpoint of the book as well as its speculative nature, I put Harlequin's mask in the context of other kinds of blackface performances in the early modern period. Why English Harlequins continued to wear the black mask well past the point where anyone really knew where it had originated or why is probably an unanswerable question, but we can observe that in the course of the Harlequin's greatest popularity on the

London stage, other blackface performances were becoming racially coded, referring to African subjects. Ultimately, I suggest that for Richardson as for other observers in mid-century, Harlequin's black mask functions as a kind of oblique referent to the complicated relationship between class and race in eighteenth-century British culture.

Chapter 5 argues that the period's concern about theatergoing apprentices—a ubiquitous worry in the first half of the eighteenth century in particular—registers the emergence of a "mass subject" who is the normative addressee of entertainment. Perhaps the first instance of a youth culture in — *no* modern Europe, the enormous cohort of apprentices in eighteenth-century London drew the attention of men of the middling sort, who believed that the spread of entertainment both geographically (as theaters proliferated across London in the wake of the pantomime boom of the 1720s) and epistemologically (as the concept of "entertainment" comprehended more and more types of performance) was a social threat, and one that was particularly concentrated in the uncertain loyalties of apprentices. Observers like the printer and future novelist Samuel Richardson (whose first published work was a conduct book for apprentices) worried about the tendency for apprentices to identify with Harlequin and other trickster or rogue heroes of the popular theater, such as Jack Sheppard and Macheath. In their anxiety about the mutual pantomimicry of spectacle and spectator, criminal topic and criminalized subject, such debates also confronted the question of *representativity* on both sides of the relation: how could the central character of a drama—a Harlequin, a Cato, or a Macheath—be said to represent the desires and fears of the individual spectator? and how could the figure of "the apprentice" be deployed to represent the audience as a whole? The place where both of these questions became most urgent is in the considerable public discourse of the period that worried about the entertainment value of the criminal justice system, in particular the considerable pleasure that witnesses took in what was supposed to be the monitory example of a state-directed, public execution.

The confusion between the spectacle of the gallows and other forms of entertainment in London points to the broader confusion between the playhouse and what was increasingly understood to be a "theater" of statecraft that manipulated the public as effectively as the showmen in the patent houses. In chapter 6, I show how public-sphere writers of the 1730s frequently equated Robert Walpole with Harlequin, a testimony to the protean capacity of both figures. I then analyze several of Henry Fielding's afterpieces of the 1730s—plays that frequently take the analogy between Walpole and Harlequin as a point of departure—to suggest that Fielding's strategy shows how the theater was also adopting logics associated with the state, attesting to a mutual influence for which narratives casting Walpole as Fielding's nemesis cannot account.

Finally, I examine the English actor David Garrick's complicated relationship to pantomime to describe the directions of the form after mid-century. Garrick probably debuted in London as a Harlequin in 1740 (a fact he tried to suppress, though could never quite deny) and profited from pantomime while managing Drury Lane in the 1750s and 1760s. But he publicly claimed to be embarrassed by its popularity and constantly tried to dissociate himself from it, aspiring to be recognized, not just as a serious, Shakespearean actor, but as Shakespeare's representative to eighteenth-century British culture. Garrick's most concentrated attack on pantomime is, ironically enough, his own contribution to the form—*Harlequin's Invasion,* first produced in 1759 and staged as a Christmas entertainment for many years afterward. Exploiting pantomime's popularity while stripping it of its populist content and critical capacity, *Harlequin's Invasion* is in effect an "antipantomime," one that casts Harlequin as a French interloper who must be driven away from British shores. Garrick's attacks on pantomime betray, however, his indebtedness to the form; in the hyperkineticism and physicality of his own performances, Garrick in effect co-opted pantomimic technique. Garrick thus represents the assimilation of pantomime into the mainstream of the theater, at which point the original entertainments themselves became, if not obsolete, somewhat archaic, available for nostalgia.

Pantomime persisted as a significant component of theatrical performance in Britain until well into the nineteenth century. Its most direct modern descendent is the Christmas "panto," an entertainment designed primarily for young children. But early eighteenth-century pantomime was considered an entertainment for adults. It was an important predecessor of the nineteenth-century music hall and minstrel show; in its use of slapstick, physical comedy, and spectacle, it stands, too, as a forerunner of the early twentieth century's silent movie comedy. Over the years and decades that followed the Faustus afterpieces of 1723, the figure of Harlequin would far exceed the London playhouses, migrating from the stage to become a familiar signifier, denominating a stance of irony, mockery, or satire, the character's protean nature permitting it to be fused promiscuously to symbols ranging widely across domains of culture that were typically kept separate: Harlequin Cato, Harlequin Jack Sheppard, Harlequin Macheath, Harlequin Horace, Harlequin Methodist, Harlequin Sheridan. Such a tendency might well serve to mark how the theater would lend itself to the concept of "the theatrical," which would, as scholars in a variety of disciplines have shown us, inflect our understandings of relationships in domains as seemingly different from each other as economics, moral philosophy, and the constitution of gendered selves.[13] But Harlequin's extraordinary popularity and ubiquity within and beyond the walls of the London playhouses also register the emergence of a phenomenon with which we are still familiar: the permeation of entertainment into almost every other domain of culture. And because we continue to inhabit the entertainment culture that was developed in the course of the eighteenth century, whether the relationship between entertaining performances and authoritative institutions like the nation and family is one of sly subversion or deadening complicity still perhaps remains to be determined.

HARLEQUIN BRITAIN

CHAPTER ONE

Perseus and Andromeda and the Meaning of Eighteenth-Century Pantomime

*W*hat was an eighteenth-century British pantomime like? What did spectators see and auditors hear? How did they understand, interpret, and critique these performances? What aspects of them gave theatergoers pleasure and gratification? Our answers to these questions will by necessity be frustratingly incomplete, limited by the fact that pantomime entertainments did not easily lend themselves to the kinds of recording available to the eighteenth century, so that even if the limited and fragmentary evidence that has survived were suddenly to be enriched by a new archive of texts, engravings, and audience reactions, we would still want to know more. (A few minutes of film of any eighteenth-century pantomime would probably tell us more than all the printed records we now have to work with.) Still, we can make some reasonable and informed guesses, not just about what early eighteenth-century pantomimes were like, but about how their audiences received and understood them. This is achievable in part by reading accounts, mocking as well as admiring, which were written by people who attended these performances, although there are fewer of these available than we would hope for, and they are generally vague or silent about just the kinds of things that we might like to know most: how, specifically, did these performances combine music and dance? to what extent did performers improvise, adding comic business or topical references? how, exactly, did the theaters achieve the magical transformations (Harlequin turning himself into a dog, or transforming another character into a piece of furniture) that were to many observers their most notable feature? We have some details about how nineteenth-century theaters accomplished such special effects, and it seems fair to assume that earlier playhouses did things in much the same way, but we have no specific accounts from early eighteenth-century Britain that would definitively confirm that supposition.[1] Bringing eighteenth-century pantomime into representation as an object of study demands that we pull together evidence of various kinds, most of which is richly suggestive but far from ideal. This indicates that a certain humility is appropriate. But pantomime is only a particularly acute case of a difficulty that confronts much research into cultural history, one reminding us that all records of the past are incomplete, and that any historical activity requires leaps of reconstruction and imagination based on evidence that will never fully satisfy our desires.

What *is* certain is not only that pantomime was enormously popular with theatergoers of all classes, but that they were often impressed by it, admiring the skill of its performers, the grandeur of its scenery, and the convincing quality of its special effects. *The Weekly Journal* for April 6, 1723 praises the mechanical effects in Lincoln's Inn Fields's production of *Jupiter and Europa*—a performance in which Jupiter was transformed into a bull "in Sight of the Audience"—claiming that "even men of the best Taste and Judgment cannot forbear being pleased at being so agreeably deceiv'd."[2] It is hard to imagine that a modern audience would be equally seduced by these spectacles. We should take this as testimony, however, not just to the superiority of our own entertainment technology—which *should* be good, considering how much money and energy has been expended on it over the last three centuries—but on the degree to which viewing is itself at least in part an historically determined activity. The first audiences of *King Kong* in 1933 were startled at how realistically it depicted an enormous ape climbing on the Empire State Building, and the special effects of the original *Star Wars* trilogy have already had to be reworked once to keep the film up to date with the visual sophistication of its target audience. Doubtless, even George Lucas's updated version, produced with all the digital wizardry that late 1990s computer technology could offer, will look hoary and unconvincing soon enough. We should not condescend to eighteenth-century performers or the spectators who admired them; when we read that the Swiss tourist Cesar de Saussure described John Rich's 1740 production of *Orpheus and Eurydice* as "altogether the most surprising and charming spectacle you can imagine," we need to take his testimony seriously, as evidence for the considerable pleasure that contemporary audiences received from these entertainments, which constituted the most sophisticated coordination of the theater's many constituent arts that most spectators had ever seen.[3]

Here at the outset of this book, I want to bring early eighteenth-century pantomime into our mind's eye by offering a reconstruction of an English pantomime that was staged in the moment of the form's greatest popularity, the 1720s and 1730s. My primary example will be a pantomime entitled *Perseus and Andromeda; or, The Spaniard Outwitted,* first produced on January 2, 1730, at the Lincoln's Inn Fields theater, which was then managed by John Rich, who, performing under the stage name "Lun," was also the century's most celebrated Harlequin. *Perseus and Andromeda* is a very rare example of a pantomime with a complete textual record of both the "comic," harlequinade sections and the "serious," operatic sections, the latter of which were written by Lewis Theobald and probably set to music (which has not survived) by Thomas Galliard.[4] Although they were published separately (as *Perseus and Andromeda* in 1730 and *The Tricks of Harlequin* in 1739), the two halves mesh so seamlessly that we can be fairly certain that they describe the same performance.[5] Most important, it seems clear from the surviving texts, descriptions, and accounts that *Perseus and Andromeda*'s success—it was produced sixty times in its first season and more than twenty times a year for several seasons after that, with revivals as late as 1780—derived in large part from the way that it so perfectly realized the shared expectations that defined the genre as it had developed over the decade and a half since the introduction of "dramatic entertainments, in dancing, after the ancient pantomimes" in the mid-1710s.[6]

In that period, the patent houses developed a generic framework within which what had previously been understood to be several different types of performance—dance, opera, commedia dell'arte scenarios—were organized into a single action. This framework proved to be extremely adaptable and repeatable, such that pantomime entertainments quickly assumed the paradigmatic two-part shape that typified the form through the 1720s, 1730s, and 1740s. First, there were "serious" sections, retelling a story that was usually drawn from classical mythology (frequently Ovid's *Metamorphoses*) and containing songs in an operatic style, though, unlike those in most operas performed in the early eighteenth century in Britain, these were sung in the vernacular. The serious sections alternated throughout the performance with "comic" or "grotesque" sections, which were organized around the escapades of Harlequin, who used all the resources of stage trickery, most crucially the ability to disguise himself and to transform objects and persons, in order to pry Colombine from the grasp of her father or husband, a character variously identified as Pantaloon, the Doctor, or, in some examples from the 1730s such as *Perseus and Andromeda* (when Britain was in conflict with Spain), "Don Spaniard."

Rich's entertainments at the theater that he also managed at Lincoln's Inn Fields and, after the company moved there in 1732, Covent Garden, were generally more popular than the ones at Drury Lane, and his most successful scenarios remained in the repertory for many years. In addition to *Perseus and Andromeda,* he performed in *The Necromancer, or Harlequin Doctor Faustus* (1723), *Apollo and Daphne: or, Harlequin Mercury* (1725), *Harlequin a Sorcerer: With the Loves of Pluto and Proserpine* (1725), *The Rape of Proserpine* (1727), and *Orpheus and Eurydice* (1740), among others. Drury Lane, after what seems to have been a period of consistent failure in its attempts to imitate Rich's entertainments, enjoyed some success with its own versions of *The Rape of Proserpine* and *Orpheus and Eurydice, Cephalus and Procris* (1733), *The Harlot's Progress* (1733), *Cupid and Psyche; or, Colombine Courtezan* (1734), and *Harlequin Incendiary* (1746).

There is probably no such thing as a fully representative eighteenth-century pantomime, just as there is no such thing as a nineteenth-century novel, a modernist poem, or a Renaissance tragedy that completely accounts for the possibilities of the form at its moment of fullest development. Pantomime accommodated very different kinds of performance within the generic framework that I have just described, and, like any genre, it changed over time. But *Perseus and Andromeda,* produced at the height of pantomime's popularity *and* its scandal, is as good a piece as any to serve as an example of the form that will indicate the nature of its appeal to contemporary spectators and its threat to contemporary opponents. *Perseus and Andromeda,* I will argue, not only provides a good example of English pantomime during the period of its greatest fame and notoriety, it also gives us access to important aspects of the period's understandings of theater, performance, and spectatorship.

My aim here is not just to describe *Perseus and Andromeda,* but to use it as a way of excavating what we can best think of as pantomime's *unconscious,* the way that it mobilized resources of memory, fantasy, desire, and anxiety in eighteenth-century British theatergoers. This can only be imagined as a collective unconscious, a level of shared experience, history, and ideology that characterized this cultural moment, such as has been defined by concepts such as Fredric Jameson's "political unconscious," Bill Brown's "material unconscious," and Eric Lott's "racial unconscious."[7] As they yoke external and internal domains, the real and the imaginary, such terms insist that we attend to the ways that references to the material and social worlds are mediated by the forms through which they are carried to readers, audiences, and spectators— the conventions, genres, and modes through which they can be apprehended. What is more, as they summon the terminology and methodology of psychoanalysis, such concepts privilege uneven aspects of the psyche and the culture, the reserves of memory and fantasy that often reside beneath the threshold of articulation but that nonetheless shape understanding and behavior. It is at such a level, I argue, that pantomime, which was sometimes said by its critics to be meaningless, or, worse, a threat to the serious productions of literary culture, registered some of its more significant meanings for its spectators. In particular, *Perseus and Andromeda* makes a theme of spectatorship itself, as it links female sexuality and state power through the trope of viewing. Such a move can be taken as an allegory for the spectatorial relations of the eighteenth-century British theater, as Perseus becomes a kind of analogue for the (male) spectator who must negotiate the hazards of spectatorship. More broadly, in its staging of the relationship between an observer and a spectacle that is at once alluring and threatening, *Perseus and Andromeda* signals the profound ambivalence inherent in spectatorship, the way that an entertaining spectacle, political and sexual as well as theatrical, can at once empower and attempt to control the viewer, inciting both pleasure and resistance.

Heroes and Tricksters: A Brief Reconstruction of Perseus and Andromeda

Pantomime entertainments became famous for surprising their audiences, but their newness derived much more from scenery, special effects, and performance than from their plots, which were typically quite familiar. The Perseus and Andromeda story was well known to the London theater before 1730, having been the subject of George Chapman's 1614 play *Andromeda liberata. Or the nuptials of Perseus and Andromeda.* It is not likely that many people remembered that play by the early eighteenth century, but the story seemed significant enough to be revived, and it was used in afterpieces as early as 1717. In that year, it became the subject of one of the first experiments in merging harlequinade with classical myth staged by the dancingmaster John Weaver at Drury Lane, a "new Dramatick Entertainment of Dancing in Grotesque Characters," entitled *The Shipwreck, or, Perseus and Andromeda.* The "grotesque characters" were the commedia dell'arte figures of Harlequin and Colombine, who "played" the roles of Perseus and Andromeda themselves, although it is impossible to know exactly how this was accomplished, as very little evidence of this performance beyond its title, cast list, and a single song has survived.[8] *The Shipwreck* was not particularly successful in 1717—it lasted only four performances—but it may have formed the basis for a Drury Lane production entitled *Perseus and Andromeda. With The Rape of Colombine: or, the Flying Lovers* that was staged in 1728. This production's printed libretto identifies its comic scenes as having been choreographed by Weaver, and also contains one song to the tune of "Thomas, I Cannot," written by the composer Christopher Pepusch, which had been part of the 1717 version. The 1728 Drury Lane *Perseus and Andromeda* conforms to what had by this point become the expected shape of the genre, interweaving three serious sections that tell the story of Perseus's defeat of Medusa and rescue of Andromeda with two comic sections (which are not described in the printed libretto) that depict the actions of Harlequin, Colombine, and the rest of the commedia cast. The Lincoln's Inn Fields production of *Perseus and Andromeda* that is our object of study here had to compete with the memory of other, similar works of the last decade and a half, which had told much the same story in a very similar format.

This production also marks a particularly acute moment in the ongoing rivalry between the two London patent theaters, or, perhaps better, it helps specify the nature of that rivalry and the kind of competition in which the theaters of this period were engaged. When it was first performed on January 2, 1730, Lincoln's Inn Fields's *Perseus and Andromeda* was going up against Drury Lane's version of the very same myth, a production that had first been mounted about a year and a half earlier. Rich's production of *Perseus and Andromeda* represents an attempt to reclaim attention and audience share back from the other house not through counterprogramming but by means of imitation, challenging Drury Lane by implicitly offering an even better, more spectacular version of the same story. This was a common practice in the London theater of the period; in addition to the rival productions of *Perseus and Andromeda,* both theaters staged versions of the Faust story, the Orpheus and Eurydice story, the Proserpine story, and others. From the point of view of either of the two theaters, this imitation must have seemed like bitter competition, a kind of one-upmanship that seemed risky and was no doubt costly, as it forced both theaters to expend resources on better costumes and stage effects. But such duplication is more a sign of the institution's extreme conservatism than of its taste for taking risks. As they avoided coming up with pantomime productions based on new and untested plots (much as they rationed out new mainpiece plays), the London theaters of this period display one of the key features of what Theodor Adorno and Max Horkheimer dubbed the "culture industry," as they offered pretty much the same thing while characterizing it as choice.[9] This is one of the less appealing ways in which pantomime can be used to mark the advent of a modern conception of entertainment, but even if we do not subscribe to the fairly gloomy version of that conception articulated by Adorno and Horkheimer, it seems undeniable that *Perseus and Andromeda* was from the moment of its inception situated in a theatrical context saturated by the logic of the market.

Here, I want to stress rather one of the less negative effects of the duplication of material that resulted from the particular kind of rivalry that the theaters engaged in, namely, the degree to which the previous and competing versions of basically the same story permitted a great deal of narrative compression. Relying on the spectators' memories of other productions based on the same myth, the theaters could tell the stories in a kind of visual shorthand, calling attention to unique features of their own production rather than devoting energy to character development and plot explication. In the case of the Lincoln's Inn Fields production, these unique features consisted largely of spectacular special effects and a high degree of integration of the serious and comic halves of the performance.

As was typical for pantomimes of this period, *Perseus and Andromeda* interweaves two plots: the rescue of Andromeda, here an Ethiopian princess, from a sea monster by the semi-divine hero Perseus (the "serious"), and a harlequinade in which Harlequin plays a series of tricks on Don Spaniard in order to lure the latter's wife Colombine away (the "comic" or "grotesque"). Theobald's script for the serious sections conflates Perseus's most famous feats—his beheading of Medusa and his rescue of Andromeda—by presenting them as one continuous narrative in three distinct episodes. The first episode begins with the Ethiopians panicked at the approach of Medusa, who threatens to turn the entire realm into what King Cepheus (Andromeda's father) calls "breathless Statues" (2). Cepheus, his wife Cassiope, and their daughter Andromeda appeal to the gods to rescue their "suffering Empire" (3) from the monster. But they know that their hopes rest in Perseus, the semi-divine hero who has already let it be known that he will attempt to slay

Medusa if he can have Andromeda as his reward. The scene changes to show Perseus reading a letter from Andromeda appealing for his help. Mercury appears and offers to equip him for his mission, and we see him receiving his sword, winged sandals, diamond shield, and magic helmet from a series of nymphs, Cyclopes, and a company of "infernals."

The second serious episode, set in the Gorgons' cave, opens with Medusa complaining about her fate, observing in particular that her former "Charms" have been replaced with horrifying ugliness in the form of the snakes that now cover a head where "Golden Tresses, that with Grace/In Ringlets flow'd" (8). She takes pleasure, though, in the power that she now has to execute the revenge of the gods by turning men into stone, which emerges as a compensation for the loss of her sexual desirability:

> Beauty delighting,
> All Eyes inviting,
> > Was my vain Glory Late.
> Now Looks affrighting,
> Terror exciting,
> > Kill my Soul with Joyes as great. (9)

Medusa, that is, was already a spectacle before she became a monster, since as a woman she was the focus of "all Eyes," the presumably male spectators whose gaze she actively courted. The pleasure she now claims to look forward to when her appearance terrifies and then, literally, astonishes men seems equal to the pleasure she took in what we have to read as typical female vanity. In the Lincoln's Inn Fields production, this memory of her own vanity aligns her with Cassiope, because Theobald's conflation of the Perseus myth specifies that Medusa's motivation for threatening the Ethiopian empire is revenge for Cassiope's excessive vanity in believing that her beauty rivaled that of the nymphs. (In this, Theobald is altering Ovid, who makes Cassiope's pride the reason that the gods dispatch a sea monster to seize Andromeda.) At the outset of the serious sections, Cepheus and Cassiope lament the latter's "arrogance" in challenging the beauty of the divine. Theobald's conflation of the story, underscored by Medusa's own lament (which has no parallel in the Drury Lane version of the myth), has the effect of *gendering* the threat to the state. Ethiopia now appears to be doubly beset by the effects of female vanity, both when it is located within the nation in the form of Cassiope and when it comes from without in the form of Medusa, who embodies the monstrous rage of women who have been stripped of their power to allure. Perseus's successful beheading of Medusa—accomplished with a lot of help from Mercury, who puts the other Gorgons to sleep—seems in the moment to have less to do with rescuing Ethiopia, or even with accomplishing the task that will gain him Andromeda, than with attacking excessive female pride; it is as if Medusa has become a displaced version or double of Cassiope herself, and is only getting what a vain woman deserves. At the end of this serious episode, Perseus, having eluded the other Gorgons by using the magic helmet to make himself invisible, flies off with Mercury to claim Andromeda as his prize.

The third and final serious episode shows Perseus, fresh off this exploit, rescuing Andromeda from the sea monster. This monster has appeared as part of Juno's continuing vengeance against Cassiope, who prays that the gods target her instead of her daughter. But her request is preempted by Perseus, who flies in and slays the monster, finally joining the rescued Andromeda in a duet. The serious section ends with the descent of the "Palace of Venus," where the gods bless the union of Perseus and Andromeda, and a dance in which the subjects of Cepheus express their joy, both at their deliverance from a series of monsters and at a marriage that will ensure the succession of the monarchy.

The comic episodes, inserted between those of the serious plot, open with Harlequin admiring a picture of his beloved Colombine. But his admiration quickly turns to despair, as he is so frustrated at his poverty (he silently mimes his anguish at not being able to afford the postage to reply to the letter that he has just received from her) that he prepares to commit suicide. As he attempts to do so, the chair that he has perched upon to hang himself turns into a magician, who tells Harlequin not to despair and gives him the magic sword that will enable him to perform the transformations that will help him get Colombine. In the remainder of the comic sections, spectators get to watch Harlequin use his new powers to trick Don Spaniard and his hapless servant, the Clown, as well as the "Petit Maitre," a foppish dancing-master who is also interested in Colombine: he transforms a chair on which the Petit Maitre is sitting into a chest and locks him in it; he replaces a letter that the Petit Maitre intends to send to Colombine with one of his own; he is shot out of a cannon onto Colombine's balcony to escape from the Clown. In what was one of Rich's most famous—or, more accurately, notorious—comic turns, Harlequin transforms himself into a dog to enter Don Spaniard's house incognito, where he proceeds to ingratiate himself to Colombine and to urinate on the leg of the Petit Maitre. A chase sequence follows, in the course of which Harlequin jumps onto an arbor that he transforms into a cupola, disguising himself by turning into a statue of Mercury at the cupola's top. Don Spaniard finally seizes Harlequin and has him hanged by a mob; Harlequin escapes by falling off the gibbet in pieces, reconstituting himself when he hits the ground. Finally, a crowd of shepherds and shepherdesses appeals to Don Spaniard to forgive Harlequin, which he does. Harlequin wins Columbine, and the cast of the harlequinade joins in a dance; it is unclear from the printed text whether this dance was combined with the one that ends the serious episodes, but it may well have been, as there are examples of pantomimes that unite the two strands of the entertainment in a final dance where characters from both serious and comic sections join together.

Combination and Compression

What significance can we derive from such a performance, a seeming mélange of farce and myth, slapstick and song? The very fact of such combining, and the kinds of compression that seem to have been required to achieve it, seems to be worth pausing over, as it points us to the relationship that these performances had to the more legitimate and established theatrical forms—comedy, tragedy, opera—that surrounded it in the London theater of the period. My brief description of the harlequinade, for example, underscores the ways in which the comic sections, like the commedia dell'arte performances from which they derive, distill the conventions of comedy, which might be summed up by calling upon Northrop Frye's description of Greek New Comedy as "an erotic intrigue between a young man and a young woman which is blocked by some kind of opposition, usually paternal."[10] Such a description is reductive enough to work for such contemporary comedies as Susanna Centlivre's *The Wonder: A Woman Keeps a Secret* (1714) and Richard Steele's *The Conscious Lovers* (1722) (among many others) as well, which is precisely the point: harlequinades presented their audience with many of the basic plot elements of the comedies that were simultaneously being offered as mainpiece entertainments. To spectators of the 1720s and 1730s, pantomimes appropriated and condensed the most notable features of the contemporary British stage: the plots of sentimental comedy, the scenery and diegetic material of Italian opera, the physical farce of Continental commedia dell'arte, and the elegance of dance.

The compression and recombination of these other forms was motivated, I think, by a desire to appeal to a broader range of theatergoers than had been possible before, to simplify the dominant modes of the contemporary theater into their salient features and then direct them toward new audience segments, in particular to members of the urban middle and working classes. For example, where pantomime plots most differed from conventional comedy was in the way that they directed attention, not to the middle-class and aristocratic lovers at the center of most mainpiece plays of the period, but to the "grotesque" characters like Harlequin and the Clown, who were typically cast as servants. In effect, they flipped the usual format of mainpiece comedy, bringing what was typically a subplot involving servants to the foreground. It is not surprising, then, that pantomime's critics worried about the appeal that these pieces had for members of the lower classes; unlike most mainpiece works, pantomimes not only provided characters with whom such audience members could identify, but gave those characters agency and power. But there was a great deal of continuity between the basic plot structure of mainpiece comedies and pantomimes, which in this respect differ primarily in the way that they placed at the forefront the characters who could become objects of identification and wish-fulfillment to a broad segment of the potential audience.

Similarly, the serious sections aimed to broaden the audience for theatrical performance by democratizing the kinds of material presented in the Italian operas that had become popular in the last generation among the elite. In the preface to *The Rape of Proserpine,* also scripted by Theobald, and performed at Lincoln's Inn Fields beginning in 1727, Rich argued that he was indeed adapting Italian opera "to the Taste of an *English* Audience," rendering it a "general Diversion" rather than an entertainment only for the wealthy. Pantomime's most significant move in this respect was to perform its songs in English rather than Italian, as was typical ever since Italian opera had become fashionable in England in the early 1700s. Despite the many satirical attacks on the unintelligibility of such performances to English audiences, operas sung in continental tongues had retained their cachet and patronage among the wealthy, and indeed had received a boost with the accession of the Hanoverian monarchs, who spoke halting English themselves and who sponsored the founding of the Royal Academy of Music in 1719 as a way to institutionalize Italian opera in Britain. Pantomime's turn to the vernacular is one of the points of correspondence between it and the other theatrical phenomenon of the 1720s, ballad opera, a boom that was kicked off by Rich's 1728 production of *The Beggar's Opera.* Both forms implicitly make the claim that English is a language worth taking seriously as a medium for organizing the entirety of a sung performance, that Britons need not reach for foreign tongues to produce significant and entertaining musical theater. More practically, Rich claimed that pantomime's particular advantage was that it enabled him to eschew the expensive foreign performers whose exorbitant salaries made opera the most expensive and therefore the most exclusive form of entertainment in this period.[11]

There is probably some measure of dissembling here, as Rich's desire to avoid paying the wages of star imports cannot wholly be attributed to altruistic motives. Indeed, one undeniable advantage of pantomime from Rich's point of view was the way it thwarted the development of the star system in general; since its primary appeals were in fixed costs that could be amortized over the long run of a particular piece such as scenery, costumes, and special effects rather than the identities of performers—with the exception of Rich, who avoided having to pay at least one performer's salary by taking the role of Harlequin himself—pantomimes were comparatively cost-effective, even given the large outlays that, contemporary accounts testify, went into their initial productions.

But the democratizing impulse that Rich expresses in the prologue to *The Rape of Proserpine* is not wholly a cover story for frugality, for it seems to be part of the intention of such performances to bring Greek mythology to a broader constituency than the comparatively small number of elite males who had had the benefit of a classical education. Where Gay moved from the vantage point of elite culture into the underclass to find the plot material for *The Beggar's Opera,* pantomimes of the same period attempted to bring simplified versions of classical myths to the widest possible audience. This desire to disseminate the story more broadly takes material form in the libretti to both versions of *Perseus and Andromeda,* which print accounts of the original Ovidian myths, in Drury Lane's case reprinting an extensive passage from Laurence Eusden's translation of the relevant section of the *Metamorphoses.* (The libretto incorrectly ascribes this translation to Joseph Addison, which was perhaps a mistake, but also perhaps a further attempt to reach for sophistication.) The comic sections were not printed in either libretto (and tend to be omitted from such texts), which might reflect the difficulty of transcribing such frenetic, wordless action, but also is consistent with the desire for respectability and gentility that the libretti express, their physicality and "lowness" embarrassing in this context even to pantomime's promoters. Indeed, to judge by the evidence of the libretto for the Lincoln's Inn Fields performance of *Perseus and Andromeda,* Rich, Theobald, and their publisher considered this to be a significant and ambitious piece; the text is printed with some care, and accompanied by two engravings by William Hogarth. Hogarth's illustrations, which depict Perseus's two most heroic actions, the beheading of Medusa and the slaying of the sea monster (with Perseus still

William Hogarth's illustrations for the text of *Perseus and Andromeda*
(*Reproduced by permission of the Huntington Library, San Marino, Calif.*)

holding the head of Medusa), probably share much the same impulse to make the libretto into an appealing object for genteel consumption, a book that records and replicates the most noble aspects of *Perseus and Andromeda*'s production. These images are also pointedly not representations of the theatrical performance, which actually makes no mention of a flying Pegasus and which almost surely did not call for Andromeda to be naked. Rather, these are idealized pictures of Perseus's feats intended for the gratification of the private reader; they bypass the theatrical production to illustrate moments in the original myth.

Another image of *Perseus and Andromeda* is both less idealizing and much less forgiving of the pantomime's populist impulses, which it takes to be a sign of vulgarity. The frontispiece to James Miller's 1731 satirical poem *Harlequin-Horace* offers us an image based in performance, one that combines several moments from the Lincoln's Inn Fields production of *Perseus and Andromeda* and embeds them in a frame that signals its location in a theater patronized by spectators who are alternately fascinated and scandalized. John Rich's Harlequin appears twice in the image, once in the foreground urinating on the leg not of the Petit Maitre but of Orpheus, and a second time

Serpentes avibus geminentur, Tigribus agni

Frontispiece to the first edition of *Harlequin-Horace* (1733)
(*Special Collections Department, University of Virginia Library*)

on top of the cupola, where he has transformed himself into Mercury. In the
middle ground, two peasants (perhaps from the group of shepherds and
shepherdesses who plead for Harlequin's life) dance, accompanied by a musi-
cian who simultaneously beats a drum and plays a flute. Behind them, several bishops have congregated; their relationship to the action of the comic
sections is unknown, since there is no mention of them in the 1739 printed
text. We do know that they were part of the first production of *Perseus and*

Andromeda in 1730, as their presence is noted in newspaper accounts of the performance. They are mocked in the notes to Miller's *Harlequin-Horace,* which objects to the attendance of clergymen at what it describes as "an obscene Dance [that] was perform'd in a Temple."[12] In the theater boxes, spectators (most of them female) display interest and also some dismay; the woman in the lower boxes, positioned closest to the Harlequin-dog relieving himself on Orpheus, lifts her fan to display her shock at this scene—but the woman at the left, at least, continues to look over her own raised fan to peek. What can this image—which, given its prominence at the beginning of what, as we shall see, was one of the period's most trenchant satires of pantomime seemingly intended more to mock pantomime than to advertise it— teach us about the kind of appeal *Perseus and Andromeda* might have had for contemporary spectators?

The caption—"serpents will lie down with birds, tigers with lambs"— offers a clue. What the caption refers to, I think, is not just the composite nature of this image, which brings together moments from different parts of the comic sections of *Perseus and Andromeda,* and throws in an image of the classical semi-deity Orpheus as well, raising the stakes of Harlequin's vulgar attack on the Petit Maitre to make it seem like an attack on music itself. But the sentiment also surely refers to the mixed nature of pantomime itself, the way it brought together classical mythology and continental commedia, operatic spectacle and physical farce. To be sure, such combinations had their precedent in Stuart court masques, with their alternate masque and anti- masque structures (some of which occasionally featured continental comme- dia figures) from which pantomime in part descends. But pantomime's inter- mixture of serious and comic modes would seem to go against the neoclassical decorums that dominated theatrical theory in the late seventeenth and early eighteenth centuries, and which argued for the strict generic separation of comedy and tragedy. Thus, for example, Theobald in his journal *The Censor* in 1715 had described "*Tragedy* and *Comedy* as Two Opposite *Glasses,* in which Mankind may see the true Figures they make in every important or trifling Circumstance of Life."[13] The figure of the theater as a mirror in which the spectator may view himself or herself is a commonplace; Theobald's refine- ment of the metaphor expresses the equally conventional desire for the integrity of tragedy and comedy, a desire that led critics like Thomas Rymer, for example, to condemn the comic moments in Shakespearean tragedy, and to have no room for the mixed form of tragicomedy. Such generic admix- tures would not gain critical acceptance until Samuel Johnson's famous pref- ace of 1765 put such neoclassical rules as the purity of genre and the unities to rest. But theatrical practice was actually well ahead of theory, and many early eighteenth-century mainpiece plays combine comedy, tragedy, romance, and farce in ways that contemporary criticism would seem to forbid. Pantomime's interweaving of comic and serious plots is not all that different in kind from the mixture of the serious, sentimental relationship between Bevil and Indiana in *The Conscious Lovers* and the farcical relationship between Tom and Phyllis in the same play, the similar combination of serious romance and farce in Addison's opera *Rosamond* (1707), or even the relationship between the political allegory and the love plot in his play *Cato* (1713).

Still, pantomime was attacked for such generic mixing, which appeared to critics to be a kind of chaos of sensation and activity that obeyed no logic and therefore did not deserve to be distinguished into even such inclusive categories as comic and serious. Using *Perseus and Andromeda* as his primary example, in *Harlequin-Horace* Miller sarcastically urges "Bards" who wish to succeed in the new poetic dispensation created by the rise of pantomime that they should

> A thousand jarring Things together yoke,
> The *Dog*, the *Dome*, the *Temple* and the *Joke*.
> Consult no Order, nor pursue no end,
> But Rant and Farce, the Sock and Buskin blend;
> Now make us dance, then doze, now weep, then smile,
> It suits the *various* Temper of our *Isle*. (24)

I want to return later in this chapter to Miller's claim that pantomime's varied attractions have their homologue in the British national "Temper." At this point, what I want to emphasize is how such an attack, launched from the high ground of Miller's neoclassical position (*Harlequin-Horace* is framed as an ironic imitation of Horace's *Ars Poetica*, a poem offering mock-advice to the poet—here Alexander Pope—on the true goals of "modern" poetry) takes pantomime's generic mixing to be, not simply a breach of decorum, but a descent beyond the borders of intelligibility itself, a jumble of "Things" that defy sorting into any more coherent order. The terms of Miller's critique were widely repeated in the 1720s and 1730s, when critics trained in the habits of classical literary criticism confronted pantomime and found it to be, not simply discordant, but frequently incoherent.

A more positive critique seems possible, however, from the standpoint of twenty-first-century taste, which has not only long forgotten neoclassical purity, but has been acclimated to the pleasures of varied attractions by forms like silent movie comedy and music video, both of which go far beyond eighteenth-century pantomime in their willingness to challenge the logics of narrative cause and effect and generic rules. From this point of view, we can see how pantomime enacted a kind of double movement whereby the two modes were, on the one hand, split apart cleanly into clearly marked sections while also, on the other hand, creating opportunities to explore the connections and shared logics of the serious and comic modes. Contrasts in tone (comic versus serious) and source material (classical versus popular or folk) such as the ones I have described in *Perseus and Andromeda* were also countered in such entertainments by visual and thematic (and, one speculates, musical and scenic as well) continuities. On the one hand, pantomime entertainments pursued the pleasures attendant on viewing rapid changes of scene, extreme disruptions in narrative logic, and the great disparity between classical and commedia modes. On the other hand, pantomimes also sought the local pleasures of discovering analogies between widely disparate plots and in exploring the possibilities of two realms where quotidian norms of cause and effect and laws of nature are equally held in abeyance. Thus, *Perseus and Andromeda* includes parallel scenes where Perseus and Harlequin read letters from the women they love and then lament their incapacity to help them; immediately following each of these scenes first Perseus, and then Harlequin is equipped with the instruments of the magic they will need to accomplish their heroic (or mock-heroic) tasks. Mercury gives Perseus a sword with which to cut off Medusa's head and the helmet that will render him invisible to the other Gorgons; in the scene that immediately follows, Harlequin receives his sword, the magic wand that enables him to transform himself or anyone else. (The helmet given by Mercury to Perseus might also be seen as an analogue to the cap worn by Harlequins, a prop that performers incorporated in a great deal of comic stage business.)[14] Later in the performance, Harlequin transforms himself into a statue of Mercury, waving the pagan god's caduceus much as he has been waving his own magic wand.[15] The harlequinade thus stands in a relationship of burlesque or parody to the serious part of the pantomime; here the "grotesque" offers a comic version of the classical plot wherein Perseus uses his god-given equipment first to kill Medusa, and then to rescue Andromeda from a sea monster, constructing a parodic analogy between the characters of Perseus and Harlequin that the performance would probably have reinforced by establishing visual correspondences or kinetic rhymes between one scene and the next.

Linkages such as the ones I have described must be understood to be associatively rather than diegetically motivated, indebted far more to visual or thematic analogies than they are to the logic of either the serious or comic narratives. Indeed, the plots are themselves so utterly conventional and predictable (who can doubt but that Harlequin will succeed in his quest to humiliate his rivals Don Spaniard and the Petit Maitre and win Colombine?) that the spectators' attention must of necessity be engaged elsewhere. In the absence of narrative suspense, the spectacle, the ingenuity of the comic routines and transformations, and the juxtapositions of serious and comic modes inevitably become the necessary object of the spectators' interest and pleasure. By contrast with mainpieces like Steele's *The Conscious Lovers,* pantomimes like *Perseus and Andromeda* almost systematically refuse to gratify the desire for plot complication and resolution; Steele's play, for example, while ultimately achieving a conventional comic ending by pairing off Bevil and Indiana, teases us with the possibility of Bevil's either being killed or ruined in a duel. Pantomime evacuated all such suspense, directing its spectators' attention away from the narrative and toward the moments of spectacle and sensation, which stood out from the story as discrete units that could be associated, compared, and entered into memory.

It is not hard to understand, then, why practitioners of serious drama, and those who were invested in its genres and conventions, took pantomime to be a kind of scandal or crime, a threat to serious drama. Pantomime parodied the conventions of serious as well as comic drama by playing them out in particularly schematic and unmediated forms. By condensing so many of the salient features of the Augustan theater, it could be taken as a form of critique on them, an argument for their insufficiency or exhaustion, as if the fact that they could be so effectively compressed was a mark against the conventions of the mainpiece repertoire. Parody or burlesque creates, of course, a parasitic or negative relationship to its host material, and seems to threaten the capacity of a performance to serve as a vehicle for positive meanings. And to pantomime's early critics, a large part of its scandal seemed to consist of the way that it seemed to evacuate the theater of meaning altogether, to substitute "show" for "sense." But if we consider more specifically how *Perseus and Andromeda* incorporated significant themes—political authority, gender, and spectatorship itself—we will be able to see that pantomime's relation to meaning was a good deal more complicated than such a dismissive account would suggest. If the form's compression and emphasis on spectacle deliberately interrupted narrative progression, it nonetheless signified powerfully to its audiences, offering the mixture of affirmation and challenge, critique and reification of its culture's assumptions, which has characterized the products of mass culture ever since.

Complicity and Resistance

In addition to reconstructing *Perseus and Andromeda,* what I have also attempted to reconstruct so far are the logics by which a work like it would have gratified an audience in 1730, the way it called upon the memory of other performances of the same and other stories, the degree to which it shared and then extended the desire for generic mixture, and most of all the nature of its appeals to the eye and ear. In short, I have tried to recover what a contemporary audience would have found *entertaining* about this pantomime, how it would have mobilized contemporary tastes in the theater to create a pleasing and engaging performance. As an entertaining diversion, *Perseus and Andromeda* would seem to have little to do, however, with political or ideological questions. Indeed, positioned as such entertainments were as the afterpieces to the five-act mainpiece plays that identified themselves as significant works, pantomime seemed to distinguish itself as a work intended to break whatever spell of serious intent had been cast over the audience before it. But *Perseus and Andromeda,* like other pantomimes of the 1720s and 1730s, is not innocent of ideology or politics. In chapter 4 I will argue that pantomime has a very specific relationship to the politics of the 1720s, and that its emergence as an object of fascination in that decade was enabled by the withdrawal of partisan politics from the public sphere. Here, I want to suggest how *Perseus and Andromeda*'s thematics of the gaze, appearing most obviously in its deployment of the Medusa myth but also present in the comic sections, indicates a more complicated relationship to questions of gendered and political authority than we might expect from a form usually considered to be mere popular entertainment.

First, *Perseus and Andromeda* reminds its audience of the ways in which spectatorship can be configured as a political issue, an aspect of monarchical rule. In effect, by fusing the Medusa story (which in Ovid occurs *before* Perseus is aware of the crisis in Ethiopia) with the rescue of Andromeda and thereby threatening Cepheus as well as Perseus with the Medusa's power, Theobald shapes the relationship between political authority and spectatorship into an object to be viewed and critiqued in its own right. Thus, King Cepheus, Andromeda's father, laments at the outset of the first serious section that Medusa's approach constitutes a particular threat to his own position as the normative object of the people's gaze:

> Still must the fell *Medusa* range
> Wide oe'r my Realms with Gorgon Terrors arm'd

And turn my gazing Subjects into Stone:
Then I in vain am call'd King;
Soon Desolation will o'er-run my Realms,
And only breathless Statues be my Subjects. (1–2)

Transformed through spectatorship from "moving" to "breathless Statues," Cepheus's Ethiopian subjects will gaze no more at their monarch, undermining the grounds of his sovereignty and rendering him in effect impotent. What is more, such a prospect already has the effect of stripping language of any force, as Cepheus realizes that there is no longer any point even to his being "call'd King." Cepheus's lament gains meaning if not pathos once we recall the lengths to which sixteenth- and seventeenth-century monarchs had gone to position themselves as the central objects of the people's gaze, understanding that their power could be measured by the degree to which their subjects were absorbed by the spectacle of their magnificence. Thus, in a much-quoted passage, Queen Elizabeth I claimed that "we princes, are set on stages in the sight and view of all the world."[16] Medusa's arrival brings the theatricality of monarchical power into discourse, which suggests that the intimate relationship between spectatorship and the feudal state was now itself an object of historical knowledge, an association that was intelligible because it had been surpassed by something else.

That something else, I would argue, is embodied in the person of Perseus himself, who rescues the Ethiopian empire not simply through his own puissance or the power he has been given in the form of the sundry magic gadgets he receives from the gods, but through the way he successfully manages the complicated problems of the gaze that Medusa represents. Perseus masters—or, more precisely, *tricks*—the gaze, successfully conquering his own anxieties to slay Medusa. In so doing, Perseus does not so much rescue Cepheus's monarchy as dramatize the terms under which it has been succeeded. By saving a realm whose king has demonstrated his inability to spare his own subjects from Medusa's threat, Perseus shows how Cepheus and the brand of monarchy for which he stands have become obsolete. Depicting a monarch unable to prevent his nation or his family from being destroyed by monsters, *Perseus and Andromeda* discovers a new locus for sovereignty in the role of the hero who successfully negotiates the hazards of spectatorship.

But of course Theobald's libretto for *Perseus and Andromeda* goes out of its way to emphasize that the threat to the state is posed, not just by any monster, but by a monstrous *woman*. As we have seen, Theobald introduces Medusa as a woman whose power is directly proportionate to her former vanity, a quality that links her with Cassiope, the woman whose egotism and pride have angered Juno into dispatching Medusa to exact vengeance. Given the fact that the entertainment is organized around the male leads Perseus and Harlequin, it is more specifically the *male* gaze that is at issue here, as *Perseus and Andromeda* makes a theme of the way that pleasure in the spectacle of femininity has frequently summoned forth a corresponding fear that mere absorption might turn into a paralyzing fixation. To observe this is to direct our attention to what we can think of as pantomime's unconscious, not only because such a fear is never expressed explicitly by the text, but because the deeply ambivalent nature of spectatorship can only be fully excavated by thinking in such terms, a fact that explains the considerable literature on spectatorial relations that makes use of psychoanalytic categories.

Thus Laura Mulvey, in a famous and enormously influential essay of the 1970s, argued that the male gaze was the structuring principle of classical Hollywood cinema, expressing what she terms a "patriarchal unconscious" that encodes the unequal power relationships between men (whose capacity for agency is signaled by their ability to gaze) and women (whose passivity is reflected in the fact they are typically the "to-be-looked-at") structuring the filmic medium itself.[17] As Mulvey puts it (using an example that is all but sent by the gods for my purposes here), "Andromeda stays tied to the rock, a victim, in danger, until Perseus slays the monster and saves her."[18] Calling upon the terms of Lacanian psychoanalysis, Mulvey argues that male-to-female scopophilia works to secure masculine identity, the woman's fixation as spectacle acting as the necessary salve to the castration anxiety that must be overcome for the male to enter what Lacan nominates the Symbolic realm of meaning. How can such an analysis be translated to our understanding of the meanings—conscious *and* unconscious—of *Perseus and Andromeda?*

We cannot equate the eighteenth-century British theater with the twentieth-century Hollywood cinema, of course. For one thing, the technological apparatus of film permits a much tighter focus on individual persons (and even, Mulvey points out, *parts* of persons) than the theater could ever permit, intensifying the power of the gaze to a point unachievable in the playhouse, where any spectator's attention is free to wander at will to any part of the stage (or to ignore the stage altogether in favor of the spectacle of his or her fellow theatergoers). But eighteenth-century Britain presents an even more patriarchal society than the twentieth-century United States, a fact that structured all its major institutions, the theater included. The misogyny that we have already seen at work in *Perseus and Andromeda*—where violence directed against prideful women saves the state, proves Perseus's heroism, and gains him a bride as a prize— is characteristic of the culture. That is to say that it is the Medusa story itself rather than (as in film) the technological apparatus that deploys the male gaze to serve as the securing principle of male identity. In her combination of attraction and horror, Medusa embodies the ambivalence of the spectatorial relationship.

When Sigmund Freud analyzed the myth of Medusa, he emphasized the way that it symbolized both castration anxiety (as the snakes stand for female pubic hair) and a compensatory reassurance (as the hardening of Medusa's spectators into stone stands for an erection). The myth thus, as Neil Hertz has argued with reference to its use in late eighteenth- and nineteenth-century France, serves an "apotropaic" function, reassuring men of their potency even while providing a frisson of anxiety.[19] This is no doubt why, as Hertz goes on to show, this myth has served so frequently to symbolize male anxiety in moments of political turmoil, where it awakens just enough fear to identify itself as relevant to the contemporary situation while offering sufficient solace to be appealing to patriarchal culture. In *Perseus and Andromeda*, the myth of Medusa works to condense the unconscious of the theatrical medium, recording the extent to which the normative spectator was gendered male, able to take pleasure in a story whose danger consisted of the threat posed by a monstrous woman to both the body and the body politic, and whose reward consisted of the political and sexual power achieved by destroying her. We can take Perseus, then, as an avatar for the (male) spectator who prompts, then conquers, the anxieties about the return of the gaze raised by the spectatorial relations of the theater.

Yet such a reading remains incomplete unless we also attempt to account for the place within such a system for the *female* spectator, to whom, the frontispiece to Miller's *Harlequin-Horace* strongly suggests, some of *Perseus and Andromeda*'s most powerful appeals were addressed. The women viewers depicted here are alternately scandalized, fascinated, and bored by the performance. In the poem, Miller takes the opportunity to mention the specific expectations and responses of female spectators:

> 'Tis not enough that Show and Sing-song meet,
> The Ladies look for something *soft*, and *sweet:*
> That ev'ry tender Sentiment may move,
> And fix their Fancies on the *Joys* they love:
> In *Perseus* this was to Perfection done,
> The *Dance* was very *moving* they must own. (33)

"The Ladies" had long been identified as a profound influence on the theater, an entity whose collective tastes formed an authoritative site of judgment, frequently credited (or blamed) for having exerted their influence to reform the theater away from its licentious excesses in the Restoration.[20] In *Harlequin-Horace,* they appear as some of pantomime's most loyal customers, admiring the sentimental quality of the serious sections. It is impossible, of course, to evaluate whether or not such a depiction tells us anything about actual female theatergoers of the 1730s and how they received this or any other performance. We have very few firsthand accounts written by women, which means that "the Ladies" remains an entity largely if not completely articulated by male writers, who may or may not have been accurately representing the beliefs of actual women spectators. In *Harlequin-Horace,* for example, the intense interest of the ladies in pantomime and other entertainments becomes the sign of the feminization of the theater and the culture more generally, its fall into a realm of sensual gratification and luxury and away from the high-minded masculinity that Miller takes to have characterized the English theater of the past. Still, such references and their invocation of the substantial discourse around the significance of women to the theater's audience serves as a warning against assuming that a character like Perseus fully exhausts the possible ways of thinking about the spectatorial position in the eighteenth-century British theater.

Finally, and perhaps most important, we have to consider the effect of the comic sections of *Perseus and Andromeda* on any attempt to read meaning into the serious parts. The comic episodes, as we have already seen, burlesque and undercut the serious part of the performance at every turn, and do so not in general, but in quite specific terms, such that Harlequin becomes an unmistakable analogue for Perseus himself. Perseus's heroism, such correspondences imply, is different in degree but not kind from Harlequin's trickery. And here, too, the thematics of the gaze play their part in thwarting the straightforward application we might make of any theoretical structure that takes patriarchy to be monolithic or easily understood. Harlequin's fixation on Colombine's picture at the outset of the comic sections, for example, underscores the ways in which *Perseus and Andromeda* thematizes the spectatorial relations that Kristina Straub has argued constitute the gendered cultural work performed by the eighteenth-century British stage. Straub calls upon the importance of the stage to eighteenth-century culture to describe "the ongoing process of naturalization by which the powerful, gendered tropes of the male spectator and the female spectacle become encoded in modern ideology."[21] In this context, Harlequin's comic address to Colombine's image parodies male scopophilia, suggesting that the process that Straub describes was more uneven and contingent than her rhetoric might imply, that the process by which modern gender identities were reified was accompanied by a counteracting desire to undercut its momentum through mockery.

To the fairly mild satire of male narcissism that this scene stages, it seems fair to add the many times in early eighteenth-century pantomime where Harlequin was transformed into a woman, decisively upending the rigidity of hard-and-fast gender distinctions.[22] Harlequin was also sometimes performed as "Harlequine" and played by a woman. This is a feature that the early eighteenth-century English stage shared with the continental commedia tradition, where female Harlequins, while almost surely a distinct minority of the role's instances, were not unusual. In the London playhouses, Harlequine typically appeared in entr'acte dances rather than afterpiece entertainments; as Elizabeth Lewis has recently shown, the role was performed most notably by Hester Santlow, who was also the wife of the tragedian Barton Booth.[23] We know too little about Santlow's performances to describe them with any degree of precision, but we can say with some assurance that they fulfilled their spectators' expectations; the German tourist Zacharias Conrad von Uffenbach wrote home that Santlow's portrait as Harlequine was frequently reproduced on snuff-boxes and that her dancing in the role "much pleases the English."[24] The popularity of Santlow's and others' performances as Harlequine testifies to the wide and continuing appeal of androgynous figures in the eighteenth-century British theater, and the pleasure that audiences took in seeing the normative codes of gender temporarily confused.

Perseus and Andromeda's relation to the state similarly identifies it as a point around which vectors of deference and resistance gather. We have already seen how its serious plot seems to tell a political allegory that makes a narrative of succession stand for something more. The passage of the monarchy from one generation of rulers to another that takes place when Perseus claims Andromeda and becomes the heir apparent to the Ethiopian throne also marks the shift from one *kind* of ruler to another. As he masters the problem that Medusa poses, he serves as the site of identification for the normative male spectator in the playhouse, a figure who is understood to have a sophisticated relation to the spectacle of state power, marking how Cepheus's brand of authority has been displaced by a more flexible kind of power. Such a narrative can be taken, I argue, as a rough-and-ready version of the historical trajectory whereby the spectacular, theatrical power of the Renaissance monarchy was succeeded by the more cunning, modern mode of agency. It is perhaps not so much that Perseus stands for the Hanoverian monarchs as he does for Whig principles: liberty, to be sure, but also adaptability, mutability, the capacity to adapt to circumstances.

The comic episodes also bring the question of the state's power into view at the moment when it appears that Harlequin will be the victim of the criminal justice system, and hanged for his crimes. I will have more to say about the relationship between Harlequin and criminality in chapter 6, but suffice it to say here that no depiction of the gallows in 1720s Britain could fail to be highly charged with contemporary application and significance to a theatrical audience. When Harlequin is pardoned by Don Spaniard at the behest of the country folk, the pantomime stages what Douglas Hay has described as a characteristic pattern under which the death penalty was administered and contained in the early eighteenth century. The period is well known for expanding the number of crimes for which the death penalty was mandated, but all the historical evidence demonstrates that far fewer people were actually executed than a strict application of the statutes would have accomplished—fewer, in fact, than a century before. One of the most important factors intervening between the statutes and their application, Hay argues, was the culture's deeply entrenched patterns of patronage and paternalism, which authorized, indeed encouraged, the gentry to intervene on behalf of the convicted, with the expectation that sufficient influence in the intricate networks of power, interest, family, and education that bind the elites of every society would produce a pardon.[25] Here the state became a mechanism by which the power of the great was displayed and, even better, magically transformed into mercy. But given that the agent of this mercy in the comic section of *Perseus and Andromeda* is the very same Don Spaniard whom we have seen mocked, humiliated, and defeated by Harlequin at every turn, the pantomime's staging of this gesture cannot have carried the meaning that Hay argues it bore in everyday practice in this period. *Perseus and Andromeda* suggests what we would like to believe anyway, that eighteenth-century Britain's paternalism had its limits, and that people were capable at times of seeing through the mechanisms of power and of expressing their skepticism, if only in displaced and "grotesque" forms.

Perseus and Andromeda's incorporation of the state as the frame within which the trajectories of both the comic and the serious plots are resolved seems particularly significant once we consider how frequently pantomime's critics described its popularity as the sign of the decline of a British culture that until quite recently had been the home of serious, meaningful drama that bore comparison with the theater of classical Greece and Rome. This is, for example, the argument of Miller's *Harlequin-Horace,* which uses its Horatian model to elaborate on the theme of nostalgia that casts pantomimes such as *Perseus and Andromeda* (his salient example of the form throughout the poem) as the mark of the culture's decay since "our Father's Days" (56). Correlating the history of British entertainment with the history of the nation as a whole, *Harlequin-Horace* claims that the introduction of politeness in the nation—an event it dates to the "*South-Sea Schemes*" of 1720—has led to the corruption of its cultural productions. In what is perhaps the poem's most elegiac moment, Miller invokes the hearty masculinity of English music before the recent onset of luxury:

> In Days of Old, when *Englishmen* were—*Men,*
> Their Musick, like themselves, was grave and plain;
> The manly Trumpet, and the simple Reed,
> Alike with *Citizen,* and *Swain* agreed;
> Whose Songs, in lofty Sense, but humble Verse,
> Sung by themselves, their homely Cheer to crown,
> In tunes from Sire to Son deliver'd down. (41)

By this point, the reader of *Harlequin-Horace* should know that any such glowing description of the past means that the present tense is going to represent a marked come-down from such a picture of an integral, harmonious society. And, indeed, Miller goes on to note that "now, since *Britains* [*sic*] are become polite," music has followed every other form of entertainment into unintelligibility:

> The *shrill-ton'd Fiddle,* and the *warbling Flute,*
> The *grave Bassoon, deep Base,* and *tinkling Lute,*
> The *jingling Spinnet,* and the *full-mouth'd Drum,*
> A *Roman Capon,* and *Venetian Strum,*
> All league, melodious Nonsense to dispense,
> And give us *Sound,* and *Show,* instead of *Sense;*
> In unknown Tongues mysterious Dullness chant,
> Make Love in *Tune,* or *Thro' the Gamut rant.* (42)

Miller's opposition between a decadent present and an authentic past maps onto a host of other distinctions that the poem assumes to be operative throughout: that between femininity and masculinity, between modern-day "Britain" and traditional "England," between unintelligibility and transparency, and between a culture riven by a distinction between a form of art that alternately appeals to high and low culture and one that expresses its culture's organic wholeness, where "*Citizen*" and "*Swain*" are able to take equal pleasure from the same performance. This is the force, I take it, of the contemptuous footnote at the start of *Harlequin-Horace* that describes the cupola scene of *Perseus and Andromeda* in full, observing that such ridiculous and improbable tricks as Harlequin's transforming into a dog, then Mercury, were greeted with "*the high Admiration and Delight of a* British *Audience*" (24n). Assuming the satirist's Olympian vantage point that enables it to speak from outside the positions of high and low or English and British, *Harlequin-Horace* identifies such contemporary entertainments as *Perseus and Andromeda* as the best possible evidence that a decisive split between traditional and modern societies, elite and popular forms of culture, has taken place in a Britain that is now cut off from the integral society of "England's" past.

Pantomimes like *Perseus and Andromeda* speak with two voices at once, combining myth with farce, opera with commedia dell'arte. But we do not have to agree with Miller and other critics of his generation who took the varied nature of these performances to be the sign that they were without meaning, even if, as I have argued, it is hard to pursue any reading of even the serious sections without some equivocation. Rather, *Perseus and Andromeda* has to be understood as having both an affirmative and a critical relationship to its culture. This is one of the tendencies that it shares with the products of the mass culture of the twentieth and twenty-first centuries. Describing the complicated mixture of what he terms "reification" and "utopia," containment and subversion in the mass-cultural products of the late twentieth century, Jameson argues that such works call upon us to "think repression and wish-fulfillment together with the unity of a single mechanism, which gives and takes alike in a kind of psychic compromise or horse-trading; which strategically arouses fantasy content within careful symbolic containment structures which defuse it, gratifying intolerable, unrealizable, properly imperishable desires only to the degree to which they can be momentarily stilled."[26] *Perseus and Andromeda* can be understood as such a mechanism. When, for example, it reiterates its period's laments about the vanity of women and their baleful effects on the state, it shares the patriarchal prejudices of its moment, and even if it does not provide the full measure of apotropaic reassurance that psychoanalytic accounts of the Medusa myth would imply, it does little to challenge or dislodge most of its spectators' assumptions about the relations among men, women, and the culture they share. But its "grotesque," comic sections consistently mock and satirize authority, including, quite pointedly, the authority of the serious sections themselves. To be sure, they hardly offered a radical critique of their culture; in particular, they retain and even condense the patriarchal plot of comedy that was normative in the theater. But they opened a space within which certain kinds of resistances—to figures of authority, to everyday laws of causality, to the stratification of class relations—could be registered and enjoyed. Jameson's formulation serves as a useful counter to the pessimism dispensed by critics like Adorno and Horkheimer, who see the culture industry as manipulating the media it controls into asphyxiating the critical capacities of its consumers. Rather, what I have suggested is that *Perseus and Andromeda* contains a utopian element, which we can apprehend both in what I have described as its democratizing impulse and its parodic relationship to its culture's norms of gender and state power.

Such an element helps explain pantomime's enormous success with its audiences, who were gratified by the various kinds of wish-fulfillments that works like *Perseus and Andromeda* offered. Perhaps the most profound of these might be located by observing that one of the things that its serious and comic episodes share is a movement toward open countryside, away from the urban milieu of the theatergoers who constituted its first audiences. The shepherds who plead for Harlequin's life and the villagers who run in fear of Medusa mark *Perseus and Andromeda*'s affinity with the genre of pastoral, a feature that it seems to have shared with a fair number of eighteenth-century pantomimes.[27] In this chapter, I have tried to reconstruct *Perseus and Andromeda* in order to situate it in its cultural context, to understand it as a performance that incorporates the ambivalences of its moment. The pastoral aspect of this entertainment identifies another node of ambivalence, that about the relationship between that moment and the past, an ambivalence that was experienced in the form of a profound nostalgia. We can map this nostalgia, I think, onto the split that Miller invokes between a contemporary Britain that is gratified by entertainments like pantomime and the hearty "England" that it has displaced. Miller's evocation of England's traditional pastimes implies a critique of the 1707 Act of Union that combined England and Scotland into Great Britain. But the constitution of the new nation-state is only a small marker of the more fundamental change that critics of contemporary culture like Miller identified, an unbridgeable (and usually lamented) gulf between the present and the past. How did such a distinction originate? The constitution of the "English stage" as an object of knowledge, debate, and satire, and of an organic, traditional culture that it succeeded and to which it is opposed, was actually a fairly recent development. In the next chapter, I want to move back a generation or so, to the 1690s, when the English stage that Collier and others wrote about was identified as a thing in its own right, distinct from, but parallel to the state or the traditional society of the past. We shall see that attention to this period will help provide a genealogy for pantomimes such as *Perseus and Andromeda,* which emerged out of the many forms of entertainment that had been common in the English theatrical tradition for generations. But, more important, it will also help identify how pantomime was originally understood as a way of bridging the newly opened divide between elite and popular cultures, and of restoring the theater to its organic roots in the classical past and the human body in motion.

Pantomime, Popular Culture, and the Invention of the English Stage

*P*erhaps no theorist has offered a harsher or more influential assessment of the modern bourgeois theater than Antonin Artaud. His angry critique of entertainment—"the notion of useless, artificial amusement, of an evening's pastime which is the characteristic of our theater"—famously led him to propose a "Theater of Cruelty," an entity whose seriousness, rigor, and appeal to "true sensation" rather than the mere "understanding" addressed by the "ordinary psychological theater" of modern Europe would restore the theater to its origins in the ritual processes that form the most fundamental aspects of culture.[1] What Artaud imagined the Theater of Cruelty might be like in practice remained notoriously vague, described by means of metaphor and allusion in his theoretical writings and only partially realized in some performances that he organized in Paris in the 1930s. But the examples of "authentic" performance styles to which he gestured as he sought to redefine the theater away from the narrow and frivolous conception of "diversion" that he took it to embody in modern society provide valuable clues. Artaud celebrates the performance practices indigenous to Bali, which he praises not for any specific technique, craft, or style, but because of the way that their combination of "dance, song, and pantomime" and concomitant deemphasizing of language restores a "physical and nonverbal idea of the theater" that permits the Balinese tradition to preserve "something of the ceremonial quality of a religious rite" (53, 60). The "true hieroglyphs" that Artaud identifies in the Balinese performance tradition serve as the evidence that Western bourgeois theater can reclaim its significance by returning to "the domain of gestures, noises, colors, movements" (70) in performances constructed as "mass spectacle," appealing to "the people" by engaging the senses through the "plastic and physical" essence of a "pure theater" (85, 71, 61). Artaud describes this theater as one of "direct Pantomime," where gestures refer not to words, but to the "Original language" of a spontaneous, authentic, and collective life not contaminated by its contact with a modernity that he everywhere associates with bourgeois philistinism and the alienating effects of advanced capitalism (39).

The relationship between "direct Pantomime" as Artaud uses the term here and its eighteenth-century version is not a direct one, of course, either formally or historically, and he probably would have seen much to dislike in the performances staged by that name as they emerged to prominence in the 1720s and 1730s in Britain. Many examples of the form might have seemed to him to be the very essence of a bourgeois entertainment, where spectacle is enlisted in the service, not of putting the audience in contact with the primal forces of nature, but of gratifying their desire for mindless diversion from serious concerns. But Artaud's critique has more in common with the culture that it attacks than he might care to admit. For all that he assails modern bourgeois culture, Artaud remains very much beholden to the same kinds of binary oppositions that it typically holds dear, opposing ritual to diversion, the primitive to the modern, the body to language, and the "people" to the bourgeoisie. Such oppositions have been common in critical analysis of theater since the late seventeenth century, the period that will be our primary focus in this chapter. Artaud's desire to rescue the theater from its status as mere diversion, to restore it to a central place in modern culture by returning it to its imagined origins in embodied performance, has been a feature of European writing about the theater since that period, which is when critics began to distinguish it from other, more traditional pastimes and modes of performance. In England, this is when critics like James Wright, Thomas Rymer, Jeremy Collier, and James Drake began to articulate the "English stage" as a thing, or, to use a word that they frequently deployed, a "case" in its own right. Artaud's critique of the modern bourgeois theater contains an important constellation of issues that are shared by contemporary observers of the seventeenth- and eighteenth-century British theater and to the pantomime entertainments that developed within it: the desire to restore the theater to its imagined beginnings in ritual practice; the belief that such a restoration might be achieved by advancing a language of gesture, physicality, and the body; and the hope that the "people," conceived as Other (ethnographic or otherwise) to the theorist, preserve an authentic relationship to the body and thus to ritual.

This chapter turns to the discourse about the theater in the late seventeenth century in England to examine how the division between the institutional theater—the "English stage"—and the much broader tradition of performances by and on behalf of the "people" was theorized. These debates set the stage for the emergence of entertainment as a public-sphere phenomenon in both general and specific ways. Again and again, critics recognized and frequently lamented the way that the London theaters had by the 1690s if not earlier become sites for mere diversion rather than important contributors to the practices that helped the culture cohere and recognize itself, the rituals of state and church with which it had (many critics argued) once been allied. The emergence of entertainment as a scandal thus seemed to be in many ways the logical if deplorable consequence of this event. More specifically, the emergence of "pantomime" entertainments in the early eighteenth century in Britain was preceded by critical attempts to reforge the broken link between theater and ritual. Where Artaud and other twentieth-century writers like Victor Turner and Richard Schechner frequently look to non-Western cultures in order to find performance traditions uncontaminated by bourgeois life, seventeenth- and eighteenth-century British theorists looked back to antiquity, when, they argued, theater had emerged from Greek and Roman ritual practices.[2] As it does in Artaud, pantomime forms an important part of that imagined tradition against which the modern theater can be defined, and to which it might return. The most ironic aspect of pantomime's modernity, I argue, is the extent to which it originally appealed to a desire to heal the wounds that modernity seemed to inflict on the social body by turning to the past to recover an original, authentic, and universal language of the human body.

Ritual, Theater, and the Emergence of "Popular" Culture

What is the English stage? The answer is less self-evident than it might seem, because any such entity is defined through gestures of inclusion and exclusion, gestures that are never simple or uninflected by other domains of culture. Thus, it is worth noting that this object of study was categorized as "English" rather than, say, "European," "popular," or "comedic" and defined as the "stage," which associates it with the permanent, professional buildings to house regular performances that only came into existence in the late sixteenth century. The English stage presumes its participants' investments in the nation-state and a degree of urbanization, which is why, while performance has existed for a long time in the British isles, the English stage as a definable entity, a topic for critical discussion and theoretical debate, is a more recent construction, dating perhaps only to the Renaissance. And it was probably no earlier than the 1680s and 1690s that the English stage became a widely shared object of historical knowledge, a topic worthy of antiquarian interest and research, and the subject of narratives that traced its origins and development.

Books such as Gerard Langbaine's *Momus Triumphans* (1688), Jeremy Collier's *A Short View of the Immorality, and Prophaneness of the English Stage* (1698), James Wright's *Historia Histrionica: An Historical Account of the English Stage* (1699), James Drake's *The Ancient and Modern Stages Survey'd* (1699), the anonymously published *A Comparison Between the Two Stages* (1702), and John Downes's *Roscius Anglicanus, or, an Historical Review of the Stage* (1708) define and study the modern English stage as a discrete entity, an institution with its own history, norms, and purposes. The books' generic markers, their self-identification as "accounts," "surveys," or "views," testify to both the ambition and the novelty of the historical enterprise, as these authors reach to other systems for organizing knowledge like bookkeeping, property assessment, and the law to gain legitimacy for their inquiries. These texts present themselves as efforts to *rationalize* the English stage, to determine its origins, its history, its repertory, its most significant authors, its most talented actors and their most striking roles. They are worth our attention, not just because they mark a moment in the historiography of the English theater, but because they show us what was involved in separating it out from the multitude of performances that permeate the lived experience of culture. Their authors worry the question of whether the English stage can best be understood as a continuation of older performance traditions such as rural pastimes and state occasions, or whether it had to be considered as something different from them, as a case in its own right. And their writings demonstrate, too, the powerful nostalgia that theorists of performance frequently feel as they contemplate the division between the theater of the "people" and that of a theater devoted to textuality and moral uplift.

That their very object of study was not a given, but a constructed thing is perhaps made most apparent in the pages of James Wright's 1699 book *Historia Histrionica*. Here, the definition of the "English-Stage" is precisely what is at issue, as Wright enlists the evidence offered by historical works like John Stow's *Survey of London* (1598) and William Dugdale's *Antiquities of Warwickshire* (1656) to demonstrate how different the "modern" theater of his own era is from that of the comparatively recent past, namely, the Renaissance stage of Shakespeare and Jonson. Cast in the form of a dialogue between Lovewit, a modern critic, and Truman, an elderly Cavalier, *Historia Histrionica* gains an elegiac tone from both interlocutors' awareness that all evidence and memory of the "last age," the era before the civil war and the Restoration, is rapidly disappearing; as the Cavalier, the embodied representative of that era, puts it in the last line of the pamphlet, "we are almost all of us, now, gone and forgotten."[3] Wright emphasizes that the stage has traditionally occupied a position of great importance to the culture; because it was an integral component of state ritual, theater once frequently engaged "Religion and Religious matters" and was called upon to mark important state events like royal weddings and coronations. But Wright understands this situation to have utterly changed by the time of his writing; his elegiac tone indicates how his book emphasizes not the continuing vitality of theater's ritual function, but rather its decay. Wright's Cavalier identifies the theater that he describes as being that of "former times"; it exists on the other side of the historical divide known as the Interregnum, when the London playhouses were closed, the theatrical companies were disbanded, and theatrical performances went underground. For Wright's Cavalier, the Interregnum constitutes not just a rupture in history but a shift in the texture of collective experience. Cut off from the Stuart court culture that once sustained him as it supported the theater, Wright's Cavalier in effect stages the excision of the stage from the broader context of ritual and collective performance that had once permeated English life.

For most of Wright's readers, as for most of the literary historians who would follow them, the "English-Stage" could by 1699 be identified with the two licensed London playhouses, which at that moment consisted of the "Old" Company at Drury Lane and the "New" Company at Lincoln's Inn Fields, so called because of its recent founding as a result of the 1695 revolt of veteran performers from Drury Lane's managers. As Wright points out, one thing that was excluded from this entity was the considerable amount of theater that took place outside the walls of these buildings and without the kind of state authorization under which the two patent companies operated. One example would be the mystery plays, which had been performed by guilds since the middle ages. Wright's Cavalier recalls that such performances, enacted on "Stages Erected in the open Street" (20), had not only displayed the guilds' talents but had been considered a legitimate component of the "noble Entertainment" organized to celebrate public events such as the wedding of Prince Arthur in 1501. To these urban performances we can add those that took place in the London fairgrounds and provincial town squares on a seasonal basis, to coincide with market days and festivals, as well as the performances of religious plays during the significant seasons of the ecclesiastical year, the liturgical plays such as the Chester Cycle, which continued to be performed well into the early nineteenth century. All of these forms of "theater" predated the establishment of professional, stationary theatrical companies in the late sixteenth century and long survived the latter's elevation to license and legitimacy at the Restoration in 1660. Wright imagines that the occlusion of extramural performances from what was normatively understood to be the theater specifies as much as anything else the difference between the contemporary stage and English performances of the "last age" and before. To equate the English theater with the licensed houses, Wright implies, is to cut it off from its origins as a vagrant and occasional mode of public performance, and from its role in a society where elite and plebeian institutions intermingled with and supported each other.

The restrictive definition of theater that Wright resists has important implications for any attempt to define the nature and scope of performance in late seventeenth- and early eighteenth-century England. We know frustratingly little, for example, about what the performances at even the London fairgrounds at Smithfield and Bartholomew Fair were like, much less about the nature of many kinds of performances that took place in the provinces. Nor does it help that no small part of what we do know comes by way of hostile observers and those who were campaigning for the abolition of, or stricter control over, fairs, pastimes, and itinerant performers.[4] Yet it seems likely, even certain, that more people witnessed and derived significance from such performances than ever attended plays or other entertainments in the London patent houses. It is of course not news to learn that some people's experiences count for more than others in the way that a culture thinks and writes about itself, but it is worth remembering at the outset that only certain types of public performance were defined as worthwhile objects for patronage by the theatergoing public and as legitimate subjects for polite critical discussion, and hence are readily available to us for historical and critical analysis. The history of performance is inseparable from the history of recording, since records are the means through which performances are preserved and brought into intelligibility to those who were not present to witness them. And to recall that these intertwined histories are always and everywhere intimately related not only to the available modes of technology, but to their culture's structures of power and strategies of legitimation is to be warned against too quickly accepting the definitions handed down to us as sufficient or normative. We need not share Wright's nostalgia to recognize the force of his implicit claim that the English stage is not a pregiven object, ready to be discussed and assessed, but a critical and historical *problem,* one that demands articulation rather than silent or unreflective acceptance. What kind of thing *was* the English stage as seventeenth- and eighteenth-century theatergoers, critics, players, managers, and playwrights defined and understood it? What was its relation to the broader traditions of performance from which it had emerged? And where can we locate early eighteenth-century pantomime, a form of entertainment that was taken by many to constitute a threat to the integrity of the English stage, within these traditions?

To ask such questions is to enter into the scholarly inquiry conducted over the last four decades into the constitution of early modern "popular culture."[5] What most studies of this topic share is the heuristic distinction between elite and popular, or patrician and plebeian class fractures, identifying a split between the great mass of the people and a much smaller group who hold the lion's share of power and influence in the culture. Such a division, most accounts argue, expanded in the course of the early modern period, such that by the late eighteenth century, the "people" were now so separated from the educated elite that they would become an object of research and study, as antiquarians and scholars began to collect the tales, songs, dances, and rituals of the common folk. Peter Burke, whose work has offered perhaps the most elegant and influential descriptions of the distinction between the two poles, as well as the shifting relations between them, sums the model up as follows: "the crucial cultural difference in early modern Europe (I want to argue) was that between the majority, for whom popular culture was the only culture, and the minority, who had access to the great tradition but participated in the little tradition as a second culture. They were amphibious, bi-cultural. . . . For the elite, but for them only, the two traditions had different psychological functions; the great tradition was serious, the little tradition was play" (28). Burke's argument has come in for criticism by writers who have wanted to break down the binary structure his model erects, arguing, for example, that neither elite nor popular cultures were as self-identical as the terms lead us to think, and that traffic between them was more mutual than even Burke's sense of the "amphibious" nature of elite members of the society would suggest. And, too, such a model tends to obscure other types of difference, such as the distinctive experiences of women, the regional variations within and between countries, or the character and affiliations of the group that identified itself as the "middling sort." But it has proven difficult to this point to replace the general terms of the schematic, to avoid using the rhetoric of what has been called a "bipolar" model even when writers wish to call attention to, and then to avoid, its biases and blind spots.

Ultimately, we might need to come up with new terms, or perhaps to think of a way to represent the social groupings of early modern culture through some medium other than language alone, perhaps through something on the order of Charles Joseph Minard's famous 1869 chart describing Napoleon's Russian campaign, which plots no less than six variables at once, allowing the viewer to see temporal, geographical, demographic, and climatological data in a single glance. In the absence of so radical a reconceptualization of early modern society (not to mention academic discourse), much recent work has attempted to bypass the limitations of the two-poles model by turning attention to the *relationship* between segments of the larger culture (a conception that itself must probably be considered carefully, as a fractured, shifting, and multiple domain rather than the singular and unified entity that a term so powerful as *culture* evokes). Thus E. P. Thompson, while adhering to the bipolar scheme of a culture divided between patricians and plebeians, offers the metaphor of a "theater" to describe the "ritualized or stylized performances, whether in recreation or in forms of protest" by means of which the "confrontations" that constitute culture take place.[6] And Roger Chartier has offered the term *appropriation* to describe the way that people below the level of elite society used materials—particularly printed works like chapbooks, Bibles, conduct books, and didactic texts of all sorts—in ways quite different from those intended by their (generally elite) sponsors, receiving them according to their own needs and adapting them to their own purposes.[7] Chartier's critical gaze focuses on the objects themselves, the materials like ballads, books, and images that are taken up and put to different uses according to local need and specific situation.[8]

Still, terms such as *appropriation* and *theater,* drawn into historiography from systems of discourse that do most of their work outside it, are imprecise and partial, instruments to help us measure the dynamic relations in a society rather than concepts that can explain everything about one. In particular, each carries with it some negative associations: in the case of *appropriation,* the sense of theft or pilferage, as well as, as Barry Reay has pointed out, a potential to become "static," to lead us to forget that "once an item, idea, or an action has been appropriated, it is no longer the 'same' item, idea, or action."[9] Thus, for example, the Harlequin who performed on the eighteenth-century London stage is not identical with the Harlequin of the Continental tradition; he shares a name, a costume, and many key features with that figure, but he developed an indigenous set of traits and conventions, the most notable of which is that English Harlequins of the first part of the eighteenth century, unlike their predecessors and continental contemporaries, did not speak. And in the case of *theater,* it is hard to avoid the sense of insincerity and artifice that seems to suggest that actions taken in such an arena are trivial, lacking long-term effects. Nor does either metaphor help us much appreciate the affective dimension of culture, the emotional freight carried along in the dynamic processes of cultural affiliation, disavowal, borrowing, and transformation.[10]

Early eighteenth-century observers tended to polarize and simplify these processes, typically arguing that the taste for entertainment rather than edifying drama epitomized the vulgarization of polite taste. By the 1720s, pantomime had emerged as one of the best indicators of this process, its popularity with all audience segments a sign of how "popular" tastes had infiltrated "elite" culture. In a kind of satirical closet "After-Entertainment"—written in the form of an afterpiece, though never meant to be staged—entitled *The British Stage* (1724), for example, a character dressed as an ass identifies himself as "the Town" embodied; a ridiculously credulous spectator, he enthusiastically leads the audience in applause at Harlequin's tricks.[11] Another contemporary satire in much the same spirit and format, *The English Stage Italianiz'd* (1727), makes it clear that "the Town" was understood to refer to a polite, rather than a plebeian formation; the anonymous author exclaims at "this hurly-burly of Coaches, this Conflagration of Glambeaux, this Circle of Belles, this crowd of Beaux" who are gathered outside a theater playing a new pantomime.[12] What becomes intelligible in such comments here is not only a concern about the decline of polite taste, but a new and more rigid conception of social class itself, one demanding that a high degree of vigilance be maintained in order not only that social ranks be kept separate, but that modes of spectatorship associated with one formation not be indulged in by another. Describing the phobias and pleasures associated with such interminglings, Peter Stallybrass and Allon White note that "a sort of refined mimicry sets into the salons and ballrooms of Europe" in the early eighteenth century at the very moment when (to cite their own example) such forms of entertainment as the commedia dell'arte were being expelled from Paris: "the imagery, masks and costumes of the popular carnival are being (literally) put on by the aristocracy and the bourgeoisie in order to simultaneously express and conceal their sexual desire and the pleasure of the body."[13] In the way it identifies mimicry as the structure of the relationship between popular and polite classes, Stallybrass and White's analysis resembles that of eighteenth-century observers, who displaced their anxiety over the psychosexual purposes of such imitation by casting their analyses in the mode of satire.

The case is more complicated than such an account would suggest. Stallybrass and White's equation of commedia dell'arte with popular culture needs to be problematized by the fact that the continental commedia was from its very inception a professional institution. From the outset, it offered a stylized version of types drawn from plebeian and bourgeois culture and frequently addressed itself to an aristocratic audience as early as the sixteenth century. Rather than the transparent representation of the common people, originating solely in sites like the fair and the street, eighteenth-century pantomime was always a highly mediated form, blending continental and native traditions that had themselves typically been subjected to professional and critical codification. Pantomime's plural and complicated history, not to mention the hybrid character of the form itself, testifies to the way that all representations of and from so-called popular cultures are stylized, mediated, and multiply determined, requiring us to assess them critically, with an awareness of their transmission through the processes of appropriation, disavowal, theft, and distantiation.

Far from giving us an accurate description of the social order, categories like "Smithfield," "the mob," and "the Town," as well as "the people" in the early eighteenth century can be taken as evidence of a new strategy for organizing the domain of the social, the application of a logic of kind that seeks to demarcate the boundaries between groups and to regulate the proper forms of traffic between them.[14] Stallybrass and White describe this as a process by which "hybrid" forms where the classes intermingled—their example is the fair—are stigmatized for their confusion so that an emergent bourgeoisie could define it as Other.[15] Much the same logic of kind extends to the categories that were deployed to describe cultural productions. The very term and concept of the commedia dell'arte itself as a distinguishable class of performance, for instance, probably dates to mid-eighteenth-century Italy, when the playwright Carlo Goldoni invented it as a means of distinguishing the improvised performances of the traditional companies from his own more explicitly scripted, *literary*, deployments of similar material.[16] The new development in the late seventeenth and early eighteenth centuries was not so much the performances themselves, but the categories for defining, classifying, and understanding them. Categories like "the people," "pantomime," and "mere entertainment" are thus in a sense brought into being by the emergence of institutions for which they became the foil: the middling sort, the individual author, and the literary.

Ultimately, the English stage can be added to this inventory, separated out from the broader context of performance throughout the culture to constitute a recognizable class and object in its own right. To specify how this happened, we need to look at the role of the state in making diversions a part of its purview, which recast entertainment into an aspect of statecraft. As it happens, pantomime's genealogy in the commedia dell'arte performances that began being staged in England in the late sixteenth century provides an excellent place to witness how the "people" became defined as the destined target of entertainment. Although the moment when it first arrived in England is unknowable, commedia's assimilation into English institutions can be traced, revealing a pattern of appropriation and distinction that helps us understand how the theater became a "case" in its own right.

From Commedia dell'arte to English Pantomime

When English pantomime came to prominence in the 1720s and 1730s, it appeared to observers as something new and striking; to many, it constituted a new kind of threat to a traditional literary culture. But pantomime's novelty had much more to do with the terms with which it was defined than with any originality in its constituent parts; considered as a form promising sheer entertainment, it seemed new and scandalous, but if we imagine it as a synthesis of dance, song, commedia dell'arte, and classical myth, we can see that it had many antecedents. As I observed in the previous chapter's description of *Perseus and Andromeda,* the basic structure of eighteenth-century pantomime, where harlequinade comic or "grotesque" sections alternated with serious sections based on classical myths, strongly resembles that of the Stuart court masque, which alternated masque and antimasque episodes. Much as in eighteenth-century English pantomime, court masques used classical myth to offer a vision of harmony and order, a vision that was periodically upended by antimasquers, figures of misrule who were ultimately routed by the royal and aristocratic masquers in attendance.[17] Regular members of the cast of such antimasques were the continental commedia characters—Harlequin, Scaramouche, Colombine, Pierrot, Pantaloon, and so on.[18]

What is more, this early seventeenth-century form had already been mediated at least once by the time it reached its early eighteenth-century manifestation. In the 1690s and early 1700s, the Anglicized Huguenot playwright and impresario Peter Motteux had used the term *masque* to describe a series of spectacles based on classical myths (e.g., *The Rape of Europa by Jupiter* [1694], *The Loves of Mars and Venus* [1697], *Acis and Galatea* [1701]) that he mounted in the public playhouses in London.[19] Edward Ravenscroft's farce *The Anatomist,* first produced in 1696, was, according to its printed text, also "Acted together" with Motteux's *The Loves of Mars and Venus,* interweaving comic business with musical interludes in a pattern that closely resembles the two-part structure of later pantomimes.[20] Motteux's masques continued to be performed at the patent houses into the 1710s, when they gave way to the "dramatic entertainments in dancing," based on many of the same stories, which John Weaver, the dancing-master at Drury Lane, staged in London starting in the middle of that decade. It was Weaver's protégé John Thurmond who choreographed Drury Lane's 1723 production of *Harlequin Doctor Faustus,* which concluded with a "masque of the deities," where the pagan gods and goddesses Flora, Iris, Mars, Bacchus, Ceres, Mercury, and Diana "express their Joy for the Enchanter's Death," marking the return of order to a cosmos temporarily upended by Harlequin Faustus's pranks.[21]

The resemblance between eighteenth-century pantomime and the Stuart masque points to the way that commedia had found itself appropriated for the purposes of advancing Stuart ideology, about which more shortly. We might thus best imagine commedia characters serving in the context of the Stuart court masque as a stylized and exoticized image of the "people," whose anarchic impulses and wants threatened the orderly progress of aristocratic rule, and whose repulsion by the aristocratic masquers at the end of the performance signified their successful containment. More immediately, the even closer link to the late Restoration "masques" organized by Motteux underscores how the degree to which early eighteenth-century pantomime emerged out of a heterogeneous mix of various kinds of afterpiece and entr'acte performances that had been common in the London patent theaters since at least the 1670s: farces, burlesques, dances, masques, acrobatics, and commedia dell'arte scenarios. From the 1670s on, the London playhouses offered a variety of performance modes and styles, multiple attractions that relied very little on plot or even language for their appeal.

We need, though, to look farther back, tracing the English theater's appropriation and transformation of commedia dell'arte characters and plot material through the sixteenth and seventeenth centuries, with a particular eye to the uses to which continental commedia was put. As theater historians have long acknowledged, commedia dell'arte characters and scenarios were a familiar feature of the English theater, both the London companies and performances in market towns and villages from the sixteenth century on. Continental commedia may have filled a partial vacuum in performance created by the attacks on traditional pastimes and revels waged by reformers throughout the late sixteenth and early seventeenth centuries. Both the London playhouses and rural plays and pastimes were affected by the suppression of many types of performance during the Interregnum, as well as by the disbanding of the London companies, which had brought performances to market towns and great houses through tours, by order of Parliament in 1642. But some kinds of performance seem to have flown under the radar of reformist critique, and commedia dell'arte seems to have been one of these, its foreignness perhaps seeming to render it less of a threat to reformers than indigenous modes of play.[22] We can be sure that commedia troupes from the continent started including England on their itineraries by no later than the middle of the sixteenth century, when the reform of native English pastimes was under way.[23] Their stock characters and scenarios were imitated by English theater companies as early as the Elizabethan period; the young Richard Burbage, later to become the leading actor in many of William Shakespeare's plays, performed in *The Dead Man's Fortune,* an adapted commedia scenario, in 1590, and John Day's *The Travailes of the Three English Brothers* (1607) stages a meeting between an Italian Harlequin and the English clown Will Kemp, here appearing *in propria persona.*[24]

English playwrights may have appropriated commedia characters (sometimes under different names) and plot elements for their mainpiece productions as well. Scholars and theater historians of the first half of the twentieth century like Edward Gordon Craig, Allardyce Nicoll, and Kathleen Lea frequently identified places where they believed that commedia influenced Shakespeare, Jonson, and other English Renaissance dramatists. Henry Salerno's 1967 translation of Flaminio Scala's 1611 collection of commedia scenarios, *Il Teatro Delle Favole Rappresentative,* similarly includes an appendix that outlines many places of overlap between the fifty plots of Scala's collection and the English Renaissance repertory.[25] But, as Kenneth and Laura Richards have more recently argued, it is difficult to make a definitive case for the direct influence of continental commedia on English plays of this period; similarities between situations and characters can frequently be explained as easily by referring to classical sources or scripted drama. Moreover, a term like *influence* seems misleading here, because it inevitably prompts one to imagine how an isolated figure—the author or actor—consciously or unconsciously assimilates material generated by an anonymous mass of performers. We might well rather stress how the English professional theater and the continental companies shared many traditions and trajectories through the sixteenth and seventeenth centuries. Each, for example, began organizing itself into the form of the company in the mid- to late sixteenth century; each developed both popular and aristocratic clientele; important works of each repertory reached print in the 1610s and 1620s (Scala's collection of 1611; Jonson's *Workes* of 1616; Shakespeare's Folio of 1623). Crucially important differences between the national traditions remained, but so too were there significant differences from region to region within each nation, as well as from company to company. What is clear is that Renaissance audiences in England were familiar with the commedia characters, and English writers were thus able to compare their public theater with the professional theater of Italy, most typically in chauvinistic terms. In *Pierce Penilesse* (1592), Thomas Nashe claims that the English theater is better than those "beyond the sea," because it stages the "true tragedies" of "Emperours, Kings and Princes," rather than the stories of "a Pantaloun, a Whore, and a Zanie."[26]

The Restoration theater's interactions with and borrowings from the Continental commedia tradition are better documented. The patent theaters staged Edward Ravenscroft's *Scaramouch a Philosopher, Harlequin a School-Boy, Bravo, Merchant, and Magician: A Comedy After the Italian Manner* (1677); Aphra Behn's *The Emperor of the Moon* (1687), adapted from a French commedia scenario; and Nahum Tate's *A Duke and No Duke,* adapted from Sir Aston Cokain's 1658 *Trappolin Suppos'd Servant,* a play probably inspired by performances Cokain took in during some Venetian sojourns in the 1630s.[27] These native adaptations followed on the heels of, and were probably inspired by, visits by two Italian theatrical companies to London in the 1670s, both of which were sponsored by the Stuart court. In 1673, Tiberio Fiorello's company performed at Whitehall for both the royal household and the general public; Charles II ordered medals and gold chains to be presented to members of the company to commemorate the event, and the company seems to have been invited back the next year. The Duke of Modena's company of players came in late 1678 and early 1679 as a gift to the Italian wife of James, Duke of York, from her brother; their visit was less successful than Fiorello's company's had been because it coincided with the early months of the Popish Plot, which made the continental and Catholic links of the Stuart family particularly suspect.

Meetings between the Stuart kings and the leaders of commedia troupes make more sense than they otherwise might when understood in the broader context of absolutist ideology, which, at least in theory, took such entertainments to be a vital part of the monarch's purview. In hosting performers from the continental companies, the Stuarts were not simply indulging their well-known taste for continental modes and emphasizing their links to other European dynasties, but also fulfilling their role as the superintendents of their people's pastimes and entertainments. As Leah Marcus has argued, Stuart kings attempted to define the theater as one of the several public pastimes over which the monarch presided. James I had articulated the theory in his *Book of Sportes* in 1618, which explicitly required that the traditional English games and pastimes be permitted on Sundays and holidays, against the desires of clerical, and particularly Puritan, attempts to stigmatize and suppress such pastimes as heathenish or papist relics; Charles I reissued his father's book in 1633 and ordered that its teachings be enforced.[28] All four of the Stuarts asserted a claim that one responsibility of the monarch was to authorize and supervise the recreation of his people in the manner of a benevolent father observing his children at play, a position that enhanced their authority by seeming to abnegate it. Marcus describes the ideological stakes and pragmatic expectations subtending the maneuver well: "By placing their official stamp of approval on the old pastimes, James and Charles I attempted to extend royal power into an area of ambivalence and instability, to channel the equivocal status of popular festival into what we can perhaps call an official 'paradox of state'—a condition of happy ambiguity in which the license and lawlessness associated with the customs could be interpreted as submission to authority."[29] Commedia dell'arte may have appealed to the Stuarts because these scenarios, depicting rustics and servants, supported the absolutist conceit of the monarch as father of his people, kindly providing for their play.

Upon his return from exile in 1660, Charles I affirmed his desire to exploit this "paradox of state" and encouraged the revival of rural revels, wakes, and rituals, as well as the theater. The simultaneous restoration of the monarchy and the playhouses represented much more than Charles's fondness for the theater, or even an expression of loyalty to a family tradition. Like many of his initial actions upon taking the throne, this was an attempt to erase the memory of the Interregnum by using the seeming permanence of such institutions to assert an essential continuity between the prewar period and the present.[30] The very timelessness of the theatrical patent as a legal instrument—it was understood to be a permanent item of property, able to be passed down like a landed estate—expressed the confidence that both the monarchy and the institution it authorized would endure. Such enduring institutions seemed to call forth the equally timeless entity of the "people" over whom the monarchs had sovereignty. Just before the Restoration, the Duke of Newcastle urged Charles II to encourage theaters and other forms of entertainment because "these Devertisementes will amuse the peoples thoughts And keep them in harmless actions, which will free your Majestie from Faction, & Rebellion."[31]

The Stuarts' embrace of the theater and other pastimes was thus an aspect of statecraft, an attempt to manage the population by the logic of what Michel Foucault, in some late writings on the science he termed "governmentality"—the application of critical reason to the organization and sustenance of the state.[32] I will have much more to say about eighteenth-century British applications of governmentality later in this book; here, I want to note the way in which the category of the people emerges as an object of knowledge in the framework of absolutist monarchy, where it becomes the object for which diversions are designed, yet whose pleasures are understood to serve, not so much its interests, but those of the feudal state. Following this logic, in her dedication to *The Emperor of the Moon,* Aphra Behn stresses that the play to follow must be understood as a "diversion," albeit one with a determinate purpose. Rather than being merely intended for "the numbers, who comprehend nothing beyond the show and buffoonery," *The Emperor of the Moon*—which was translated from a French adaptation of commedia material—has been, Behn writes, "calculated for his late majesty of sacred memory," Charles II, who had died in 1685. Behn's point, then, is not only that Charles would have enjoyed *The Emperor of the Moon* had he lived to see it, but that he also would have taken pleasure in presiding over an entertainment that diverted his people. As Behn puts it, the "magnificence" of the diversions "of old" was the "sign of a flourishing state."[33] Behn thus offers *The Emperor of the Moon* as an example of an entertainment that will correctly channel the attention of great "numbers" of persons in directions that will be to the advantage of the Stuart dynasty and the state that it rules. She presents the English people as a mass to be apprehended from a position of rational detachment, conceptualized as "the numbers" who cannot be counted on to understand what is best for them, and who must therefore be wisely supervised and shepherded by the aristocracy.

It is a little heartening to realize, perhaps, that the Stuart monarchs' attempts to appropriate the theater as an aspect of their rule remained an ideal rather than reality, as the reception of one of their attempts to appropriate commedia dell'arte makes clear. In the 1670s and 1680s, Charles and James opened their private theater at Whitehall to a general audience as a way of ostentatiously performing their role as superintendent of the people's sports and pastimes. But the evidence from reports by observers close to, but not formally aligned with, the court suggests that this was only partly successful, and that the conditions of theatrical performance in the city, at least, demonstrated how the traditional absolutist theory was confronting a new commercial economy of money and exchange with which it was incompatible. In his diary, John Evelyn commented on having seen an "Italian *Scaramucchio*" perform at Whitehall, and found "very Scandalous" the fact that people were paying money to attend.[34] The scandal, as Evelyn sees it, is not that the common people were allowed into the Banqueting House, but that they were expected to *pay*, which he observed to be a new thing "at Court Diversions." Andrew Marvell's account of the Fiorello company's performances records how the occasion seemed to undermine the distinction between the private court entertainments and performances at the public theaters; observing how the king had made certain that "even a twelve-penny Gallery is builded for the convenience of his Majesty's poorer Subjects," Marvell also noted that "all Sorts of People" came to Whitehall and paid to enter, "as at a common Playhouse."[35] And even from the point of view of the playhouses themselves, Stuart loyalists such as Behn could not help but notice how such performances now had to compete in a broader arena of debate and opinion, one over which the monarch had little control. Indeed, her dedication to *The Emperor of the Moon* gains a special urgency because of the kinds of entertainments that have filled the void created by the death of Charles II. For against such useful diversions as the play she offers, Behn opposes the current interest in "public controversies in taverns, coffee-houses, &c.," the debates over politics and religion that occupy the attention of Londoners to the point that they have lost interest in the theater.

Marvell, Evelyn, and Behn understood well the purpose behind such royal appropriations of continental commedia, but they also began to see, if not with great clarity, how and where the monarch's authority over popular "Devertisements" was being supplanted. On the one hand, the very playhouses for which Charles II had granted patent rights at the start of his reign were increasingly pursuing a logic quite different from the one under which they had been founded. If to the monarch the patents were a means of institutionalizing his traditional role as supervisor of entertainment, to the managers they were the conditions of the London stage's becoming a money-making cartel. From this point on, the conditions of the market—for example, the cost of new productions versus their expected revenues, the differential popularity of works with the audience, the strict rationing of innovation characteristic of cartel systems more generally—would mediate between performances and the audiences, readers, and critics who receive, enjoy, and assess them, transforming popular traditions and literary culture alike into something that could be sold for a price. This is a particularly pessimistic way to put it, but there is no point in denying that by the late seventeenth century, the London theaters were recognized to be commercial ventures that were unable, and frequently unwilling, to hide the fact that they were money-making enterprises, their managers often exercising their authority with a breathtaking and shameless degree of crassness.

On the other hand, Behn's remark that her play had been shunted to the side by the diverting talk of political debate points to how the theater and the court that it entertained and supported had by now become one of many objects of attention in what scholars in the last decade and a half, informed by the early work of Habermas and the many theorists and historians writing in its wake, have come to call the bourgeois public sphere. Emerging as a recognizable entity in the late seventeenth and early eighteenth centuries in Europe, the bourgeois public sphere constituted a domain of opinion, debate, and dissent that explicitly set itself apart from the absolutist court, promoting its own standards of taste, judgment, and manners. As an ardent monarchist and a Stuart loyalist to boot, Behn laments this turn of events, understanding it to be a diminution of the Crown's authority as the monarch's voice is drowned out by what she can only perceive to be a cacophony of unregulated voices pouring out of the City's coffeehouses.

But the emergence of this public sphere of debate and discussion would have more significant and permanent effects on cultural productions such as the theater than just the attenuation of their relationship to the monarch. By the late seventeenth century, the English stage had become defined as an object of critical discussion, an institution with a history that could be reconstructed by scholars and norms that needed to be articulated by critics. To invoke a term used by contemporary writers, the English stage was now apprehensible as a "case" in its own right, distinct from the feudal state and from popular culture alike. In this critical framework, the pastimes of the common people became, as they are in Wright, modes of performance existing at the other side of an historical break, and inhabiting a domain of culture that was largely distinct from the performances offered at the London playhouses. At the same time, such a separation prompted desires to reinforce, or, perhaps more accurately, reinvent the terms of the linkage between the theater, the state, and the lives of the "people," now conceived as an object of nostalgia. Writers of the 1690s debated whether the ancient performance practice known as "pantomime" could be appropriated to imagine how the theater could be returned to its origins and ritual and brought back under the purview of the state. The debate achieved material form in the blizzard of pamphlets constituting the "Collier controversy," which, more than anything else, registers the culture's profound ambivalence about this abstraction of theater from ritual, its unmooring from the institutions of belief and compulsion. It is to this separation, and the critical context within which it was articulated, that we now turn.

The Roman Pantomimi and the "Case" of the English Stage

As Habermas describes it, the bourgeois public sphere is a place devoted to text, relying for its emergence and its continuing existence as an object of historical study on the written and particularly the printed word. After the lapse of the Press Licensing Act in 1695, the quantity and availability of printed materials in England increased greatly, and it is no mere coincidence that the first intense public-sphere debate concerning the London playhouses—the controversy set off by the publication of Jeremy Collier's *A Short View of the Immorality, and Prophaneness of the English Stage*—would begin only three years later. What I want to stress here is how the new prominence of print shaped the terms of the emergent critical discussion on the theater, prompting observers to define the stage at least partly in its terms. Writers like Gerard Langbaine and John Downes tended to imagine the theater as a domain of language and textuality, whose most important expressions were the words spoken by actors and preserved in the pages of printed playtexts.[36] Langbaine's *Account of the English Dramatick Poets* (1691), for example, lists all the authors of English plays, and describes, not their biographies, but the editions in which their work appears and the sources upon which they drew. As he constructs books designed "so that the Reader may at one glance view each Authors Labours," Langbaine equates the English stage with the printed drama and identifies its central agents as the "Poets" who have created its repertoire.[37] John Downes's *Roscius Anglicanus* (1708) similarly offers a catalogue or account of the theatrical repertoire of the London patent houses, one crafted to cast attention on the performers rather than the writers. As the prompter at virtually all the major houses in the course of a career that started in 1642 and ended in 1706, Downes

enjoyed the prompter's customary rights over the theater's texts, most important, its promptbooks, but also its accounts and performance records.[38] Thus
he describes himself as, not the author, but rather the "Editor of the ensuing
Relation," which was compiled from other written texts in order to catalogue
the plays produced at the patent theaters from 1662 on, along with lists of
their casts. For both of these first-generation historians of the English stage,
the theater is first and foremost an institution constituted through language
and best realized in print.

When the theater is imagined this way, it is easy to disavow or ignore its
material components: scenery, spectacle, dance, song, and the human body
that performs them. To critics like the author of *A Comparison Between the
Two Stages* (1702), who claimed that the English stage had "kept its purity a
hundred years" by excluding "unnatural Ornaments" like dancing and
music, the fact that they had recently become "the very staple Commodity of
the Stage" was "scandalous," an indication of the contamination of a realm
normatively devoted to language.[39] The *Comparison's* version of theater history is misleading at best, for, as we have already seen, such "unnatural" elements had always been part and parcel of the English performance tradition.
But its claim makes explicit what other works of these years assume, that the
English stage was primarily a domain of language, and it also shows how
such a conception goes hand in hand with the idea that the English stage
could be equated with the two stages of the *Comparison's* title, the patent
theaters of London. Both assumptions mark a kind of double abstraction
that helped define the English stage as an entity in its own right, as the theater's language was disaggregated from all its other components and the English stage was distinguished as a separate thing from the broader performance
traditions out of which it had emerged.

That so narrow a definition of the stage can be put in the service of a more
ambitious project of cultural ordering and redefinition than a mere history
of the institution is indicated by the programmatic imperatives of Jeremy
Collier's *A Short View of the Immorality, and Prophaneness of the English Stage*
(1698), which shares with other works of the fin de siècle a desire to define
the English stage as primarily a medium for verbal performances. Readers of
Collier's *Short View* have for three centuries had good reason to feel betrayed
by its title, for at 288 pages, Collier's work is far from short. And it is fair to
say that Collier's rhetorical style makes his book seem even longer than it is;
sarcastic, argumentative, and frequently repetitious, his prose forms no small
barrier of its own to the reader's engagement and sympathy. Nor for that
matter does his book offer much in the way of a "view" of its subject; the

𝔅𝔶 𝔱𝔥𝔢 𝔖𝔱𝔞𝔤𝔢.

st? Sir without presuming to have an ex-
traordinary Opinion of my Figure, give me
leave to tell you, if you had seen as many
Lords as I have done, you would not think
it Impossible a Person of a worse Taille then   Relaps.
mine might be, a Modern Man of Quality.   p. 84.

I'm sorry to hear *Modern Quality* de-
generates so much. But by the way, these
Liberties are altogether new. They are
unpractised by the Latin *Comedians,* and
by the *English* too till very lately, as the   p. 24.
Plain Dealer observes. And as for *Moliere*
in *France,* he pretends to fly his Satir no
higher than a Marquis.   L' Ombre
de Mo'iere

And has our *Stage* a particular Privilege? Is their *Charter* inlarg'd, and are
they on the same Foot of Freedom with
the *Slaves* in the *Saturnalia?* Must all
Men be handled alike? Must their
Roughness be needs play'd upon Title?
And can't they lash the Vice without
pointing upon the *Quality?* If as Mr.
Dryden rightly defines it, a *Play ought*
to be a just Image of Humane Nature ; EssayDram
Why are not the Decencies of Life, and Poet.
the Respects of Conversation observ'd? p. 5.
Why must the Customes of Countries
be Cross'd upon, and the Regards of Ho-
nour overlook'd? What necessity is there
to kick the *Coronets* about the. *Stage,* and
to make a Man a Lord, only in order to
make

Page from Collier's *Short View* (*Special Collections Department, University of Virginia Library*)

Short View contains no illustrations and attempts very little if any description of staged performances or actors, scenery, or costume design. Rather, Collier fixes his attention rigorously on the *language* of the plays he discusses, subjecting them to the kind of detailed analysis that, as Simon Shepherd and Peter Womack have noted, had to this point been reserved for scriptural texts. Collier translates the professional habits of a clergyman trained in the exegesis of scripture to the contemporary repertory of the English stage, which he approaches primarily by means of printed editions rather than his memory of performances. Collier's book appropriates the form of a biblical commentary in its very layout and design, identifying the passages it discusses by scene and line in the margins.[40] Why does Collier's title go against the grain of the material embodiment and the critical procedure of the book that follows?

Collier's title alludes to another book, and, as several critics have noted, can best be understood as a kind of quotation of that of Thomas Rymer's treatise *A Short View of Tragedy*, published in December 1692.[41] But Collier's gesture to Rymer does more than acknowledge the latter's influence and declare Collier's affiliations to Rymer's neoclassical project. The quotation of Rymer's title facilitates what I believe to be Collier's most important critical move, which is to define the English stage as a kind of genre, on the model of a literary genre as it was understood by neoclassical theory. In effect, Collier takes Rymer's title and redefines its object as the national theater, which can now be defined as an institution that has its own norms, rules, and examples. Collier offers the "English Stage" of his title as a kind of genre or *thing* in itself, a concept that can be abstracted out from other literary and social domains in England. Translating Rymer's generic frame into a national one, Collier defines the English stage as a case in its own right, one that can be judged according to whether or not it fulfills the norms established by that sort of case. Thus, his *Short View* begins by positing that "the business of *Plays* is to recommend Virtue and discountenance *Vice*," and asserts that "this Design has been oddly pursued by the English *Stage*" (1). The contemporary English theater is found lacking by virtue of the fact that it fails to fulfill the purpose of its *kind* of thing, violating the generic norms of an institution that to Collier's mind is bound by rules in the manner of a literary genre. Such a logic of kind informs Collier's text throughout. He invokes it, for example, to explain why it is that he is particularly offended at "smutty" language when it is uttered by female characters. Collier argues that an author who makes women speak "smutty" language will "throw them out of their Kind" by representing women as anything other than modest, which is the "distinguishing Vertue of that Sex" (10-11). So too, Collier objects to the presence of foolish clergymen on the stage because such depictions typically "endeavour to expose not only the Men, but the Business" (97), mocking not individuals, but the clergy as a class or kind. When, then, Collier claims that "the Roman and Greek *Theatres* were much more inoffensive than ours" (15), his key term must be understood to be *ours*, for it demonstrates how fully he has appropriated the neoclassical logic of kind as deployed by Rymer to define the English stage as an object of study, comparison, and censure.

Even more explicitly than most of his contemporaries, Collier articulates that the English theater had by this time become intelligible as an entity in its own right. But he emphasizes the degree to which the theater has been segregated out from other domains of its own culture such as the church and the court mostly as a way of lamenting, or even castigating, that separation, decrying it as the mark of modern corruption. Collier's attack on what he perceived as the excesses of the Restoration stage derives from his desire to reclaim the theater as an institution of state, which would once again place it under the purview of churchmen like himself. A Stuart loyalist who had lost his place in the church for absolving several Jacobite traitors on the scaffold in 1696, Collier wants to reforge the traditional link between the theater and the feudal state that the Stuart monarchs had asserted. To Collier, the English theater's newfound autonomy from the state and the church is the very essence of its corruption, its abnegation of a traditional responsibility that the English stage of the present shares with the theaters of the ancient world.

Collier takes the classical genealogy of the theater as part of the state's ritual function to mean that the theater must be considered, not as a "Diversion," but as a serious institution, a form of ritual derived from and normatively inseparable from religious ceremony (199). For this reason, he cites— often at great length—passages where the church fathers declaim against the theater, not because the theater is inherently opposed to religion, but because in its current state as a form of "entertainment," it profanes the ritual practices that had originally supported faith by engaging the sensoria of its votaries. There is some self-interest at work here, as Collier's desire to bring the theater back under the purview of the church-state apparatus would enhance the authority of men like him over against the authority of the licentious "Poets" who constitute the most consistent target of his attack. Collier's *Short View* thus frequently derides English playwrights who go for laughs by including foolish clergymen in their works, claiming that priests were never an object of ridicule in the theater of the ancient world (122). But Collier's ultimate goal in defending the authority of the church is to heal the breach between ritual practices and mere diversion that he takes the English stage of his own era to epitomize, to return to what he claims was the more fully integrated culture of the ancient world, when entertainment was placed in the service of religion, which was in turn intimately connected to the life of the state. At stake, then, in the broader Collier controversy to which the *Short View* gave rise was a question of the historical *situation* of the modern theater, which Collier typically framed as a question of the degree of similarity between the English stage and the theater of ancient Greece and Rome: was it, to use the term that Collier and others frequently deployed, a parallel *case* with the classical theater, an institution that occupied much the same location in the culture that the theater had in ancient Greece and Rome? Or, rather, were these cases so utterly different as to call for distinct critical, historical, and theoretical approaches?[42]

The conflict between these two positions became most intelligible in the argument between Collier and Drake over the status of the Roman pantomime dancers, the *mimi* and *pantomimi*. Their debate at first might seem to be merely a side-argument in the larger controversy catalyzed by the publication of Collier's *Short View*, but it is more significant than that. Their dispute would help set the terms for the defense of English pantomime in the early part of the eighteenth century. And it also demonstrates how the discourse around pantomime would be a proxy for the much more significant question of the place of the theater within the culture as a whole, whether it was normatively a serious institution of state or potentially a site for mere entertainment.

Toward the end of the *Short View*, Collier offers what appears to be a bit of preemptive self-criticism, anticipating the objections of readers who would not agree that what he terms "the parity of the Case" (276) that he has constructed between the modern English and the ancient Roman stages applies:

> But it may be objected, is the Resemblance exact between Old *Rome* and *London*, will the Paralel [*sic*] hold out, and has the *English Stage* any Thing so bad as the *Dancing* of the *Pantomimi?* I don't say that: The *Modern Gestures* tho' bold, and Lewd too sometimes, are not altogether so scandalous as the *Roman*. Here then we can make them some little Abatement. (277)

James Drake seized upon Collier's passing reference to the Roman pantomime dancers as an opening that undermined the *Short View*'s entire argument. By admitting that the English stage offered nothing as profane as the pantomime dancers, Collier demonstrated that he had disingenuously misidentified his very object of study. Drake argues that the church fathers had opposed, not the theater as a whole, but only those "Heathen Shows" that had clearly and deliberately exploited the sensual resources of the stage, conflating religion and theatricality in such a way as to seduce spectators who understood "almost all its acts of Devotion but so many entertainments of their Senses" (14). The Roman *mimi* and *pantomimi,* dancers who wordlessly performed stories drawn from pagan mythology, were the most egregious offenders, since their productions so obviously and unavoidably exploited the stage's materiality; in such performances, Drake argues, "the Amours of the Gods or Heroes were not related only, but sung to Musick in luscious fulsome Verse, mimickt in lewd dances with obscene Gestures and naked Postures, and even the very Adulteries and Rapes themselves express'd by scandalous actions" (28). The *pantomimi* were for this reason, according to Drake, the sole targets of the church fathers' attacks on the theater. To Drake, Collier's brief mention of the pantomime dancers is the sign of a guilty conscience; it is in effect Collier's return to the scene of his crime in having deliberately taken the church fathers to be making a general argument against theatrical representation as a whole rather than a restrictive argument against a particular species of performances.

Most important, Drake takes Collier's distortion to mark how far he has to go to argue that the English theater ought to be considered to be the equivalent of the ancient stage, to occupy much the same situation within contemporary English culture as it did in the classical world. By the terms of the rhetoric of casuistry that both men use, this would be to consider the English stage as a case, one so similar to that of the classical theater that the critiques of it leveled by the church fathers are still applicable. Drake argues otherwise, charging Collier with mistranslating critiques of the theater in antiquity to suit his argument, translating Tertullian's "Theatro" as "*Dramatick Bawdy-house*" precisely in order to condemn the theater as a whole with the crimes of the pantomimes alone: "in changing the Terms he has chang'd the state of the case, and made the Author accuse the *Drama* of those enormities, which were peculiar to the Shews of the *Mimi*" (31). When, then, Drake asserts that "the Authority of the Fathers ought to affect us no farther than their Reasonings will come up to our case" (33), his point is that the situations of the ancient and modern theaters within their own cultures are almost completely different. Hence, as Drake sees it, the arguments upon which Collier has based the entirety of his *Short View* are no longer relevant.

Collier's dispute with Drake could never be ranked as one of the most brilliant exchanges in the history of criticism; each man is contentious and self-serving, tilting evidence to support his own position and shamelessly distorting that of his opponent. But the dispute over the Roman mimes and pantomimes is significant, for it helps us identify some crucial questions about the nature of the English theater that would continue to resonate even after the public-sphere event known as the Collier controversy had more or less played itself out. First, their conflict demonstrates how the definition of the theater as a place of language and textuality sits uneasily with what we know to be a much more comprehensive history of performance, one where the human body was the main, even at times the only, means of communication. The controversy's focal concern about, and fascination with, the impact of the pantomime dancers on their spectators registers the powerful ambivalence that the theater's materiality incites, an anxiety that the physical elements of staged performance will overwhelm the ideas that are normatively transmitted by language. For Collier, the "bold Liberties and Luscious Pleasures" of the stage are located primarily in the way that it appeals to the imaginations of its spectators by virtue of its sensuality, its embodied liveness and materiality, which renders it a more powerful form of idolatry than any painted or sculpted representation could be: "Sence [sic] is stronger than Memory, and Life, than Painting."[43] The pantomime dancers, whose "gross Entertainments" were wordless, are thus only a particularly concentrated example of a universal and transhistorical problem of theatrical representation, the essential characteristics of which are to Collier's mind unchanged since the time of the ancient theater.[44] This is why Collier's seemingly offhand comments about the Roman pantomime dancers reveal that the controversy he set off is to some degree a conflict about the nature of modernity itself, whether the modern era operates according to a fundamentally different set of laws than held true in the past, or whether older norms are still fully applicable. Hence, as Drake implies, Collier's attempt to restore the theater to its putative origins in ritual process is essentially a *nostalgic* and anachronistic move, an attempt to turn the clock back to a period long past, when English culture might actually have presented a parallel case to that of the ancient world.

But this was not merely an academic argument. By the 1710s, the London theaters had begun staging afterpieces described as being "in imitation of" the ancient pantomime dances. The first of these is generally credited as being *The Loves of Mars and Venus,* composed and produced in 1717 by the English dancing-master John Weaver. Probably adapted in part from an earlier masque by Motteux, *The Loves of Mars and Venus* and Weaver's follow-up production, *Orpheus and Eurydice* (1718), were serious attempts to revive the ancient art, ones accompanied by scholarly introductions by Weaver and designed to give material form to the theories about the history of dance that he had advanced in his *Essay Towards an History of Dancing* (1712). The following chapter will analyze Weaver's program in further detail, but here I want to place his work in the context of the period's debate about the historical situation of the theater that we have been tracing by means of the Collier controversy. Weaver's attempted revival of ancient pantomime dancing can be understood as one of many aspects of the eighteenth century's neoclassicism, as he presents a return to the classical models—at least insofar as they are described in the small number of surviving ancient texts that discuss the theory and practice of dance—as a way of restoring an art that has fallen into decay and whose respectability as a liberal art has been forgotten.

To judge from the descriptions of these performances that Weaver published to promote and explain them, these entertainments reveled in the stage's physical and material elements, calling upon all the sensory resources of the medium to entertain their spectators; they would probably have horrified Collier had he lived to see them. But Weaver is in accord with Collier insofar as he takes the ancient stage to be a good model for the English stage because they occupy similar positions within their own cultures. Weaver argues that the ancient pantomime emerged as a way of reforming a stage that had grown corrupt and depraved, its tragedies and comedies "lost in Noise and Show" and the theater dominated by "the pompous Passage of a Triumph, Rope-dancing, and many other foolish Amusements."[45] Weaver's implication is that the English stage, its mainpiece repertory in some disrepute from the efforts of reformers like Collier, and similarly dominated in recent years by a variety of nondramatic amusements, offers a parallel case to the Roman theater. What is more, Weaver links that theater's decline and the "Depravity" of its audience's taste (119) with the nation's recent imperial conquests and the "Asiatick Luxury" (118) that they brought with them. Reading ancient Rome as a fitting allegory for contemporary Britain, Weaver promotes "pantomimic" dancing because of the way that it countered what he takes to be a similar enervation of both the stage and the state.

Neither *The Loves of Mars and Venus* nor the 1718 *Orpheus and Eurydice* incorporated a Harlequin or other commedia dell'arte figures. But, as we saw in the previous chapter, Weaver did combine harlequinade with classical myth in 1717 in *The Shipwreck; or, Perseus and Andromeda,* which he billed as "a Burlesque Entertainment of Dancing in Grotesque Figures," joining ancient myth with what his *Essay on the History of Dancing* identifies as a kind of dance—"the merry conceited Representations of Harlequin, Scaramouche, Mezzetin, Pasquariel"—that is merely "a faint Imitation of the *Roman Pantomimes*" (163).[46] *The Shipwreck* featured the silent Harlequin who would become conventional in the English "pantomimes" that were to come over the next years and decades; although there are examples of speaking

Harlequins in some entertainments of the late 1710s, English Harlequins would remain silent in the 1720s and 1730s, which was the most significant way in which they kept faith with their putative classical model and ancestor. Weaver's appropriation of the term *pantomime,* which would eventually be adopted for performances that had long forgotten the theoretical basis of his classicizing impulse, is a particularly sophisticated item of nostalgia, as it uses the parallel to ancient Rome to argue for a return to a more integrated public culture, a world where public performances represented the best traditions of the nation rather than offering mere sensual gratification.

For it is not really the passing of the classical period that these performances truly mourn, however much they appropriate its terms and cast of characters. Rather, I would argue that they mourn the more recent past of England itself, an imagined past before urbanization, commerce, and the emergence of the very public sphere of debate upon which Collier and his combatants relied had changed the nature of daily experience, leading to a desire to construct the people as an object of spectacle and nostalgia. Such a desire arose in part because of the suspicion on the part of urban, elite, literate culture that the process of politeness and reform, which they had counted on to save them from the vestiges of archaism and superstition that they associated with the feudal and Catholic past, as well as from the excesses that had led to civil war in the seventeenth century, had perhaps gone too far. Witnessing—with the distance created by aesthetic formalization and stylization—the actions of the common people might now act as a corrective to the very separation from the traditional rural culture that early Enlightenment intellectuals had worked so hard to achieve. Thus the antiquarian Henry Bourne praises many country folkways as worth emulating by city dwellers so obsessed with "secular business" as to fear the "Loss of Time" that would be expended on customary practices, particularly those that could be associated with ritual and devotion. Such village traditions as leaving off work on Saturday afternoon to prepare for the Sabbath run counter, Bourne observes, to "the politeness of the Age" (115), which is a good thing; they are just the kind of practice that urban sophisticates need to undertake in order to halt the secularizing and homogenizing effects of politeness.[47] Taking as his object the "common people," Bourne specifies and names an entity against which the "Town" could define itself, and demarcates the domain of society that figures in the eighteenth century's "revival" of pantomime such as Harlequin, Colombine, Pierrot, and Scaramouche—typically cast as servants and rustics and thus figures drawn from the great body of the common people—would represent.

More specifically, the character of Harlequin, as he was performed by English pantomime artists like John Rich, Theophilus Cibber, and Henry Woodward, drew on the association between the *Volk* and nature to recover an authentic discourse of the body. No character in the commedia tradition enjoyed a closer relationship to the most elemental needs of the body— eating, drinking, sexual intercourse, rest—than Harlequin, a figure of pure neediness, whose tricks were always in the service of his basic desires for food and sex. Many of Harlequin's customary *lazzi*—short set-pieces of comic business that interrupted the (often flimsy) plots of commedia performances—revolve around food, such as the "lazzo of eating oneself," where a hungry Harlequin consumes his own body, starting with his feet and working his way up, or the "lazzo of eating fruit" (whose first recorded performance is in mid-eighteenth-century London, though it almost certainly was performed earlier on the Continent), where Harlequin consumes imaginary fruits and berries, drawing out the process in order to make his imagination assuage his hungry belly.[48] Harlequin's neediness and his physicality, also expressed in his skill at slapstick comedy and his dancing ability, and focused in the case of English pantomime of the first half of the eighteenth century by the custom that he never spoke, made him an emblem of the great body of the hungry common people, one sufficiently stylized to place his association with the masses at a safe remove, but sufficiently convincing to mobilize the theater's capacity for direct engagement with the spectator. As Erika Fischer-Lichte puts it in her analysis of eighteenth-century European theater's desire for embodied performance, "in that the theatre aimed to restore the original language of gestures in the art of acting, it served as a corrective force in the civilizing process which, under the influence of court society, had spoiled and deformed this language to the point that it had been almost completely lost in European culture."[49]

Typically cast as the manservant to a pompous member of the bourgeoisie and often identified as a foreigner because of his Continental heritage, Harlequin was doubly "natural" to an English audience, a figure who put spectators back in touch with the codes of gesture and performance that they had sacrificed for the sake of modernity. This was, to be sure, an extremely stylized figure, one whose reliance on an elaborate set of conventions enabled spectators to put several layers of mediation between them and the real. An eighteenth-century Artaud, if we can imagine such a person, might well have decried the way that the attempt on the part of critics to invoke classical ritual dancing as a way of redeeming the theater's seeming fall into irrelevance was co-opted by that institution and rendered tame and comparatively innocuous; when it was staged in early eighteenth-century Britain, "pantomime" offended the self-appointed guardians of literary culture, but it hardly brought about the kind of revolution in thought and feeling that Artaud sought for both his and our times. Still, Harlequin's physicality, which serves as a marker of his low-class status, also gives him access to what Artaud himself would likely have called a "language" of the body, what theorists of English pantomime such as Weaver defined as a "mute rhetorick" that permitted Harlequin to "speak" across the divides of nationality and class. This mute rhetoric, or "wit corporeal," will be the subject of the following chapter.

CHAPTER THREE

Wit Corporeal

THEATER, EMBODIMENT, AND
THE SPECTATOR

*G*aze for a moment, if you will, at the following image of the eighteenth-century English pantomime artist John Rich, a print that depicts him in his signature role of Harlequin Doctor Faustus. Rich's body, equipped with the characteristic particolored bodysuit, black mask, cape, slapstick, and cap of a Harlequin, appears twice in this image. In the background, Harlequin duels with a miller in front of his windmill in a famous scene from *The Necromancer, or Harlequin Doctor Faustus,* the afterpiece entertainment of 1723 that has often been taken to have initiated the boom in pantomime productions of the 1720s and 1730s. In the foreground, Rich's Harlequin fills the frame, well exceeding the situation and plot of *The Necromancer* to emerge as an object of attention and absorption in his own right.

This print enacts the attempted fusion of media that it describes; like many eighteenth-century prints a composite of image *and* text, it translates the most salient feature of Rich's performance to the printed page. Yet it would be hard to deny that there is a considerable short-

John Rich as Harlequin Doctor Faustus (*Harvard Theatre Collection*)

fall between our experience as spectators/readers of this print and the experience of early eighteenth-century London theatergoers. For a good part of the point of eighteenth-century pantomime, this print tells us in more than one way, lay in its *embodied* nature, the fact that Harlequin's body was present to the assembled spectators. The verse printed under the image offers a particularly useful gloss on Harlequin's significance to his first spectators, describing his originality as having everything to do with his sheer physicality:

> Thank you Genteels, These stunning Claps declare,
> How Wit corporeal is your darling Care.
> See what it is the crouding Audience draws
> While Wilks no more but Faustus gains applause.

"Wit corporeal": the verse construes Harlequin's silent motion as a form of language in its own right, a discourse of dance, gesture, and the human body that constitutes a form of "wit" comparable to the dialogue uttered by an actor like Robert Wilks, who was one of the most famous English comedians of the early part of the eighteenth century. Linking Harlequin's astonishing popularity to his corporeality, the print gestures toward a theory of the theater as it attempts to record the force of Rich's intervention in the London playhouses of 1723; the theater, it implies, must be understood as a sensual medium, where vision, sound ("stunning Claps"), language, and above all the bodies of performers summon the attention of the spectator.

The relationship between the live performer and the spectator had a privileged place in early eighteenth-century thinking about the theater, entertainment, subjectivity, and culture. In the way that it focused its spectators' attention on the moving body of performers like Rich, pantomime represented the limit case of a desire felt more generally in the period: the wish to use the human body as a vehicle for transmitting meaning to equally embodied spectators, whose engagement with the onstage action constituted a form of entertainment in a particularly physical sense—entertainment as mentation, the spectators' processes of thought as they have been seized by the sensual stimuli projected by the performer. What the verse above calls "wit corporeal" had at least three interlaced senses: the embodied performer, whose motions, like Harlequin's, "spoke" a language of their own to theatergoers; the embodied spectator, whose mind was conceived in similarly plastic terms as a kind of machine for mentation; and finally, the material aspect of language itself, the sense in which, as Richard Kroll has argued, seventeenth- and eighteenth-century theorists conceptualized language, not as a transparent medium, but as a physical force, "a

tissue of such almost-concrete elements" whose materiality had to be acknowledged, accounted for, and either put to work in the service of underscoring the
constructedness of human knowledge, or transcended in the interest of making
an author's ideas fully intelligible to the audience.[1] Such an overdetermined concept acquired a certain urgency because of the perceived changes in the size and
constitution of the theatergoing public, the expansion of the audience pointed
to by the adjective that this print uses to describe it: *crouding.*

The first part of this chapter will describe how early eighteenth-century
observers responded to this shift by coming up with new strategies for classifying, categorizing, and conceptualizing the theatergoing public. The most
significant of these, I will argue, was the figure of the spectator, imagined as a
general rather than a particular position, a theatergoer who would be an ideal
against which the different kinds of spectators who actually attended the playhouse could model themselves. In the second section, I will attend to the texts
where the position of the spectator is addressed and articulated most fully in
this period, the writings of Joseph Addison and Richard Steele, not the least
important of which is the journal entitled *The Spectator.* Finally, I will consider the writings of one of that journal's contributors, John Weaver, the
dancing-master and performer, who was also, as we saw in the previous
chapter, one of the most prominent theorists of dance and pantomime in
early eighteenth-century Britain. In both his contributions to *The Spectator*
and a series of books on dance, Weaver promoted "entertainments, in emulation of the ancient pantomimes" as a way of bypassing cultural differences
through an appeal to the body, which assumes the place of a universally
accessible plane of understanding. One premise of this chapter, then, is that
The Spectator actually has something important to say about spectatorship.
My more significant claim is that the forces of the eighteenth century's cultural
revolution—the spread in the scope and availability of printed material, the
demographic shifts entailed in the migration from the country to the city and
the expansion of the middling sort, shifts felt in a democratization of the theater audience that was noted at the time and since—made the materiality of
embodied performance newly intelligible and desirable, and prompted a
desire to use the human body as a way to overcome cultural difference.

"Shoals of Exoticks": The Eighteenth-Century Audience

We will probably never know as much as we would like to about eighteenth-
century theater audiences, for reasons that are not hard to imagine. Little or

nothing in the way of statistically useful records about audience composition has survived. We have a very good idea of *what* was performed in the patent houses and many of the smaller, unlicensed theaters after 1702 owing to the presence of advertisements in the *London Daily Courant,* which began publication that year, as well as other newspapers. And we have some understanding of *how many* people attended the theater and how much they paid from theater plans and some scattered records of receipts, both of which provide valuable clues, since it is fair to assume that how much one is able to pay for a seat is a measure of one's income and social standing. But our knowledge about *who* the audience actually was is likely to remain fragmentary and incomplete, based not on hard evidence but on the contemporary discourse about the stage and its constituency.[2] Because we must rely in large part on the recorded memories and impressions of contemporary observers, whose positions and motivations are varied and often biased, our understanding of the eighteenth-century London theater audience better reflects what was said about it rather than what it actually may have been. This understanding cannot take the place of the kind of record that would satisfy a cliometrician, and should not be described as doing so, but it is valuable in its own right, as it was on the basis of such a conception of the theatergoing public that playwrights fashioned their works, managers programmed a repertoire, performers developed their craft, and critics of the theater offered reformist solutions to perceived problems.

There is one point on which many sources from the period agree: that the theatergoing public became broadly *democratized* in the course of the late seventeenth and early eighteenth centuries, expanding to include citizens and their families, single young men (such as Templars), apprentices, and footmen, who were frequently sent ahead by their employers to hold seats and in the early part of the century had a gallery of their own from which to view the performance.[3] Contemporary observers noted how the London theaters had become available to what was often described as the "middling sort," a group that comprehended merchants, artisans, and urban professionals more generally. It was a class whose aspirations and anxieties might be apprehended in the term through which the verses under the image of Rich address them: "genteels." Here used in a fairly rare vocative stance, *genteel* denotes a "rank" situated (as the *OED* puts it) "above the commonalty on the ground of manners or style of living" but beneath the aristocracy on the ground of lineage. A seventeenth-century coinage, the word serves to mark not only the emergence of a new social class but a new conception of social status as well, one based on distinctions of culture rather than nature, the product of social performance rather than blood.[4] As a result, *genteel* would frequently carry with it, as the *OED*'s definitions and usages indicate, the hint of sarcasm, as if to remind its designated bearer that his or her rank was conditional, subject to review or revocation. This was, many sources concur, the group that increasingly became the theater's main constituency and source of financial support in the first half of the eighteenth century.[5]

But such a generalization, while probably on the whole accurate, should be treated with some caution, in part because it is impossible to measure the pace of this broadening of the audience with any confidence and thus to speak with assurance about its composition at any particular moment. As early as 1662, less than two years after the reopening of the public playhouses following the restoration of Charles II, Samuel Pepys was complaining about the intrusive presence of citizens and apprentices in the theater. By 1668 he was already looking back nostalgically at the days before there were so many "ordinary prentices and mean people in the pit."[6] When *were* those days? Alongside whatever changes there surely were in the composition of the theatergoing public from the Restoration to the middle of the eighteenth century runs a fairly constant lament about the decline of the audience that compares the current, mixed crowd of the moment unfavorably with an idealized, more uniformly aristocratic and genteel, audience of the past. It is not that the theaters ever really were the exclusive province of the court and its coterie, but rather that this model was a norm against which the actual composition of the audience always, and increasingly, seemed to be at odds. The gap between the rhetoric about the theater and the reality of its changing composition, then, may be hard to measure, but it has a consistent shape in the form of a long-running complaint about the way that royalist patronage and aristocratic norms were in decline, replaced by the cruder tastes of the public at large. How to account for, describe, and thus to begin to *manage* this change was a matter of considerable importance to critics of the early part of the eighteenth century in Britain, who understood that the Stuart ideal of the theater as one of the many popular pastimes over which the monarch presided was now so attenuated (particularly in the face of royal indifference to the theater after the 1688 Revolution) as to be an artifact of history, a situation that might have held true for a while in the "last age" but that could only function now as an object of nostalgia.

The playwright and critic John Dennis, for example, lamented the shift from a court-dominated institution to one with a broader constituency as a decline largely attributable to the political and economic events of the last generation. Writing in the early 1720s about the period of Charles II, when the "True entertainments of the stage" were supported by "audiences that understood what They saw and Heard," Dennis claims that

> We had then none of those shoals of exoticks, that came in by the Revolution, the union, and the Hanover Succession, which tho they were events that were necessary all, and without which we had been undone; yet have They Hitherto had but an evil Influence upon the genuine entertainments of the stage, and the studies and arts of Humanity.[7]

Here and elsewhere, Dennis laments a general decline in the audience's taste and discrimination, a decline that he attributes to demographic changes caused by political events: the audience is larger than ever before because the population of London has greatly expanded, and the influence of an educated court coterie has become greatly diluted owing to the introduction of "a new and numerous gentry [that] has arisen among us by the Return of our fleets from sea, of our Armies from the Continent, and from the wreck of the South Sea."[8] The newcomers in the audience that Dennis describes are pointedly not plebeian; rather, they are gentlemen, but of a new and unfamiliar species. As early as 1702, he had decried how the center of gravity in the theater had shifted from a coterie of court-affiliated wits who understood the literary protocols and models that ideally shaped the drama to gentlemen whose minds are now so concerned with "Business" that they have no leisure to attend to the authentic "Pleasure" that the stage offers. Indeed, they are so "full of great and real events" that they cannot "receive due impressions from the imaginary ones of the Theatre."[9] Dennis understands the theater to be a domain normatively subject to a definition of pleasure that could only be indulged in a culture of leisure. Such a culture, it is worth noting, would not only provide the context within which critical debate could prosper and collective norms be articulated, but which would also form the proper subject for viewing, hearing, and assessing the works that culture produced, the mind capable of properly receiving "impressions" made by the stimuli of the playhouse. We shall see in the following section how Addison and Steele would develop such an interest in the viewing subject into a full-fledged theory of spectatorship.

Because of the association between theater and the court, citizens, apprentices, footmen, and other "outsiders" of the middle sort and lower were felt as a much greater intrusion than their sheer numbers might ordinarily admit had the institution been unmarked by royal and aristocratic associations. This was all the more the case because many constituent parts of the audience understood it to be their right as free-born English subjects to make their opinions heard in the theater, and thereby frequently made their presence felt in excess of their numbers. Footmen in particular were notorious for being noisy and obstreperous, and there was frequent conflict between them and the politer fractions of the audience. The most famous and decisive crisis in this ongoing conflict within the audience at the patent theaters took place in February 1737—just before a performance of Addison's *Cato*—when members of the pit at Drury Lane rioted against the footmen, demanding of the management that they be driven out of the theater once and for all. Exiled from a gallery that they claimed to be "our Property" by customary right, the footmen broke down the doors in the middle of the first act of *Cato* and proceeded to shout down the afterpiece, Henry Fielding's *Eurydice*, upon which the Riot Act was read and soldiers were called in to restore order.[10] From reading contemporary accounts, it is clear that what was most distressing about the footmen's behavior was not just that they made a lot of noise—although they did, sometimes interfering with the audience's ability to hear the play—but that their noisy judgments put them in the position of usurping the role of their employers as arbiters of plays and actors' performances. Hence *The Daily Journal*'s account of the 1737 riot argues that the footmen's transgression rested in the way that they "have assumed the Province of their Masters, and erect themselves into Judges and Directors of publick Spectacles."[11] The footmen's gallery was eliminated soon thereafter, though the members of the audience who occupied the inexpensive seats to which it gave way clung to their right to interfere if the performance did not please them, or if they felt that some aspect of the staging—such as the pricing or the casting—violated the customary rules of the theater.[12]

The many laments about the behavior of the audience accompanied and supported a substantial reformist literature, a near-constant attempt to improve audience behavior and promote the theater as a site for moral uplift rather than mere entertainment and spectacle. But the unruliness that reformers saw when they gazed upon the broadened audience served important social purposes, which helps explain its persistence in the face of repeated efforts to tamp it down. In their very form, the London playhouses effectively staged a model of urban society to itself, displaying the hierarchy of the social order and thus affirming the vertical and horizontal relations between classes. This was an unexpected way in which the eighteenth-century British playhouse expressed the etymology of *theater* as a "place of seeing"; it served as a site within which relations between classes were made visible, and violations of norms of deference and behavior became particularly clear.

A certain kind of visibility within the theater was facilitated by the design of the playhouses, which were arranged to display the audience as much as the performance onstage. English theatergoers were notorious for ignoring the action onstage in favor of observing the other members of the audience, an exercise facilitated by the fact that until the 1760s or so, there was no difference in the level of lighting between the stage and the auditorium.[13] Foreign observers often commented on the way that London spectators took the opportunity to interact with other members of the audience rather than to attend to the performance, and theater reformers—particularly those with a stake in the audience's actually hearing their words—consistently urged theatergoers to be quiet. As John Macky observed, the performance in the audience rivaled that on the stage: "between the Acts you are as much diverted by viewing the Beauties of the audience, as while they act with the Subject of the Play."[14] And like a play, this was a diversion with a formal structure, with different orders of people distributed in the different levels of the theater. The epilogue to Susanna Centlivre's *The Basset Table* (1705) compares the "goodly Fabrick" of the playhouse to a "Three Deckt man of War," with pit, boxes, and gallery arranged in order:

> Abaft, the Hold's the Pit, from thence look up,
> Aloft! that Swabber's Nest, that's the Main-Top.
> Side-boxes mann'd with Beau, and modish Rake,
> Are like the Fore-castle, and Quarter-Deck.
> Those dark disguised, advent'rous, black-nos'd few,
> May pass for Gunners, or a Fire-ship's Crew.[15]

In Centlivre's conceit, the constituent parts of the audience—beaus and rakes, orange-ladies, and members of the pit—are each comparable to a part of a ship's crew, such that every one gains an intelligible function in the larger whole. Superintending the analogy, though never expressed, is the topos of the ship of state, the comparison between the nation and a seagoing vessel that was likely to be particularly pertinent to British writers at the time of Centlivre's writing in 1705, a key year in the War of the Spanish Succession, whose prosecution depended on the success of the British Navy. The epilogue restates the common understanding of the theater as a model for the state, describing it as a place where the nation's various orders and the relations between them are intelligible in a particularly clear way.

That ideal of the theater as a site where the society's "different and distinct Classes" would be on display persisted throughout much of the eighteenth century.[16] This visibility was thought of as one of the customary rights of the audience, which went to the theater in part with the expectation that it would not only see a play but that it would see an image of the nation arranged in front of it, the various orders joined together viewing an entertainment in a playhouse licensed by the Crown, an ideal "mimic state" that resembled the political state not only in its frequent dramaturgical focus on dynastic affairs but in its material form.[17] Such attempts to describe the theater's audience in terms of the state held true even when the traditional logics that governed the latter were breaking down. As late as the 1750s, the actor-manager Theophilus Cibber tried to explain "the Town," the amorphous term that was frequently used to describe the constituency of the playhouses, with reference to an ideal model of the state: "I think, the Town may be supposed to include all Degrees of Persons, from the highest Nobleman, to the lowly Artizan &c. who, in their different Stations, are Encouragers of dramatic Performances:—Thus all persons, who pay for their Places, whether Noble, Gentle, or Simple, who fill the Boxes, Pit, and Galleries, in a theatrical Sense, form the Town, as K--g, L-rds, and Commons, in a constitutional one, make that great Body, the nation."[18] Cibber's supposition calls on political theory to balance competing wishes: on the one hand, the theater preserves and even enhances the identifications of individuals with a small number of "degrees" and "stations"; on the other, the audience merely consists of those who are able to "pay for their places." His metaphor does not stand up to much scrutiny (if one were willing and able to pay enough for one's political "place," could one get to be king?), but it testifies to a continuing cultural desire to link the theater to the concept of the nation-state even in the face of the money economy, which tends to dissolve traditional degrees, replacing them with its own, quantitative rankings.

Like the nation, the public and the "town" were in part fictional, imaginary constructs, summoned into being through their repeated articulation, but lacking easily comprehended material form. They needed (and still need) to be supplanted by symbols and bodies that bring them to the realm of the senses. The most significant and influential of these that was developed to conceptualize the eighteenth-century theatergoer was the "spectator." Given the close association between the theater and the feudal state, it is not surprising to discover that this is a construct whose lineage can be traced to the ideology of absolutist monarchy, in particular to the concretization of absolutism in the architecture of seventeenth-century theater buildings themselves. The temporary theaters erected for court masques of the early seventeenth century were typically designed to privilege a single viewpoint—the

One of James Thornhill's scenes for the opera *Arsinoe* (1706)
(*The Victoria and Albert Museum, London*)

king's—as a way of underscoring his singularity and sovereignty. His was the one seat from which the single-point perspective scenery achieved its full effect, a position that created an analogy between his perfect vision in the theater and the comprehensiveness with which he could "view" his realm and its subjects. As Julie Stone Peters has put it, the idea of a single vanishing point, which locates the prince in the ideal position for spectating, corresponds closely to the way that the "body politic" was also "ideally subject to the surveillance of the Prince's omniscient eye."[19]

Late seventeenth- and eighteenth-century theaters similarly materialized a singular spectatorial position in the way that their perspective scenery—introduced after the Restoration when Charles II's courtiers, in particular William Davenant, brought Continental designs and tastes back with them—assumed the presence of an observer positioned in the ideal place from which to view the effect at its maximum impact.[20] To be sure, the effects of such scenic design did not exhaust the possibilities for theatrical performance in this period, as accounts of performance frequently stress the intimacy of these theaters, the close interaction between audience and performers, who frequently performed in the downstage areas between the proscenium arch and the pit, breaking any illusionistic spell created by the perspective scenery. Still, the general structure of the playhouses constitutes an example of how the absolutist monarchy continued to shape the experience of Britons for generations after it had ceased to wield real power in the political domain, and might serve as a case study in how a residual formation can impress its logic on a future that would no longer even recognize the terms under which it had been developed in the first place.

Indeed, there are signs that the singularity of the viewpoint created by perspective scenery and the proscenium arch may have been enhanced in the course of our period, as performers gradually moved back from the audience. In his *Apology*, published in 1740, Colley Cibber lamented the 1690s renovation of Drury Lane, which took away several feet of forestage, depriving the performers of a significant portion of the space between the scenery and the spectators that he and other actors had long exploited.[21] These renovations were not performed so much in order to follow through on some ideological program that would reaffirm the importance of a single spectating position as to create room for more seats. There is a certain irony involved here, in that the expansion of the audience prompted a desire to appropriate the most exclusive of all conceptions of the theatergoer. But the "spectator" as used by Addison, Steele, and other eighteenth-century writers is fashioned to comprehend the entire theatergoing public, and does so by being couched in general rather than specific terms, by being a figure that sheds its particularity in order to become available to all the people in the theater.[22] In fact, the persistence of a model derived from an earlier conception of the relationship between the viewer and the spectacle testifies less to the continuing authority, real or symbolic, of the monarchy and of the singular "perspective" it may have retained, but rather to the proliferation of multiple and fragmented perspectives both inside and outside the playhouse. Even in the Restoration, the unitary position that might be occupied by a single observer was understood to be at best an ideal, one whose existence was marked by nothing so much as the fact that dramatists so frequently called attention to the limited perspectives possible for any individual character. The conception of "the spectator" that developed in the early eighteenth century in part out of this older framework would thus mediate between the ideal model of a singular, Olympian position and the emerging reality of multiple and subjective viewpoints. Ultimately, it would describe spectatorship in terms of a radically subjective model of the theatergoing experience, one that focused on the *entertainment* between the onstage performance and the mind of the spectator in the theater. The best place to gain access to this conception is in the pages of Addison and Steele's journal *The Spectator*, which, I want to suggest, actually has a great deal to do with the material as well as the ideological components of spectatorship.

"What Machines are We!" The Spectator *and the Mechanics of Viewing*

It would probably be fair to say that nothing has done more to revive interest in Addison and Steele's journalism than the promulgation in the English-reading academy since the late 1980s of Habermas's concept of the bourgeois public sphere, the abstract realm of opinion and debate, distinct from the court or the absolutist state, for which, in Habermas's own account, *The Tatler* and *The Spectator* serve as early signs, contributors, and materializations. But Habermas has little to say about that prominent actor in the emergent public sphere, the spectator itself. Such a figure was widely taken up beyond Addison and Steele's *Spectator* series, spawning various imitators and successors such as *The Universal Spectator* (1728–46) and Eliza Haywood's series *The Female Spectator* (1742–44), all of which adopted the original publication's program of articulating a general position, a transcendent viewpoint above the fray of the crowd and the market from which critical judgment might be rendered. As Michael Warner describes it, such a position offers authors and readers a "prosthetic person" in whom they can surrender their own particularity in order to imagine themselves as a public rather than as individual persons. Such a conception posits a single figure—the "spectator"—as a category that could comprehend many different types of spectators. Warner perhaps overstates the case, however, when he argues that this entails the deliberate and thoroughgoing "disincorporation" of both the figure and the reader, the latter of whom is led to identify with "a disembodied public subject that he can imagine as parallel to his private person."[23] Rather, it is clear that, for Addison and Steele at least, spectatorship must be understood as a material process, an exercise that engages the body's apparatus for viewing and its machinery for mentation. By describing this figure in terms of a human body whose operations are (in theory) common to all, Addison and Steele attempt to bypass the particular identifications that individuals and groups brought with them to the theater, establishing proper spectatorship as a natural rather than a cultural relationship.

This conception of spectatorship is nowhere outlined programmatically, and is, in the event, shot through with ambivalence and inconsistency, not least because it is clear that Addison and Steele differed on some fundamental points, and conceived the theater itself in subtly, but nonetheless significantly different ways. Steele seems to have taken their differences to center on the proper use of the human body onstage. In his last, unfinished play *The School of Action* (c. 1723–26), Steele's representative Humber asserts that Addison's avatar (Severn) "must beware of standing as if you were a thinking statue, a case for a spirit to reflect in, and not a mind and body acting together. You improve the soul only in your colleges—you neglect the body."[24] Steele in effect mocks Addison's abstraction from his own body, his academic predilection for thought and ideas over physical action, a disposition that Steele takes to be a liability in the theater, and that, as much as anything else, marks the difference between his approach to the stage and Addison's. A close reading of *The Spectator* more or less confirms the wisdom of this assessment, showing, as we will see, that Steele was on the whole more accepting of the theater's status as a material medium than Addison, who worried more openly about the way that the physical aspects of the medium—scenery, music, costumes, special effects, the bodies of the performers, and the materiality of language itself—can interfere with the smooth transmission of meaning. For Addison, ideas are what count, and the theater's materiality constitutes a threat, as it increases the viscosity of the medium through which ideas are communicated from the author to his audience, enhancing the chance that they might be blocked, deflected, or misunderstood. Nonetheless, even the "thinking statue" that we might indeed associate with the voice of Addison's *Spectator* essays does not so much "neglect" the human body as enlist it as an ally, a key if sometimes obtrusive participant in his broader project of producing new techniques for achieving critical judgment.

Addison's relationship to the theater is particularly vexed, shot through with the mixture of attraction, repulsion, and anxiety that defines the state that we have learned to call ambivalence. His wariness of the way that the theater's materiality could act as a barrier to the unimpeded transmission of an author's ideas and could fool credulous spectators into mistaking the stage performance for reality dates back to his earliest published writings, from his Oxford days in the 1690s. In his early poem "The Play-House," Addison mocks the duplicity of theatrical representation, the ability of stage mechanism to absorb the spectator so thoroughly as to mislead him.[25] "The Play-House" takes the reader "behind the scenes" of a performance centering on the conflicts in and around a royal family, a production where "the pomp and pageantry" of the stage convincingly mimic kingly power and feminine charm. Hence when the actor playing the king "tears his lungs with verse," he convinces the spectators that he really is a prince: "His subjects tremble, the submissive pit,/Wrapped up in silence and attention, sit." Likewise, a "callow 'squire" just arrived in London from the provinces "feeds his eyes,/And silently for paint and patches dies" when he gazes on the "painted charms" of the actress playing the endangered princess. But readers of "The Play-House" will not be so easily fooled as these unsophisticated spectators, because Addison brackets such brief vignettes of spectatorial absorption with descriptions of the actors first putting on makeup and costumes and then shedding them after the performance in order to "quaff away" their cares in the alehouse next door. Making the inexperienced spectator into an object of spectacle in his own right, Addison's poem aims to expose the artifice that sustains the illusion of political and sexual power, displaying how the "gaudy plume" and "purple train" of a royal costume merely overlay the stinking "vile tatters" that more properly belong to such "rabble of the stage."

"The Play-House" prompts its reader to think of absorption in the theatrical mimicry of royal power as hopelessly naïve and archaic, the practice of the rustic and unsophisticated spectators who by the testimony of most observers were coming to the theaters in greater numbers by the end of the seventeenth century. Such absorption calls to mind the sense in which, as many critics writing under the banner of the new historicism have taught us, Tudor and Stuart monarchs understood "theatrical" display to be an essential component of royal authority. The point gains a particular force if, as the poem's recent editor believes, the performance that Addison has in mind is of a production of Peter Motteux's *The Island Princess* (1698), an "opera" adapted from John Fletcher's 1617 play of the same name, and thus a lineal descendent of the early Stuart theater. What saves the narrator of "The Play-House," a kind of Mr. Spectator *avant la lettre,* is that he is not really scandalized by the theater's duplicity because he is able to render the theater building and the artifice it contains *transparent,* imaginatively seeing through the duplicitous makeup, costumes, and scenery to the humble flesh that it conceals.

The Spectator's famous attacks on Italian opera, as well as its discussions of English tragedy (in both cases, largely Addison's work) extend this critique of the stage's "mechanick" nature. What scandalized Addison about Italian opera was not the occasional absurdity of its plots, the foreignness of the performers, or the expense of the productions—all of which figure prominently in the many contemporary attacks on the form—but the sheer materiality of Italian opera, its indulgence in spectacle at the expense of meaning. Such materiality extends most crucially to language itself, which is as one with the other elements of theater in that it has volume, weight, and heft. Addison takes the word to be a type of thing, an object in the world that has a physical dimension as well as being a vehicle for meaning. Hence, because they were performed in a language that its audience did not understand, Italian operas raise the specter of language degenerating into mere sound, at which point it becomes merely dross, inert nonsense that constitutes so much wasted matter. By much the same logic, when he describes English tragedy as

"Performances of a much higher Nature, and capable of giving the Mind a much nobler Entertainment" than opera, Addison begins by considering the proper style for the language of tragedy, an exercise that, it becomes clear in the course of a series of *Spectator* essays on the form, has to do with constructing the proper relationship to the materiality of language itself. Thus the playwright must avoid allowing the hero's thoughts to be lost in "a Cloud of Words," and must above all avoid "*rant*," which fills "the Mouths of our Heroes with Bombast" and proceeds "rather from a Swelling than a Greatness of Mind."[26] Filling the mouth and swelling the mind, bombastic language exceeds the natural boundaries of the performer's body, making it monstrous because it is now *merely* a body. The entertaining gift that tragedy offers to the mind is only worth accepting if the performance does not indulge too greatly in material aspects of the stage such as rant, costumes, and scenery, the "Mechanical Method[s]" for "Adding Dignity to Kings and Queens" that divert the spectator's attention from the nobility of the action to a mere "Train of Robes or a Plume of Feathers" (1:179).

This concern about the materiality of the theater, extending down to the materiality of language, finds its programmatic expression in the form of Addison's plays, all three of which display considerable restraint in using the material components of the theater. Thus, following much the same logic as *The Spectator's* essays on opera, Addison's comedy *The Drummer* (1716) satirizes the materiality of language in the form of the excessive and therefore meaningless rhetoric of stage lovers. Abigail, a scheming maid, urges the fortune-hunter Tinsel to "pour forth a Volley of Rapture and Nonsense, till you are out of Breath."[27] A far better-known example in Addison's dramatic oeuvre of his resistance to spectacle occurs at the end of *Cato,* which stages Cato's suicide out of the spectators' view. In *Spectator* 44, Addison forecasts this ascetic ending, explaining why English tragedies should avoid representing violence. The decorum he outlines is explicitly neoclassical (imitating "the Practice of the ancient Poets, who were very sparing of their publick Executions") and pointedly nationalistic (attempting to define a British aesthetic that would be more "natural" than that of the excessively rule-bound French) (1:190).

What is particularly important to note here is the extent to which the Spectator's eye focuses on the physical props of staged violence, the "Daggers, Poniards, Wheels, Bowls for Poison, and many other Instruments of Death" that lead to the "Carcasses" littering the stage at the end of, say, a Jacobean revenge-tragedy. What Addison's Spectator takes to be shocking to real spectators is not the morality or injustice of staged violence, but its brute materiality, which diverts the attention of spectators in the audience away from the ideas of the play and toward the objects that were intended merely to convey them. At its extreme, Addison's dramatic oeuvre might even be considered as an *antitheatrical* mode of drama; his plays programmatically resist recourse to stage machinery and sensuality, aspiring to the plane of the literary as an act of resistance to the materiality that the theater is always in danger of indulging to excess.

Addison's program calls attention to, and attempts to diminish, the potentially baleful effects of the theater's material components on the audience's sensibilities, which are all too easily led astray, diverted by the physicality of performance. What this cannot explain, though, is why Addison devotes so much time and attention to the theater, why he returns to it again and again as a topic of critical inquiry, and why he writes works—notably, one each in the genres of comedy, tragedy, and opera—for a medium he considers so suspect. One obvious answer is that the theater remained an institution with great critical authority to early eighteenth-century British culture, so that any writer who wanted to intervene in that culture had to direct his or her energies toward the playhouse; thus, Addison had little choice, this line of argument would say, but to write *Cato* for the playhouse rather than as an epic poem or a novel. Such an answer is too negative, however; it obscures the positive reasons why Addison, in spite of his concerns about the playhouse's duplicities, would have wanted to take advantage of the medium. The theater was also recognized to be early eighteenth-century culture's most important institution for live, embodied performance, a phenomenon that was believed to be the most powerful means of moving a spectator. Addison's ambivalence about the theater derives from his profound respect for it, and, in particular, his understanding that, as a "place of seeing," the theater created a space for harnessing the considerable power of vision as a vehicle for ideas, its capacity literally to *impress* meaning on minds imagined, in the best Lockean fashion, as blank tablets, malleable media awaiting sensations from the outside world.

Addison's *Spectator* series on the pleasures of the imagination, published in 1712 but first drafted in the late 1690s when he was a fellow at Oxford and thus contemporary with "The Play-House," presents what is probably the period's most detailed articulation of the linkage between vision and mentation. It is no surprise to discover that the model of the imagination that Addison offers there gives pride of place to vision, "the most perfect and most delightful of all our Senses." Adopting the conception of vision articulated by Descartes, Addison describes spectatorship in material terms, analo-

Schematic model of sight in Descartes' *La Dioptrique*
(*Reprinted with the permission of Cambridge University Press*)

gizing it to tactile experience: "Our Sight," he proposes, "may be considered as a more delicate and diffusive Kind of Touch" (3:536).[28] This conception of vision is illustrated in Descartes' *La Dioptrique* with the image of a blind man finding his way in the world through sticks held in front of him.

As Jonathan Crary elaborates, "this is *not* an image of a man literally blind; rather it is an abstract diagram of a fully sighted observer, in which vision operates like the sense of touch."[29] Hence the images with which vision "fills the Mind" can be considered as "Objects," material things that occupy space and cause effects in a mind that *feels* their presence. Inner and outer worlds mirror each other; each is conceived as a space of material things, objects whose most important features are not, say, their colors, intensity, or brightness, but their shapes and mass. Vision serves as the primary conduit between outer and inner domains, opening the chambers of the mind to the objects outside it.

This materialist, corporeal conception of vision is part of Descartes' influential argument that the human body can be conceived as an automaton, a "machine" propelled by an inner "ghost."[30] In this model, the mind was conceived of as part of this mechanical person, functioning as the destination point of nerves that Descartes had originally analogized to the pipes that moved the automatons in the royal gardens.[31] Hence, to describe how memory can "heighten the delightfulness" of an image, Addison calls on the Cartesian model of the machine-man:

> The Sett of Ideas, which we received from such a Prospect or Garden, having entered the Mind at the same time, have a Sett of Traces belonging to them in the Brain, bordering very near upon one another; when, therefore, any one of these Ideas arises in the Imagination, and consequently dispatches a flow of Animal Spirits to its proper Trace, these Spirits, in the Violence of their Motion, run not only into the Trace, to which they were more particularly directed, but into several of those that lie about it. (3:563)

Addison makes a point of distancing himself from this account (which continues for several more sentences), describing it in the printed version of this essay in *The Spectator* as what "a *Cartesian*" might say rather than something to which Addison firmly subscribes himself; in the original manuscript of the late 1690s from which the *Spectator* essay was drawn he subscribes to the Cartesian model without equivocation.[32] Yet the language of "animal spirits," "traces," and "channels" worn in the mind through visual stimuli appears frequently enough in Addison's published works to show that he continued to consider mentation to be a mechanical process; the mind has a sensuality that is plastic, corporeal, and traceable. At the beginning of his *Spectator* series on English tragedy, Addison asserts that "Diversions of this kind wear out of our Thoughts every thing that is mean and little," because they are "capable of giving the Mind one of the most delightful and most improving Entertainments" (1:164, 163). The series goes on to claim that a tragicomedy, or a tragedy with a double plot, is inferior to a tragedy with only one plot because the diffusion of the spectator's interest "breaks the Tide of Sorrow, by throwing it into different Channels" (1:171). Drawing on the Cartesian model of the mind, Addison imagines entertainment as a form of mentation, an exercise of the individual's mental machinery that would in effect enable the spectator to measure the difference between an improving

"Horror and Ravishment," from *The Conference of Monsieur Le Brun* (1701)
(*Typ 705.01.514, Department of Printing and Graphic Arts,*
Houghton Library, Harvard University)

performance and an ill-conceived one by tracing the paths worn in the mind
by the various stimuli they inspire. Ultimately, so powerful is the absorption
engaged by this mental mechanism that it can be imagined as autotelic, having no need for subject matter or purpose beyond its own operations: "The
working of my own Mind," Mr. Spectator (here voiced by Steele) observes,
"is the general Entertainment of my Life" (1:21).

The eighteenth-century theater's use of Cartesian theory well exceeded
The Spectator's appropriations. As Joseph Roach and others have documented,
Descartes' codification of internal motivation into six universal passions—
horror, fear, sorrow, astonishment, ravishment, and awe—was translated
into a professional doctrine for the Augustan performer, who was expected to
be able to "hit" each of these passions (as well as others derived by combinations of these primary six) with recognizable, striking gesture and mien.[33]
The French painter Charles Le Brun, a student of Descartes, either did performers and critics a great service or created a great burden by drawing clear
and easily reproducible images of the six passions, images that were widely
circulated, cited, and used as points of reference and comparison, standards

against which actors were to measure themselves and audiences were to use to assess a performer's skill. Ventriloquizing the greatest English actor of the period, Thomas Betterton, Charles Gildon argued that performers should study Le Brun. Barton Booth, successor to some of Betterton's roles and the first actor to play Cato, collected prints derived from Le Brun that displayed the passions, images that he trained himself to mimic precisely in his staged performances.[34] Codified and reproduced in print and onstage, the passions constituted a shared vocabulary, a universally accessible taxonomy of emotion. Such a taxonomy downplayed idiosyncratic variation and individuality. In effect, a performer like Booth succeeded to the extent that he made *himself* into a kind of machine, replicating the lineaments of the passions as precisely as they were reproduced on the page. Ideally, the performer and the spectator mirrored each other, the one a mechanism for transmitting meaning and emotion, the other a mechanism for receiving and understanding it.

The theory that informed facial expression extended itself to the body as a whole, a fact exploited by the early eighteenth-century theorist of dance John Weaver. In his *Essay Towards an History of Dancing* (1712), a book that was promoted by Steele in the pages of *The Spectator,* Weaver argues that dance in the ancient world served as a form of "mute rhetorick" precisely because of the way that it permitted dancers to raise "the Passions of Anger, Pity, Love, Hate, and the like" in the "Spectator," something that "Poets or Orators" could merely "pretend to effect by all the Force of their Tropes, and Figures."[35] The printed texts of Weaver's pantomime dances of the 1710s narrate, then, the various passions that characters display through their expressions, gesture, posture, and movement. Thus, for example, Venus's "*Contempt*" for Vulcan in *The Loves of Mars and Venus* (1717) "is express'd by scornful Smiles; forbidding Looks; tossing of the head; filliping of the Fingers; and avoiding the Object"; later, "the left Hand thrust forth with the Palm turn'd backward; the left Shoulder rais'd, and the Head bearing towards the Right, denotes an *Abhorence,* and *Distaste.*"[36] Some accounts of eighteenth-century pantomime suggest that Harlequin acquired a simplified taxonomy of the passions of his own, a set of positions expressing admiration, flirtation, contemplation, defiance, and determination.[37] Most important here, what is implicit throughout all of Weaver's texts is a claim that all such embodied performances are much superior vehicles of the passions than the spoken drama because human bodies offer a direct form of communication, capable of displaying emotion without the equivocations of language.

Weaver also underscores what *The Spectator* makes clear as well, that the Cartesian model was valued in part because of the way it advanced what we can think of as the *phatic* function of the passions, the degree to which they served not only to transmit ideas but to maintain social contact between the stage and the audience. The system inscribed the actor's body as the instrument for conveying a stable and universal set of meanings that were intelligible to author, performer, and spectator because they represented emotions that exceeded the specifics of any particular situation and were therefore universal. Spectator and performer enjoy a mimetic relationship to each other, as spectators come to feel the emotions portrayed by the performer, and thus participate in a concentrated engagement of the passions. Hence Steele praises the Italian castrato Nicolini, not because of the beauty of his singing, but because "every Limb, and every Finger, contributes to the Part he acts, insomuch that a deaf Man may go along with him in the Sense of it."[38]

More than Addison, Steele takes this model to insist on a live, embodied performance, as if the mind demands direct stimulation from the world of objects in order to be fully engaged. When, in the preface to the first edition of *The Conscious Lovers* (1722), Steele reminds the reader that "a play is to be seen and is made to be represented with the advantage of action nor can appear but with half the spirit without it," he expresses what is more often implicit in his theatrical criticism, that "the Representation of the Closet," the performance of solitary reading in the privacy of one's home, is a poor substitute for that of the playhouse, to which he grants a unique capacity to engage the spectator's sensory and therefore his or her cognitive apparatus.[39] Steele's journalistic descriptions of performances that he has witnessed frequently speak of the "irresistible Force" with which a well-crafted play "impresses" itself on the sensorium.

Here is one example of many. *The Tatler* quotes his friend Eugenio comparing the art of painting (his specific example, by no mere coincidence, is a work of Charles Le Brun's) to that of the theater, which is much more powerful precisely because it is embodied by a living performer: "How forcible an Effect this would have on our Minds, one needs no more than to observe how strongly we are touch'd by meer Pictures. . . . If the Painter and the Historian can do thus much in Colours and Language, what may not be perform'd by an excellent Poet? when the Character he draws is presented by the Person, the Manner, the Look, and the Motion of an accomplish'd Player: If a Thing painted or related can irresistibly enter our hearts, what may not be brought to pass by seeing generous Things perform'd before our Eyes?"[40] Steele's recourse to the category of the "Thing," which seems here to comprehend not just the persons and places that might be represented in a painting, a poem, or a play, but the sentiments and passions that a mise-en-scène in each of these forms attempts to convey, emphasizes the extent to which different media are challenged by the need to account for the materiality of the real itself, the physicality of the lived world that is necessarily to some degree lost in the translation from reality to representation. By a logic that takes the human sensorium as a material medium in its own right, the "thingness" of a live, embodied performance impresses the mind with a material force that exceeds the capacity of even the best history painting to act as a spur to mimetic desire.

If Addison's dramatic oeuvre programmatically resists indulgence in the materiality of the stage, Steele's brings to the fore how human performers can "touch" the sensoria of spectators without words at all. The two most significant scenes in *The Conscious Lovers,* for example, exploit the power of silent, "mechanick" performance. In the fourth act, the moment where the hero and heroine Bevil and Indiana realize that they are in love with each other is accompanied solely by music, as the two communicate their feelings through gesture, glance, and physical attitude. Later, in the scene that Steele claimed the entire play "was writ for the sake of" (299), Bevil finally and definitively proves his moral stature by refusing to duel Myrtle. Neither man speaks; rather, they circle around each other, pantomiming their intentions and the shifts in their attitude via expression and motion. In both scenes, physical action replaces dialogue, as characters communicate their intentions and positions through gestures, facial expressions, and significant gazes, as if the meanings they are trying to express would only be cheapened by being verbalized. Such reticence has frequently been taken as one of the hallmarks of that sentimental discourse for *The Conscious Lovers* is often described as a point of origin, an indication that the sentimental hero is dealing in emotions so real and overwhelming that language is unable adequately to represent them. But Steele's recourse to dumb-show here can be equally well positioned within the discourse of the human machine.

When, then, during the climax of his encounter with Myrtle, Bevil exclaims, "What machines are we!" he states what Steele's theory and practice assume, that the emotions both men have been experiencing pulse through mechanistic nervous systems that resemble those of their audience, and are indeed linked to them through the visual apparatus. One might say that this is a moment where Bevil fulfills the title of the work in which he stars; he brings to the threshold of conscious expression a model of the human subject that more frequently remains *unconscious* and unarticulated in so many words. More generally, Steele understands that silent action ensures universal communicability because it appeals directly to the human mechanism that it mimics; when Steele claimed in the preface to *The Conscious Lovers* that the dumb-show scenes in the play were designed to impress the "Goths and Vandals" who now attend the London theater, his point is not just that he hopes that Bevil's restraint will serve as a good example to spectators, but that, because the performance here takes the form only of embodied action, even those who might not understand Bevil's "sentiments" will be engaged in the scene by virtue of the correspondence between the onstage entertainment and the entertainment taking place in their mind. Steele understands that the broadening of the theater audience demands that playwrights appeal to a uniform and consistent site of address, a general rather than a particular spectator, a figure that can be conceptualized by appealing to the human sensory apparatus.

The conception of the theater as an embodied medium, one that linked spectator and spectacle in a kind of spell held together by sensory stimuli, was widely shared in this period, informing the decorums of playwriting, criticism, and performance. It is accessible to us in descriptions of performance such as those offered by the actor-manager Colley Cibber in his *Apology.* Cibber remembers Thomas Betterton, the leading actor on the London stage from the Restoration until his death in 1710, as having achieved the full "possession" of the minds of theater spectators, and puts forth Betterton's performance in the role of Hamlet as the model that actors should emulate if they wish to "to keep the attention" of the spectators "more pleasingly awake."[41] Following much the same logic as had been articulated in *The Spectator,* Cibber's description emphasizes, not Betterton's interpretation of the role, but rather the sensual force of his voice and physical attitude, which made a sense of their own that was independent of the meaning of the words he was speaking, and that together arrested the audience in a way that no other English actor ever had: "he seemed to seize upon the eyes and ears of the giddy and inadvertent! To have talked or looked another way would then have been thought insensibility or ignorance. In all his soliloquies of moment, the strong intelligence of his attitude and aspect drew you into such an impatient gaze and larger attention, that you almost imbibed the sentiment with your eye before the ear could read it" (62).

As reconstructed in memory by Cibber, Betterton's first appeal to the audience—particularly to its "giddy" and "inadvertent" members—rests not in the substance of what he says or does but in the grace and force with which he moves. Betterton's body holds the gaze and seizes the attention of the entire theater, fulfilling Addison's concern in "The Play-House" that the unwary spectator might be seduced by mere materiality. Between them, Addison's poem and Cibber's description mark the negative and positive poles of the period's ambivalent relationship to the embodied performer:

nothing was more capable of engaging the minds of spectators, but for that reason no element of the theater was better able to mislead them, claiming their attention so fully as to divert them from the play's meaning.

The ambivalence about the materiality of the theater that I have charted here expresses itself in *The Spectator*'s peculiar tendency to imagine spectatorship in terms of the act of reading, and vice versa. In the series on English tragedy, for example, Addison argues that playwrights should resist the common practice of inflating the importance of stage monarchs by adding a handful of retainers who are supposed to stand in for a whole army, for "it is impossible for the Reader's Imagination to multiply twenty Men into such prodigious Multitudes" (1:170). The slip of the pen here, where the "reader" takes the place of what should more logically be the "spectator" occurs at several points in these essays. It testifies not only to Addison's ambivalence about the materiality of the stage, but the extent to which he contains that ambivalence by projecting it onto a scene of reading. Addison characteristically mobilizes this conception of entertainment to describe the relationship between the reader and the text, in particular, the text of periodical essays themselves. Such writings offer what we might call a kind of *virtual* spectatorship; they co-opt the theater's capacity to sustain attention while being spared the burden of the stage machinery that can, like static over a radio frequency, interfere with the transmission of its meaning. By describing reading on the model of seeing, *The Spectator* participates in the economy of embodied sympathetic entertainment whose paradigm is the relationship between the staged performance and its viewer; as Mr. Spectator puts it in the tenth number of the journal, "I have resolved to refresh [my readers'] Memories from Day to Day" by printing texts that "tend to the wearing out of Ignorance, Passion and Prejudice" from the mind (1:44). Here, the reader has become a virtual machine-person, the grooves or traces of his brain subject to the inspiration of animal spirits that have been stimulated by their entertainment with a text that has become a kind of spectacle in its own right.

Most important, Addison's deployment of spectatorship as a model for reading harnesses the inescapable sociability of the theater to an activity that risks becoming a solitary business, conducted by lone readers in the privacy of their closets. Recently, William Warner and Ronald Paulson have both argued that Addison's conception of entertainment in effect paves the way for the hegemony of private reading as the culture's primary form of diversion.[42] But such an outcome must be understood to be deeply ironic. For I would argue that Addison rather wishes to offer his conception of entertainment as a hedge against the atomizing effects of print, privacy, and individual or factional interest; whether it is performed on the stage or through the page, it is inherently a *social* activity, one that mounts an act of resistance toward indulgence in individual agendas or solitary gratification. Entertainment is thus explicitly and necessarily political, an exercise of commonality that should ideally take place in a world shared by others engaged in it at the same time. Hence Addison's frequent attempts to imagine the number of people who read *The Spectator* every day, or to suggest that its subscribers all share it over the breakfast table.[43] These are not only (as they have been described) attempts to puff sales or to reconstruct domestic space, but also to prod individual readers to imagine themselves as at all times engaged in a common task, a nationwide performance that takes the engagement of the minds of an audience with a properly staged drama as its model.

Addison and Steele cross text and image, attempting to overcome the limitations of each by calling upon the logics that are native to the other's medium. The stubborn textuality of *The Spectator*—a work that includes its narrator's haunting vow "to Print myself out, if possible before I Die" in its inaugural issue—that marks the atomization of solitary readers is hedged by a recourse to visuality; meanwhile, the potent yet dangerous spectatorial relations of the stage can be mitigated by recourse to the figure of reading (1:5). But Addison's slips of the pen betray the difficulty that this aspect of *The Spectator*'s project poses to a conception of culture that ultimately gives the word priority, taking it as the normative medium for transmitting meaning; when push comes to shove, Addison in particular reaches for the safe haven of language. A different relationship to language and materiality was, however, imaginable in this period, one that, while it took the word as a metaphor for the motions of the human body, which could be fashioned into a kind of "language," nonetheless saw the body as the best vehicle for meaning because it was universally shared and therefore more democratic than the word itself. This was, it turns out, the prime rationale for the promotion of pantomime entertainments in the early eighteenth century in Britain, and to understand fully the argument by which "wit corporeal" was advanced as the solution to the alienating effects of urbanization and the marketplace, we need better to assess the works of its leading promoter, the dancing-master John Weaver.

John Weaver and Pantomime as Universal Language

It would be an exaggeration to say that *The Spectator* and the drama that Addison and Steele produced to demonstrate its programmatic reconceptualization of the relationship between performance and spectator forecast or fully account for the emergence of pantomime as a dominant form in the London theater in the generation after Addison's and Steele's deaths. The one known response to the form by either man—a jotting of Steele's suggesting that he planned to write a play that in part satirized *The Necromancer*—would lead us to think that they would have sided with the many writers of the 1720s and 1730s who attacked pantomime because they understood all too well the kind of threat that it posed to a traditional conception of literature and the place of the theater in the culture.[44] But a different account of the place and significance of these entertainments is implicit in their writings, and was therefore available to early eighteenth-century Britons, one that has been eclipsed by the considerable authority that has attached itself to the negative evaluations and attacks by virtue of the fact that they were frequently mounted by the victors of the period's debates over the theater and entertainment. In this version, eighteenth-century English pantomime was not so much a deviation from as a certain kind of fulfillment of its medium's goals and norms. It exploited the theater's obvious materiality—both its most signifi- cant advantage over other forms of cultural production and its greatest liability—in a particularly concentrated and effective way. To those who were familiar with the mechanistic model of spectatorship that I have described above, "pantomimic entertainments" were not the cause or sign of the theater's decline, but rather a basis for its cure. Steele, for example, endorsed Weaver's *Essay Towards an History of Dancing*, asserting, in very much the terms of the Cartesian machine-man outlined above, that the silent pantomimic spectacles that Weaver was proposing there "would be a mechanick way of implanting insensibly in Minds not capable of receiving it so well by any other Rules, a sense of good Breeding and Virtue" (4:148). More generally, the revival of ancient pantomime that Weaver called for held out the hope that Britain might develop an art form that was both indige- nous and classicizing; it would revive the theater by returning it to its origins in the display of the human body in motion.

We can gain a glimpse into how the distinctive Britishness of pantomime and its positivity were mutually supported in a rare endorsement offered by the *Grub-Street Journal*, which, as a journal following the lead of Alexander Pope's critique in *The Dunciad*, frequently attacked pantomime. Yet the *Journal* also occasionally endorsed it as another means by which the stage might accomplish its assigned "business" of offering simultaneous "pleasure and instruction. Our *Pantomime Entertainments,* if rightly managed, might be no less useful than our best Plays: for as these improve our discourse, so might those our carriage; and a well-chosen Subject, properly represented by genteel action and graceful attitudes, would, I doubt not, make a considerable alteration in the outward behaviour of the attentive spectator."[45] The "Our" of the *Grub-Street Journal*'s atypically sympathetic account is significant, because it points to the way in which the invention of *"Pantomime Entertainments"* as a distinguishable form in the 1720s and 1730s supported a conception of Britain as possessing a distinctive national culture, one capable of being compared to the cultures of Greece and Rome. To its first advocates, the emergence of pantomime was to be understood, not as the sign of the stage's decline, but as a harbinger of its reform and a vehicle for engaging the attention of spectators untutored in more traditional literary forms.

As we have already seen, the central figure in the effort to advance "pantomimic dancing" as an enlightened science, a liberal art rather than just a mechanical craft, was John Weaver. His treatises—*An Essay Towards an History of Dancing, Anatomical and Mechanical Lectures up on Dancing* (1721), and *The History of the Mimes and Pantomimes* (1728), as well as several contributions to *The Spectator*—collectively aim to construct the kind of theoretical basis that mimetic media such as painting and drama had long enjoyed in order to support his central claim that dancing is "worthy the Regard and Consideration, as well as Reflexion, of the learned World."[46] Issued by the Whig house publisher Jacob Tonson (perhaps with the mediation of Steele and Addison), these essays participate in *The Spectator*'s program to bring "Philosophy out of Closets and Libraries, Schools and Colleges, to dwell in Clubs and Assemblies, at Tea-Tables and Coffee-Houses" (1:44). Throughout his work, Weaver offers dance as a uniquely comprehensive art, embracing the figural quality of painting, the expository capacity of rhetoric, and the emotional power of music. Crucially, dancing brings the role of the human body in theatrical performance to the fore, not only because of the obvious ways in which it orients itself around the bodies of its performers, but also because of the assumption, drawn ultimately from the Cartesian physiology articulated above, that the minds of spectators are particularly prone to being "impressed" in a physical sense by their attention to the body in motion.

For Weaver, a scientific and historically based approach to dance is the means by which the "Human Machine" might be harnessed as an expressive medium because it offers the hope of subjecting the body to the kind of "Regulation" that the theater demands by virtue of the particularly concentrated spectatorial relationship that it creates and exploits. If, as he says, such "external objects of Sensation" as the "Regular or Irregular Position, and

Motion of the Body" are enough to (literally) *inform* the "Soul" or "Mind" of the spectator as to the difference between a "fine Gentleman" and an "unpolish'd Peasant," or "the graceful Mien of a young Lady" from "the ungainly Carriage of her Maid," how much more powerful would proper and professional "Regulation" of the human body be to the minds of spectators gathered in for the express purpose of viewing an embodied performance?[47] Here, proper classification through spectatorship becomes the touchstone, or even the lure, by which a new disciplinary impulse toward the body—well-catalogued by Norbert Elias, Michel Foucault, and Joseph Roach, among others, as a salient feature of the eighteenth century's self-appointed "civilizing" mission—might be advanced as an enlightened art.[48]

Weaver brings a version of history to bear on his claim that dance might become a central component of modern cultural life, turning to the example of classical Greece and Rome, where, he argues, dance was understood to be every bit as expressive and intelligible to its spectator as spoken language (*Essay,* 16). Drawing his evidence from classical texts (particularly Lucian's *Peri Orcheseos*) and seventeenth-century scholarship into antiquity, Weaver urges that modern dancers imitate the ancient *pantomimi,* the "universal Actor[s] in Dancing" (*Essay,* 139), who were reputedly able to transmit any story through gesture and movement alone. As we saw in the previous chapter, seventeenth- and eighteenth-century English writers on the stage such as Jeremy Collier, Thomas Rymer, and James Drake frequently held up the Roman pantomime dancers as a point of comparison to the English stage. Where Weaver departs from these predecessors is that he does not use the ancient mimes and pantomimes as a way of underscoring the origins of the theater in ritual processes. Rather, he emphasizes how their motions constituted a form of communication that transcended time, place, and culture, approximating a universal language. The limit case of such communicative ability is offered in Weaver's account of a barbarian who was so impressed at the performance of a pantomime dancer in Rome that he asked the emperor Nero to be able to take the performer with him so as to be able to interpret to the surrounding tribes, "since by his Movements and Gesticulations he could inform him of all they should negociate" (*Essay,* 135). This story, which comes from Lucian, was widely cited in the period, appearing, for instance, in Gildon's *The Life of Mr. Thomas Betterton* as an illustration of the power of acting.[49] The frequency of its repetition bears out the degree to which embodied performance had become a locus of the period's desire to discover or produce a universal language system, a means of cross-cultural communication.

Pantomimic dancing was not so much a diversion as "a Science imitative, and demonstrative, an Interpreter of Aenigmatical Things, and a Clearer of Ambiguities" that offered, not senseless stimulation, but rather a uniquely clear route of access to knowledge (*Essay*, 124). By such a logic, pantomime dance in effect spoke to the "barbarians" within Roman culture itself, the spectators whose tastes had been weakened by the nation's imperialist over-reaching. Most important, by imitating Rome's invention of a "serious" and "instructive" mode of pantomime performance, Britain could, Weaver implies, rediscover a form of communication that would appeal to spectators of all kinds. He gives the most detailed articulation of a desire that, as we have seen, was strongly felt within the eighteenth-century theater, the hope that motion alone could constitute the most basic and universal form of eloquence, a hope prompted by the felt need to address and civilize diverse audiences. As James Ralph waggishly put it in *The Touch-Stone*, his satirical guide to contemporary London entertainments, "the only Method of attaining an universal Language, is to be Dumb."[50]

Weaver dramatizes both the hope embodied in and the resistance likely to be mounted to his own project in the 1718 "Dramatick Entertainment in Dancing" entitled *Orpheus and Eurydice*, a work whose title page announces how the performance was "Attempted in IMITATION of the Ancient *Greeks* and *Romans*."[51] In his preface, Weaver offers a scholarly discussion of the story of Orpheus (the role that he performed), who emerges in this account as perhaps the quintessential Enlightenment philosophe *avant la lettre:* he is reputed to have written tracts on the motions of the stars and histories of the labors of Hercules; he "instructed the *Grecians* in the Ceremonies of their Divine Worship, and taught them the Being, and Beginning of the gods"; he introduced law to Thrace; finally, and most important, he "Civiliz'd the *Grecians*" (2) through the taming influence of music. With the Orpheus story, Weaver stages the origins of theatrical performance in the "*Bacchanalian* Rites" (2) that his subject had introduced, rituals that, he points out, were always accompanied by ceremonial dance. Like the Faustus story that would set off the boom in pantomime a few years later, *Orpheus and Eurydice*—which would be one of the most popular subjects for eighteenth-century pantomime, with two new productions staged in 1740 alone—is a tale of contract and catastrophe; it's because Orpheus is, as Weaver puts it, "forgetful of his Contract" (14) with Pluto not to look back at Eurydice as he leads her from the underworld that he is dismembered by Thracian women infuriated by his indifference, an affective stance caused by his mourning for Eurydice. In Weaver's hands, the Orpheus story can be read as a cautionary tale about the reception that the enlightened artist is likely to receive. But in the utopian ideal it holds out, *Orpheus and Eurydice* stages what Weaver's theoretical texts argue, that music and dance might alone accomplish a civilizing mission.

It is fair to say, however, that the pantomime performances that came to dominate the London theaters in the 1720s and 1730s were not precisely what Weaver had in mind when he urged a revival of Roman pantomimic dancing, and it is clear that contemporary writers, whether or not they knew of Weaver's work, were aware of the claim that English pantomime was simply the re-creation of a classical form. The question of whether or not the entertainments advertised under the name *pantomime* in those decades represented a modern version of the ancient practice became part of the public debate over their utility and propriety. Journals took sides: *The Weekly Journal,* usually sympathetic to Rich's company at Lincoln's Inn Fields, praised that theater's 1723 production of *Jupiter and Europa* as being "after the Manner of the *Pantomimes,* a kind of Actors amongst the *Grecians,* who made themselves understood by Dance and Gesture, without speaking a Word."[52] The rival *British Journal* denied that such afterpieces "are truly *Pantomime*" because "there is neither Moral nor Fable in any of their *Raree-Shows,*" performances that merely cause the spectators to "stare our selves out of our Senses."[53] Weaver himself registers what we might well read as his disappointment in the course taken by the London theater at the outset of his 1728 *History of the Mimes and Pantomimes* (in large part a reprinting of the sections from his *Essay on the History of Dancing* that related to Roman pantomime), where he complains that those "*Dramatick* Entertainments, consisting of *Dancing, Gesture,* and *Action,* intermix'd with *Trick* and *Show*" that "the Town" currently calls pantomimes rarely rise to the level of their classical precedent.[54]

Yet it would be short-sighted to dismiss Weaver as either an isolated idealist or a mere self-promoter, even if his work was unsuccessful and forgotten, constituting the kind of legacy that leads a person to be labeled (as Weaver has been) "before his time."[55] Rather, we can take Weaver's lament as testimony to the difficulty of imposing any such form of discipline on an audience who could not be forced into accepting, much less enjoying, performances staged with the express purpose of reforming their judgment. Real spectators refuse to become "spectators," a normative ideal, smoothed to enlightened civility and uniformity by their engagement with the spectacle. The sheer multiplicity of tastes, desires, memories, and experiences that theatergoers now brought with them ensured that attempts to legislate their response would ultimately be resisted and upended. In the last production he mounted in a long career, Weaver made a final attempt to stage an "instructive" entertainment with a revival of William Congreve's "masque" *The Judgment of Paris* in 1733. Reverting here both to a classical subject and to the icon of literary respectability in the English theater, Weaver scored a modest success. But after a few performances on its own, *The Judgment of Paris* was joined to a new harlequinade composed by Theophilus Cibber, *The Harlot's Progress,* a "grotesque Pantomime entertainment" inspired by, and no doubt intended to capitalize on the success of, William Hogarth's popular series of prints.

Staging each of the first four prints in the series as a tableau that proceeds to come alive, *The Harlot's Progress* recasts Hogarth's narrative of the fall of an innocent country girl come to London as a harlequinade, with the young woman in effect a Colombine figure and Harlequin taking the role of the young suitor. Cibber proclaims his admiration for Hogarth's series, but *The Harlot's Progress* undercuts the moral point of the images at every turn. Harlequin upends each tableau with his tricks and transformations; in the scene where the young woman, now arrested for prostitution, beats hemp on blocks in Bridewell, for example, Harlequin, Scaramouche, Pierrot, and Mezzetin suddenly appear on each block, and each takes one of the female prisoners off to a *ridotto.* Hence, rather than Hogarth's instructive and pathetic scene of the harlot's final illness and death, *The Harlot's Progress* pantomime closes with a festive dance, as the English and the commedia characters join together with a "Variety of People" (the cast list calls for "Hungarians" as well as "Fingalians") in dancing to "English, Scotch, Irish and French Tunes."[56] Cibber's move out beyond the theater's walls to the broader expanse of urban entertainment has the effect of pretty much erasing the instructive and uplifting goals of Hogarth's original series of prints. Still, in its multiethnic dances and its efforts to democratize Hogarth's series, *The Harlot's Progress* does follow through on some of the goals that Weaver pursued, if in a rather different register. But when it was staged as the accompanying "serious" part to this performance, *The Judgment of Paris* may not have come across as a satire, but it cannot have appeared as an unequivocally uplifting spectacle, either. The outcome of Weaver's program testifies, perhaps, to the truth-value of a premise that eighteenth-century English pantomimes never tired of staging: that the public sphere and the material world upon which it rests constitute an ironic place, prone to overturn, misuse, and appropriate for its own ends the most enlightened of intentions.

Weaver's utopianism about the potential for pantomime to bridge differences of culture and class, whether or not it was wholly realized in practice, can be taken as a signal of his awareness of the new demands placed on public performance by the conditions of the present tense, the breakdown of absolute claims to authority over language and political power, and the growing diversity of interests and perspectives in his culture. In short, this conception of pantomime as the logical performance medium to seize and gratify the eye of the spectator is self-consciously *modern,* as it recognizes the difference between its own moment and the culture of the past. The following chapter will suggest that such an awareness could be woven into the fabric of pantomime entertainments themselves. I will argue that the Faustus pantomimes that initiated the boom in pantomime of the 1720s in London can be understood as marking the presence of modernity in at least two different senses. To their detractors, the enormous popularity of these entertainments and the imitators they spawned signaled the dangerous hegemony of entertainment itself, which now threatened to siphon attention away from literary culture as it had been understood. There is an element of truth in this, and I will suggest that this "event" actually does serve to mark important shifts in the public sphere that point to changes in the place and authority of the literary. And in their subject matter and the way that these entertainments staged the rivalry between the performative body and the written word, the Faustus entertainments also, I will suggest, function as an allegory about the emergence of modernity, as Harlequin Faustus's protean capacity identifies him with the magical arts that distinguished the enlightened presence from the benighted past.

CHAPTER FOUR

Magic and Mimesis

HARLEQUIN DOCTOR FAUSTUS AND
THE MODERNITY OF EIGHTEENTH-
CENTURY PANTOMIME

*O*n November 26, 1723, London's Drury
Lane followed its performance of John Fletcher's
1624 comedy *Rule a Wife and Have a Wife* with
a new afterpiece entertainment, *Harlequin Doctor Faustus,* a comic retelling in dance, song, and
spectacle of the Faust story, in which the scholar-
antihero of legend was played by a Harlequin.
Choreographed by the dancing-master John
Thurmond, a protégé of John Weaver, *Harlequin Doctor Faustus* consisted largely of a series
of tricks performed by Harlequin Faustus after
he signs the contract with Mephistopheles and
is given his magical powers. For example, Harlequin cuts off his own right leg when confronted with a usurer, but then replaces it with
a woman's leg that flies in from the wings; he
makes the money he has given a prostitute disappear; he makes ass's ears appear on the heads
of Scaramouche, Pierrot, and Punch, who are
dressed as scholars. The entire entertainment
concludes as Harlequin Faustus, his time up, is
carried away by devils, followed by a "masque
of the deities" in which the pagan gods Apollo,
Mars, Mercury, Diana, et al. dance to "express

their Joy for the Enchanter's Death."[1] Less than a month later, on December 20, the rival patent theater at Lincoln's Inn Fields countered with its own afterpiece version of the Faust legend: *The Necromancer, or, Harlequin Doctor Faustus,* which was performed following Joseph Addison's 1716 comedy *The Drummer.* Much like the entertainment at Drury Lane, the Lincoln's Inn Fields production burlesques the myth of Faust receiving magical powers in return for his soul by having Harlequin Faustus perform a number of tricks, including conjuring up the spirits of the classical lovers Hero and Leander, who sing of their love, virtues, and constancy to one another. At the end of this entertainment, his tricks accomplished and his magic spent, Harlequin Faustus is dragged away by a dragon.[2]

Both of the Faustus afterpieces were successful, particularly *The Necromancer,* which became one of the most popular staged pieces of the eighteenth century, revived again and again over the next years and decades. Why it distinguished itself as, by most accounts, the more successful of the two entertainments is impossible to reconstruct fully at this remove, but accounts suggest that *The Necromancer* did a better job of integrating its classical elements with the commedia characters, and it also had the benefit of John Rich's performance as Harlequin, which became one of the most applauded pairings of performer and role in the eighteenth-century British theater. But what is more important than the sheer popularity of these works is the way that the two afterpieces were collectively taken to change the nature and significance of such afterpiece performances. To the theater's observers, the two Faustus entertainments assumed the status of a significant *event,* in the sense of an incident that divides a narrative—here the story of the eighteenth-century British theater—into a distinct before and after.[3] They marked the start of the boom in afterpieces that would continue through the 1720s into the 1750s at least, a period when pantomime was arguably the most popular form of entertainment on the British stage, and was certainly one of the most commented-upon phenomena in the public sphere. Depending on the degree of the observer's investment in the current state of the stage, Harlequin's seemingly sudden rise to notoriety either promised to restore the theaters' fortunes or threatened to destroy them once and for all. What made such afterpieces collectively seem so distinctive that their presence was felt to mark a distinct change in the history of the London theater, dividing it into a nostalgically remembered past and a degraded present?

This chapter argues that we can only answer a question like this by thinking about the relationship between the story told by these entertainments and the public sphere in which they gained significance. Specifically, I want to think about how the Faust story as it was understood by eighteenth-century Britons would have resonated with an audience in the early 1720s. Early eighteenth-century Britons frequently believed the Faust story to be an account of the seemingly magical origins of printing, in which they believed the historical John Faustus to have played a key role. The Faustus entertainments thus thematized the invention of a technology that a wordless form like pantomime seemed to threaten. But the invention of the printing press was also understood in epochal terms, as one of the primary acts by which a traditional culture was transformed into a modern one. My claim will be that the Faustus entertainments both narrated and marked the emergence of certain aspects of modernity. As they invoked Faustus's association with printing, they identified how modern, technological "magic" had displaced superstition. Meanwhile, the Faustus afterpieces seemed to represent something new to the culture, a kind of entertainment that threatened to displace both the traditional pastimes of the rural past and the urban literary culture of the present. And we shall see that both of these displacements help us specify crucial shifts in the shape and constitution of the public sphere, which was undergoing a transformation of its own, one that enabled entertainment to move to center stage.

Faustus, Pantomime, and the "Event" in the Public Sphere

First the theater was one thing, then, seemingly in the blink of an eye, it was another. Whether or not the Faustus entertainments of 1723 deserved to be called a scandal, there is no question that collectively they were understood to constitute a significant *event,* a break in the narrative of the English theater. More than any afterpieces before or after, they brought the mode of performance that John Weaver had promoted in the 1710s as an entertainment in "emulation" of the ancient pantomimes into intelligibility as a thing in its own right, a recognizable form that could henceforth be critiqued, admired, attacked, and entered into history. But most of the components of the Faustus entertainments were hardly new to the theater in 1723. The Faust story had been in circulation for more than a century, and had been staged in a variety of ways since the first production of Christopher Marlowe's *Doctor Faustus* in the early 1590s. As we have already seen, commedia dell'arte characters had appeared in English performances since the sixteenth century and had been commonplace in the London patent theaters since at least the 1680s, if not earlier. What is more, the Faustus story had already been burlesqued on the London stage with the use of commedia dell'arte characters by William Mountfort's farce *The Life and Death of Doctor Faustus* (c. 1684), which included a speaking Harlequin and Scaramouche, as well as "Songs and Dances between the Acts."[4] The singing, dancing, and stage effects featured in these productions were familiar components of the early eighteenth-century British stage; none of the various accounts of the Faustus entertainments describes any radically novel formal and technical innovations. To be sure, the synthesis of dance, song, spectacle, commedia, and classical mythology that the Faustus performances achieved represents something new in its own right, and that synthesis established a paradigm that could be recognized as a specific performance genre, one that was, crucially, *repeatable* in a number of pantomime entertainments staged over the course of the next two decades. The Faustus entertainments, and particularly *The Necromancer*, which would become one of the most popular productions of any kind in the century, with more than 300 recorded performances between 1723 and the retirement of its star John Rich from acting on the stage in 1753, represented a new synthesis of elements that had been present in the London theater before, and thus reworked what we can think of as the generic structure of the afterpiece entertainment as it had been established over the previous few decades. This is the aspect of the Faustus entertainments that contemporary accounts noticed most frequently, and we must rely on their testimony for clues as to how Thurmond and Rich created a new paradigm for afterpiece performances by their shrewd and striking appropriations of the kinds of songs, dances, story, and spectacle that the theaters had been using for some time. But the internal logic of these pieces, to the extent that we can reconstruct it from contemporary descriptions and accounts of their production, is not sufficient to explain the enormous impact they had in their moment, the way that they seemed to have changed the course of the stage itself. Why these performances, and why did they constitute an event when they did?

To ask this is to be forced to think not only about the content of these productions, the responses they provoked, and the imitators they spawned, but also to think critically and skeptically about the category of the event itself, and why these productions were construed under its sign. Instead of simply reaffirming the standard account that casts the Faustus performances as central and transformative events, we need rather to examine the terms of the debate that seized on them to bring the afterpieces that London theaters had promoted as "pantomimic entertainments" or "dramatic entertainments in dancing" into a new kind of intelligibility. The event must be understood as a doubled concept; although it is in an obvious sense an empirical thing that can be said to have happened and that would go on to influence people's understanding of the medium and affect their decisions within it, the event is also a mode of recording and classifying, a dynamic process rather than a static object. The anthropologist Marshall Sahlins offers a useful description of the concept of the event that emphasizes its transitivity: "the event," he says, "is the relation between" mere "happenings" and larger "structures," a relation that confers "meaning and importance" on incidents that might otherwise never reach the threshold of significance.[5] Thus, the "happening" of the Faustus pantomimes in the fall of 1723 might very well have been ignored had they not appealed to meaningful "structures" in British culture. These performances were so striking to contemporaries in part because of the way that they were overdetermined by virtue of their implication within several different structures at once: social, political, and affective, collectively constituting what Raymond Williams described as a "structure of feeling."[6]

What Sahlins's formulation suggests but does not articulate is the reciprocal quality of this relationship, by which an event not only represents the elevation of a happening to significance but can also help identify shifts in the constitution of the larger structure. The Faustus entertainments did not have to offer all that much that was new if the context within which they took place had changed in such a way as to make such performances newly intelligible as an event. The seemingly sudden emergence of pantomime as a topic of public discussion is indebted, I would argue, to significant changes in the shape, scope, and possibilities of the bourgeois public sphere itself, which is itself less a stable object than a shifting relationship between people, classes, and the media through which they communicated. Perhaps because Habermas's model is typically imagined in terms of spatial rather than temporal metaphors—prompting its readers to imagine a sphere or forum of debate rather than, say, a chronicle or diary—it can lead us to ignore or downplay changes in the nature and possibilities of public discussion over time, creating a somewhat static image of the possibilities for political and cultural debate, as if these were constant over the period. But to its participants, the early eighteenth-century public sphere was extraordinarily contentious, dynamic, and unstable. Indeed, the very reason why so many voices and venues were introduced into the public sphere was that the political and economic issues of the first decades of Parliamentary rule were so divisive, pitting clearly defined interests against each other and offering such stark choices (Stuart versus Hanoverian monarchies; Catholic versus Protestant state religions; a land-based versus a credit economy) that a substantial *infrastructure* of debate developed, as if it were summoned into being to spell out in detail the full implications of every move in the game. An enabling condition for this infrastructure was the lapse of the Press Licensing Act in 1695, which had the effect of unleashing a torrent of printed materials. These tended to organize around specific crises and controversies, but also to catalyze them, giving them a shape, intensity, and impact that was difficult if not impossible to achieve before.

The pamphlet war known as the Collier controversy was one of these crises, and it is worth returning briefly to the aftermath of that debate to understand some of the changes in the public sphere that enabled the Faustus pantomimes to become objects of public attention and scandal. One irony of the Collier controversy of the late 1690s and 1700s is that Collier's reformist program was taken up most energetically by figures who occupied the opposite end of the political spectrum. Collier was a Tory with strong Jacobite sympathies who not only refused to take the oath of loyalty to William and Mary but who climbed a scaffold in 1696 to grant absolution to conspirators convicted of treason for plotting to assassinate William. This was a public performance that caused Collier to lose his place in the church, a fact that may have its own part to play in his becoming a polemicist on behalf of theatrical reform, as it in effect freed him to write for an audience larger than his own congregation.[7] But it was primarily Whig writers—Addison, Steele, William Congreve, George Farquhar, John Vanbrugh, Nicholas Rowe, Colley Cibber, and Susanna Centlivre, among others—who publicly aligned themselves under the banner of reform with which Collier was associated, even where they professed to disagree strongly with the specific terms of his attack.

Thus Centlivre admitted in the prefatory material to her very first play, *The Perjur'd Husband* (1700), that Collier had so altered the environment for playwriting that she had in effect learned to censor herself away from innuendo.[8] Richard Steele attested more than once to the influence of Collier's critique on his own work, and fashioned his early plays to appeal to and consolidate the taste for a comedy that would be reformed away from the excesses that Collier had identified in Restoration comedies. Even John Vanbrugh and William Congreve—two of Collier's main targets in the *Short View*—sought and obtained a theatrical license in 1705 on the basis of their professed desire to reform the theater.[9] To be sure, party labels could be fluid and imprecise throughout this period—Jonathan Swift, by most lights a Tory, considered himself to be a Whig who held on to the faction's original principles while others changed; Daniel Defoe was notoriously said to write for whichever side would pay him best; and their mutual patron Robert Harley successfully switched back and forth according to political expediency. Yet it seems fair to say that few of the Whig reformers of the 1700s and 1710s would have shared much common political ground with Collier, however eagerly they aligned themselves with the program for which he served as the public voice.

But the more significant irony about Collier is that his attack on the licentiousness of the London playhouses laid the terms under which his own program could be turned on its head by the next generation of reformers. As we saw in chapter 2, one of the fundamental premises of Collier's attack on the English stage was that playwrights, managers, and performers had forgotten that the theater was a constituent part of feudal state/church apparatus, subject to supervision by the Crown and clergy, and therefore available to be assessed by the norms of morality developed under the central authority of the state. By the 1710s, however, Whig writers who publicly subscribed to the program of reform and politeness described the theater as a place apart, a domain that was distinct from the state and should therefore no longer be considered according to its norms or subject to its rules. In effect, they turned Collier's rhetorical move in defining the English stage as a genre or thing in order that it might be compared to the contemporary national theater of France or the classical theaters of Greece and Rome upside down, using his definition of the English stage as a "case" to argue that it should be considered a separate and distinct realm *within* British culture. By framing the English stage as a kind of genre or thing in its own right, Collier would in effect facilitate the next generation's efforts to redefine the British theater as an institution to be evaluated by a wholly different set of norms than his own, and to be reinvested with very different purposes than those which he had imagined for it.

Whig writers from the 1690s on gravitated to the theater because they saw it as a cultural domain that they could readily appropriate for their program of politeness and refinement. The theater would thus be weaned away from its association with the absolutist state and, at the same time, could be reformed without the divisive controversies that had typified seventeenth-century debates on the stage. Such a program demanded that the theater be depoliticized, at least in the sense that it would be protected from the contentiousness of partisan conflict, segregated away as a distinct, nonpartisan domain of the public sphere. No writer better articulates the stakes of the reformist program than Joseph Addison. In his journal *The Freeholder* for April, 16, 1716, for example, Addison describes how "the bitterness of Party-

Rage" has come to saturate domains of the culture that he wants to claim had once been uncontaminated by partisanship.[10] Writing in the wake of a failed Jacobite insurrection in 1715 and in the midst of continuing protests and riots over its aftermath, Addison laments the politicization of the London theater, casting the division of audience sympathies by party as a violation of its history and its norms. The controversies surrounding recent events like the Hanoverian succession and the Jacobite uprising, his journalistic avatar the Freeholder asserts, have recently come to saturate "all the most indifferent Circumstances of Life," including "our Parties of Pleasure . . . our Diversions, and . . . most of our publick Entertainments" (40, 39). He illustrates the problem by telling the story of his recent visit to a Drury Lane production of John Crowne's 1685 comedy *Sir Courtly Nice*. Revived at this moment of "dangerous Dissension," Crowne's satire has, according to the Freeholder, been misconstrued to have such pointed political content that the audience took sides, the Tories cheering on "Hot-head" (clearly intended by Crowne as a satire on people who overreact to religious enthusiasts) and the Whigs applauding the character named "Testimony" (a satirical version of just such an enthusiast).

To Crowne, these two characters represent the extremes of the mid-1680s political spectrum, positions that must be rendered equally the subjects of satire in order to construct the kind of moderate position from which a new consensus might be achieved. But to Addison's Freeholder, the "wise Posterity" attending the theater in 1716 have appropriated Crowne's characters for the purpose only of confirming their own extremist positions. The Freeholder construes this mistake in spectatorship as a violation of the national interest. The "Parties and Divisions" revealed at this performance may "bring Destruction upon our Country" in a way that no "foreign Enemy" ever could, and he urges his readers to set aside their "Party-Rage" in order to think of themselves as a "*British* Audience," rather than one divided into Whig and Tory factions.[11] Addison's essay is extraordinarily disingenuous, disavowing the aggressively partisan character of *The Freeholder* itself, the shamelessly Whig bias that has rendered it among the deadest of all of Addison's periodical writings to the critical posterity that much prefers the suave moderation of *The Spectator*. But it nonetheless expresses well the discomfort that political application prompted among those who wished to redefine theater as a space of entertainment, and also demonstrates how such a program called for a reappropriation and reevaluation of the Restoration theater that had long been the locus of reformers' animus, a recasting of history to show that the playhouse had been an innocent institution all along.

Hence Addison offers a myth of origin for the theater, one reaching back to a Stuart defense of public amusements as a useful diversion from serious matters that had originated as a riposte to Puritan attacks on recreational activities, particularly rural games, sports, and holidays:

> The Institution of Sports and Shows was intended, by all Governments, to turn off the Thoughts of the People from busying themselves in Matters of State, which did not belong to them; to reconcile them to one another by the common Participations of Mirth and Pleasure; and to wear out of their Minds that Rancour which they might have contracted by the interfering Views of Interest and Ambition. (192)

Note how Addison imagines the participants of "Sports and Shows" as machine-men on the model of the Cartesian spectator outlined in the previous chapter, their minds worn into moderation by a well-conceived entertainment. More important, Addison here invokes, and then alters, an older defense of pastimes in English culture. As we saw in chapter 2, this argument had perhaps its definitive articulation in James I's *Book of Sportes,* which considered sports and shows as traditional English customs, virtually part of the ancient constitution of the state itself, and vital components of the monarch's role as the benign father supervising the pastimes of his people.[12] Addison obscures the absolutist ideology that this theory expresses, however, one that would align the theatrical and the political as two aspects of monarchical rule. He silently shifts the locus of sports and shows from the country to the city, alters the source of authority from the Crown to "Government," and presents public sports and shows as the alternative, not to the Puritan conformity of the seventeenth century, but to partisan bickering in the present moment.

The position of neutrality that the essay maps out as the ideal site for entertainment is occupied, it turns out, by the figure of Harlequin. The Freeholder observes that Harlequin—featured in the afterpiece to the performance of *Sir Courtly Nice* that Addison is describing in this essay—has not "violated his Neutrality" by taking any side (even though at least one Whig theatergoer apparently mistook Harlequin's characteristic checkered suit for "Highland Plad" and applauded when he climbed a ladder, as if he were miming an ascent to the scaffold, an allusion to the Jacobite Scottish Lords then on trial for treason). Harlequin pinpoints the neutral, moderate position that Addison wishes to define, embodying an ideal of apolitical entertainment that Addison advances as the desirable alternative to bitter partisanship. Here Harlequin's foreignness—we can, in fact, identify the performance that the

Freeholder is thinking of as a production on April 11, 1716, of a commedia play entitled *La Guinquette; or, Harlequin Turned Tapster* that was staged by a visiting French troupe—helps make him available as a figure for *British* unity because it absolves him of any association with the divisive partisanship that permeates the national life of actual Britons.

There is, of course, no direct causal relation between Addison's passing description of a Harlequin as the embodiment of neutral entertainment and the emergence, several years later, of Harlequin as one of the most famous figures in the public sphere in Britain. But the very emptiness, the freedom from particular and controversial positions and associations that permits Addison to nominate him, however ironically, as a figure of national unity, helps account for how a character that originated in Continental theater would become so enormously popular in British culture over the next few decades that he would become a kind of emblem of the national theater. More immediately, we can think of Harlequin's presence in an essay that laments the confusion of politics and entertainment as a kind of foreshadowing of some of the unintended consequences of the Whig reform program that Addison was attempting to advance. Addison's hopes that the intensity of partisan debate would diminish were fulfilled, though probably not in the way he could have expected or would have chosen. Partisan rancor diminished in the 1720s, but this cannot be taken as a sign of the advance of civility or the health of the public sphere. For by the early 1720s, the public sphere was in crisis, and indeed, if we adopt the strictest terms of Habermas's definition, a pretty good case could be made that the normative bourgeois public sphere, the domain of open debate and discussion that he heralds as a counter to the more restrictive context of the absolutist monarchy and its court, had already become extinct. For the arena of public debate in which *The Spectator* and its many imitators had flourished was threatened by the government's attempts, not merely to harness print media, but to manage or even control it.

The free-wheeling, bitterly partisan atmosphere that had taken hold since the advent of party divisions in the dynastic contests of the 1680s, and which had become particularly virulent in the unsettled political context of the 1710s, was dramatically transformed in the 1720s. The South Sea Bubble, the astonishing rise and fall in the value of shares in the South Sea Company that took place in the spring and summer of 1720, serves as a convenient marker of the shift, in no small part because it was in the Bubble's aftermath that Robert Walpole seized power on the basis of his ability to manage a financial crisis—and to cover up, or, to use the contemporary metaphor, "screen" the involvement of high-ranking members of the government, including the king and his mistress, in the scheme. In the aftermath of the South Sea Bubble and the rise to power of Walpole and his "Robinocracy" that attempted to co-opt, buy out, or suppress opposition and the dissenting voices that articulated it, partisan political debate greatly decreased in frequency and intensity. (This was perhaps particularly the case after the trial in 1723 of Francis Atterbury, the bishop of Rochester, in connection with a failed plot to restore the Stuart dynasty to the throne the year before, an event that Walpole exploited as a way of uncovering some of his more powerful and well-protected adversaries in order to move against them.) The space had thus been cleared for a new object of public attention, one that might mimic the craze surrounding the South Sea Bubble in intensity and seeming universality, but, unlike the Bubble, would be wholly free of partisan associations. That is, the conditions were now present for the modern phenomenon of a *fad*, a phenomenon that seemed to unite the nation in a common interest, an object whose irrationality and ephemerality were the very conditions of its appeal. The Faustus entertainments became that fad.

Contemporaries recognized that the expansion of the entertainment culture in the 1720s that Harlequin widely symbolized seemed to have its precedent in the public fascination with stock-trading in the late 1710s. A character in James Ralph's 1730 mock ballad opera *The Fashionable Lady, or Harlequin's Opera* comments that the recent "national Phrenzy" over ballad opera in the wake of the astonishing success of John Gay's *The Beggar's Opera* is not only "intirely owing to Whim and Caprice," but must be compared to "that of purchasing South-Sea Stock, in the Year Twenty, or the Gape at Doctor Faustus ever since."[13] The ability for public culture in London to generate and foster theatrical fads was enabled by the infrastructure for debate that had been developed during the intensely partisan controversies of the last generation, debates that had had their oxygen cut off by the emergence of one-party rule in the early 1720s. In that sense, the "national phrenzy" or the "British Frenzy" over the new entertainments that dominated the London theaters in the 1720s may be said to have followed from, and taken the place of, the "rage of party" of the decade before.[14]

The change in the public sphere and the media that helped constitute it did not, of course, stifle politics, and it would be an exaggeration to say that oppositional voices were fully suppressed or drowned out by Walpole, who was never as successful as he wished to be. By no later than the mid-1720s, opposition journals like *The Craftsman* had established an active and frequently combative public debate on the Walpole government, and, as we shall see in chapter 6, the theater would generate a considerable oppositional body of work of its own, a satirical program that is frequently associated with, but not exhausted by, the dramatic and journalist writings of Henry Fielding. But the emergence of pantomime as a highly visible entity in the public sphere in the wake of the Faustus entertainments is indebted, I would argue, to the changes in the scope and possibilities for print media that occurred after 1720 with the shifts in the political context, such that the Faustus pantomimes might be considered an example of what William Warner has recently termed a "media event." Such an event is manufactured by and within the media that observe it and confer it with significance. But the kind of significance recorded at the time may have the effect of distorting or disguising other important aspects of phenomena so entered into the public sphere. Warner argues, for example, that the media event surrounding the publication of Samuel Richardson's *Pamela* in 1740—sometimes taken, in retrospect, to mark the moment of the emergence of the English novel—needs to be understood as a "primal scene" that "overwrites" the more complicated history of prose fiction that preceded it.[15] Something of the same thing can be said about the emergence of pantomime in the early 1720s, which can be understood as a media event prompting debate about the nature, propriety, and cultural location of performed entertainment. To the extent that it shared common concerns about the democratization of cultural authority and the popularity of forms designed for pleasure rather than for moral uplift, the debate set off by pantomime preceded and in some ways set the terms for the debate about narrative fiction that would follow almost two decades later. But the Faustus afterpieces constituted a media event in another sense as well. These performances can be understood as, in part, allegories about the medium in which they were performed; they staged the rivalry between theater and text, stage and page that had become acutely intelligible with the invention of printing. To understand how the Faustus afterpieces thematized the relationship between the medium in which they were performed—theater—and the medium through which they were critiqued—print—we need to understand the constitutive role that their hero was understood to have played in the invention of printing, and the modernity that printing ushered into existence.

The True History of Doctor Faustus

John Faustus was widely believed to have been a real man, an historical figure of fifteenth-century Germany. But to the early eighteenth century, he was not quite the same man as the legendary scholar-turned-wizard usually available to literary history through Marlowe, Goethe, or, to those interested in tracing such narratives to their earliest textualizations, the *Faustbuch,* published in Germany in 1587, and translated into English as *The History of the Damnable Life and Deserved Death of Doctor John Faustus* soon thereafter.[16] Rather, that familiar story was frequently combined with a now largely forgotten story of *another* Faustus, a man who was less a magician than a thief and a trickster, a con artist who simply deluded others into *thinking* that he had magic powers. This is the version of the story as told by the anonymous author of "A short Account of Doctor *Faustus;* and how he came to be reputed a Magician," which was prefaced to the libretto for the Lincoln's Inn Fields production of *The Necromancer* in 1723. The "short Account" debunks the notion that the historical Faustus ever really possessed magic powers, much less the ability to conjure up the dead. Such a stance would seem to undercut the entertainment to which it is prefixed, which follows the more familiar Faust legend by having its title character sign a contract with Mephistopheles and raise the spirit of Helen of Troy. But it reflects its author's desire to offer Faustus as a touchstone of modernity, and as a case study for demonstrating the improvement in historical understanding since Faustus's own time.

It is not that the author of the "short Account" doubts the existence of the historical Faustus. Rather, he takes the story that this man possessed magic power as merely a "*Fable,*" one exploited if not invented by Faustus himself "both to propagate his *Reputation,* and enhance his *Profit*"; this fable, uncritically accepted by modern writers guilty of the same lack of skepticism displayed by Faustus's contemporaries, was wrongly cast later in the form of historical fact.[17] Faustus's reputation as a conjurer is thus significant here as a symptom of the "*Ignorance*" and "*Credulity*" that dominated the "Period of Dullness and Barbarism" in which he lived, a period from which both author and reader now stand apart, at the critical remove that more than anything else constitutes enlightened modernity (iii). Faustus functions in this account as an index for the modern historian's critical capacity, as well as a marker for this author's construction of differing periods, an ignorant "before" and a more sophisticated "after," which Faustus himself straddles, a self-aware modern exploiting his situation among uncultured barbarians. But the widespread belief in his magic powers, though false, is explicable by virtue of Faustus's association with the institution that, by the logic of this short account, demarcates and to a great extent *caused* the break between an enlightened modernity and a credulous past: the printing press.[18]

The association can be understood as the confusion of Faustus with the actual historical figure of Johann Fust, a goldsmith and money lender in Mainz who had at one time sold manuscripts in universities and was one of Johann Gutenberg's financiers (and who eventually successfully sued Gutenberg for debt, gaining control of some of his presses).[19] By the early eighteenth century, the few remembered facts about Fust had become fused with the legends about Faustus to invest the invention of printing with historical significance, making it into the mark of the difference between the modern era and the barbarous past. This Faustus, the story went, was either the apprentice or the partner of John Coster, who was believed by most eighteenth-century historians to have invented the printing press in Mentz during the fifteenth century. Stealing Coster's types, Faustus printed an edition of the Bible and brought it to Paris, where it amazed onlookers, who could not understand how he was able to produce so many virtually identical copies of the same text, each of which they believed was done by handwriting, "A Labour that would have requir'd more Time to accomplish, than the Life of a Patriarch could be done so consistently, and so cheaply, as they thought, by *one* Hand" (vii). To the ignorant Parisians, the most plausible explanation for this astonishing feat was that Faustus must have made a deal with the devil. Accused of trafficking in the black arts and fearing for his life, Faustus fled to Germany, where he met up with one Johann Gutenberg. Together, they perfected the craft of printing.

This account of Faustus's theft and subsequent display of print technology as a form of magic, adapted for the preface to *The Necromancer* from Michel Mattaire's *Annales Typographie* (1719–25), was broadly circulated (with considerable variation) in early eighteenth-century Europe; as Adrian Johns has shown, it became an essential and characteristic part of the story the period told itself about the history of printing. In his *History of the Principal Discoveries and Improvements* (1727), Daniel Defoe, for example, attempting to explain the person about "which so many Books and Ballads, Tales and Harlequins have been made," narrates much the same "Tale" of how the historical Faustus took his pilfered texts to Paris and was almost hanged there "for a Necromancer and a Witch."[20] To these accounts, Faustus embodied what became known as the printing revolution not only because he was believed to be a central figure in the story of how the printing press was invented and its technology disseminated, but because his performance registered how that revolution fit into a broader narrative of how print transformed culture, how it became identified as, in Adrian Johns's words, "the indispensable cusp separating Descartes, Bacon, Newton, and modernity from corruption, superstition, ignorance, and despotism."[21] Faustus's magical transformations, the wonder of benighted medieval peasants, indexed the real metamorphosis that print was understood to have accomplished in human history, the transition from ignorance to enlightened modernity.

When his story was staged in the spectacular entertainments of 1723, Faustus staked the claim to the theater's also being a fully modern institution. This is why, to the anonymous author of *Round about our Coal-Fire; or, Christmas Entertainments* (c. 1730), the Faustus pantomimes and the magical performances that followed in their wake are an ideal reference point to identify the difference between the popular entertainments of "former Days" and those of the present.[22] An account of the changes in "hospitality" and popular pastimes in the last generation or so, *Round about our Coal-Fire* compares the "conjurers" of the past to modern "wizards," the most successful of whom is none other than John Rich, the "Conjurer General of the Universe" (and dedicatee of *Round about our Coal-Fire*), whose stage magic has all but supplanted the traditional, folkloric forms of mystery "that the old Folks used to relate of Friar *Bacon* and the Sorcerers in the Days of Yore." The author's central example of a conjurer of the past is, however, not Bacon, but Dr. Faustus who, in this account, exploited the fact that "he had the first Knowledge of Printing" (25) to convince "Fools" (27) of his magic powers, that "he could eat Loads of Hay, had fiery Dragons stew'd for Breakfast, had fry'd Toads and broil'd Serpents for Dinner, and, by way of Desert, would change Mens Noses into Bunches of Grapes, or Bunches of Grapes into Noses, which was the same thing" (26). The author adopts an ironic stance to such beliefs, of course, treating them as evidence of the way that prior generations were too willing to indulge in magical thinking when more rational explanations are available. Indeed, he goes to great lengths to demystify wizardry, describing at one point precisely how to create a spectacular entrance for a devil or witch by combining tartar, sulfur, and nitre, and he goes on to identify a chemist in Southampton-Row who can provide the key ingredients, evacuating all the mystery from this kind of wizardry by making it seem, not so much scientific, as hopelessly mundane and prosaic. But the author also seems to view the replacement of the people's traditional pastimes and beliefs by the modern stage magic of pantomime with as much nostalgia as satisfaction. While Rich's performances represent a kind of advance in that they are available "daily" rather than only at certain, festive, times of the year, and harness rather than are cowed by magic, they also mark a demystification of the world that carries with it a sense of loss. More than anything else, *Round about our Coal-Fire* identifies how the Faustus pantomimes seemed to epitomize the emergence of a new and identifiably modern culture of entertainment, one that was recognized to be different in kind from that of a traditional rural society, its seasonal pastimes, and its superstitions.

What is more, by imagining Faustus not merely as a role played by Rich but as a fitting analogue for him, the author of *Round about our Coal-Fire* underscores the *performative* nature of the Faust story as early eighteenth-century Britons understood it, the ways in which it was already suited to the medium of theater even before it was ever staged. For while Gutenberg has of course long since eclipsed Fust's reputation in the historical record (not to mention Coster's), there is a sense in which "Faustus's" role in the history of printing was always a poor fit with the medium of the printed text and the forms of historical writing and scholarship that would develop with it. As described by Defoe and the writer of the "short Account," Faustus is a con artist who indeed might have begun his career as that most compelling and threatening of early eighteenth-century rogues, the bad apprentice (about which much more in chapter 5). His medium was public, embodied performance rather than print; indeed, the texts he was said to have displayed to the credulous citizens of Paris were pointedly understood by them to be, not printed books, but manuscripts generated by a hand that they imagined was capable of reproducing texts with a speed and exactitude that could only be explained by magic. Faustus was thus always an eminently theatrical rather than a textual figure even where he was most closely associated with the institution that would spread texts to the point where they threatened, and then usurped, the primacy of theater.

The Faustus entertainments pointedly relied upon the kinds of magic that were unique to the theater, signaling the way that pantomime would advance the theater's superiority to print; as *The Weekly Journal*'s favorable review of *Harlequin Doctor Faustus* put it, "words cannot give a full Idea" of the event as it is experienced in the theater.[23] Writing in 1700, Thomas Brown had described the playhouse as "the land of enchantment, the country of Metamorphoses," and it was precisely this transformative capacity that the Faustus entertainments exploited.[24] To cite one of numerous instances from Drury Lane's *Harlequin Doctor Faustus:* Harlequin Faustus, Scaramouche, Punch, and Pierrot try on clothes in a shop until the master demands payment; Harlequin Faustus transforms the master into a woman; the master's wife enters and at first thinks the woman must be her husband's mistress, so she attacks all the men; the four commedia figures escape when Harlequin Faustus transforms them into "the Shapes of a Cat, a Hob, a Goat, and an Owl."[25] Such transformations of persons to animals or things (items of furniture, for example) and back again became the hallmark of the comic sections of pantomime afterpieces. As it coalesced into a recognized genre in the course of the mid-1720s, English pantomime condensed the metamorphic

Scene from the Lincoln's Inn Fields production of *The Necromancer*, 1723
(© *Copyright The British Museum*)

capacities of its theatrical medium into a specific and repeatable form. The chief agent of transformation, as here, was Harlequin himself, whose magic wand or bat served as the instrument through which all transformations took place. It is almost too easy to point to the phallic resonances concentrated in a prop that defined the power of Harlequin and the world he dominated in these entertainments; here, the degree of mediation is not impressive. And indeed, eighteenth-century pantomimes frequently reminded their spectators of the magic bat's centrality lest any of them forget it; a typical set piece of English harlequinade was the scene where Harlequin receives the bat from a devil, wizard, or sorcerer, and thereby gains his power to transform himself and his surroundings as needed.

The Faustus entertainments fused this scene with the moment where Doctor Faustus signs the contract with Mephistopheles pledging his soul in return for receiving the power to transform the material world and to raise the dead. The fullest visual record we have from *The Necromancer* casts the origins of its protagonist's magic power as a scene of writing, an act performed by the very "hand" that the citizens of Paris had believed was capable of astonishingly rapid and precise reproduction. Such a gesture, that is, demands Harlequin Faustus's physical presence; it underscores the corporeal essence of these entertainments as it reminds its viewer that the law demands the live presence of participants in order to secure a contract. As scenes from the Faustus entertainments go, this one is among the least visually interesting; it is much less spectacular than, say, the conclusion of either piece, when devils or dragons came onstage to drag Faustus to hell. But this is a shrewd choice nonetheless, for it records the moment when the legal, textual, spiritual, and corporeal themes at stake throughout the performance are in play at once. Inscribing the moment when Harlequin Faustus gains his transformative power, the image also pointedly locates him firmly within the proscenium arch of the Lincoln's Inn Fields theater, stressing that this is the record of a live, staged performance, here presented to the ideal spectator occupying a central point in the playhouse, one floating somewhere above the actual seats in the middle of the pit area.

Most important, the image suggests what the performance goes on to elaborate, demonstrating that Harlequin Faustus's magical powers are comparable and complementary to that of the theater as an institution. Faustus's magic powers literally give Harlequin's magic its *motivation,* enabling him to perform the various tricks and transformations that constituted the "grotesque" or comic parts of both entertainments; it is pointedly when Harlequin Faustus is taken to hell at the end of each afterpiece that the pagan deities arrive for a concluding masque, their presence the sign that order has been restored to a cosmos disrupted by his illicit magic. And the association between Harlequin and Faustus also reminds us that theater can be considered as a form of necromancy in its own right, raising the dead on a nightly basis. This is a fact that was well appreciated by the author of the libretto to *The Necromancer;* in its preface, the author makes explicit the profound connection between the entertainment's subject and its medium, observing how the London theaters had magically "reviv'd the Memory of *Faustus*" through their performances (viii). Such linkages between the themes of these performances and their medium would indicate that contemporary observers of early eighteenth-century pantomime took it to be a potentially metatheatrical form, one that rendered the medium's characteristics—its memorial capacity, its appeals to the eye and ear—into objects of interest and attention in their own right. Bringing the purported inventor of printing into the live, embodied realm of the playhouse, the Faustus pantomimes pointed to the performative nature of writing, reversing the desire to make the theater into a subset of the word by making the word into an aspect of theater.

Yet this does not necessarily mean that the Faustus story mounted a conflict between the stage and the page so much as it displayed the complex relationship between text and image, word and the body, which has characterized theater in the West since at least the Renaissance, a relationship that is sometimes antagonistic, sometimes admiring, and frequently imitative, the one medium calling upon the resources of the other. For as it was popularly understood in the early eighteenth century, the Faustus story underscored not so much the tension between theater and the printing press as their fundamental similarity. Here, both appear as fundamentally *imitative* institutions, cultural systems by which unique items are (as if by magic) duplicated, performed over and over again. In her recent study *Theatre of the Book, 1480–1800: Print, Text, and Performance in Europe* (2000), Julie Stone Peters has articulated what the Faustus entertainments demonstrated, but never brought to the level of explicit expression: that the histories of post-Renaissance European theater and that of the art of printing are deeply intertwined and interdependent. As Peters puts it, "in disseminating volumes of Terence and Plautus and Seneca and identifying them with gesticulating actors on stages, with painted streets and trees, in promoting standards against which the multitude of local performance genres could measure themselves, in textualizing the singing of the *jongleurs,* the dance of acrobats, the playing of *histriones,* in circulating images of 'scenes' and 'theatres,' in supplying performers with playbooks, in identifying 'comedy' and 'tragedy' as the paradigmatic performance genres, print was at the heart of the Renaissance theatrical revival. . . . The printing press had an essential role to play in the birth of the modern theatre at the turn of the fifteenth century. As institutions they grew up together."[26] To the early eighteenth-century British spectators who flocked to performances that fused these two forms of modern magic, Faustus embodied what we might think of as the essentially *pantomimic* desires that motivated both the printing press and the theater, negotiating their rivalry by making them appear to be engaged in much the same task.

The complex interplay of text and performance—the mutual dependence and bitter rivalry between them—that the Faustus story condensed took its most lasting material form in the very texts that serve as our best evidence of what these entertainments were like, the printed libretti and other accounts of performances that seemed to refuse the benefits of language, not least of which is the ability to be recorded in well-established and widely available media. The difficulties of recording, preserving, and transmitting embodied performance in forms that were always somewhat alien to it were felt at the very moment when pantomime first came to prominence. John Weaver was

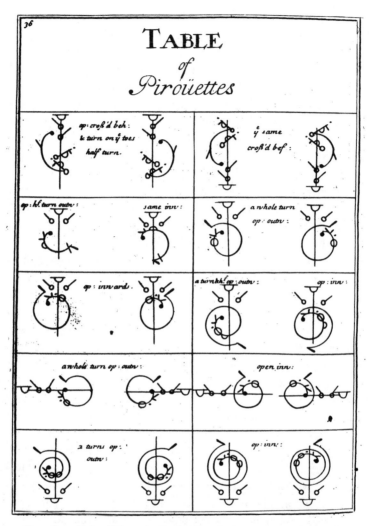

Page from John Weaver's *Orchesography* (1706) (*British Library*)

sufficiently motivated by the desire to use print to preserve his entertainments to translate a French book describing a system for transcribing dance in 1706 as *Orchesography, or, the Art of Dancing, by Characters and Demonstrative Figures.* An attempt to promote dance by advancing a system by which it might be permanently recorded, a "Universal Character" that would put it on a par with spoken language and music, this system was used in a number of eighteenth-century texts by Weaver and other dancing masters.[27]

It was one of the ways in which dances were disseminated from metropolitan centers like London and Paris out to the provinces. But the system of notation never achieved the status that Weaver clearly desired for it, to become something on a par with musical notation, understood by amateurs as well as professionals; it remained a fairly arcane knowledge to which primarily dancing-masters had access. What we are left with for most pantomimes are the short printed libretti, which preserve the songs, the spoken words (of which there are few if any in the harlequinade sections), and at times attempt to offer a short description of the action.

As Peters teaches us, brief libretti such as these had long been a feature of the English theater, and seem to have been particularly common, as we might expect, with performances of masques and other spectacles, for which they "served as advertising, souvenir, supplement, not as competitive entertainment in their own right."[28] By the early eighteenth century, it was expected that the London playhouses would sell short, moderately priced (generally 6d) libretti to their entertainments, pamphlets that typically contained descriptions of the action and, perhaps most important, the verbal (and sometimes the musical) text of the songs.[29] Descriptions of the onstage action are generally very sketchy, as can best be appreciated by reading this brief excerpt from *The Necromancer*'s climax: "*Doctor* waves his Wand, and the Scene is converted to a Wood; a monstrous Dragon appears, and from each Claw drops a *Dæmon,* representing divers grotesque Figures; several Female Spirits rise in Character to each Figure, and join in Antick Dance. As they are performing, a Clock strikes, the *Doctor* is seiz'd, hurried away by spirits, and devour'd by the Monster, which immediately takes Flight; and while it is disappearing, Spirits vanish, and other *Dæmons* rejoice in the following words;

> Now triumph Hell, and Fiends be Gay,
> The Sorc'rer is become our Prey." (15)

Specific enough to identify characters and describe certain fundamental relationships between them, such texts nonetheless seem designed not to replace the live performance but to serve as an aide-mémoire for those who have already seen it. In so doing, they acknowledge, and attempt to erase, the distinction between the onstage performance that the spectator has witnessed, and the performance that he can reconstruct in memory, prompted by a text provided by the magical art with which *The Necromancer*'s hero was associated. Devoting a great deal of its space to recounting the legendary Faustus's association with the printing press, the curious libretto of *The Necromancer* seems to make a point of its status as a printed document that has much stronger natural affinities with the medium it embodies than that which it describes. In a sense, such texts promote the value of print by proposing to realize the performance in a way that the theater itself—hindered by the many kinds of interference that an ideal performance sustains from the physical world—never can, allowing the reader to create a perfect performance in the theater of his or her mind's eye. Here, print media reasserts its own virtues of memorialization and idealization, virtues it would be ungrateful to downplay, especially considering that these texts remain the best records we have of such elusive performances.

Literary history has recorded the Faustus pantomimes as a kind of crime of writing, an attack on literature itself. The best-preserved responses to the Faustus entertainments are the many attacks their astonishing success prompted, most of which are memorable for the verve of their negativity and the decisiveness with which they describe these performances as heralding the ruin of the English stage. In the first version of *The Dunciad,* published in 1728, Alexander Pope identifies the actor-manager John Rich's performance as Harlequin Faustus as the example *par excellence* of the boom in afterpiece entertainments that was one of the signal indications of how the "*Smithfield* muses" were on the move from the fairgrounds near the City of London to the domain of polite culture located to the west:

> He look'd, and saw a sable Sorc'rer rise,
> Swift to whose hand a winged volume flies:
> All sudden, Gorgons hiss, and Dragons glare,
> And ten-horn'd fiends and Giants rush to war.
> Hell rises, Heav'n descends, and dance on Earth,
> Gods, imps, and monsters, music, rage, and mirth,
> A fire, a jig, a battle, and a ball,
> Till one wide Conflagration swallows all.[30]

The "sable Sorc'rer" is Rich wearing the characteristic black mask of a Harlequin, and the description here more or less correlates with that of the conclusion of *The Necromancer* as given in its printed libretto, saving of course Pope's formal medium and, perhaps even more to the point, his tendentiousness. The "He" of this passage is Lewis Theobald, by 1728 collaborating with Rich at Lincoln's Inn Fields, where he composed the libretti for *The Rape of Proserpine* (1727) and *Perseus and Andromeda* (1730), among other pantomime entertainments. At this point in *The Dunciad,* Pope's disgust with Theobald probably has as much to do with his part in the continuing dominance of pantomime in the London theaters as it does with the latter's attack on Pope's edition of Shakespeare, which is more frequently remembered as the source of Pope's resentment. In critiques like Pope's, the dual productions of the Faustus pantomimes assume the status of a defining event in the course of eighteenth-century cultural history, the spectacular transformations for which they became famous in effect mirroring the transformation of the British theater itself from a morally uplifting medium that understood language to be its most important component to a profit-hungry institution devoted to spectacle. Samuel Johnson summed up this line of analysis succinctly at mid-century in the prologue he wrote for David Garrick to deliver at the opening of the 1747 season at Drury Lane: "great *Faustus* lay the ghost of wit."[31] By mid-century, the Faustus performances could be cast as being single-handedly responsible for the decline of the theater and be used to mark the fall of the word into degrading spectacle and materiality.

What I hope to have shown in this chapter is that such accounts simplify and flatten a much more complex history. The emergence of the Faustus afterpieces and the rise of pantomime as perhaps the dominant theatrical form of the 1720s and 1730s teaches us not only about the intervention that they made in the history of the eighteenth-century British theater but about how that event in turn teaches about the history of the public sphere and the media through which it is constituted, disseminated, and recorded. As Pope, Johnson, and other critics of pantomime such as Henry Fielding and William Hogarth attacked it as a threat to British culture, they were expressing much the same ambivalence about the relationship between language and spectacle, the idea and materiality that we saw in the works of Addison and Steele in the previous chapter. But their attacks had greater urgency because the public sphere had been reconfigured in such a way as to provide them an object to aim at, and a rival against which to articulate their own conception of a *literary* model of culture, one where language and an individual author's ideas are paramount. Because literary history's agenda has been set by such figures, we generally share their investment in texts over spectacle, and have typically accepted their version of history as true. Their account obscures, however, both the ingenuity of the performances themselves and what we might call the medial logic by which they seized the public imagination.[32] And if we take seriously, as I think we should, the notion that the Faustus story, however much it was burlesqued in these entertainments, was understood as being in part about the emergence of the modern world, we might also take the opposition to pantomime as a complaint about modernity itself. With the Faustus afterpieces, a modern understanding of entertainment as a cultural product with no more serious purpose than its audience's sensual gratification had become intelligible, perhaps for the first time, and it is no surprise that those with a stake in the political and ethical components of culture would find themselves looking at it with a skeptical eye, and wondering just how much of the public sphere it might eventually consume.

Entr'acte

*T*oward the end of his 1741 handbook for letter writers, now generally known by the title *Familiar Letters on Important Occasions,* Samuel Richardson includes several sample letters describing the diversions of the metropolis, letters written from correspondents in London to family members in the country. The largest group of these letters is from a young woman narrating her first visit to London to her aunt and uncle; although they express a sensibility that could best be described as middle class, they display a combination of innocence and shrewdness reminiscent of Pamela, the serving-girl turned fine lady who became the heroine of the work of fiction for which Richardson famously put aside the draft of this letter guide in order to write. Such a combination means that the young woman of *Familiar Letters* comes across as naïve, but in the best possible sense. Her ignorance demonstrates that her judgment has been uncorrupted by city living, and her questions only gain credibility and significance by their being offered from a position of innocence. Her London itinerary is comprehensive to the point of exhaustion: in the course of the half-dozen or so letters, she visits the Tower of London, St. Paul's, the Monument to the Great Fire, the Custom House, the Guildhall, Westminster—Hall *and* Abbey, Somerset House, St. James's Palace, Whitehall, Chelsea Hospital, Bethlehem Hospital, a concert at Vaux Hall, and any number of squares, parks, and promenades in between. Finally, in her last letter, she describes an evening's program at a London theater, a performance consisting of *Hamlet* followed by a pantomime afterpiece. As we might expect, the young woman admires *Hamlet,* but she actually has a lot more to say about the pantomime that comes after it. Or, rather, she has a lot of questions *about* the pantomime, and she turns to her city cousin William, who has agreed to chaperone her to the theater, for answers. Appalled at the way that the effect of Shakespeare's tragedy is so quickly dissipated by the pantomime that follows (a "dismal piece of farcical dumb shew"), she wants a fuller accounting of Harlequin, asking why he never speaks, why he jumps, why he is so successful with women despite his ugly face, and why he carries a wooden sword. One of her questions in particular seems to demand explanation. Referring to Harlequin, she asks William, "Why is his face black?"[1] Like her other questions, "Why is his face black?" is a good question *because* it is a naïve one, resonating with the force of the knowledge that a culture takes for granted and therefore need not bring to the level of explicit expression or even full consciousness.

The young woman in Richardson's scene is not the only person in eighteenth-century Britain who took notice of Harlequin's black mask. Writing in 1740, at about the same time that Richardson was composing his *Familiar Letters,* Henry Fielding referred in his journal *The Champion* to Harlequin's "sooty countenance."[2] In *The Dunciad,* Alexander Pope described John Rich's Harlequin as the "sable sorcerer" of *The Necromancer,* the afterpiece entertainment that, as we have seen, marked the start of the pantomime boom in the 1720s.[3] Similarly, an anonymous 1745 verse satire on pantomime entitled *British Frenzy* described Harlequin as a "Black Magician."[4] These last two references, associating Harlequin with diabolical magic, invoke the long-standing link in European culture between blackness and the devil, a linkage that was exploited in Plough Monday plays and other popular performances from the middle ages on.[5] Some instances where English performers wore black faces were clearly intended to invoke these associations. Thus, as E. K. Chambers noted in the 1930s, the devils in miracle plays frequently "wore vizards, or were, like the bad souls themselves, painted black."[6] Black faces signified devils on the Continent as well, and some scholars have found specific associations between such figures and Harlequin. Early in the twentieth century, for example, the German historian Otto Driesen asserted that Harlequin derived from a twelfth-century devil figure named "Hellekin," who claimed the souls of the unrepentant.[7] Antoni Sadlek has recently argued that one early manifestation of Harlequin can be identified with a devil figure called "Alichino" who appears in the *Inferno* (1314), and may have originated in religious plays that Dante witnessed in Paris.[8] Whether or not these figures are indeed the ancestors of the character named Harlequin who took his recognizable form as Arlecchino in Italian popular comedy more than two centuries later, and whether or not either figure was ever incorporated into English performances is a question that is probably unanswerable. But it seems safe to suppose that when the character of Harlequin emerged in commedia dell'arte performances during the sixteenth century, his mask associated him with the black-faced devil figures that had been featured in European performances for many generations. And that association was probably mobilized as well for many London spectators of the Faustus pantomimes of 1723, which not only have the masked title character dealing in the "black" arts, but which concluded with actual devils— probably wearing black faces or masks themselves— dragging him to hell.

But although its link to traditional folk performance suggests that eighteenth-century London spectators would have recognized certain conventional meanings for the mask, Harlequin's black mask also violated *other* conventions in the eighteenth-century British theater, an institution that, as we have already seen, put great value in intelligible facial expression and in recognizable performers. In his *Apology* (1740), Colley Cibber wonders why English harlequins continued to wear "that useless, unmeaning Masque"; having changed so much from the Continental commedia dell'arte tradition already, why did English performers not discard this as well?[9] Cibber knows that any kind of mask went against the grain of what was already a well-developed star system, in which actors and actresses developed careers by willingly becoming typecast. The effect of this was that theatergoers always saw the performer as well as the character; an actor like Cibber or David Garrick was never fully subsumed by whatever role he was playing. To eighteenth-century theatergoers, used to recognizing not just familiar character-types, but individual performers as well, such a deindividuating device marked a disruption in the economy of the performance that viewers noticed and critics felt called upon to account for. As a way of answering his own question, Cibber offers the story of one Harlequin who tried to perform *without* a mask, William Penkethman, who played the role of Harlequin in Aphra Behn's *The Emperor of the Moon* in the 1690s. When, at the request of

"several Gentlemen (who inadvertently judged by the Rules of Nature),"
Penkethman performed without the black mask, he discovered that "he was
no more *Harlequin*—his Humour was quite disconcerted! his Conscience
could not, with the same *Effronterie* declare against Nature, without the
cover of that unchanging Face, which he was sure would never blush for it!"
Cibber takes the mask to be an instrument and sign of the character's alien-
ation from "Nature," a boundary violation that turns out to be, to Penkethman's and his gentlemanly spectators' surprise, the enabling condition of the
physical comedy that defined the role. But for Cibber, "Nature" seems
roughly cognate with "human nature," as he naturalizes the boundary that
the black mask breaches by associating it with the division between human
beings and the animal world; he goes on to observe that the Harlequin mask
"resembl[es] no part of the human species," and claims that it represents the
face of a black cat.[10] If, to the young woman of Richardson's *Familiar Letters,*
the black mask represents a referential excess that generates an unanswered
"why?" to Cibber it marks a *deficit* of referential capacity, a blankness that
causes him to ask in effect "why not?" And if, as Cibber concludes, the role
of Harlequin requires the mask, that is only so because the character exists
out of the realm of human meaning—here nominated "Nature"—altogether.
What Cibber and Richardson's young woman share is a desire to speculate
on the black mask's relation to *reference,* what it stands for, to what extent it
might anchor the performance to the meaningful world outside the playhouse that we might designate as the real.

Why *was* Harlequin's face black? Why did English harlequins continue to
wear a black mask well past the point at which anyone could remember what
it had originally meant, or indeed where and why it originated? What did it
mean to the spectators who enjoyed their performances? This chapter—
which I dub an *entr'acte* to mark both its place at the midpoint of this book
and its speculative key—will take Harlequin's black mask as an occasion to
consider the question of *reference* in the context of entertainment, how and
what such an object as Harlequin's black mask might have signified to a spectator in an eighteenth-century London playhouse. I should state at the outset that it would be a fruitless quest to identify any single and fully articulated cause of or referent for Harlequin's black mask. For one thing, as I shall
argue more fully in chapter 6, eighteenth-century English pantomime seemed
to mark a retreat from the direct referentiality of earlier, "Aristophanic"
satire, taking the theater in the direction of farce and fantasy. But it is possible to define the contours of what we can think of as the referential field of
force that the mask inhabited for its performers and activated for its specta-

tors. It is certain that not every possible referent constituting such a field would have registered with each member of the audience, and it is equally certain that its significations changed over time. If we could watch the history of English performance in the form of a film made through time-lapse photography, one that would enable us to see the progress of decades in the span of a couple of minutes, we could probably observe with ease how the significance of blackness changed in the course of the eighteenth century; at one time primarily associated with the devil, black faces would increasingly, though not necessarily, refer to African subjects. But whatever meanings we might assign to Harlequin's black mask, particularly for the first half of the eighteenth century, will surely have to be multiple and perhaps contradictory, and will flicker at the threshold of expression, recording, and conscious recognition as well. Because its origins were uncertain, Harlequin's black mask was free to be filled with meaningful content, unconscious as well as conscious, by observers who brought their own understandings of performance, personhood, class, and race to bear on each viewing. But this content was not wholly random, either; as will become clear in what follows, Harlequin's mask frequently helped Britons conceptualize the similarly faceless mob of the "people," understood as at once a timeless entity without any origin and as the contemporary subjects of a modern nation.

It is of course necessary to recognize that skin color signified differently to the eighteenth century than it does to us. This is particularly the case for the first half of the eighteenth century, when the link between skin color and race—indeed, the very concept of a race itself as a meaningful category for grouping humans—was much less fully articulated than it would be later. The way that eighteenth-century writers explained the variation in human complexions does not easily map onto later conceptions of racial difference, and in fact does not map onto any single system or theory. In her recent book *The Complexion of Race,* Roxann Wheeler has demonstrated the lack of coherence in eighteenth-century European theories about how different human populations acquired different-colored skin, an incoherence that results from a split between emerging attempts to explain skin color in terms of what we would now think of as anatomical science, and more traditional understandings based on the model of a body infused with humors.[11] Scientific understandings of skin coloration were, Wheeler shows, beginning to be available by the middle of the seventeenth century, and while they lack the explanatory power of later theories, they nonetheless represent significant attempts to harness the tools of the scientific method to understand human anatomy and development. Thus, for example, Sir Thomas Browne, writing in the 1640s, attempted to explain why the "Blacknesse of Negroes" is passed down from generation to generation by proposing that it is transmitted via sperm, though he confessed that he still considered the origin of dark human skin to be "yet a Riddle, and positively to determine it surpasseth presumption."[12] Beginning in the late seventeenth century, however, anatomical research had gotten presumptuous, and had determined that skin color was, literally, superficial, confined only to the upper layers of the epidermis, a discovery that seemed to undermine explanations that took dark skin to be the expression of the body's internal humors, in particular a preponderance of black bile. We have in fact already seen this traditional explanation invoked in this chapter; it supports the understanding of the relationship between surface and selfhood expressed in Colley Cibber's observation that William Penkethman's "Humour" was "disconcerted" by not wearing the black mask in *The Emperor of the Moon,* and it is symptomatic of the theory's persistence that Cibber was able to say this as late as 1740, long after it had been challenged if not wholly discredited by official science. For alongside the scientific interrogations that drew their evidence from experiments ran considerably older explanations, of which the theory that skin color was determined by the balance of humors in the body would remain prominent and widely shared even into the nineteenth century.

The ultimate referent for this system was not race but climate. Given the permeability of the humoural body, its sensitivity to the conditions of its physical environment, such an explanation took the differential skin colorations of groups of humans to be closely linked to the climate of the geographical region in which they lived. Thus people in the tropics were darker because their humours were warmed by virtue of being closer to the sun, and northern peoples were fair because the coolness of their climate resulted in a preponderance of lighter-colored humours. What Wheeler sums up as the "climate theory" of human skin color serves as a good case study in the slow and uneven course by which Enlightenment science displaced traditional explanations of worldly phenomena, as for most of the eighteenth century, elements of older and newer theories were combined and appropriated as called for to explain a particular condition or situation. The persistence of the climate theory suggests that Harlequin's black mask would not have carried racial content in the way that we might imagine it to an early eighteenth-century spectator. As Wheeler puts it, race did not "anchor" European understandings of cultural difference and thus cannot serve as the primary category for understanding colonialist ideology until much later, so that our

Tobacco trade card (© *Copyright The British Museum*)

conception of the significance of racial codes cannot be read back into periods before the nineteenth century at the earliest.[13]

Still, the question of the extent to which Harlequin's black mask might be read as a racial sign gains a certain urgency when we recall that the period of pantomime's greatest popularity in the eighteenth century, the 1720s and 1730s, were years during which Britain's share of the colonial trade in African subjects destined to become slaves in the Americas greatly expanded. To be sure, it was not until at least the 1760s that the moral implications of Britain's involvement in this trade prompted the emergence of a substantial abolitionist discourse, one that would dramatically increase the frequency and intensity with which African persons were individually and collectively constructed as objects of public knowledge. But African-born and -descended subjects had resided in England, particularly in London, since the sixteenth century. By the 1720s, their presence was felt to be on the increase both in terms of the actual number of persons, and, even more so, in the number of representations of Africans in media such as advertising. *The Daily Journal* for April 5, 1723, claimed that "'Tis said there is a greater number of Blacks come daily into this City so that 'tis thought in a short Time, if they be not suppress'd, the City will swarm with them."[14] By the early 1730s, this "swarm" was taken to be a threat to the jobs of native workers; in 1731, the Lord Mayor of London banned "*Negroes* or other *Blacks*" from being bound apprentice to any of the City's companies.[15] And observing how the presence of black persons was supplemented by a profusion of black faces in shop signs and advertising, David Dabydeen has claimed that, at least in respect to its commercial iconography, London was "*visually* black" in the early eighteenth century.[16]

There were also, of course, black-faced performers in the legitimate theater of London ever since it had been given permanent institutional form in the Renaissance. Men described as "Moors" appeared on the English public stages, notably in the form of Shakespeare's Aaron of *Titus Andronicus* and Othello, a blackface role that was frequently performed throughout the eighteenth century. As an enormous volume of literature on Othello in particular has demonstrated, the signifier *Moor* indicated both less and more than skin color, and cannot be fully assimilated to a modern conception of race. Anthony Barthelemy observes that *Moor* was an uncertain signifier in the early modern period, more typically, "a general term for those who were strange" to European people than a specific reference to an identifiable race or group. Frequently, the term also implied dark skin, but Barthelemy argues persuasively that people so described were generally distinguished from Africans who came from the southern and interior reaches of the continent.[17] Such a distinction between the Moors of northern and coastal Africa and darker-skinned Africans from the interior of the continent persisted into the early eighteenth century. Julie Ellison has argued that Joseph Addison's *Cato* (1713) exploits both this distinction and the general uncertainty about the continent and its peoples, factors that together "gave 'Africa' a particularly fluid cultural meaning in British plays. When North Africa is configured as the antithesis to or opposite of Rome, or Venice, or Britain, it becomes 'Africa'—Europe's other—and Moors speak as, and for, 'Africans.' In other dramatic contexts, when North African characters refer to sub-Saharan Africans, it is important to discern the degrees of attributed savagery that become progressively greater as the interior of the continent is approached."[18] For Ellison, this fluidity enables the character of Juba—a dark-skinned Numidian who nonetheless also desires to be like the European Cato—to serve as a surrogate for British imperial ambivalence.[19] An even better-known example of a dark-skinned African was the character of Oroonoko, introduced to English readers through Aphra Behn's short novel of 1688, and known to many eighteenth-century Britons primarily by way of Thomas Southerne's stage adaptation of 1696, which was one of the staples of the repertoire in the London theaters into the 1760s. Like Cato, the figure of Oroonoko complexly figured the emotional component of imperial traffic, the mixture of sentimentalism, violence, and, as Srinivas Aravamudan persuasively indicates, absurdity, which are inseparable from the interrelation of embodied performance, Whig ideology, and trans-Atlantic history.[20]

Other examples of blackface appear in Stuart court drama of the early seventeenth century and in street pageants sponsored by the London companies. Ben Jonson and Inigo Jones's *The Masque of Blackness,* produced in 1605 following the request of James I's wife Queen Anne for a piece in which she and her ladies could dress as "Black-mores," is the most fully articulated and the best-known example from a tradition that goes back at least to Henry VIII in which courtiers and hired players impersonated African persons.[21] Jonson's script negotiates potentially hazardous territory to flatter both queen and king. For Anne and her ladies, who went beyond simple masks to blacken the skin of their faces and arms with makeup, Jonson overcomes the associations of blackness with sin and ugliness by crafting a plot that casts the court ladies as the daughters of the river Niger who seek to restore their skins to a prelapsarian whiteness that will match the purity of their souls. And as a way of flattering James, Jonson has the goddess Aethiopia inform Niger that his daughters will be made wholly white by visiting Britain, which is "ruled by a sun"

> Whose beams shine day and night, and are of a force
> To blanch an Ethiop and revive a cor'se.
> His light sciental is and (past mere nature)
> Can salve the rude defects of every creature.[22]

As Barthemely details, actors dressed as Africans continued to appear in court entertainments until the Civil War, where they served as the ultimate example of the Other, the outsider to the enchanted world of a court that was held to be as spiritually pure as its residents were physically pale. After the Restoration, black and blackfaced men in particular, some of whom were by this point actual Africans brought to England as a result of burgeoning colonial trade, continued to function as "exotic paraphernalia" in Lord Mayor's pageants.[23] Examples are so numerous as to be beyond cataloguing or critiquing thoroughly here, but it is probably safe to say that such performers—who rarely if ever spoke—typically figured the exotic regions from

For the Benefit of Mr. ESSEX.

By His Majesty's Company of Comedians,

AT the Theatre Royal in Drury-Lane, this present Thursday being the 9th Day of May, will be presented, A Comedy call'd, LOVE's LAST SHIFT: Or, The Fool in Fashion. The Part of Sir Novelty Fashion by Mr. Cibber; Lovelefs, Mr. Wilks; Amanda, Mrs. Porter; Sir Will Wifewou'd, Mr. Johnson; Elder Worthy, Mr. Williams; Worthy, Mr. Mills; Snap, Mr. Cibber, jun. Sly, Mr. Miller; Narcissa, Mrs. Thurmond; Hillaria, Mrs. Heron; Flareit, Mrs. Mills. With select Pieces of Musick between the Acts, and several Entertainments of Dancing, viz. At the End of the 1st Act, La Jeuntiss, by Mr. Rainton and Miss Robinson, fen. At the End of the 2d, a new Dance by Miss Robinson, jun. a Scholar of Mr. Essex. At the End of the 3d, a new Dance of Ethiopians by Mr. Essex, Mr. Lally, Mr. Haughton, Mr. Rainton, and by Mr. Burney. End of the 4th, the Sultana by Miss Robinson, jun. particularly at the End of the Play, the Huffars by Mr. Essex and Mrs. Booth.

N. B. Tickets to be had at Mr. Cook's the Boxkeeper.

At the particular Desire of several Persons of Quality.

For the Benefit of a Gentleman in Distress.

By His Majesty's Company of Comedians,

AT the Theatre Royal in Drury-Lane, on Monday next being the 13th of May will be presented, A Comedy call'd, The FUNERAL: Or, Grief A-la-mode. The Part of Lord Brumpton by Mr. Williams; Lord Hardy, Mr. Cibber; Mr. Campley, Mr. Wilks; Trusty, Mr. Mills; Cabinet, Mr. Wm. Mills; Sable, Mr. Johnson; Counsellor Puzzle, Mr. Shepard; Trim, Mr. Miller; Lady Brumpton, Mrs. Horton; Lady Charlot, Mrs. Porter; Lady Harriet, Mrs. Booth: Madamoiselle D'Epingle, Mrs. Brett; Mrs. Fardingale, Mr. Norris; Kate Matchlock, Mr. Harper. With Entertainments of Dancing by Monf. Roger, Mrs. Booth, Mrs. Brett, Miss Robinson, fen. and Miss Robinson, jun. particularly the Pierraite.

Tickets to be had at Mr. Cook's the Boxkeeper.

Not Acted this Season,

For the Benefit of Mr. WREXHAM,

(Who sustained great Losses in the Year 1720.)

By His Majesty's Company of Comedians.

AT the Theatre Royal in Drury-Lane, on Thursday the 23d Day of May, will be presented, The Tragical History of King RICHARD The Third. Alter'd from Shakespear. With Dancing by Mrs. Booth.

Mr. Wrexham returns his sincere Thanks to his Friends for their Favours last Year, which has enabled him to begin his Trade again. The Gentlemen Managers of the Theatre Royal, in Order to carry it on successfully, have generously and voluntarily given him the entire Profits of this Play, it being the last Time he designs to trouble his Friends on this Occasion, but being conveniently situated at his Shop at the Blackmoor's Head in Taviftock-ftreet, he will always be desirous to serve his Friends in the Mercery Way, being what he was brought up to, and will use his utmost Application, that they shall be accommodated with the best of Silks, and at the lowest Rate.

Tickets are deliver'd at his Shop, and at Mr. Cook's, Boxkeeper in the Playhouse Passage, where Places are taken for the Boxes and Stage.

At the particular Desire of several Persons of Quality.

For the Benefit of Mr. CHETWOOD.

By His Majesty's Company of Comedians.

AT the Theatre Royal in Drury-Lane, on Friday the 17th Day of May will be Acted the following Entertainments: The WHAT D'YE CALL IT, A Tragi-comick Pastoral Farce of Two Acts, written by the Author of the Beggars Opera, with the Original Ballads. The Part of Timothy Peascod, by Mr. Miller; Sir Roger, Mr. Griffin; Sir Humphrey, Mr. Harper; Squire Statute, Mr. Shepard; Filbert, Mr. Johnson; Peter Nettle, Mr. Norris; Kitty Carrot, Mrs. Mills; Aunt, Mrs. Sherburn; Parish Girl, Miss Robinson jun. HOB; Or, The Country Wake. The Part of Hob, by Mr. Miller. The Pierraite, by Monf. Roger, and Mrs. Brett. The STROLERS, A Farce of one Act. Bindover, Mr. Griffin; Carbine, Mr. Bridgwater; Buskin, Mr. Cibber jun. Spangle, Mr. Corey; Macahone, Mr. Miller; Jeremy, Mr. Oates; Betty Kimbow, Mr. Harper; Fidelia, Miss Lindar. The Harlequin Dance, by Master Lally and Miss Brett.

To which will be added, A Grotesque Entertainment, call'd, Harlequin Doctor Faustus, with the Grand Masque of the Deities, Harlequin, Mr. Clark; Bawd, Mr. Harper; Mephostophilus, Mr. Rainton jun. Time, Mr. Rainton fen. Death, Mr. Ray; Statue, Mr. Cibber jun. Pierot, Monf. Roger; Ufurer, Mr. Norris; Firft Countryman, Mr. Miller; Scaramouch, Mr. Haughton; Diana, Miss Robinson fen. Mars, Mr. Thurmond; Mercury, Mr. Lally; Bacchus, Mr. Boval; Ceres, Mrs. Mills; Flora, Mrs. Walter; Iris, Mrs. Brett. The Scenes, Machines, Flyings and Sinkings carefully revised. With an Epilogue by Miss Robinson jun. spoke at the Head of her Lilliputian Company.

Tickets and Places to be had at Mr. Cook's the Boxkeeper.

Front page from *The Daily Post*, May 9, 1728 (detail)
(*British Library*)

which London's merchant companies were acquiring the commodities that they traded.[24]

English Harlequins, then, came to prominence in a period when other black faces suffused the public imaginary, invoked in the public sphere in ways both fundamental to the national economy and seemingly trivial, the stuff of afterpiece performance and street advertisement as well as of serious, literary drama like Addison's *Cato*. By the 1720s, many of these had clear associations with African persons and the slave trade, and had become deeply interwoven into the fabric of everyday life, a claim supported by the contiguity of three advertisements in a single issue of the *Daily Post* in May 1728. Three forthcoming benefit performances at Drury Lane are advertised in a single column: one, a performance of *Harlequin Doctor Faustus,* intended for the benefit of the theater's prompter William Chetwood; second, a performance of Cibber's revision of *Richard III,* for the benefit of a Mr. Wrexham, a mercer (perhaps a supplier of cloth for theatrical costumes) whose shop was located "at the Blackmoor's Head in Tavistock-Street"; third, a performance of Cibber's *Love's Last Shift,* to be followed by "a new Dance of Ethiopians." Given the additional fact that Wrexham's benefit was intended in part to make up the "great Losses" he had sustained in the South Sea Bubble almost eight years before, that speculative boom and bust in stock in the company set up to provide African slaves for Spain's colonies in the Americas, we might say that the three advertisements collectively comprehend many of the ways in which black persons were deployed in these decades, both in public performance and in the economic practices whose material reality was generally kept below the threshold of representation, or, perhaps more precisely, were represented only by shares of stock that abstracted the South Sea Company's activities into virtual invisibility.

None of these contexts, however, seem to have encouraged Britons to consider the relationship between real and represented Africans consciously or critically, or to interrogate their own relationship to the broader systems of exchange and conquest given local materialization in commodities like tea, chocolate, and coffee. This is not to say, though, that they could not be *used* critically, mobilized in contemporary discourse to figure complex social relations and problems. I want to offer here the example of the group widely referred to as the "Blacks." These were rural gangs of poachers and deer-thieves who were active in Waltham and Windsor Forest in 1722 and 1723. The Blacks, who began disguising their faces probably for the sake of anonymity, were never a very large group, perhaps less than one hundred men in all, and maybe as few as sixty, loosely organized into several gangs that had no fixed membership and whose leadership remains obscure. But the Blacks attracted an extraordinary amount of sympathy in the countryside and considerable interest in London; the newspapers of these years are filled with references to the Blacks, to their prosecutions and, in several cases, eventual executions. In his book *Whigs and Hunters,* which is largely devoted to analyzing the scanty historical evidence about the Blacks, E. P. Thompson makes the case that they were in effect attempting to uphold the moral economy by which common land and the fauna that lived on it were, by custom, the property of all, over against the Whig regime's desire to appropriate common lands as private property.[25] The Blacks were thus responding to the Walpole government's incursion on the customary relations of the country-side, harassing government officials charged with enforcing land-claims, breaking down walls to restore free egress across fields, stealing deer to underscore their character as public rather than private property. The official response from the Walpole government came, most notoriously, in the form of the Black Act of 1723, which made it a capital crime to "black" one's face, an act that stayed on the books well into the nineteenth century.

Obviously, the black faces served the purpose of disguise, one that was particularly effective given the gangs' modus operandi of conducting their raids mostly at night. But that cannot account for the way that the group took such disguises as a badge of honor and raised them to a theme in their self-descriptions. Popular accounts of the Blacks make it clear that they took a kind of pleasure in describing their disguises in terms that, if not fully assimilable to the racial ideology that would assume its full definition only much later, are clearly prepared to use racial difference as a way of making distinctions between groups of English people. In an anonymous pamphlet of 1723, *The History of the Blacks,* the group is described as "the *Black Chief* and his *Sham* Negroes," a characterization that, it is clear, comes from within the gang itself.[26] Other accounts refer to their leader as "his Ethiopian Majesty," or, in a particularly detailed and spirited description of group rev-elry and mock-ceremony, "Prince Oroonoko, King of the Blacks."[27] These conflations of monarchical and criminal identities are playful and sardonic; they *use* racial difference as a way of casting the authority of the gang's leader as a festive inversion of royal power. But it is also a kind of restoration of it; the "King" of the Blacks presents himself in these accounts as a monarch who understands what the Hanoverians implicitly do not, that the king's first responsibility is to his people, the ordinary subjects whose interests are being ignored by corrupt ministers. As a group, the Blacks identified themselves with Africans as a way of signifying their status as common people, staging an act of resistance to the new regime's attempt to change customary prac-tices, and to separate themselves from a tradition that, at least in theory, understood that fields, parks, and the wildlife they supported were held in common by the gentry and the people alike. Theirs was a public-sphere per-formance in which the appropriation of racially coded black masks became a way for people to stage a kind of resistance to power, to mark themselves as loyal to the rural plebeian class in opposition to the new ruling order.

There is no record of any London theatergoer taking Harlequin's black mask as a reference to the Waltham and Windsor Blacks, though the coincidence between the passage of the Black Act and the sensation caused by the Faustus pantomimes, both of which occurred in 1723, is tantalizing. And it *was* recognized in the press that theatrical and masquerade performance was the only medium in which it was legal to wear a black mask; in theory, a Harlequin in the theater was a form of entertainment, while one standing in a field in the country could have been arrested and charged with a death-penalty offense.[28] We might say that early eighteenth-century pantomime and the Waltham and Windsor Blacks shared a common strategy by which black faces helped mark the pleasure that each took in representing the common people as a collective entity. And these performances also mark the way that such an entity was being brought into a new kind of intelligibility in the 1720s by the emergence of new distinctions of class and rank both inside and outside the playhouse.

The example of the Blacks suggests that by the early eighteenth century, racial difference could be enlisted to serve as a surrogate for distinctions in status; in the absence of a critical language of class, it provided a symbolic repertoire for describing the differences between elite and plebeian formations, one that could be appropriated by the lower orders themselves to redefine the terms of their opposition. Writers in the same period used racial difference as a way of identifying the Italian comedy's origins and its place in the culture. For these writers, Harlequin's black mask became a crucial piece of evidence. Writing in the late 1720s, the Italian actor-manager Luigi Riccoboni traced Harlequin's costume, including his black mask, to those worn by the *pantomimi* dancers of ancient Rome. He took the mask to be a reference to African slaves captured by Roman armies in wars of conquest and brought back to the seat of empire. Riccoboni was probably excited in part by the recent (1727) discovery of a statue at Herculaneum that was quickly taken to be the figure of "Maccus," a character in Roman farce, whose humped back and grotesque features seemed to resemble commedia figures like Punchinello and Harlequin.[29] But the groundwork for associations had been laid in place long before, by the body of research into performance in antiquity that we saw mobilized in the debate between Jeremy Collier and James Drake over the relationship between the contemporary English stage and theatrical performances in the classical period. Thus as evidence for his linkage between the ancient and modern Italian theaters, Riccoboni cites brief descriptions of Roman pantomime dancers. These are far from precise, such as the phrase "mimi centunculo" ("patchwork mimes") from Apuleius,

which he takes to be confirmation that the modern Harlequin costume orig-
inates with the Roman mimes and pantomimes.[30] Like Collier, Riccoboni
imagines that there is a continuous tradition linking the ancient theater and
the modern stage, but given the lack of records describing medieval performances, he cannot rely on texts to bridge the two periods. Harlequin and his
costume serve for Riccoboni as the evidence for a continuous tradition of
performance in Italy. Riccoboni's ultimate goal differs from Collier's; rather
than using such a connection to argue that the modern theater should consider itself as an aspect of the state's ritual performances, Riccoboni's claim
that Harlequin is the descendent of the ancient *pantomimi* dancers seems to
support the desire, articulated by writers like the English dancing-master
John Weaver, to advance eighteenth-century pantomime as the revival of an
ancient form, and thus as another dimension of a fully neoclassical public
culture.[31] Even more important from his own point of view as an Italian
writer trying to advance his national culture, Riccoboni's association between
Harlequin and ancient black-faced performers gives the popular Italian comedy a status comparable to that of the scripted comedies of other national
traditions—the works of Molière, Calderon, and Shakespeare, for example—
by virtue of its having the kind of classical pedigree that France, Spain, and
England can only envy.

After Riccoboni, eighteenth-century attempts to link the commedia character of Harlequin to the classical theater would frequently articulate a racial
connection, claiming with even greater confidence that the Roman originals
frequently referred to African subjects. In the *Encyclopédie,* Jean-François
Marmontel follows Riccoboni in tracing Italian commedia to the ancient
Romans, and extends Riccoboni's argument by claiming that "an African
slave was the original model for this role."[32] By the nineteenth century, such
suppositions had been extended to trace the origins of Roman pantomime
back into Greek farces, at which point supposition hardened into dogma.
Maurice Sand's 1860 *Masques et Bouffons* (published in English in 1915 as *The
History of the Harlequinade*) asserted a direct line of descent between Roman
comedy and the Italian commedia dell'arte, a line for which Harlequin
becomes a kind of linchpin, his black mask the object that establishes continuity from Greece to Rome to Renaissance Italy: "this Sicyonian phal-
lophore, his countenance blackened with soot or concealed under a papyrus
mask, is transformed into a *planipes* in Rome and becomes in the sixteenth
century the Bergamese Harlequin."[33] By the later nineteenth century, such
explanations were being treated with skepticism, as eighteenth-century historiography's assumptions no longer met the needs of readers and critics. In

the introduction to his English translation of the memoirs of the eighteenth-century Italian dramatist Carlo Gozzi, published in 1890, John Addington Symonds dismissed as "uncritical" the idea that one can posit an "uninterrupted descent" of characters like Harlequin from the classical period to the Renaissance. (Symonds's explanation for the similarity between Roman and Renaissance characters is, however, scarcely more critical, as he proposes that Italians in both periods "possessed the same mimetic faculty," substituting an ethnic stereotype for a historical fantasy.)[34] Notwithstanding such skeptical evaluations, eighteenth-century historians like Riccoboni were cited again and again in twentieth-century histories of the commedia dell'arte such as Pierre Duchartre's *The Italian Comedy*, first published in French in 1929. Duchartre thus claims that Harlequin is the descendent of Roman clowns who took on the part of African slaves in ancient comedy.[35]

A second myth of origin for the black mask is implicated in Sand's adjective *Bergamese* and Symonds's assumption about the essentially imitative nature of the Italian people. In this tradition, the character of Harlequin is believed to have originated in the town of Bergamo; he would have represented a bumpkinish servant from the countryside to the town audiences that would have first seen him.[36] Thus for the eighteenth-century Italian playwright and sometime commedia scenario writer Carlo Goldoni, the black mask can be accounted for by the origins of the character in the hilly regions of Bergamo, and, according to his *Memoirs*, "is a caricature of the colour of the inhabitants of those high mountains, tanned by the heat of the sun."[37] Goldoni's attempt to support the tradition that Harlequin derived from Bergamo with the climate theory of skin coloration underscores the gap between that theory and modern conceptualizations of race, while also using a discourse designed to articulate the difference between various ethnicities to draw class distinctions within a single national tradition. Taking the dark mask to be the mark of a rural peasantry that he conceives of as a very different order of person than himself or his readers, Goldoni provides a rational explanation for his color that definitively marks him as a class subject who is wholly and physically unlike the bourgeois spectators who enjoyed him.

By the early twentieth century, the two different myths of origin for Harlequin and his black mask would appear to be a contradiction, and it became necessary for writers on the Italian comedy like Winifred Smith, J. A. Symonds, and Pierre Duchartre to argue either that Harlequin was descended from masked characters in Roman drama who represented African slaves, or that he was a representative peasant from Bergamo, but not both.

But eighteenth-century writers seem not to have felt the contradiction so powerfully. This perhaps testifies not only to the complicated and uncertain way in which the category of race was articulated, but also to the ways that these seemingly incompatible explanations served many of the same purposes. Eighteenth-century attempts to identify the origins of Harlequin's black mask in either antiquity or the Italian countryside serve equally to define commedia itself as a form of the people, a mode of performance that emerged from the culture of the common folk, and that now represents them to the urban middle classes. As such, commedia's origins were understood to be both in need of—and, because of their possible classical pedigree worthy of—recovery by historians and middle-class intellectuals. Attempts to trace the origin of the figure back to the Roman theater express a desire to credentialize the "popular" theater of the Renaissance by showing that it ultimately derives from classical models, and is therefore worthy of scholarly attention. And associations such as Goldoni's between Harlequin and the peasantry of Bergamo help distinguish between the commedia dell'arte—a form of the common people—and the more distinguished, textualized theater of the middle class (for which Goldoni was a leading dramatist). Both narratives speak to the developing distinctions between elite and popular cultures, and for the way that Harlequin was cast in the public sphere as a representative of the common folk—playful and mischievous, occasionally a petty criminal, articulating desires through the body rather than by speech.

What I have held back until this point is the response that Richardson's young woman gets from her cousin William to her question about Harlequin's black mask. As it happens, William has no good answer to *any* of her questions about the pantomime, which is not surprising in a sense given his general fatuousness; as the young woman reminds her parents, "Billy has no great capacity." But William's ignorance does not negate the significance of her questions, either. The young woman clearly deserves better answers than her cousin is able to give her, and his stupidity is symptomatic of more than an isolated character flaw. To her query about the reason for Harlequin's black mask, William responds simply that "Harlequin's was never of any other color," an answer whose evasiveness and brazen inadequacy are both characteristic of the man and symptomatic of the form's tendency to forestall critical interrogation. That is all the young woman can get out of him.[38] In fact, the question is never given a fuller answer in the course of Richardson's *Familiar Letters* but is left hanging along with the others. Unanswered in terms that would satisfy Richardson's model spectator, they collectively mark the kinds of nonsense that he takes to be endemic of pantomime as a form.

The young woman serves as Richardson's surrogate here, her disgust with her cousin and with the performance no doubt expressing his own suspicions about the theater. Describing how the frisson of ethical and epistemological doubt created by *Hamlet* (the conclusion of which, she testifies, "had shaken my soul") was thoroughly dispersed by the pantomime afterpiece, the young woman proposes that her parents can "guess at my entertainment," invoking the sense of "entertainment" as a form of mentation that, as we have seen, informed discussions about the phenomenology of spectatorship such as Joseph Addison's. Having had her mental apparatus disconcerted by such a yoking of serious with buffoonish modes of performance, she swears off theatergoing altogether, and proclaims herself ready to return home to the country for good.

Yet in the context of this series of letters on the great variety of diversions in mid-century London, William's ignorance as to the reason for the black mask, as well as his inability to imagine the possibility that Harlequin might not need a mask at all signifies more than his own dimwittedness. It also marks the degree to which William and London residents like him have been anesthetized by their constant exposure to modern diversions; here, they have become so accustomed to the absurdities of pantomime that they no longer make an impression on their own machineries for mentation. William's ignorance demands to be read, not just as the sign of his own stupidity, but of the level of his generation's saturation by what Richardson refers to as "entertainment," both (as here) in the sense of a psychic process and (elsewhere) a mode of performance. Now that "entertainment" is the sign under which theatrical performance is received, such objects as Harlequin's mask seem to refer to nothing at all, to float freely merely as vehicles for sensation.

To be sure, William's answer, "Harlequin's was never of any other color," while inadequate for the purpose of answering his cousin, is not wholly without content or meaning. It suggests that William, and, more important, his author, was aware of the arguments about the origins of commedia dell'arte and its constituent characters that were being published in these decades by Riccoboni, Marmontel, Goldoni, and others. For all of these mid-century observers of the culture of entertainment, Harlequin's black mask was indeed always there, always black, referring back to its origins in a distant historical epoch. Such explanations occlude not only the contemporary referents that the mask might have—to the Blacks, or to the Africans then being shipped to the Americas on British slave ships—but also secure the status of the performance as a frivolous trifle, a representation of the stylized but for that reason stereotypical behavior of the common people.

But they also signal something more, for the desire to invoke the common people in this way is itself testimony to the fact that the traditional culture that Harlequin seems to represent was dissolving, which is why it can be stylized and offered as an object of nostalgia. In its place, as many theorists have argued, is the modern conception of the nation, and I believe that it's ultimately British national identity that Harlequin, his mask, and the way both were used and described in this period, work to secure. Here I want to invoke Homi Bhabha's argument about what he calls the "double-time" through which a concept like "the people" or "the nation" is articulated, how, in his words, "the scraps, patches and rags of daily life" get turned into "the signs of a coherent national culture," through "a complex rhetorical strategy of social reference."[39] Bhabha posits that there are two axes along which a nation or a people have been constituted in the modern world, axes of temporality and address that he terms the "pedagogical" and the "performative," which have to be imagined as working simultaneously. By *pedagogical,* Bhabha refers to the authority derived from locating the origins of the nation in the past, establishing the nation as a permanent object that has always been the same, identical with itself, able to be identified and referred to as a known quantity. This is the solidity and permanence summed up in the notion that Harlequin's face was "never of any other color," a notion that, as I have argued, ultimately derives from contemporary research into the origins of the character and of pantomime that was designed to give it a classical pedigree and to identify him as the product and expression of, originally, the Italian people, and then the common people more generally. The eighteenth century's desire to pose the question of Harlequin's origins, however that question might be answered, is indebted to the contemporary effort to secure the concept of the nation-state and to define the human component of its domain. Harlequin becomes enlisted in the pedagogical aspect of articulating the nation the moment that his significance is entered into the discourse of history, which aims to fix the meaning of its objects. But this, Bhabha argues, does not fully exhaust how a people is constituted, for any such entity needs also to be brought into discourse in the present tense, and indeed needs to be repeatedly summoned into being. Hence, by *performative,* Bhabha intends what he calls the signs of "the *present* through which national life is redeemed and iterated as a reproductive process."[40] Here Bhabha attempts to account for the way that a people is in part created through articulation and repetition, by being realized again and again in performances that in effect constitute the object that they address. It is through the double-movement of pedagogical and performative modes of referring to a people that a concept like the nation becomes reified, made into "an empirical sociological category," but the process leaves a residue, Bhabha argues, of ambivalence and anxiety that testifies to the ultimate incoherence of the concept (140).

The two axes intersect, I want to argue, in a single afterpiece composed by David Garrick in 1759 entitled *Harlequin's Invasion,* a work that uses Harlequin's blackness as a vehicle for national definition and celebration. I will offer a fuller account of *Harlequin's Invasion* in chapter 7, but certain key features of this production are worth considering here, because of the way that Garrick in effect internalizes the significance of Harlequin's blackness that had been developed by writers on the theater and its history in the previous half-century. Garrick's text contains the first explicit description from within a pantomime itself that would identify Harlequin as an African, as it refers to him twice as "that Blackamoor man."[41] Garrick may simply be recording in words what others had understood or imagined before, but his identification of Harlequin as a "Blackamoor" specifies his meaning in a direction that follows the course of eighteenth-century historiography in assigning national identities to persons. It positions Harlequin as the ethnographic Other against which Britishness can be defined.

It is no coincidence, then, that *Harlequin's Invasion* is also the most aggressively and openly nationalist eighteenth-century English pantomime, at least until the 1790s, when the French Revolution and the Napoleonic wars spurred the London theaters to stage highly patriotic performances. Produced in the middle of the Seven Years' War, *Harlequin's Invasion* is a rousing celebration of British military and cultural puissance, one that casts Harlequin as an alien presence on British soil—he is both African *and* French. Most important, he also functions as the embodiment of a *principle* of national identity that needs to be displaced by the most powerful of all the theatrical figures that might articulate the British nation—William Shakespeare. *Harlequin's Invasion* concludes with a spectacular tableau in which a statue of Shakespeare rises to banish Harlequin from the stage. Garrick appropriates the pedagogical aspect of Harlequin as he was understood by this point, his status as a timeless figure of a people, as a way of conferring those qualities onto Shakespeare as the embodiment of British culture.

The performative, reiterative aspect of this comes in the way that Garrick installed this performance as an annual tradition. *Harlequin's Invasion* was performed annually in London for more than fifteen years, its militarism and Francophobia long outliving its original occasion as a patriotic celebration. It inaugurated the tradition, which exists to this day, of offering pantomime as a Christmas entertainment. Up until this point, pantomime had appeared throughout the year, and had no particular association with any season. Garrick instituted the custom, which endures to this day, of having pantomimes premiere on Boxing Day, December 26. By changing the performance schedule to associate pantomime with the Christmas season, Garrick in effect installed Harlequin in a different order of time than that inhabited by Shakespeare, the man for all seasons; he contained Harlequin by segregating him to a specific season that was now marked as a time of festivity *unlike* the normal, homogeneous time of the workaday world. In a sense, Garrick would seem to be merely returning to a much older tradition in which certain kinds of pastimes and entertainments were associated with particular periods of the year, with many of them (such as Stuart court masques on the one hand, and holiday mumming on the other) associated with the Christmas season. But there is a key difference. By the 1750s, such performances were clearly marked *as* such a return; tinged with a kind of nostalgia, they offered customary, festive time as a commodity to audiences who believed their experience of temporality to be considerably more homogeneous than that of their ancestors. To pick up Bhabha's distinction, Harlequin was now a way of *performing* that older tradition, staging it within a very different context in order to ensure that pantomime came to be understood as part of merrie old England, a pastime that reproduced Britishness, on cue, every year. Garrick's sole pantomime marks the point when Harlequin most clearly was racialized as an African figure, and also when such a figure is decisively identified as Other to a British people whose origins are similarly both permanent and in need of constant re-creation.

After this, an African identity was clearly available as a referent for Harlequin's black mask. By the end of the eighteenth century, English Harlequins could readily be racialized as Africans, as expressed in, for example, the titles of both a 1789 pantomime called *Harlequin Mungo*—"mungo" being a typical name for a slave in the late eighteenth century, and thus a slang term for Africans in general—and *Furibond, or Harlequin Negro,* produced in 1807. In the 1830s, English pantomime became fused, at least for the moment, with American minstrelsy. After a series of appearances in London by the famous minstrel performer T. D. Rice, the theaters rushed to capitalize on his success by adding Jim Crow dances to their pantomimes, as in an entertainment entitled *Cowardy, Cowardy Custard; or, Harlequin Jim Crow and the Magic Mustard Pot;* such dances appeared in pantomimes for many years.[42] Here, however, "Harlequin Jim Crow" does not refer (as we might have assumed) to any fusion between the characters of Harlequin and Jim Crow. In *Cowardy, Cowardy Custard,* for example, Jim Crow changed into the Clown, who was by this point the star attraction of most pantomimes; in many other cases, Jim Crow songs and dances were simply added to afterpiece entertainments that increasingly became variety acts in the manner of a music-hall show. "Harlequin" in such cases referred less to the character himself than to the idea of entertainment that he embodied; he was the emblem of pantomime, even when, as was increasingly the case, his own role was much diminished from what it had been in the first half of the eighteenth century.

Crucially, pantomime had by this time become identified as a characteristically British form. However much we might admire the inclusion of, for example, American minstrelsy in nineteenth-century pantomime, the entirety of such a performance structured the presence of Jim Crow dances as an appropriation that inevitably to some degree altered their original significance, making them into part of what was understood to be "that peculiar British institution," a species of entertainment whose uniqueness is proven by the fact that it has never caught on anywhere else.[43] By the nineteenth century, Harlequin's black mask had served its purpose, consolidating pantomime's distinctive identity as an aspect of British national culture so fully that it need not refer to anything in particular at all, or even appear onstage. Its most important theater, we might say, was in the memories and fantasies of Britons, their shared conception of themselves as constituting a distinctive people, one that had always been entertained by Harlequin's antics, but that also wanted—or needed—to be reminded of that fact every year.

CHAPTER FIVE

"Infamous Harlequin Mimicry"

APPRENTICES, ENTERTAINMENT,
AND THE MASS AUDIENCE

*I*n his first published work, a conduct book entitled *The Apprentice's Vade Mecum* (1734), the London printer Samuel Richardson attacks the theater as an illicit form of diversion. Winding himself up to a fever pitch of contempt for the current productions on the London stage, he warns his readers against "the horrid Pantomime and wicked Dumb Shew, the infamous *Harlequin Mimicry*, introduc'd for nothing but to teach how to cozen, cheat, deceive, and cuckold."[1] In the course of the discussion that follows, it becomes clear that Richardson's term *Harlequin Mimicry* fuses several related but distinguishable operations. Most obviously, it refers to pantomime itself, and in particular to the frequency with which such entertainments cast Harlequin—originally a servant-figure himself and for that reason a potential object of identification for apprentices—not just as a trickster, but as a criminal, and typically took pleasure in his ingenuity, daring, and ability to humiliate authority figures. More broadly, Richardson's term also embraces the recent mainpiece productions staged at the patent theaters that had represented criminal activity. In the previous decade, the playhouses had mounted a series of plays such as *The Beggar's Opera* (1728), *The Quaker's Opera* (1728), and *The Prisoner's Opera* (1730), each of which staged and celebrated the activities of highwaymen, pickpockets, cutpurses, fences, and burglars. Richardson believes that all such works should be kept away from such an "*underbred* and *unwary* Audience" as young apprentices (17), naïve spectators who are particularly liable to draw the wrong lessons from any representation placed before them.

For the term *Harlequin Mimicry* also gestures toward a particular understanding of spectatorial relations that motivates Richardson's rage against the theater. Entertainments in which Harlequin and other characters mimic the behavior of the urban underworld are dangerous to him because he assumes that such performances will in turn prompt their spectators to mimic *them*, becoming criminals themselves in emulation of what has been presented to their sensoria. This is particularly significant because it obstructs what Richardson assumes to be the normative path of mimesis in the apprenticeship system, one that imagined the apprentice to be copying the skills and virtues of his master. His concern relies upon the Aristotelian claim that, as Edmund Burke would later put it in his own first book, *A Philosophical Enquiry into the Origin of our Ideas of the Sublime and the Beautiful* (1757), the "pleasure in imitating" leads human beings "to copy whatever [men] do."[2] And as would Burke, Richardson specifies that the desire for imitation is bound up in what the former calls "our natural constitution," the apparatus of the human body itself. Following the model of spectatorship that, as we saw in chapter 3, was richly articulated by Joseph Addison in *The Spectator*, Richardson situates the dangerous effects of pantomime entertainments in the viewer's mechanism for mentation. Here Richardson worries about the "Mind" of the apprentice, which will be fatally disengaged from "his Business" because it has, like a blank sheet of paper, been "impress'd" by the sensual force of these diversions: "the Musick will always play upon his Ears, the Dancers will constantly swim before his Eyes" (13). To Richardson, the sensuality of pantomime makes it an especially dangerous species of performance because it appeals in a particularly direct and unmediated way to the human cognitive apparatus considered as a site of "entertainment" in the sense of mentation, taking it over by filling and then overwhelming its critical capacity. He imagines the entertainment between the apprentice whose mind has been "unhinged" from business and the performance that is placed in front of him as a scene of mutual pantomimicry, a *mise-en-abyme* of imitation run wild.

The mimetic relationship between the spectator and the performance is our object of study in this chapter, and the figure of the theatergoing apprentice will be our exemplary case to illustrate how that relationship was brought into public discourse in the 1720s and 1730s. Imitation, central to conceptualizations of the theater from antiquity, constitutes both its power and its danger, and when the imagined audience included apprentices, it was its danger that came to the fore in public-sphere discussions about the place and propriety of theatrical representation. Richardson's attack on pantomime is typical of bourgeois observers in the 1720s and 1730s, who took its extraordinary popularity as the sign of the degradation of traditional literary culture and the reduction of the theater's scope to mere spectacle and show. His concern about the apprentice as the person to whom such performances were addressed was also widely shared in the 1730s, when apprentices were often described as the audience fragment most at risk in the epistemological and geographic spread of entertainment into hitherto untouched areas of the city and the culture.[3] The frequency with which theatergoing apprentices were invoked in these decades marks the awareness on the part of men like Richardson of the existence of an urban mass culture to which the new phenomenon of entertainment appealed. Such an entity demanded a figure through which it could be comprehended, understood, and managed. The apprentice became that figure. To early eighteenth-century observers worried about the impact of theatrical performances, "the apprentice" was a figure capable of standing in for the mass audience; he represented the collective body of spectators whose responses to entertainments could be neither predicted nor fully controlled.

This construction, through the figure of the apprentice, of what we can call the "mass subject" was an important event in the emergence of entertainment that I have been tracing in this book.[4] In this chapter, I want to assess the nature and significance of this event by analyzing works that were associated with apprentices, either as the central figures of the performance, as the normative spectators, or both. The most important texts will be Edward Ravenscroft's *The London Cuckolds* (1681) and George Lillo's *The London Merchant* (1731), which were the plays customarily produced for apprentice audiences on designated days each year, with Lillo's play supplanting Ravenscroft's farce at the instigation of men like Richardson who wanted to ensure that the young men who witnessed these performances would be edified rather than corrupted by them. As Richardson's singling out of pantomime suggests, that form plays a significant part in the story I will tell here. Pantomime's stunning popularity catalyzed public awareness of the autonomy of entertainment from the traditional pedagogic function of art, the extent to which it seemed to justify itself by appealing to audience taste. It prompted a new need to consider not just the site of production, but the site of consumption as well, to theorize the kind of subject to whom such entertainments appealed and to devise new ways to guide their responses. But we shall see that the performance history of *The London Merchant* also dramatizes how difficult it is to determine in advance how an audience might respond even to so obviously didactic a work, to ensure that spectators learn to imitate good rather than bad examples, and to receive a work as instruction rather than as mere entertainment.

Apprenticeship, Performance, and The London Cuckolds

Why were apprentices so important to observers of eighteenth-century British society? Of all the social groups and subgroups in contemporary London, apprentices were among the most visible and most fretted-over, and they became the subjects of a substantial literature that ensured that they would be a continual source of great fascination and some fear. As Lucinda Cole has put it, the apprentice became an "emblematic figure" of the period, a proxy for broader concerns about the relationship between work, play, time, generational relations, and the orderly transmission of property.[5] For example, the debate about the several new unlicensed theaters that opened in London in the late 1720s and early 1730s—a debate in which, as we shall see shortly, Richardson played a part—frequently invoked the figure of the apprentice as the person whose loyalties were most at stake in the migration of programmed diversion into new areas of the City. Did apprentices actually desert their jobs in great numbers, devoting themselves to entertainment at the expense of business? We cannot know, as there are no records of either hours worked or plays attended by apprentices that we might use to determine the answer to such a question. The tone of my question, however, implies that a certain skepticism is merited about whether or not the crisis over apprentices in the 1720s and 1730s was real, or, perhaps more usefully, in what sense it was real. The concern that apprentices would learn the wrong lessons from staged entertainments, particularly as those stages moved closer to their places of work, was widely shared and expressed, prompting real responses in the public sphere, and almost surely a completely unknowable number of responses in individual households, as masters clamped down on the freedom of their charges. Whether or not apprentices really were a threat to the fabric of early eighteenth-century society is probably beyond our capacity to know for sure at this remove; what is most important is that "the apprentice" is at the focal point of an enormous public discourse that has been preserved, and through which we can gain access to some of the culture's most significant anxieties.

For like other entities of the public sphere, such a figure is not so much a given as something produced in and through public discourse, and indeed we can consider the production of the apprentice as an emblematic figure to be another aspect of the process of *classification* that we have witnessed elsewhere, the division of the sious into separate and definable groups as a way of making the culture intelligible to itself. Thus the term *apprentice* is a little misleading, since it was frequently used in the eighteenth century as a shorthand term for all young unmarried urban men, whether or not they had been formally indentured; it was the label under which such men were frequently classed.[6] The size of the apprentice cohort, difficult enough to figure out in any case, thus partly depends on how "apprentice" is defined, although the class was a large one any way it might be computed; one estimate suggests that there may have been as many as 20,000 apprentices at any one time in all trades in early eighteenth-century London, and an even larger number of young men living and working outside the guild system but who might still be referred to as "apprentices" in some contexts.[7] In spite of such instability in its constitution, the apprentice cohort nonetheless was typically written about as being fully coherent and, strikingly, traditional and customary, as if it had existed in much the same contours from the beginnings of time. One reason for this was a well-articulated system of ritual and ceremonial performances that were believed to have been passed down from generation to generation of apprentices. Apprenticeship was an institution that was saturated with traditions, customs, and unwritten but nonetheless seemingly intractable rules and practices that were believed to be of immemorial origin, and well exceeded the written terms of service. The relationship between individuals and the guild system was actually governed by an explicit law, the Statute of Artificers and Apprentices of 1563, which set the formal terms for the relationships between apprentices and their masters until its repeal in 1814. But the apprentice system's regular practices struck observers as being derived more from what Joseph Moxon in his *Mechanick Exercises* referred to as "the Custom of Time out of mind."[8] Such customs have led historians to suggest that the London apprentices of the seventeenth and eighteenth centuries may have been the first example of a youth culture in Europe, a group large enough and sufficiently self-aware to constitute a subculture of their own.[9]

Both to its own members and to the public at large, the identity of the apprentice subculture was consolidated and reinforced by being repeated through performances so long established that they were understood to be customary, their origins forgotten. For example, every type of workplace had its own customs and traditions, systems of rules, fines, and quasi-ritual performances into which apprentices were indoctrinated along, of course, with their knowledge of the trade to which they had been indentured. Print shops had some of the most elaborate and (not surprisingly) best-documented customs. When an apprentice entered a London print shop such as Richardson's, for example, he would have been expected to pay a fine known as "bienvenue" to the journeymen printers, a fee of 2s 6d that they most likely would spend on drink. He would also have been initiated as a "deacon" or "cuz" of the workshop "chapel"—the self-governing body of the workmen— in a performance that involved carrying a wooden sword (like a composing stick?) around the workshop three times, at the end of which he would have been ritually "anointed" when the senior or "father" journeyman printer of the chapel squeezed a sponge of beer over his head while giving him a new title (e.g., "Deacon of Pissing Alley") and exhorting him to keep the rules and preserve the secrets of the shop. The other journeymen and apprentices would then have marched around him incanting the "Cuz's Anthem," a song that a contemporary account in *The Craftsman* described as being put together "by adding all the *Vowels* to the *Consonants* in the following Manner. *Ba-ba; Be-be; Bi-be; Ba-be-bi; Bo-bo; Ba-be-bi-bo; Bu-bu; Ba-be-bi-bo-bu*—And so through the rest of the Consonants."[10] That is, the journeymen printers were chanting the very letters of the alphabet through which the products of their trade were, literally, *composed*. Such ceremonies and customs clearly have a parodic and playful dimension, as they mock the seriousness of the linguistic medium that their trade advanced and upon which it relied. But this does not mean that they were not also to be taken seriously; when Benjamin Franklin, who worked as a journeyman printer in London in the 1720s, initially refused to pay his bienvenue upon moving up from the press room to the compositing room on the grounds that he had paid his dues in the downstairs chapel already, he found that he was "considered as an Excommunicate" and eventually complied, "convinc'd of the Folly of being on ill Terms with those one is to live with continually."[11]

Many customary performances were associated with specific feast days and holidays. In the seventeenth century, apprentices notoriously took the lead in riots at brothels and theaters on Shrovetide, just before Lent, and sometimes on May Day.[12] Ben Jonson's Lanthorn Leatherhead in *Bartholomew*

Fair remembered "the rising o' the 'prentices; and pulling down the bawdy houses" of his youth, which at times included attacking theaters as well, the two institutions being linked together as sites of sexual transgression that had to be closed down in preparation for Lent. In 1617, three years after Jonson's play was first performed, a crowd of apprentices destroyed a playhouse in Drury Lane, burning the playbooks and tearing apart the costumes.[13] Apprentices licensed such violence by casting it as, in James Harrington's words, "the ancient administration of justice," claiming a traditional right to regulate public morals.[14] Given the intrusive, even spectacular quality of such acts of "administration," the London apprentices could be understood as one of the public faces of custom itself, the self-appointed representatives of tradition. In seasonal as in everyday performances, they reminded Londoners of the traditional patterns of social organization that were being challenged by the modern, capitalist reorganization of the city, time, work, and play.

One scene of performance associated with apprentices that offers insight into some of these changes has been preserved in print in the form of the text of Edward Ravenscroft's 1681 farce *The London Cuckolds*. Ravenscroft's play quickly became the occasion for apprentices to display their group solidarity, as they attended en masse special performances designated for them at Easter time, the Christmas season, and the Lord Mayor's Day. These designated performances quickly took on the status of a time-honored tradition, such that even while Richardson and his peers worried about their apprentices' attendance at the theater, they understood that their servants had a customary right to go to the playhouse on specific days and seasons of the year. We will consider later in this chapter how bourgeois observers of the mid-eighteenth century sought to transform, or even perhaps to co-opt, this custom by substituting a text more to their liking for these performances, but here I want to devote some attention to Ravenscroft's play, which will provide a point of comparison that will help make their intentions more perspicuous. As we saw in chapter 2, Edward Ravenscroft is already of interest in the history of pantomime as one of the Restoration England's many appropriators of Continental commedia dell'arte material, authoring *Scaramouche a Philosopher, Harlequin a Schoolboy, Bravo, Merchant, and Magician* in 1677, a play whose use of commedia characters, Robert Hume has plausibly suggested, may have been prompted by the success of Tiberio Fiorilli's company of Italian performers at Whitehall in the early 1670s.[15] Although *The London Cuckolds* includes no commedia characters, it draws freely upon the same stock of social stereotypes, plot formulas, and slapstick routines as commedia did and eighteenth-century pantomime would. This ensured that

Ravenscroft's play would remain below the radar of literary criticism, and on those few occasions when it has been discussed, *The London Cuckolds* has generally been classed as a mere farce, one that, in Hume's words, "is rollicking good fun with no ulterior point whatever."[16] My argument will be that the contours of "good fun" come to a very sharp point in *The London Cuckolds*, a play that encourages its spectator to think of the City businessman's obsession with the productive application of time as ridiculous, and to identify with the fortunes of figures who give themselves over to play, farce, and fortune itself.

The structure of *The London Cuckolds* is straightforward and symmetrical: three City businessmen (Wiseacres, Doodle, and Dashwell) are cuckolded by three younger men (Ramble, Townly, and Loveday), who face a number of logistical and physical impediments to acquiring time alone with the businessmen's three wives (Peggy, Arabella, and Eugenia), but have very little difficulty convincing the women to have sex with them once they do. *The London Cuckolds* clearly stages, and takes sides in, a generational conflict, as the younger men are conferred a kind of right of conquest largely on the basis of their youth and energy. Only Loveday, who was once promised in marriage to Eugenia, has a specific romantic claim to advance; the marriage was impeded by their two families, and Eugenia was married against her wishes to Dashwell, giving her liaison with Loveday something of the character of an injustice finally set right. Most important, the women are treated for the most part as objects within the conflict between the older businessmen and the younger rakes. They offer a kind of set of female types, none of them realized with great depth or sympathy; Arabella is a sharp-tongued shrew, Peggy is an ignorant country girl (deliberately kept so by Wiseacres, who has raised her in the country to be his wife since her childhood), and Eugenia has masked her loathing of her husband through religious hypocrisy, retreating to prayer whenever he makes an advance on her. Given the short shrift with which the women characters are treated in the play, it is no surprise to discover that *The London Cuckolds* was said to be disliked by women audiences; in the prologue to *Dame Dobson* (1683), Ravenscroft admitted that "some squeamish Females of renown / Made visits with design to cry it [*The London Cuckolds*] down," and promised that his new play took special efforts not to offend women in the audience. Ravenscroft's prologue has been taken as evidence for the influence of women spectators in reforming the bawdiness of the Restoration stage, but it seems equally plausible to suppose that women would have understood *The London Cuckolds*'s misogyny to rest more firmly in its structures of address and identification than its language;

it's a play about the relations between urban men, and its salient categories are class, profession, and generational cohort.

What pleasures might an apprentice take from this play? To ask this is to think about the question of *identification,* since there are no apprentice characters in *The London Cuckolds,* and even the servant figures have comparatively small roles. If women protested in part because their only representatives in the play were depicted so negatively as to make any identification painful, apprentices might be expected to feel that they had relatively little stake in the play, since the rakish gentlemen who cuckold the City businessmen are of a wholly different class from them. A certain space from which identification might be possible for apprentices might be imagined, however, once we consider the interbraided, and to that degree highly contested, relationships between women and apprentices, not so much in the playhouse as in the households from which such spectators would have come. For the cuckolding of the three men of business in *The London Cuckolds* signifies the degree of disorder within their households, an institution in which apprentices were nominally members. Apprentices had a stake in the orderly management of the families to which they were indentured, and stood to suffer if a master was negligent or incompetent. Their identity as part of the master's household perhaps also explains the comparative hostility that the play displays to the three wives, who might be expected to elicit more sympathy. Wives, like apprentices, were under the authority of the master of the house, but they could assert authority over the apprentices as well. This was a situation ripe for resentment and rivalry, as both wives and apprentices found themselves mutually dependent on the intelligence and benevolence of the master, and simultaneously competing for his attention and the household's resources. One eighteenth-century handbook for parents contemplating putting their sons out as apprentices warned against letting their children enter families where the wife seems to have "got the better of her husband" because she also "must of course rule his apprentice; the youth must be Madam's slave."[17] *The London Cuckolds* thus sets up a kind of system of identification by which young men in service might identify with the three gallants who are otherwise so unlike them in terms of social standing. Associating himself to some degree with the neglected wives by virtue of his shared status as a member of the family, an apprentice spectator would nonetheless quickly reach the limits of his capacity to identify with their situation and would be free to cathect his attention and aspirations to the three rakes.

At the moment of the play's first production in the wake of the Exclusion Crisis, the difference between the businessmen and the cuckolders probably had a partisan dimension, as the former could easily be identified with the Whigs, the City party. (This is a linkage made most clear not in Ravenscroft's *The London Cuckolds,* but in a contemporary ballad with the same name, which taunts Whigs as having left home to pursue a new "covenant," leaving the Tory "bully" in their place.) But the play's continuing popularity well past that occasion—with City Whigs no less—suggests that its more pressing interests lie elsewhere. I would argue that *The London Cuckolds* identifies the root cause of the businessmen's ability to be cuckolded in their mismanagement and poor allocation, not simply of their households and businesses, but of time itself. Wiseacres, Doodle, and Dashwell are consistently shown to be devoting so much time to the "business" of earning money that they neglect what characters frequently refer to as the "business" of sexual pleasure, leaving their wives frustrated and creating opportunities for other men to take their place.[18] The second line of the play, spoken by Doodle to Wiseacres, indicates some of the dimensions of the problem; agreeing to accompany Wiseacres to his wedding, Doodle observes that he "will dispense with business, since 'tis on this occasion."[19] To men like Doodle, "business" normatively claims all time and energy, except for that which might be allocated to a unique "occasion," after which business once again takes priority. The play encourages us to think of such an overinvestment in business as foolish, a misapplication of energies. This is stressed most obviously in the scene where Wiseacres leaves Peggy alone on their wedding night in order to transact "some great business" as soon as he hears that a ship on which he has "concerns" has docked; left to her own devices, Peggy is easy prey for Ramble.[20]

We must, however, also consider how the opposition that *The London Cuckolds* constructs between "business" and "occasion" refers to a larger problematic of temporality, a distinction between a conception of time as homogeneous and seamless, and a sense of time as differential, punctuated by discrete events. It is fitting, in this context, that the man who cuckolds Wiseacres, the most obsessive man of business in the play, is Ramble, who frequently announces how he places his trust in "Fortune"; unlike Wiseacres, Ramble accepts time itself to be random and chancy, marked by occasional good luck and bad. In a broader sense, the play uses the opposition between Whig and Tory, cuckold and cuckolder, to register a distinction, not so much between parliamentary party affiliations, but between rationalizing and more carefree approaches to time itself. It marks the confrontation that, as E. P. Thompson argued, the late seventeenth and early eighteenth centuries witnessed between a traditional, "task-oriented" relationship to the use of time and a more modern, "clock-oriented" disposition, in which time is understood to be a precious commodity, to be measured, hoarded, and devoted in the first instance to work and business.[21] As Benjamin Franklin (whose opinion of *The London Cuckolds* is unfortunately not recorded) would put it, "*Time is Money.*" And projected onto the span of the year, the conflict between Wiseacres and Ramble registers the difference between a homogenized calendar and one organized according to the differential schedule of work, play, and festivity.

Ravenscroft's farce exploits the comedy inherent in the clash of social types—the City businessman, the rake, the shrewish wife—each of which in turn points to broader social and political structures, such as the workplace and the family. This is no doubt why the play endured for so long in the repertory, until being displaced in the 1750s. As we shall see, such a displacement involved, among other things, a new and radically different conception of the "representative" character from that which Ravenscroft uses, a conception that we will later see articulated in some of Richard Steele's writings about the nature of comedy, and exemplified in, by no mere coincidence, George Lillo's *The London Merchant,* the play that would replace *The London Cuckolds* as the expected performance for apprentice audiences. The confrontation between pleasure and business, embodied in the conflict between the rake cuckolders and the City cuckolds, would not, however, remain static throughout the period. More to the point, the broader cultural revolution of which it is a part, the slow but inexorable spread of capitalist relations and the concomitant reordering of the logic of virtually every institution that they touched—the workplace, surely, but also the family, the state, and the individual—continued to the point where, by mid-century, *The London Cuckolds* probably looked, not just licentious, but archaic, a prompt to nostalgia as much as anything else. By that time, changes in the workplace and the institution of the family had put apprenticeship into a kind of crisis that would summon forth new ways of representing time, diversion, and apprentices as well.

Pantomime, Criminality, and the Bad Apprentice

Apprenticeship was, historians agree, under particular pressure throughout the eighteenth century, as the guild system in which it had been invented and under which it had thrived was breaking down under the pressures of capitalist reorganization. The "ritual" performances of massed groups of apprentices and other young men at Shrovetide seem to have ended by the early eighteenth century, suppressed after years of effort by the civil authorities. More comprehensively, what Christopher Brooks has described as "the transformation of the traditional culture of the middling sort" undermined the apprenticeship system by creating new professions that fell outside the traditional guilds and thus carving out different paths for social advancement; many young men were now able to enter professions without being formally indentured.[22] The institution of apprenticeship registered these shifts in the broader economy internally as well. As Jocelyn Dunlop's dated, but still useful history of the institution puts it, apprenticeship in the eighteenth century was being "transformed . . . from a close personal relationship between masters and pupils into commercial arrangements between employers and their hands."[23] Dunlop's account hums with a certain nostalgia for the paternalistic order that, as she demonstrates, was being replaced by a more transparently financial system, one based on the cash nexus; "close personal relationships" can be destructive as well as enriching, and there are enough records of masters who beat, harassed, neglected, or otherwise abused their apprentices to suggest that there were advantages to the more impersonal system, mediated in part by rules negotiated through trades unions rather than the norms of the patriarchal family. Nonetheless, it clear that during a period in which a broad reorganization of urban working culture took place, apprentices occupied a particularly uncertain position in the professional and patriarchal orders. No longer fully protected by the institution of the family nor completely a part of the culture of adult urban working men, apprentices were objects of intense interest, concern, and fear.

This is the context within which we can understand the production and promulgation in popular culture by the 1720s of the figure of the bad apprentice, the servant who, to use the formulation popularized by William Hogarth's popular series of engravings (1735), preferred idleness to industry, disobeyed his master, abandoned his articles, turned criminal, and, inevitably, ended up swinging on the end of a rope at Tyburn. As we shall see, the period's most notorious criminal, Jack Sheppard, was a celebrated instance of the bad apprentice, having broken his articles to a London carpenter. So too was the most enduring fictional hero of the 1720s, the surgeon's apprentice Lemuel Gulliver, who abandoned his master well before his term was up, only to suffer well-known dire consequences in his singularly unlucky career as a ship's surgeon; Swift's hero simultaneously exemplifies and satirizes the figure. Perhaps most important here, such figures as Hogarth's Tom Idle, Jack Sheppard, and Gulliver testify to the desire, not just to embody a certain class of urban men in the figure of "the apprentice," but to bring such figures into representation in the public sphere as the central figures of fiction and drama.

Made into an object of representation in his own right, the apprentice-gone-bad would become the focus of certain concerns about the propriety and purposes of entertainment, as it was hard to be sure whether such figures served as monitory examples to be avoided or as charismatic models to be imitated. And pantomime, the most popular form of urban entertainment in the 1720s and 1730s, would play a key role in catalyzing the desire on the part of middle-class observers to redefine the terms of exemplarity, representation, and entertainment itself.

For the figure of the bad apprentice was readily fused with that of Harlequin, a fact that in part explains Richardson's animus toward the character and his particular concern about the degree to which apprentices might identify with it. Like apprentices, Harlequins were nominally servants; in the Continental commedia tradition from which they came, Harlequins typically played the role of the manservant to one of the characters who occupied a higher social rank, such as the Doctor or Pantaloon. As we saw in chapter 4, one version of the Faust story as it was told in the early eighteenth century cast Faust as an apprentice, a servant-gone-bad who stole the art of printing from his master and passed it off as magic. The character of Harlequin Faustus was in that sense an easily accomplished linkage of the "historical" Faust's believed social position and the commedia figure's traditional rank. Yet even in the commedia tradition, Harlequins were servants of a particularly unfixed kind, notable more for their tricks than for their loyalty and service to their masters. They were probably never seen actually doing work. Harlequins crossed barriers of rank, age, and even gender, mocking the figures who supposedly had control over them, indulging their anarchic desires for food, fun, and sex. It is not hard to imagine that young men who found themselves under the constant supervision of their employers must have enjoyed viewing such tricks. Harlequins offered the possibility for a certain imaginative freedom and resistance to authority, and it is perhaps not surprising that a master like Richardson would have felt them not only to be a general menace but a specific challenge to his authority.

An association between pantomime and criminality was reinforced again and again, as early eighteenth-century harlequinades frequently cast their hero as a petty thief, and often brought him into contact with the criminal justice system. The titles of two now-lost afterpieces of the 1710s are suggestive, even through all record of their content has evaporated: *Harlequin turn'd Judge* and *Harlequin Executed* (both 1717). Several pantomimes of the 1720s and 1730s portray Harlequin being subjected to a mock-trial; in at least one instance, he is sentenced to death. In the comic section of one version of

Orpheus and Eurydice, the Pantaloon figure "Don Spaniard" sentences his servant Pierrot to death for letting Harlequin get away, but Harlequin turns a trick and the Don ends up in the pillory, where he is pelted by a mob of outraged onlookers. The last act of *Harlequin Hydaspes,* a 1719 satire on the popular opera *Idaspe,* presents Harlequin lamenting his fate from inside a prison cell; with songs set to tunes from Italian opera, it's a scene that anticipates, and may have served as a model for, the more famous tableau of Macheath in prison toward the end of *The Beggar's Opera.*[24] Similarly, in the comic part of the Rich/Theobald version of *Perseus and Andromeda,* the scene opens and "Discovers *Harlequin* Hanging" on a gallows. But he is not killed by the rope; his body falls from the gallows in several pieces, which are magically reconstituted on a bier, and he rises to get his revenge.[25] A sign of how common the association between Harlequin and criminality had become is the tendency of pantomime's opponents to appropriate the theme, satirizing the court scenes that pantomimes had often used to mock the criminal justice system. David Garrick's 1759 *Harlequin's Invasion,* which, as we shall see in chapter 7, might be considered to be an "antipantomime" for the way that it seems designed to undercut the most salient features of the form, saw Harlequin declared a vagrant by a group of English judges, and ultimately condemned and exiled by the even more powerful force of *literary* judgment in the form of William Shakespeare, whose statue rises onstage while Harlequin sinks into a trapdoor. Henry Fielding's 1736 satire on pantomime, *Tumble-Down Dick,* not only shows Harlequin being committed and then escaping when Colombine bribes the judge, but justifies the trick by having the theater manager "Machine" (a figure for John Rich) claim "that Aristotle, in his book concerning entertainments, has laid it down as a principal rule, that Harlequin is always to escape."[26] A certain mockery of the criminal justice system's efficacy and finality was, it seems, all but built into early eighteenth-century pantomime as a form, becoming so integral a part of the expectations that theatergoers brought to it that Fielding is able to construct a joke invoking the premier authority on generic rules to signal how typical such satire had become.

The crossing of apprenticeship, criminality, and entertainment reached perhaps its consummate expression in the November 1724 production of Drury Lane's *Harlequin Sheppard,* a burlesque reenactment of the career of Jack Sheppard, the famous housebreaker and escape artist who had been executed at Tyburn a few weeks earlier.[27] Sheppard had apprenticed as a carpenter, but he broke his articles and turned to crime, engaging in a series of break-ins in pursuit of fencible goods. Sheppard's fame, however, derived not

Frontispiece to *Harlequin Sheppard* (1724) (*Reproduced by permission
of The Huntington Library, San Marino, Calif.*)

so much from his crimes as from his extraordinary ability to break out of
prison cells, including, most incredibly for contemporary observers, both the
"condemned hold" at Newgate and the even more secure cells of the New
Prison in Clerkenwell, where he had broken through thick chains, lowered
himself down twenty-five feet into an adjoining yard, and then climbed a
twenty-two-foot wall to freedom. Sheppard's resourcefulness and his flair for
the dramatic—he began to steal with an eye for flashy clothing and made

some triumphal progresses through the city by coach, practically daring the authorities to catch him—rendered him a figure of widespread fascination and even admiration. It is not surprising, then, to discover that Richardson identified *Harlequin Sheppard* as an especially toxic example of the criminal entertainment; he complains in *The Apprentice's Vade Mecum* how "the Characters of *Shepherd, Jonathan Wild, Blueskin*" were exhibited in the theater, "not for the Sake of Poetical Justice, in their *Execution,* but to divert the Audience by their *Tricks* and *Escapes*" (12–13).[28] Fusing Harlequin with the figure of Jack Sheppard, England's most famous apprentice-gone-bad, *Harlequin Sheppard* underscored the association between apprenticeship and criminality that the Faustus entertainments had exploited but had not brought to the level of explicit expression.

The connection between all three bad apprentice figures—Sheppard, Harlequin, and Faustus—is enacted at the end of the *Authentic Memoirs of the Life and Surprising Adventures of John Sheppard* (1724), a hastily published criminal biography that details Sheppard's crime-spree and escapes. Observing that he has actually "been writing a sort of a *Tragedy*" in the course of telling Sheppard's story, the anonymous author closes his "*Play*" with "an imaginary *Speech*" where Sheppard fantasizes himself playing a role similar to that of Harlequin Faustus in the arena of public opinion:

> Like Doctor *Faustus,* I my Pranks have play'd,
> (By Contract with his *Master* long since made)
> Like him liv'd Gay, and revell'd in Delight,
> Drank all the Day, and Whor'd the live-long Night.
> To raise my Name above all Rogues in Story,
> I've made Chains, Bolts, and Bars fly all before me:
> But, heark, the Dismal Sound! the Clock strikes One:
> The Charm is broke, and all my Strength is gone:
> The Dragon comes, I hear his Hideous Roar;
> Farewel, my Friends, for now Poor JACK's no more.[29]

Linking his escape artistry with the theatrical magic of Harlequin Faustus, this Sheppard advances his motivation as the desire for fame and notoriety, the wish to "raise his Name" in the public sphere as the example of the urban rogue *par excellence.* To many in the urban working classes, Sheppard became a figure of admiration and wish-fulfillment, in part because of the way that he channeled the skill set learned in the course of his apprenticeship into entirely different uses than the ones for which they had been intended. As Peter

Linebaugh has pointed out, Sheppard applied the knowledge of tools and materials he had gained as a carpenter's apprentice, not to house-building and joinery, but to the crafts of house-breaking and escape artistry. Described in the *Authentic Memoirs* as "a perfect *Don Quixot*" for the way that he undertook increasingly hazardous "Romantic Adventures" even as the authorities were mobilizing against him, Sheppard became an object of public interest and discourse whose meaning could be interpreted in several different ways, as monitory example or as emblem of resistance.[30] What the specific association with Harlequin Faustus brings to the fore is how these wayward servant characters came together as a kind of constellation of related figures in the urban public sphere of the early 1720s, their prominence and persistence indebted to the new media of debate and dissemination that such criminal biographies as the *Authentic Memoirs* exploited and exemplified.

The "Jack Sheppard" of the *Authentic Memoirs* also recognizes that the theater, and specifically its new and astonishingly popular form of pantomime, is the institution that his readers will recognize as the culture's most effective site of publicity, such that his own claim to fame is best signaled by the degree to which he can claim himself to be "like Dr. Faustus." This gesture, however, would seem to reverse the usual terms of the relationship between the theater and the real world; here, an actual person seems to model himself on a theatrical character, rather than the other way around. The seeming reversal of cultural authority from world to stage would prove profoundly troubling to men like Richardson, who understood this to imply that criminal exploits could be cast as entertaining. The possible confusion of fictional and real, entertaining and pedagogic, called forth a desire to devise new modes of entertainment. Significantly, these would be constructed to accommodate and display a new type of character, one that would represent the audience to itself in a wholly new way. With the continuing concern over "the apprentice" as the normative site of address for entertainments that might lead young men astray, it is not surprising that the best example of a play constructed on these principles would be another play about a bad apprentice, George Lillo's *The London Merchant,* to which we now turn.

The London Merchant, *the Representative Character, and the Conceptual Spread of Entertainment*

The reform of public culture in the early eighteenth century would cast Restoration-era farces like *The London Cuckolds* as old-fashioned and primitive, too sexually frank and unrepentant for modern taste. In the 1750s, the traditional performance for apprentices was changed to George Lillo's *The London Merchant; or, the History of George Barnwell,* first staged at Drury Lane in the summer of 1731. The precise moment when this shift assumed the status of a custom in its own right is impossible to pin down, although the available evidence suggests that it was David Garrick who began to remove *The London Cuckolds* from the repertoire for the Lord Mayor's Day in the early 1750s.[31] But efforts to change the conditions of entertainment for working people began much earlier, and indeed one occasion that we can identify for Samuel Richardson's attack on pantomime in the *Vade Mecum* is very likely the controversy over the opening in the late 1720s of unlicensed theaters located to the east of the patent houses, in particular Thomas Odell's, which opened in Goodman's Fields in 1729 and was taken over by Henry Giffard in 1731. Because it was situated closer to the City than the patent houses (particularly after the move of John Rich's company west to Covent Garden in December 1732), Giffard's theater was well positioned to draw a substantial audience from the shopkeepers, tradesmen, journeymen, and apprentices who worked in the industries located nearby. The success of Giffard's theater and others, including the Little Theater at the Haymarket and a new theater at Sadler's Wells, constituted what Hume has accurately described as a "boom" in London theatrical production in the late 1720s and 1730s, a rapid expansion not only in the number of theatrical entertainments, but of the range of genres they staged and the geographic scope of programmed performances across the city.[32] Prompted by the success of pantomime and then by the vogue for ballad opera following the unprecedented sixty-two-night run of *The Beggar's Opera* in 1728, staged performance enjoyed a level of frequency and prominence in these years that it had not achieved since the closing of the public playhouses in 1642 and would not reach again until perhaps the 1790s. Richardson joined in a public debate in the mid-1730s over the propriety and the legality of Giffard's and other such enterprises, publishing, besides the *Vade Mecum, A Seasonable Examination of the Playhouses* in 1735, a pamphlet that attacked the new theaters as a threat to business and "a very improper Diversion to be planted among the Working Class of People, particularly."[33] Richardson's writings, particularly the *Seasonable Examination,* contributed to a broader attempt on the part of men of his own class in London to regulate the London stage in the mid-1730s, an effort that led to the introduction in 1735 of "Sir John Barnard's Bill,"[34] which was an important forerunner of the Stage Licensing Act;[34] the bill did not pass, but the debate it summoned forth helped facilitate the passage of the Licensing Act two years later.[35]

The replacement of *The London Cuckolds* by *The London Merchant* marks a moment when the urban middle class recognized entertainment as a phenomenon in its own right, one whose sway over spectators who were believed to lack the capacity to discriminate between good and bad examples of behavior induced them to assert more direct control over its course. When they directed apprentices to Lillo's domestic tragedy rather than Ravenscroft's farce, men like Richardson were attempting to seize control of urban entertainment, and to fashion it according to new understandings of temporality, imitation, and exemplarity. It is important to recognize that this alteration in the theaters' annual programming co-opted and then reconstructed the older, seasonal pattern of work and diversion, a pattern that was newly intelligible in the early eighteenth century precisely because it was being replaced by one that was more rationalized and homogeneous. By superimposing their own, chosen piece on the traditional performance schedule, theatrical reformers were consciously appropriating what they recognized to be the power of custom to regulate behavior. Richardson provides a useful gloss on the way that the shifting seasonal pattern of entertainment registers broader changes in the relation of work to play in British culture. In *The Apprentice's Vade Mecum,* he recalls that "there was a Time when publick Spectacles, and Shews, Drolls, and Farces (and most of our present Theatrical Performances are no better) were exhibited once a Year," at an annual fair, a customary schedule that, he asserts, was "productive of Trade" because it provided necessary relief after months of labor (14). By contrast, the daily, scheduled performances of "the present age" do not so much "relax" the mind in order that it be keener upon its return to work as "detach" it from work. This is at best a fine distinction, the erasure of which Richardson blames, not (as we might expect) on the growing depravity of the workforce, but on a fundamental change in the disposition of social and individual time. Richardson's prescription that apprentices should attend *The London Merchant* "once a year" (16) needs to be taken as an attempt to reclaim the beneficial effects that he imagines an older mode of temporality had on the psyche.[36] With the expansion of the playhouses in the early 1730s, the spread of entertainment into new domains of the culture could literally be mapped. In order to forestall the acceptance of Giffard's Goodman's Fields theater, Richardson reaches to the past, attempting to turn the clock back on the advance of sites for programmed commercial entertainment. Reminding his readers that players are "by our very Laws . . . deemed Vagabonds" (17), he invokes the "ancient Custom" by which the theaters in London were limited to two alone.[37] Richardson presses what would seem to be an anachronistic understanding of the theaters' origins and authority for the local purpose of resisting Giffard, but it expresses his nostalgia for an older relationship between work and diversion, one threatened by what seems to be their increasing indistinguishability in an era when, on the one hand, theaters are being built "in the very midst of the middling sort of Tradesman" (18), and, on the other, when entertainment seems to be staking a claim for the time and attention of workers.

Even as it appropriates the older discourse of "custom" to justify its attack on the new theaters in London, Richardson's rhetoric also situates his *Seasonable Examination* as well as *The Apprentice's Vade Mecum* in the emergent social discourse that Foucault termed "police," the eighteenth century's attempt to apply rationality to affairs of state, in particular to the administration of the people. By police, eighteenth-century theorists of the art of government meant, as Foucault puts it, "not an institution or mechanism functioning with the state but a governmental technology peculiar to the state—domains, techniques, targets where the state intervenes."[38] "Police" thus signified much more than its modern meaning of a body of men organized to keep public order and investigate crime; rather, it described the comprehensive attempt to use critical reason to address social issues. It is what Tobias Smollett in *The Expedition of Humphry Clinker* (1771) referred to as "civil regulation."[39] Crucially, the doctrine of "police" addressed itself less to questions of individual persons than to the population as a class, taking as its object the entire population within a particular state, which could then be divided into subgroups for the sake of investigation and management. While it was much more highly developed in the centralized state systems of France and Germany, such a conception of police is nonetheless invoked in an English context in the title of Sir John Fielding's *Account of the Origins and Effects of a Police Set on Foot by His Grace the Duke of Newcastle in the Year 1753, upon a Plan presented to his Grace by the Late* Henry Fielding, *Esq.* (1758). Here, John Fielding outlines his half brother Henry's schemes to reduce the rate of crime in London, plans that included, but were far from limited to, the establishment of a professional force of officers deputized to pursue and investigate crimes against property. John Fielding expresses the central doctrine of the art of governmentality when he asserts at the start of this pamphlet that "The Riches and Strength of a Nation are the Number of its Inhabitants; the Happiness of that Nation, their being usefully and constantly employed."[40] As he goes on to describe his late half brother's efforts to reduce criminal behavior by addressing the social conditions that cause it, Sir John Fielding demonstrates how those plans fulfill the central goals of police in its broadest meaning, as he identifies and then addresses the problems of the various classes of people whose mis- or under-employment is a threat to the nation: young boys, "deserted Girls" (41), gamblers. The discourse of police, which neither Richardson nor Lillo may have known by that name but which nonetheless informs their thinking about the relationship between urban entertainment and the "Working Class of People," addresses itself to the population conceived in the aggregate, as a body that could be represented in numerical, statistical terms. When its logic is incorporated into a work like *The London Merchant* that is addressed *to* a specific class—here the class included under the term *apprentices*—the discourse of police takes the shape of a new conception of character, one that, as we shall see, consciously attempts to comprehend the largest possible number of its class in the construction of a character who fully represents them.

Staged in the patent theater at Drury Lane rather than one of the new unlicensed houses, *The London Merchant* is a self-conscious counterattack on rogue plays like *Harlequin Sheppard, The Beggar's Opera, The Quaker's Opera,* and *The Prisoner's Opera.* It was fashioned to displace entertainments like pantomime, Restoration farce, and particularly performances that made heroes out of criminals into something new and more suitable for emulation. *The London Merchant* can be understood as the product of a class that was newly intelligible to itself as such, a group that consisted of the upper level of urban artisans across professions, who collectively were eager to reform and redirect patterns of play as the logical correlative to their reformation of patterns of work. Harry Pedicord has even managed to specify further that Lillo's play is a text deeply imbued with the rhetoric and ideology of "speculative Masonry," an institution abstracted from the craft guild of "operative masonry" that had originally been composed of men who actually built things to become a "fraternity where all could meet on a democratic level."[41] Organized in 1717, English Masonry claimed as members not just Lillo, but also John Rich, Theophilus Cibber, and Henry Giffard—that is, the managers of the prominent London theaters in the 1730s.[42] Pedicord makes a good case that Masons not only frequented the theaters en masse, but in particular supported Lillo's play in substantial numbers, frequently calling for its performance. Pedicord goes on to argue that it is possible to discover Masonic doctrine being uttered in *The London Merchant,* but my point is not so much to identify Masonry as the keystone for the play's ideology and success as to observe that the emergence of speculative Masonry in these decades testifies to the existence of a self-aware bourgeois class, one that recognized a shared set of interests. As a representative cultural production of a new cohort, *The*

London Merchant not only reflects a new set of beliefs and values, but calls for and makes use of a new conception of representation.

Much the same logic of anachronism as Richardson would use in his *Vade Mecum* informs *The London Merchant,* which consistently defines *time* itself as the merchants' most essential commodity. In the first scene, Thorowgood instructs Trueman to settle as many unpaid bills as possible immediately, lest "artificers lose their time, so useful to the public and their families, in unnecessary attendance."[43] Trueman's assimilation of this lesson pays off in a much more crucial scene later, when Barnwell, having stolen money from their employer, laments that the deed cannot be undone, because "never yet did time, once past, return" (28). Trueman amplifies the sentiment—"the continued chain of time has never once been broken"—and immediately extends this cosmic point to its local application: "business requires our attendance" (28–29). Such words might have been indebted to careful readings of Richardson's book or, even better, of *A Present for an Apprentice:* "Above all Things learn to put a due Value on *Time,* and husband every Moment, as if it were to be your last: In Time, is comprehended all we possess, enjoy, or wish for; and in losing that, we lose them all" (20). Trueman and Thorowgood project this contemporary understanding of temporality onto the play's Elizabethan-era setting, collapsing the difference between present and past as if to insist that no other conception of time had ever existed. When its subject is commerce, Lillo's play imagines the past as virtually continuous with the present. Lillo projects his plot back to the moment just prior to the event that could be credited with being the origin of Britain's preeminence in the Atlantic trading system, the defeat of the Spanish Armada, enabling his audience to draw a parabolic arc from that moment to their own. The point is made most emphatically at the outset of the play, when Thorowgood rejoices at the news that the bankers of Genoa have broken their contract with Spain for a major loan at the behest of the merchants of London, forcing the Spanish king to delay his invasion until he can get the money he needs from the New World, and giving Queen Elizabeth the "time" she needs to outfit her navy. The moral of this story, according to Thorowgood, is that "merchants, as such, may sometimes contribute to the safety of their country as they do at all times to its happiness" (11), a point phrased so generally ("as such"; "sometimes") as to be exportable from its historical context and applied to gratify the interests of its audience in the present tense.

We can make a distinction here between the formal logic of Thorowgood's and Truman's speeches on commerce and their content. Both the how and the what of what they say will help articulate aspects of the play's ideology and structures of address, with the formal issues ultimately clarifying questions of ideology and the play's content—its advocacy of free-market capitalism in particular—actually speaking to questions of form, especially the way that Lillo goes about constructing his hero. Formally, Thorowgood's speeches, typically addressed to Trueman, invoke a traditional model of imitation, as he hopes and expects to hear his beliefs and sentiments mirrored back to him by his apprentices. Here Lillo in effect adopts Richardson's argument that the key to the merchant class's success lies in the mimetic relationship between the master and his apprentice. Trueman, the good apprentice of the play, enacts the logic of moral duplication that Richardson advanced in his *Vade Mecum;* he is the perfect "copy" of his master Thorowgood, mimicking the latter's pieties about trade, thrift, diligence, and the ability of commerce to "tame the fierce and polish the most savage" (40). Such mimicry was conceptualized in extremely concrete, material terms. In the culture of the eighteenth-century print shop, for instance, "to copy" resonated with the particular force of a figure of speech whose typographic literalization is close at hand. Just a few pages before his attack on "Harlequin Mimicry" in his *Vade Mecum,* Richardson had made clear the degree to which he understood copying as a material process in the first instance by the way in which he traced the origins of the indenture, the (typically, printed) document that formalized the relationship between a master and his apprentice: "*Indenture,*" he writes, "is derived from the French *Endenter,* to *jag,* or *notch,* and signifies an Agreement between different Persons, wherof there are two Copies, which being cut, *waved* or *notched,* tally to one another when put together, and prove the Genuineness of both" (1–2).[44] The duplication of such a contract in physical form confers material support and legitimacy to the more abstract duplication of moral value that *The Apprentice's Vade Mecum* attempts to enact and that *The London Merchant* models, the replication of virtues like thrift, sobriety, and diligence from master to apprentice.[45] And by the logic of spectatorship that Richardson invokes in his critique of the contemporary theater, where theatergoers naturally desire to imitate those who are placed before them, Trueman would serve in turn as a model for the apprentices in the audience, a figure whose fidelity to his master should be faithfully copied.

But the same figure of "copying" that Richardson invokes to promote socially and economically desirable virtues could also, in the hands of workmen themselves, be deployed to identify what seems to be its antithesis, a parodic imitation of such desiderata that could cast them as fronts for bourgeois hypocrisy. In his book *The Great Cat Massacre,* Robert Darnton describes how apprentice printers in Paris in the same decades frequently mimed "burlesque reenactments in the life of the shop"; such performances, known in the argot of the print shop as *"copies,"* constituted "a major form of entertainment for the men," one that gave the apprentices symbolic power by enabling them to mock the eccentricities of others in the workshop: fellow apprentices, journeymen, the master's wife, or the master himself.[46] The form of imitation figured in the print shop as *copying,* then, described a form of resistance to authority as well as the exercise of authority itself. This is a case where what we might think of as the theater of the everyday teaches us a lesson worth keeping in mind when considering the eighteenth-century theater as an institution; the workmen's burlesques point to the way that programs for regulating behavior can be received, appropriated, and used quite differently from the way that they are intended, and demonstrate how modes of performance organized "from below" might be used to counter the influence of the structures that seemed to have authority over them. In terms of the theater, it reminds us that spectators cannot always be counted on to receive representations in the way they were intended by their makers, that they might find themselves inclined to copy, say, a Harlequin rather than a Trueman. We shall shortly see that Lillo understood the problem well, and took steps to forestall just this kind of resistance.

Indeed, it is the content of the play's many sententious speeches on capitalism, in particular the mismatch between the ideology they profess and the historical moment in which *The London Merchant* was performed, that will lead us to the new understanding of character that informs both Lillo's understanding of modern economics and his innovation in the theater. Trueman's ode to capitalism's civilizing function echoes not only his master, but Montesquieu, who articulated what Albert Hirschman has called the "doctrine of *doux commerce,*" the claim that trade works to soften the influence of the human passions, replacing the lust for glory, conquest, and war with the more civilized pursuit of profit.[47] Lillo makes a point of linking the play's explicit statements about the centrality of trade to its implicit claim that the ideal union of master and apprentice best advances Britain's interests in a world organized by commerce by staging arguments about the virtues of the London merchant class in the form of dialogues between Thorowgood and Trueman, who together articulate the ideology of trade in much the same language as it was being deployed by contemporary theorists. Yet Trueman's expression of the *doux commerce* argument also brings us to the fault line of the play's colonialist ideology, the fact that European commerce with what he calls the "fierce" and the "savage" was increasingly a one-way affair.

European traders did not just take away the "superfluities" of "savage" nations, but their people as well, a practice that accelerated in the 1730s, which was, as Teju Olinayan has pointed out, the decade that witnessed the most rapid increase in the British slave trade in the entire century.[48]

The play refers to slavery when it has Millwood speak admiringly of the practices of the "Spaniards in the New World, who first plundered the natives of all the wealth they had and then condemned the wretches to the mines to life to work for more" (16). Millwood's goal is to claim for women the power that she takes men to have already; they have made women "slaves" to them, denying them "property . . . even in themselves" by right of "conquest" (15). Millwood here alludes to what we can think of as the doctrine of slavery-by-conquest, the argument that slavery was a traditional practice by which conquered peoples became the property of the victors of war. The uneasy coexistence of this older rationalization of slavery with the play's openly expressed rhetoric of *doux commerce* is registered by Millwood's maid Lucy's comment that her mistress is "strangely arbitrary in [her] principles" (16), as Lucy is much more ready to understand relations between the genders according to a logic of commercial exchange, with women trading sexual intercourse for money. In effect, Millwood expresses *The London Merchant*'s bad conscience, exposing the hypocrisy at the heart of *doux commerce* doctrine. Such a displacement of the play's most glaring contradiction onto its most unequivocally malicious character is perhaps not surprising, indeed almost inevitable given the degree to which Lillo localizes agency in individual persons rather than broader systems or movements. The criminality of Britain's global capitalism in the 1730s gains a scapegoat in Millwood, her will-to-power the monstrous foil against which Thorowgood and Trueman's benevolent trade defines itself—and upon which it secretly relies.[49]

But I take Lillo's insistence that commerce is driven by such intimate personal relationships as a sign, not of the continuity between the period of the play's action and that of its first production, but of the profound difference between them. For by the 1730s, the heroic age of capitalism had passed and the age when corporations like the South Sea Company and the Africa Company dominated commerce was ascendant. Such a system, in which faceless companies carried out the business of the state, eclipsed the ability of individuals to represent the activities and failures of the commercial order in the way that Lillo wants his characters to do. My point can be clarified by returning to the play's dedication, offered to the subgovernor of the South Sea Company, the institution that had been incorporated to fulfill the terms of the *asiento*, the contract to supply the Spanish colonies in the Americas with slaves that was one of the concessions of the Treaty of Utrecht in 1713. Like the play that follows, the dedication reaches back to the Elizabethan period, citing a cut-and-paste version of Hamlet's address to the players, extracting the sections that pertain particularly to how *The Mouse-Trap* will expose Claudius as the murderer of Hamlet's father. What Lillo selects as important from this speech, though, are not any sections that might describe the play's address to Claudius in particular, but those that speak to the theater's more universal capacity to "amaze indeed / The very faculty of eyes and ears" (5). By contrast with Shakespeare's hero, Lillo is more interested in "the general ear" than he is in Claudius's, theorizing how the theater's liveness and sensuality endow it with what Lillo calls an "irresistible force" that impresses itself on any member of the audience. Lillo's interest here in the general rather than the specific character of theatrical representation supports his claim elsewhere in the dedication that *The London Merchant* has been designed to democratize tragedy by describing "the circumstances of the generality of mankind" (3). Hence his hero, as observers from the play's first production to the present have noticed, is bourgeois rather than the typically noble hero of tragedy, as such a figure better reflects the audience to which the play is addressed.

But Lillo understands the problem of Barnwell's representivity as a central character to be more complicated than that, a fact revealed by the difficulty he encounters when he comes to the question of offering "the character" (6) of his dedicatee, Sir John Eyles. The "character" was, to an eighteenth-century reader, a genre in its own right, one that, as Diedre Lynch has put it, forms "a semantic complex in which the ethical, the physiognomic, the typographic, and even the numismatic merge."[50] In her book *The Economy of Character,* Lynch brilliantly shows how eighteenth-century critics and writers exploited the puns latent in the term *character,* underscoring the visual and material dimensions of writing and printing, and the degree to which the significance, or (staying within the metaphor's field of force) the *value,* of a literary character was understood to lie in its public intelligibility. What a reader of 1731 would expect here is a brief articulation of Eyles's virtues, one that draws his character on the page, in typographical characters, such that it forms a legible pattern. Lillo claims that he cannot produce such a thing, and in so doing, he signals how the traditional conception of the character would not only be insufficient for his dedication but for the play that follows. The problem for Lillo is not, as we might expect, that Eyles's merits exceed the capacity of language to create such a pattern, but that his character has *already* been sufficiently attested to by the fact that others—his Parliamentary constituents and the proprietors of the South Sea Company—have seen fit to choose him as one of "their representatives" (6). The uncountable "numbers of persons" in both bodies take the place of Lillo's testimony as to Eyles's virtues. They render the very form of the "character" description archaic, no longer an adequate representation of a man whose virtues have made him the representative of economic and political corporations.

Lillo's recourse to economic and political understandings of representation extends beyond his modest description of Eyles to his conception of character in *The London Merchant* itself. To this point, I have barely mentioned Lillo's hero George Barnwell, the bad apprentice offered as an example to be avoided (for falling into the traps of sensuality and criminality) and then admired (for recognizing the error of his ways and undergoing a full Christian repentance). This has been strategic rather than accidental, a sign of the way that Barnwell seems fashioned to preclude the kind of shorthand character description that would sum him up in a few lines or paragraphs. Rather, I take Barnwell to be constructed on the basis of the new logic of character, one that we can glimpse at work in Lillo's address to the play's dedicatee. Unlike, say, the three young men who cuckold the burghers in *The London Cuckolds,* or even the bad apprentice figures of the Jack Sheppard stories, Barnwell is fashioned, not as a cultural type, but as the representative of a segment of the audience, the London apprentice cohort from which he came, which he mirrors back to itself. This is why Barnwell is a notoriously empty figure (less interesting by far than Millwood, for example); he is almost wholly lacking in specific traits or quirks that would make him notable or memorable, but that would also reduce the number of spectators able to identify themselves with him. The critical history of the play is for this reason filled with complaints about his inadequacy as a tragic hero, the difficulty of either admiring his nobility or condemning his perfidy. The problem, I want to suggest, is that Lillo is deploying a new conception of the dramatic character, one that fits uneasily with traditional theories of the tragic hero, but one that was called for by the broader shifts in the concept of representation that are brought into view by the delicacy of Lillo's approach to his dedicatee Eyles. The theoretical basis for such a conception was best articulated in critical discussions about the nature and purpose of exemplarity, particularly as it related to comedy, discussions that turned on the propriety of offering a "vicious" or, at the extreme, a criminal character as the hero of a comic entertainment.

This was not a new question, of course, but it gained a particular salience in the early eighteenth century, motivated in part by the production of plays featuring criminal heroes that we have already looked at and raised to a more abstract level in a critical discourse about the nature of comedy in general. A useful example of a work that to some degree sits between theory and practice, and one that is particularly germane here because of the criminal—Jack Sheppard—to whom it refers, is the frame play of *The Quaker's Opera*, performed at Bartholomew Fair in September 1728, and then brought to the indoor theater at the Haymarket later that fall. Usually assigned to the authorship of Thomas Walker, the original Macheath of Gay's *The Beggar's Opera*, whose title and ballad opera format it emulates, *The Quaker's Opera* is for the most part an adaptation of *The Prison Breaker*, a play on the career of Jack Sheppard that was planned for performance at Lincoln's Inn Fields in 1725 but for unknown reasons was never staged.[51] In the opening frame added to *The Prison Breaker* for its fairground performances three years later, an Old Quaker and a player discuss the propriety of pieces like this one that display the criminal deeds of malefactors like Jack Sheppard, thereby setting "odious and abominable Characters off in the most Ornamental Colours" and encouraging "Lewdness and Immorality." The Old Quaker testifies that he has read *The Quaker's Opera* and found it to be harmless, though he admits some of his more scrupulous "brethren" might be offended. More important, the discussion about the propriety of such a play prompts him to lament how the "Stage, which in it self is a well-instituted thing . . . has been often of late debas'd and revert from its Original Intention," which he takes to be "the exposing of Follies and Vice in an agreeable manner, and generally concluding with some Instructive Moral, beneficial to Mankind."[52]

The Quaker expresses the traditional view of the purpose of comedy, that it should identify transgressions against social norms by representing them within a pedagogic frame that identifies individuals who pursue them as examples to be ridiculed and avoided. By the time of the Old Quaker's lament, however, this understanding of the purpose of comedy was in many respects as archaic as he is, which enables *The Quaker's Opera* to present his argument as itself a kind of comic complaint, spoken by an eccentric whose words need not be taken too seriously, and cannot be expected to have any material effect. The Quaker's name in the title of the play has much more to do with the performers' desire to mimic the title of Gay's extraordinarily successful hit than it does with his own authority over the performance that follows; the Old Quaker disappears after the framing introduction to a performance that celebrates Sheppard's career. By the 1720s, as theater historians have long shown, dramatic theory was calling for playwrights to offer *positive* examples for the spectator to imitate. A full account of the debate over the nature of this change is beyond the scope and needs of this book; rather,

I would like to examine how any such shift needs to be placed into broader conceptions of temporality and representation of which it takes part. A good place to analyze how such conceptions informed early eighteenth-century debate over the nature of comedy is located in the argument conducted between Richard Steele and John Dennis in the pages of *The Spectator* and a series of pamphlets surrounding the first production of Steele's last comedy, *The Conscious Lovers*.

By the time it premiered in 1722, *The Conscious Lovers* was embarrassingly long overdue, since it had been preceded by more than a decade of anticipatory promises, puffs, and essays by Steele intended to clear a space for a comedy that was designed not just to exemplify a new type of comedy, but to advance a redefinition of the concept and purpose of character itself. Steele began the buildup in 1711 by devoting *Spectator* #65 to a reassessment of Sir George Etherege's *The Man of Mode,* the 1675 play that by Steele's testimony had come to serve as "the Pattern of Gentile comedy" to early eighteenth-century critics and audiences.[53] The problem with Etherege's play, Steele argues, is that the hero Dorimant is too licentious to serve as a model for the spectator to imitate, more "a direct Knave in his Designs and a Clown in his Language" than a "fine Gentleman" (278–79). Steele's essay is the opening move in a larger plan to discredit the Restoration comedies that he uses *The Man of Mode* to represent, in order that *The Conscious Lovers* could take their place as a model for comedy, and its hero Bevil could replace Dorimant as the culture's model for "the fine gentleman" (which was, by no mere coincidence, the original title of *The Conscious Lovers.*) When Steele's play was finally in rehearsal in 1722, Dennis responded to Steele's essay of a decade earlier, making a preemptive strike against *The Conscious Lovers* by defending *The Man of Mode.* At stake in their dispute is what Dennis calls "the Nature of true Comedy"; should a comedy offer positive models for imitation, as Steele claimed? Or should it teach through "ridicule," by, in Dennis's words, exposing "Persons to our View whose Views we may shun and whose Follies we may despise; and by showing us what is done upon the Comick Stage, to show us what ought never be done upon the Stage of the World."[54] The relation can be understood in terms of the model of entertainment as mentation as articulated by Addison that I described in chapter 3. By such logic, the ridiculous character fails, literally, to entertain because his example alienates the spectator, breaking the spell of the theater's absorptive power in order to prompt critical reflection, thereby teaching him through the repulsive force of a negative example.

By the lights of Dennis's largely neoclassical theory, this is not entirely a bad thing. For Dennis, Etherege's Dorimant is a successful hero because he is marked, on the one hand, by all the "distinguishing strokes" of the comic character as defined by Aristotle, and on the other hand he reproduces the traits of contemporary individuals so precisely that no member of the audience could mistake the reference. Dennis's figure of "strokes" indicates how thoroughly his argument is grounded in the traditional understanding of the concept of character that Lillo would renounce in his 1731 dedication to *The London Merchant.* When, for example, Dennis observes that "the violent passions which are the subject of tragedy are the same in every age and appear with the same face," his metaphor invokes the physiognomic associations of character that were also expressed, as we saw in chapter 3, in such anatomically based taxonomies of the passions as that created by Descartes' student Charles Le Brun. This was a universal repertory of facial expressions and gestures, a grammar of signs shared by audiences and performers, and therefore offering assurance that the emotions they expressed would be readily understood.

In this conception of the theatrical "character," a figure like Dorimant can be understood as occupying—ideally—the intersection point of what we might think of as the horizontal and vertical axes of temporality. In one direction, Dorimant is merely the current incarnation of what Dennis calls "an allegorical and universal" figure ("the young man"), motivated by a set of passions appropriate to that type and therefore capable of giving "general instruction." But in another direction, he gains relevance to contemporary spectators by taking on readily identifiable traits of individual young men of his time (Dorimant, for example, was frequently taken for Rochester). As we have already seen, Steele frequently invokes the system of the passions, and seems to subscribe to its goals of universal intelligibility. But his reformist program reappropriates and radically alters its application, and *The Conscious Lovers* in effect turns Dennis's categories inside-out. What makes Bevil an exemplary character for Steele is precisely his idiosyncrasy, manifested most obviously in a lack of interest in his own financial welfare, a high-minded willingness to set aside his own best interests in order to accede to his father's wishes. Critiquing the play after it opened, Dennis describes Bevil's filiopiety as a species of "particularity" that renders him an illegitimate hero for comedy. Because he goes against the Whig ideology of self-autonomy and the priority of individual property rights over all else, Bevil appears to be, in Dennis's words, an "inconsistent" character, one whose pattern is illegible because it violates social norms without at the same time directing the spectator or reader to any more specific referent. Yet for Steele, this very idiosyncrasy is what enables Bevil to be universally interesting, because it strips him of the excess referentiality that interferes with the spectator's identification.

Bevil's abstraction from any particular historical situation renders him an object of interest whose character can be construed by the broadest possible range of spectators.[55] In effect, the "vertical" plane of history has dropped out of the equation; even though Steele's play is loosely modeled on an original by Terence, he thinks of Bevil not so much as the current instantiation of a universal, timeless type as a figure embodying the collective ideal of a fine gentleman in his own moment. Steele has begun to separate "character" from its typographic and literal support, to float it free so that its value might be determined by the audience itself.

Steele's final attempt to create an extramural set of expectations for *The Conscious Lovers* suggests that we can best understand his innovation, not so much in terms of sentiment, but in terms of a new conception of representativity, one that aims to produce a character who can be seen as a fair representation of the audience segment to which it appeals. In the third issue of his last periodical series, *The Theater,* published in the winter and spring of 1720, Steele proposes "a new Scheme for the Government of the publick Diversions," a "Body" of "Auditors" who will serve as "real Representatives of a *British* Audience."[56] The candidates that his own representative in this series, Sir John Edgar (who will be renamed Sir John Bevil and cast as Bevil's father in the forthcoming play), advances for the panel turn out to be the rest of the cast of *The Conscious Lovers:* Myrtle, who will represent the students at the Temple; Lucinda, who will represent "the Boxes" (where fashionable women sat); the merchant Mr. Sealand, who will stand for the pit (the preferred seating for such citizens); and Sir John's valet Humphrey, who will represent his fellow-servants in the gallery. *The Theatre* brings to the level of expression what the play leaves implicit, namely that *The Conscious Lovers'* claim to its spectators' interests is not simply that it accurately represents the audience, but that it does so on the principle of a new understanding of what it means to be representative. Rather than representing either a transhistorical figure or a particular contemporary, each of these characters is understood to represent a contemporary group or class, to stand in for them by virtue of the way that each embodies the norms of that class of person.[57] The cast of *The Conscious Lovers* is able to do this because they represent a composite or average of the features of demographic group from which they are drawn; they thus lack individualized quirks of character that might prevent someone in their class from identifying with them.

In *The London Merchant,* George Barnwell similarly represents the class of apprentices to which he belongs, and does so to the greatest possible extent precisely by embodying collective and general rather than individual and specific norms. Any specific character traits that might satisfy the critical objections that he is lacking in the kinds of strengths of character that make him an interesting hero would also, by the logic of representation that Lillo is pursuing, make it more difficult for Barnwell to represent "the generality of mankind," because it would reduce the sheer "numbers" of spectators who would be able to identify with him. Lillo's expectation is that spectators would be more able to insert themselves in Barnwell's place if he offers as blank as possible a screen for the projection of their own self-images. It is only in this way that Lillo will be able to reach the great mass of spectators who require the monitory influence of such an example, the apprentices and other young men in London who might otherwise be swayed by the popular entertainments that romanticized the exploits of criminals. Invoking the "numbers" of spectators he wishes to reach and the "proportion" of remedy that *The London Merchant* will offer to the "disease" of criminality, Lillo appropriates the language of statistics in the service of theatrical characterization. George Barnwell is a place where literary and political models of personhood intersect. On the one hand, he fits the terms of a new conception of character as it was theorized in literary-critical terms as the modern replacement for a now-archaic model based in the power of ridicule. On the other hand, he also is calibrated to appeal to the largest possible number of spectators, a concern that, as Lillo's rhetoric indicates, is indebted to the contemporary discourse of police and its protocols for imagining, classifying, addressing, and managing the population by applying rational calculation.

But if literary, economic, and political modes of discourse share common features at this moment, the correspondence between their understandings of agency, representation, and imitation was far from frictionless. In fact, the spread of "entertainment" in the eighteenth century, here in the theoretical and epistemological as well as in the physical senses, would emphasize the risks involved in linking such discourses conceptually, as it would become more difficult to determine, for instance, whether a particular representation could be considered an entertainment or not. The problem might be illustrated by considering one of the curious facts in the performance history of *The London Merchant.* Just before the play's 1731 premiere, Lillo excised what would surely have been the most spectacular and absorbing moment in the entire play, the climactic scene at the gallows, where Barnwell and Millwood are finally brought to justice, the one appropriately repentant and accepting of his fate, the other defiant to the end. Lillo wrote such a scene, depicting the condemned criminals, a gallows, and a "crowd of spectators," but left it out "in the representation" on the "advice of some friends," advice that Lillo

Frontispiece to George Lillo, *The London Merchant* (*Special Collections Department, University of Virginia Library*)

describes no further. Although it was never performed in the theater, the scene was nonetheless illustrated in a frontispiece that was printed with the text beginning with the play's fifth edition in 1734. Why was this scene cut "in the representation"?

In a shrewd article, Helen Burke argues that this scene must be considered as a discarded keystone that, when restored to its proper place, reframes the entire play's architecture and reveals *The London Merchant*'s historical significance as a play about the violence of early modern capitalism and imperialism. Burke argues that Lillo's goal is to legitimate the resort to capital punishment on the part of Britain's "men of property," by "rationalizing" their claims to possession and empire.[58] The gallows scene was thus cut because it crossed a line of decorum surrounding this claim, "displaying the harsh reality" of the costs that the bourgeoisie's desires exacted on the underclass and exposing the brutality that the ruling class rather wished to veil under a cloak of benevolent sentiments."[59] My reading of the play and sense of the ideological work it performs is close to Burke's, but I want further to specify the nature of the spectatorial problem that this excised scene raised, and that accounts more fully for its removal. I would agree that Lillo and his "friends" perceived, or perhaps just sensed, that the play's attempt to appeal to the "general" spectator reached a crisis of representation when it drew within proximity of the gallows. But this is not just because the scene revealed too spectacularly the harsh discipline undergirding the emergent capitalist order. That system was, in fact, never very well disguised in the period, and the play makes no effort to hide the fact that Millwood and Barnwell will pay for their crimes with their lives. Rather, the problem is that the usual scene at the Tyburn gallows was already too much like the mise-en-scène of *The London Merchant* itself, too "entertaining" in its own right to serve as the monitory example that it was intended to be. While such a scene might be safely read in the privacy of one's closet, it must not be *seen* in the live, embodied space of the theater, where the performance so closely resembles the spectacle of justice itself as to imply that the latter, too, might be just another form of entertainment.

That Lillo recognizes this to be the case is proven, I think, by the way he uses the term *entertainment* throughout the course of *The London Merchant*. What is striking is not only how frequently the word appears, but how it is almost always used anachronistically, typically in the older sense of entertainment as a banquet. Thus for example in the second scene, Thorowgood asks his daughter Maria if she has "given orders for the entertainment" (12), the meal that they have prepared for a throng of her suitors; later, Millwood claims that she was too interested in Barnwell to "observe the entertainment," that is, the supper that her servants have prepared for them (21). Millwood also euphemistically refers to her brothel as a "house of entertainment" to the innocent Barnwell, luring him in by leading him to think that her business is no more dangerous than an inn. These anachronistic uses of the term remind us that Lillo has deliberately set his play a century and a half in the past; like Thorowgood's references to the Spanish Armada, they help to abstract the action of the play from the present tense, situating it in the English history from which the ballad that serves as Lillo's source had come. That of all words, it should be "entertainment" that serves this function attests to its prominence, not in the Elizabethan period where the play is set, but in the Augustan moment in which Lillo is writing, a moment in which, as I have been arguing throughout this book, *entertainment* was a keyword whose emergent understanding as a self-authenticating mode of mass-cultural performance was profoundly disturbing to those who wanted to preserve a monitory function for art. It is only in what would turn out to be the final scene of the play that the modern confusion to which the concept of entertainment is prone becomes manifest when Maria laments that Barnwell's march to Tyburn will "give a holiday to suburb slaves and, passing, entertain the savage herd" (77). Maria's words, which all but close the play as it was actually performed in the eighteenth century, shed the patina of archaism that the play has to this point conferred on the term *entertainment;* in the context of the 1730s, they cannot help but refer to a more widely felt confusion between the ritual performances of the state and the mere entertainments of the playhouse that mimicked them.

Literary and cultural historians like John Bender and Peter Linebaugh have recently concurred with Maria's concern about the theatricality of the eighteenth-century British penal system, in particular the extent to which, as Linebaugh has put it, the public executions of eighteenth-century London can be construed as a kind of "drama" crafted by the state to elicit the traditional Aristotelian responses of "rage, glee, pity, terror and fear."[60] The analogy between the stage and the gallows was acutely felt in the 1720s and 1730s, becoming a staple of journalistic accounts. *The Weekly Journal*'s review of *Harlequin Sheppard,* for example, invoked the comparison to explain the pantomime's failure in its first production (it lasted only seven nights), observing how it was "dismiss'd with a universal Hiss—and, indeed, if Shepherd had been as wretched, and as silly a Rogue in the World, as the ingenious and witty Managers have made him upon the Stage, the lower Gentry, who attended him to Tyburn, wou'd never have pitied him when he was hang'd."[61] The satisfaction that the *Journal*'s writer takes in *Harlequin Sheppard*'s early demise (although, as Richardson's attack on it in *The Apprentice's Vade Mecum* demonstrates, it stayed active in the public imaginary for more than a decade afterward) would, however, provide little comfort to the many observers who would be made uneasy by the homology between theatrical and criminal justice that their comparison relies upon. The Swiss tourist Cesar de Saussure was struck on a visit to London in the 1720s by the superiority of English public shows to the spectacle of English justice. In a letter to his family, he compared the types of "entertainment" offered by the Lord Mayor's Show and the sight of "thirteen criminals all hanged at the same time," deciding in the end that the spectacle of justice was less "magnificent" than the City pageant.[62] These descriptions point to the fundamental problem that occurs when justice appears to be indistinguishable from theater, namely that it is difficult if not impossible for the state to ground its authority in anything more fundamental than representation. The penal system in effect risks becoming *mere* theater, and therefore of being potentially less absorbing and effective than staged representations that are not so closely bound to the messy contingencies of the real.

Probably the most sustained critical inquiry in this period into the relationship between entertainment and the gallows is found in Bernard Mandeville's *An Enquiry into the Causes of the Frequent Executions at Tyburn* (1725), which stages an internal debate about whether "the meanest and most abject part of low Life" is a proper object "for entertaining" a reader.[63] Deciding not only that it is, but that such a spectacle is best rendered by pushing the analogy as far as it can go, Mandeville uses the structure of the standard London theatrical program as it took shape in that decade to organize the "Scene of Confusion" at the scaffold into an intelligible performance. He thus describes the moment after an execution when friends and family members of the victim fought with surgeons over the disposition of the corpse as a mainpiece drama and its afterpiece pantomime: "The Tragedy being ended, the next Entertainment is a Squabble between the Surgeons and the Mob, about the dead Bodies of the Malefactors that are not to be hanged in Chains" (26). Considering a public execution as a form of entertainment—indeed, as a tragic mainpiece followed by an afterpiece—Mandeville's characteristically scandalous analysis (which claims, in short, that the middle class is itself the cause of the increase in crime because of its misplaced pity for the criminal classes, which has led them to collaborate with thief-taking middlemen like Jonathan Wild rather than simply trusting to the law) proceeds in much the same terms as those that had been used by Dennis and Steele in their dispute about the nature of exemplary heroes of comedy. Because he anticipates that his essay will be attacked by those "Men of Taste and Politeness" who believe that they ought not to be "troubled with" a "Scene" like "the Inside of *Newgate,* either on an Execution Day, or any other," Mandeville argues that he cannot "raise [the] Indignation of his audience " or give it an "Aversion" to the reality of life inside Newgate unless he offers a "general Idea" of it (A5).

The root metaphor of Mandeville's argument is drawn from the theory of painting; he analogizes his *Enquiry* to a Dutch still-life, scrupulously devoted to documenting the real, however repulsive that might be. This too is a theory of spectatorship, and his basic claim—that it is necessary to represent behavior that you would wish an audience to avoid—reiterates the essence of Dennis's argument against Steele. Immediately, however, Mandeville, in a characteristically ironic and disarming move, undercuts the theoretical support undergirding his own essay, attesting that he must in the end "plead guilty" to no desire more noble than sheer mimetophilia: "the Pleasure there is in imitating Nature in what Shape soever is so bewitching, that it overrules the Dictates of Art, and often forces us to offend against our own judgment" (A6r). Here Mandeville echoes, not Dennis, but rather Steele and Richardson, both of whom assume, as he does, that spectatorship creates a particularly powerful scene of mimetic desire, so much so that the observer invariably wishes to imitate what is placed before him.

Mandeville's confession underscores his self-assurance in the agility and correctness of his textual "Performance" in the *Enquiry* (a4v), where he casts himself as a kind of Harlequin of the printed page, a trickster who takes a perverse sort of pleasure in upending the pieties of bourgeois culture. Yet his account also fits into a long-standing literary tradition in which the brutality of the gallows might be seen to be not so much the antithesis of theater as a pretty good figure for its essence. Virtually every generation of writers on the theater have been deeply troubled by the sheer excessiveness of tragedy, its reliance on representations of violence to produce effects on the spectator. The Aristotelian concept of catharsis, frequently, even obsessively invoked in descriptions of public justice, has also proven to be a durable tool for recovering an ethical purpose from the violence of tragedy. Yet Timothy Murray has recently gone so far as to assert that "the profound turn of subject and socius against themselves" depicted in tragedy evokes such an "ambivalent pathos" that it exposes the most troubling dimension of the link between representation and the constitution of the self: *"mimesis is the theatricalization of masochism."*[64] Murray's somewhat cryptic formulation points to the profoundly unsettling effects that the seeming indistinguishability of entertainment and violent justice, coming into view in the entertainment culture of early eighteenth-century Britain, had on the individual subject. Such a confusion calls forth an equally powerful disavowal, an attempt to claim that there is no real pleasure in the spectacle of suffering. It leads, for example, to the fastidiousness with which even observers as usually shameless as Mandeville took care to separate out the individual observer, what he calls "the best-dispos'd Spectator," from the "Scene of Confusion" upon which he gazes, shoring up the integrity of the subject over against a painfully confounded spectacle. Similarly, a certain "thinking person" who describes an execution at Tyburn in the series of letters describing London entertainments that appears toward the end of Richardson's *Familiar Letters* separates himself from the mob that takes pleasure in the sight, stressing that this was "a scene that was no way entertaining to me."[65]

The scene of execution, located as it is at the border between life and death, the individual subject and the state, has remained a particularly vexed locus of spectatorship and mimesis. (This is perhaps particularly the case in the United States, the culture that has pursued the logics of both entertainment and state-licensed execution more thoroughly than any eighteenth-century British writer could have imagined.) As we continue to experience the confusion that results from the way that entertainment and punishment seem at times interchangeable with each other, we might well sympathize with Richardson's observer at Tyburn, who preempts any possibility that his reader might think that he took any pleasure from the theatrical spectacle of justice. For no one, it seems, is immune from the suspicion that they, like the apprentices of eighteenth-century London, might draw the wrong lessons from a monitory example.

Coda: Harlequin Methodist

The concern about how the geographical and conceptual spread of entertainment posed a danger to the working class extended itself beyond the institution of apprenticeship and the criminal-justice system. In this brief coda, I want to suggest how and why another discursive deployment of Harlequin was used to figure anxieties about a different emergent phenomenon of the 1730s and 1740s: Methodism. A broadside issued around 1750 depicts a Methodist preacher dressed as a Harlequin. He speaks to a crowd largely composed of old women and the poor, which is in turn the object of curiosity by a group of fashionable people, who are themselves part of a scene staged for our benefit, one whose theatricality is literalized by the presence of the curtain, proscenium arch, and chandeliers. The anonymous creator of this broadside takes Methodism to be a form of theater, and its famous founding figures George Whitefield and the Wesley brothers to be as much entertainers as men on a religious mission:

> *Wh-tf---d* he needs no farther Art,
> A perfect Comedian to be,
> And th' *W--st--y*'s may both top their Part
> To make *Farce* and *Religion* agree.

Such a critique of Methodism was widely shared in the years after its emergence to national prominence in the late 1730s. William Hogarth's late engraving *Credulity, Superstition, and Fanaticism* (1762) draws the same analogy to Harlequin as that made in the broadside, and the conflation of religion and entertainment that it figures was frequently invoked to dismiss Methodism as a form of diversion, its preaching a mode of performance indistinguishable from that appearing in the London playhouses. The author of the satirical poem *British Frenzy: Or, the Mock-Apollo,* a 1745 attack on pantomime, imagines Whitefield taking lessons on how to use theatrical effects to impress a crowd: "See! Burning Hell! W--tf--d, stand though amaz'd/How with Hell-fire dull Sinners can be pleas'd."[66] Abraham Adams of Fielding's *Joseph Andrews* (1743) encountered another aspect of the comparison when he tried to sell some of his sermons, only to come across a bookseller who informs him that sermons suffer from the same conditions of overproduction as plays, and that "unless they come out with the Name of *Whitfield or Westley*" they are simply not worth trying to bring to market.[67]

If the spread of unlicensed theaters cast into the areas of the City where the working class spent most of their time was a source of worry to bourgeois observers, the emergence of Methodism in the 1730s and 1740s was an even greater concern, and for some of the same reasons. Methodism's appeal to the poor, the young, and the disaffected seemed to be a distressing return of religious enthusiasm to a culture that had long cast a suspicious eye on such fervor, and also suggested that a large swathe of the population had needs that were unmet by the traditional institutions of church and state. Crucially, Methodist preachers like Whitefield and Wesley were seen, like the unlicensed theaters, to be threatening to disengage working people from their duties. In a remarkable moment in the epilogue to Thomas Cooke's *The*

Harlequin Methodist broadside (E294) *(From the Rare Book, Manuscript, and Special Collections Library, Duke University, Durham, North Carolina)*

William Hogarth, minister dressed as a Harlequin. *Credulity, Superstition, and Fanaticism* (detail) (© *Copyright The British Museum*)

Mournful Nuptials (1739), a Harlequin attacks Whitefield and Wesley for drawing people from the workshop to the fields where they preached:

> For them the shuttle's left by lazy weavers;
> And butchers drop their marrow-bones and cleavers;
> And, while the weaver's wife forsakes the loom,
> *Susan* leaves half unmop'd the dining-room:
> These are the dregs, the rubbish, of mankind,
> Sightless themselves, and guided by the blind,
> Strangers to virtue, as unknown to schools:
> As ev'ry like its like, fools cherish fools.[68]

One might suppose that Harlequin's presence here is deeply ironic, that he would be the last one to complain about people leaving off work for entertainment. But I take the logic of his presence here to be a way of registering the full outrage of Methodism's sudden incursion on the public sphere; even *Harlequin,* it seems, is disdainful of the Methodist preachers, who have become, in a way, his rivals for this audience's attention. From the point of view of a serious playwright like Cooke, both pantomime and Methodism are dangerous because their appeal to "the dregs" will lead to the disruption of orderly workplaces.

The analogy between the early Methodist preachers and the various forms of entertainment that had proliferated in London in the previous two decades gained a certain degree of traction from a temporal coincidence that did not go unnoticed: Whitefield began to draw tens of thousands of auditors to Moorfields to hear him preach in the summer of 1739, just over two years after the passage of the Stage Licensing Act had placed severe restrictions on the theaters, subjecting plays at the patent houses to prior censorship and shutting down some of the unlicensed houses. With many of these theaters closed, Whitefield's sermons seemed to fill a gap in public performance. There is probably no direct cause-and-effect linkage worth trying to establish between Whitefield's astonishing success at this moment and the restriction of the theaters less than two years earlier, but I would suggest that Methodism, like pantomime before it, became an object of public-sphere fascination, the focus of attention in pamphlet literature and periodicals in part because it entered a kind of vacuum created by the removal of something else. In the case of pantomime, that object was, as I argued in chapter 4, the intense partisan squabbling of the 1710s, which found itself neutralized by the early 1720s in the wake of the collapse of the South Sea Bubble and the rise of Robert Walpole. In the case of Methodism, that object was the London theater, which had retreated from controversy as a result of the Licensing Act, giving way to this new form of public theater as a focus for attention.

Whitefield's rhetorical gifts only advanced the analogy, as his capacity to seize the attention of his audience merited comparison with the best stage performers. Garrick was on record as saying that he "would give a hundred guineas if I could say 'O' like Mr. Whitefield," and another contemporary claimed that "every accent of his Voice, every Motion of his body *speaks.*"[69] These descriptions of early Methodism's theatricality are in a sense supported by the well-known hostility that Whitefield and Wesley bore to actors and the actual theater of their day. In his published journals, Whitefield recalled being dressed as a girl in school theatrical performances, a "remembrance" which, he said "has often covered me with confusion of face."[70] He preached against the theater and other forms of diversion throughout his career, most famously in 1759, when his attacks on the playhouses drew forth Samuel Foote's *The Minor,* a satirical attack on Methodism in which Whitefield appears as Dr Squintum. John Wesley (who claimed John Rich's wife as one of his devoted London followers) also discouraged his followers from attending the theater.[71] In his own journal for November 1743, Wesley took satisfaction in the story that a Newcastle performance of a satire called *Trick upon Trick, or Methodism Displayed* had to be called off when the stage collapsed under the performers' feet, as if it were a sign confirming the Lord's disapproval.[72] Whitefield and the Wesleys also seem to recognize the playhouses as rivals for the hearts and minds of potential followers. As Henry Abelove has pointed out, Methodists frequently rented old theaters, some of them put out of business by the Licensing Act, to serve as their chapels, and in London, they each opened chapels in Long Acre, quite close to the theaters.[73] And the players responded to the threat, not just with satires like *Methodism Displayed* and *The Minor,* but also more directly. As early as 1740, Charles Wesley was confronted by a group of actors who claimed "that the Gospel has starved them" and threatened to burn the house in which he was staying.[74] Whitefield complained to his patron the Countess of Huntington and then to the authorities that the playhouses were sending people to make noise outside his chapel at Long Acre in order to disrupt his sermons.[75] The Methodist founders and the playhouses took themselves to be engaged in a kind of competition, their mutual animosity fueled by an understanding of the ways in which they were similar. Abelove puts it well: "Perhaps the Methodists disapproved of adult play, and especially theater, because they had an ongoing theater of their own, which they liked better than the one that dramatists provided" (105).

The conflation of early Methodism with the theater suggests how the movement from ritual to entertainment that I described in chapter 2 had been turned on its head by mid-century. Now, religion was perceived to be following the example of the entertainment culture it had once excoriated, appealing to the masses by mimicking the theater, and by this means moving into its physical, conceptual, and psychic spaces. Methodism's emergence in the late 1730s and its extraordinary success over the next decades was not of course caused by the state's successful efforts at clearing the public sphere of other forms of theater. Rather, the frequent deployment of the analogy of the theater to early Methodism marks well how the imaginative scope of "theater" had spread over the course of the early eighteenth century, and how it would continue to blur the boundaries between the serious and satirical domains of culture.

CHAPTER SIX

Harlequin Walpole

PANTOMIME, FIELDING, AND THE
THEATER OF STATE IN THE 1730S

$\mathcal{T}$his is a chapter about the political public sphere in the 1730s, a decade that witnessed considerable civil and political unrest in Britain. The 1730s were also a decade in which the London theaters became increasingly politicized, to the point where, as is well known, the government imposed prior censorship in the form of the Stage Licensing Act of 1737 as a way of squelching political satire directed against it. Pantomime's relationship to the political events of this decade is complicated, or, perhaps more accurately, bifurcated. On the one hand, pantomime performances seem largely to have steered away from direct political commentary. As far as can be reconstructed from the available evidence, pantomimes of the 1730s did not join in the wave of pointed name-calling, a mode of staged satire that has long been associated with the Greek Old Comedian Aristophanes and that helped prompt the Licensing Act. But, on the other hand, pantomime's extraordinary prominence in the public sphere made it political in ways that far exceeded the content of the performances themselves. As we have already seen, pantomime became a focal point of the *cultural* politics of the 1720s, in particular the Scriblerian counterattack against the seeming debasement of culture that the prominence of these entertainments represented and furthered. More to the point for my argument in this chapter, pantomime was drawn into partisan political debate by opposition writers as a symbol for the corruption of the Walpole regime, with Harlequin occasionally serving as a figure for Walpole himself.

The analogy between the period's most notable form of public performance and the administration of the government identifies another place where the confusion between entertainment and what was supposed to be a serious domain of culture was felt in this period. Like the scene of execution or early Methodism, the state itself now seemed to be a kind of diversion, as the Walpole government was seen to be cynically manipulating the public in the manner of theatrical managers. One of the writers who advanced the analogy most frequently and cogently was Henry Fielding, who made the close conceptual relationship between the "political" and the "theatrical" into one of his favorite satirical targets, the object of a sustained critique that increased in intensity over the course of the decade. For Fielding, pantomime frequently becomes the symbol of the way that politics and entertainment had become confused, indistinguishable from one another, once-separate domains of culture that now seemed to be operating according to the same kinds of logic. Fielding was not alone in mounting this critique, nor was he above exploiting this confusion in his own works. One of the goals of this chapter is to contextualize Fielding's own theatrical afterpieces of the 1730s within the wider discourse over the place of entertainment that was catalyzed by pantomime. In the first part of this chapter, I describe the ways in which pantomime figured in public-sphere debates of the 1730s as a proxy for the Walpole regime. Then I offer an analysis of Fielding's afterpieces of that decade, which take the infiltration of entertainment into matters of state as the most important cause of the culture's decay. The dual critique of entertainment and administration that Fielding and others mounted in this decade offers a compelling forecast of the way that modern politics has been frequently disparaged as a form of diversion.

Pantomime and Politics in the 1730s

At the end of Henry Fielding's *The Historical Register for the Year 1736* (1737), the character of Quidam leads the other figures remaining onstage in a dance, a ridiculous performance so manic that it enables Quidam to pick up the money that spills from their pockets, a move described by the character of Medley as "a pretty pantomime trick, and an ingenious burlesque on all the *fourberies* which the great Lun has exhibited in all his entertainments."[1] This interpretation of Quidam's dance as a satire on John Rich ("Lun") may be enough to satisfy Medley, who as one of Fielding's many author figures has staged the scene as part of a play-within-the-play. But for Medley's creator Fielding and for the audience of *The Historical Register,* the joke cuts more deeply, as by this point in the play it has become abundantly clear that Quidam is also to be taken as a figure for Robert Walpole, the first minister of the government and a man whose craftiness and appetite for graft were well known. The analogy of Walpole to Rich and thence to the role of Harlequin in which he starred mocks Walpole as both greedy in the manner of a theater manager and also as cunning in the manner of a Harlequin himself, able to cheat others out of their money by using their own gullibility against them.[2] The originality of Fielding's analogy of Walpole to Harlequin in *The Historical Register* lies more in its framing as a performance within another performance than in the novelty of the comparison, for in many respects it merely invokes an equation between the two figures that had become commonplace in the course of the decade. Such a relationship would seem, however, to run somewhat counter to my argument in chapter 4 that pantomime was a comparatively nonpolitical form, and that it can be used to index a more general toning down of political content in the theaters and the public sphere more generally. To explain what changed, we have to look to the course of pantomime in the 1720s and 1730s and, even more important, to the course of the public sphere as well. By the 1730s, the nature of the relationship between the stage and the government had shifted in such a way that it would become possible to use pantomime as a figure to describe the operations of government itself.

Very few pantomimes of the 1720s and 1730s seem to have contained much explicit political, much less partisan, content. This is actually no surprise if, as I have argued, pantomime can be considered as a kind of replacement for partisanship in the public sphere of the 1720s, when, in the aftermath of the South Sea Bubble, the Walpole regime's rise to power had the effect of at least temporarily neutralizing the intense partisanship that had characterized public discourse in the first two decades of the century. It is instructive to compare *Perseus and Andromeda* (1730), which I described in chapter 1, with *Harlequin a Director,* a 1720 pantomime staged at Lincoln's Inn Fields that, given its title, no viewer could have mistaken for anything but a satire on the South Sea Company's directors and the bubble they inflated in the course of that year. No text or image of *Harlequin a Director* has survived, so we do not know exactly what its take on the Company was, or how it went about enacting that critique. But a contemporary newspaper review testifies to the pointedness of its satire on the Company's directors, as well as how effectively *Harlequin a Director* exposed financial dealings that had to a large extent been covered up, or, to use the contemporary metaphor, "screened" by the Walpole government. In *The Weekly Journal,* an anonymous reviewer claimed that *Harlequin a Director* "does not only ridicule the awkward Vanity of those imaginary great Men, who from Pigmies, were, of a sudden swelled up to Giants; but it also lets us into the most secret and iniquitous Part of the Management. . . . We learn as much of that Matter by this Dance, as by any Thing made publick to us."[3] Emphasizing the way that this performance indicates how pantomime might have political applicability, the reviewer goes on to argue that *Harlequin a Director* should be taken as a model for the construction of a "System of *political Dancing,* in which all the Intrigues, or State Arcanas may be represented," claiming that such a system would keep the theater from being suppressed by "the Hand of Power" because "what is not to be spoke, or writ, may be danced, without incurring the Penalty of *Scan. Mag.*"[4] The kind of direct applicability that such a system implies seems to have diminished by the time that pantomime achieved its greatest popularity a few years later. It would, for example, probably be impossible to extrapolate or even to imagine such a system based on the example of *Perseus and Andromeda,* which, I argued in chapter 1, contains only a general allegory of the relationship between political power and the spectator in the story of Perseus's defeat of Medusa, one that is as much an allegory of spectatorial relations in the theater itself as it is a story with a contemporary political application.

And *The Weekly Journal*'s waggish thought experiment remained no more than that; no such system by which dance steps could be used to convey partisan content was developed, and all the evidence suggests that, like most of the other performances on the stage in this period, pantomimes avoided explicit political statement. Such a claim seems counterintuitive, as we might, with the *Weekly Reviewer,* suppose that pantomime's nonverbal nature would permit it to evade censorship and thus to offer a certain degree of political content. This was the case, for example, in eighteenth-century France, where, Angela Goodden has asserted, satirical mimed performances flourished precisely in those moments when the authorities clamped down on the legitimate theater, providing a vehicle for political satire when it was being disallowed in mainpiece drama.[5] But in Britain, pantomimes exploited their nonverbal character by offering sexually suggestive physical action, rather than political satire, a feature that seems to have been inherited from the commedia tradition. In 1720, Richard Steele complained that the Harlequin and Colombine of a visiting company of Italian commedia performers all but simulated sexual intercourse onstage, to the great scandal of the audience, and it seems to be the case that English pantomime performers occasionally made bawdy or sexually suggestive gestures as well.[6] The *Grub-Street Journal* dryly mocked the frontispiece of *Harlequin-Horace,* which represents a scene from *Perseus and Andromeda* (reproduced in chapter 1) for having underplayed that performance's salaciousness ("in which the most lascivious acts, nearly tending to copulation itself, were repeatedly represented"), showing the women's skirts as being much lower than they were during the performance, and having the bishops looking away, "when it is certain that at the time of its being represented onstage, they were as observant of it as any Bishops could possibly be."[7] The most common complaints about pantomime on the grounds of its content seem to be about its bawdiness rather than its politics.

To be sure, there were exceptions to the general rule that pantomimes steered away from partisanship. During a performance of the pantomime *Love Runs all Dangers* in 1733, an actor improvised a joke about Walpole and his current Parliamentary battle over an excise tax; at the end of the performance, Walpole's son came backstage, and, after discovering that the words were not in the written scenario (which would have meant that the author could be prosecuted), "his Lordship immediately corrected the Comedian with his own Hands very severely."[8] This was just about all that Walpole junior could do, since the law did not readily admit prosecution where there was no text to put into evidence. And there were occasions when managers programmed performances that could have been taken to have political meaning, as, for example, in the fall of 1737 when Henry Giffard staged *Harlequin Shipwreck* every night for several weeks during a time when George II—then extremely unpopular because of the Gin Act—was expected to be returning to Britain across the Channel, a program that, Vincent Liesenfeld has suggested, "may have been seen as a morbid prediction of the king's fate."[9] But I have discovered no records of spontaneous political references being offered within performances. At best, it seems, pantomime afterpieces were suggestive without being explicit, offering the kinds of coded references that could not easily be prosecuted. The author of a 1738 pamphlet entitled *The Usefulness of the Stage* observes of pantomime performers that "I have often thought both their Dress and Meaning very Hieroglyphical, and seem to point to Particulars," that is, to specific public persons. But the author fails to offer examples of any such "Hieroglyphical" performances, and generally thinks of pantomime as a medium more popular with "School Boys, City Prentices, and Old Women" than the "Men of Sense" who would be interested in political satire.[10]

But if pantomime itself seems to have avoided direct political commentary, its extraordinary prominence in the 1720s and 1730s ensured that its most distinguishing features, most notably its star performer of Harlequin, would be deployed in public-sphere debates. As early as 1723, Harlequin and Walpole were understood to be the joint beneficiaries of a transfer of the political nation's collective attention from politics to entertainment. This is the burden of the lead article in *The Weekly Journal, or Saturday's Post* for June 15, 1723. The article is composed in the format of a short play, entitled "The Metamorphosis: or *Harlequin Cato*."[11] A satire on contemporary politics and political journalism, "The Metamorphosis" imagines Cato in very different terms than the ones put forth by Joseph Addison in his hit 1713 play, or even those advanced in John Trenchard and Thomas Gordon's extraordinarily popular (if occasionally dyspeptic) oppositional series *Cato's Letters* (1721–24). In these works, Cato is the ultimate figure of integrity and disinterested virtue, the emblem and focal point of resistance to the state's power over the individual. But through the logic of transformation offered by pantomime, the Cato of "The Metamorphosis" proves to be every bit as corruptible as any other "Man of the Times," quite willing to sacrifice principle to self-interest. At the start of the "play," Worthy and Johnson, two "honest Gentlemen," are observing how little actual news there is in spite of the ubiquity of newspapers and journals, a phenomenon that they clearly understand to be a new and distressing thing. They lament the resulting dullness of public discourse, in particular the way that dissenting voices have become increasingly rare as the government has bought them off.

Cato, once a reliable voice of dissent, proves no more able to resist temptation than anyone else. Led by "Doctor van Ticklenburgh" (a figure for Walpole) into an enchanted closet and plied with "the Argument of Arguments," that is, a generous bribe, Cato is transformed into a Harlequin, and proceeds to dance and jump over a stick at the Doctor's urging. Specifically, the act refers to the shift in loyalties of *The London Journal*, which had until recently been the home of *Cato's Letters*, but which had been bought by the government to become a propaganda organ for the Walpole ministry, forcing Trenchard and Gordon to move their antigovernment essays to *The British Journal*.[12] More broadly, by yoking Harlequin, the culture's marker of the theatrical, the protean, and the performative, with Cato, the symbol of self-identity and disinterestedness, "The Metamorphosis" describes the way that the money economy destabilizes human character into pantomimic excess, and turns politics into mere entertainment. To *The Weekly Journal*, affiliated at this time with the Tory opposition, "Harlequin Cato" sums up the substitution of popular entertainment for political dissent. In effect, it has already noted the shift in public discourse away from partisanship and politics that the Faustus entertainments would, as I argued in chapter 4, bring into much greater visibility a few months later.

To other observers of the public sphere in this period, pantomime not only served as a useful figure for describing the transformation of political discourse in the 1720s and 1730s, but as a piece of evidence about significant shifts in the contours of the culture as a whole. For Fielding's friend and occasional collaborator James Ralph, for example, pantomime's lack of personal, Aristophanic satire emblematizes a sea-change in the nature of public performance that repeats a similar change that took place in antiquity. Ralph's satirical survey of the "reigning Diversions of the Town," *The Touch-Stone* (1728), identifies pantomime as a sign of the depoliticization of the stage. Clearly drawing upon the research into the origins of theater in antiquity that, as we saw in chapter 2, late seventeenth- and early eighteenth-century writers used to argue that the theater emerged from ritual practices, Ralph narrates a story of how the "old Grecian COMEDY" had discredited itself by "abusing nominally Persons of the highest Stations and brightest Characters."[13] Forced to invent "feign'd Stories, which were confin'd to the meanest Events in low Life, after the Manner of our Modern Comedies," the Greek theater also began including more "Interludes of Singing and Dancing, in the way of *Mimickry* and *Buffoonry*" as an appropriate complement. From these comic interludes, "the *Mimes* and *Pantomimes* in *Greece* sprung up; from whence they were usher'd into *Rome* with vast Applause" (95).

Ralph's account of the transition from old to new comedy is hardly his own invention, and something close to this version of the story remains a standard paradigm for the history of the ancient Greek theater. But the close correspondence between the Greek theater as Ralph describes it and the recent history of the London stage suggests that his story has a locally applicable point. Ralph's account, I would suggest, offers the classical period as an allegory of early eighteenth-century Britain. In *The Touch-Stone*, Greek Old Comedy's practice of identifying specific individuals stands in for the abusive, name-calling, and scandalous early eighteenth-century public discourse that was succeeded by the considerably more quiescent public sphere of the 1720s. The modern pantomime emerges as the equivalent to the Greek mimes and pantomimes, not just as a mode of silent, comic performance, but as the replacement for scandalous, Aristophanic modes of satire. If my reading is correct, *The Touch-Stone* has to be seen as a *coded* work, one that offers a history of the Greek theater as a figure for the present. Ralph's recourse to allegory might be taken as testimony not only for his own inclinations but as a mark of the dangers that might still have been involved in describing the diversion of the theater from politics to mere entertainment more directly. What *The Touch-Stone* underscores more than anything else is that any discussion of the shift in dominant modes of comedy needs to be placed in a broader context than that of the theater alone, and understood as the sign of complex political and historical changes.

If pantomime's emergence as a mass-cultural fad in the early 1720s is indebted, then, to the clearing of other objects of attention from the public sphere, its content would do little to jeopardize this apparent divorce from politics, as the performances themselves typically retreated from partisanship and affairs of state, turning to myth, fairy tale, and romance in their stead. But its seemingly sudden rise to popularity at roughly the same time as that of the one-party rule of Robert Walpole—not merely a beneficiary of, but a primary agent behind the comparative clearing of the public sphere of the 1720s and 1730s of direct political reference and particularized critique— suggests that pantomime's apparent abstraction from its immediate context, its depiction of a timeless fantasy-land of nimble servants, gullible masters, and magic belied its opportunistic exploitation of a very particular set of conditions in its own political and cultural moment. Within a very short time, however, that very abstraction from politics would lead to a reversal, as it would appear that politics was encroaching on entertainment rather than the other way around.

This is the point of the line of critique about the rival "states" of the theater and the nation in these decades that we have already seen Fielding deploy, one in which Harlequin and Walpole are made to stand as analogous figures. Perhaps the fullest articulation of the comparison before Fielding's is offered by a 1731 satirical print on pantomime, "The Stage's Glory," which closely mirrors a 1730 panegyric, "To the Glory of the Rt. Hon. Sir Robert Walpole." Most of Walpole's propaganda took verbal form, making "To the Glory of the Rt. Hon. Sir Robert Walpole" a rare thing, a pro-Walpole *image*. "To the Glory, etc." displays the first minister, accompanied by his "Guides" "Fame" and "Policy," receiving a Duke's coronet from Minerva, whose speech-banner announces (in Latin, translated in the explanation on the side) that "It equals not his labors." The conceit is that Walpole's efforts on behalf of the nation

"The Stage's Glory" (© *Copyright The British Museum*)

"To the Glory of the Rt. Honorable Sr. Robert Walpole"
(© *Copyright The British Museum*)

resemble those of Hercules; having destroyed a hydra whose heads are labeled "Envy," "Detraction," "Impudence," and "Disquiet," Walpole's strength fulfills the "Anagram" made of his name: "Thou England that fear nothing by Land may boldly sail ye Seas; WALPOLE who is the Strong WALL that guards thee there shall be thy POLE at Sea." "The Stage's Glory" similarly associates Harlequin with Hercules, claiming that he can "kill the Spleen" as the other destroyed the hydra. More to the point, the print associates Harlequin with Walpole, and uses the most notable qualities of each to serve as a comment on the other. Thus Harlequin's guides "Pierro" and the Doctor attest their loyalty to "Folly" and "Fortune," rather than the "Fame" and "Policy" that the other print identifies as the source of Walpole's success, thereby undercutting them. In turn, "Folly" and "Fortune" reward Harlequin with a shower of gold rather than a ducal coronet, an act that suggests that both figures have profited from their positions.

The print repeatedly attributes Harlequin's prosperity to his skill at "Craft," making "Craft is my Lot" into the motto of Harlequin's coat of arms (which features a devil from the Faustus pantomimes, a dog drawn from Rich and Theobald's *Perseus and Andromeda,* and a monkey, the emblem of Harlequin's mimicry.) In the oppositional discourse of the 1730s, "Craft" was a heavily laden term, referring—with a strongly negative connotation—to Walpole's unmatched skill at the art or "craft" of political maneuvering; for opposition journals like *The Craftsman,* it described how the government had withdrawn debate from the public sphere, where political issues could ideally be argued by disinterested citizens, and replaced it with cynical manipulation and horse-trading, most of which was conducted behind a screen of state-subsidized propaganda (of which "To the Honor of Sr. Robt Walpole" would be a prime example).[14] The close mimicry between the careers of Walpole and Harlequin on display in "The Stage's Glory" shows how the "glory" of each derives from their ability to fool a credulous public. Both men's place at the center of the public sphere depends on the fact that so much has been shunted away from it, removed from public view. This is why "The Stage's Glory" uses the emblems in the columns at the side to display scenes where Harlequin clearly puts profit ahead of art: choosing "Momus" (the god of mockery) over Apollo, leading players to a realm of "Plenty and Coin," destroying the works of Shakespeare. These scenes, depicting most of the crimes of which pantomime's opponents accused it, visually dramatize the otherwise-hidden operations of the 1730s culture industry, pulling the screen away from the practices of the patent theaters as *The Craftsman's* writers were attempting to do to the practices of the Walpole regime.

Yet as it analogizes Harlequin to Walpole to expose the self-interest at the heart of theatrical and political craft, "The Stage's Glory" identifies an ironic reversal in the relationship between politics and entertainment; having accomplished the separation from partisanship that Whig playwrights and theorists desired, entertainment now seemed to provide models for political practice, and to figure the operations of state power. Given the way that entertainment served as a model for politics, it was reasonable by the 1730s to wonder how it might be possible to tell them apart. Where is the boundary line, and how could we know it if we were to see it? Fielding's afterpieces of the 1730s can be understood as a sustained meditation on this question.

Fielding's Entertainments, the Critical Gaze, and the Violence of History

There is a sense, of course, in which the Stage Licensing Act of 1737 defined the line between entertainment and politics in a particularly stark way. By demanding that the London playhouses submit to prior censorship, the Walpole government was in effect claiming that the theaters' productions had crossed the line into impermissible areas, as they were now taking on subjects that were more properly the purview of the state; from this point of view, the act "restored" the relationship to its normative condition. Fielding's relationship to the act was in some respects brutally simple: by in effect forcing him out of business as a playwright, it changed the direction of his career away from the theater and toward fiction and the law. But in most ways, his relationship to the act, and, more important, to the state that issued it, was more complicated than that summation would suggest. As a number of critics have shown over the last two decades, it oversimplifies the situation to claim, as was sometimes argued in the past, that Fielding's political satires of the 1730s are more or less enough to account for Walpole's successful prosecution of the act, which needs rather to be attributed to a number of interbraided causes.[15] There *was* an increase in the number and intensity of satires against the government, Fielding's included, in the 1730s, and the government had already intervened to stop theatrical productions that it believed were openly hostile to it, such as *Polly,* the sequel to John Gay's *The Beggar's Opera,* which was halted in 1729, and *The Fall of Mortimer,* an allegory of the Walpole regime that was banned in 1731.

But Walpole's concern and his ability to marshal support against such plays, and ultimately to pass the Licensing Act, were also prompted by the widespread public agitation and occasional rioting over the effects of the Gin Act in 1736. And, too, these scenes of unrest were the culmination of a more inchoate discontent that had been observable since at least the time of Walpole's attempt to pass the Excise Act in 1733–34. Finally, we could, with the eyes of an economic historian, identify how these discrete events were collectively stoked by weakening economic conditions owing in part to overproduction in the colonies, a political-economic crisis that first led the Walpole regime to adopt a more aggressive and costly military stance and which would ultimately drive it from power.[16] The oppositional theater of the 1730s fed, focused, and became particularly obvious and actionable expressions of a more general discontent. To the extent that the event that we might call "Fielding's silencing" has dominated understanding of the Stage Licensing Act, it simplifies more complex histories and formal trajectories.

One of the things that is lost in that narrative is how fully Fielding's critique of the government is intertwined with his critique of contemporary entertainments. As Thomas Lockwood has argued, at the start of the 1736–37 season—which turned out to be Fielding's last as a working playwright and theatrical manager—he set out with two roughly equivalent objects of satire in view: pantomime and the Walpole government.[17] In fact, throughout his career as a playwright, Fielding frequently mocked pantomime, beginning with the puppet-show that closes *The Author's Farce* (1730), where a silent "Monsieur Pantomime" (a proxy for John Rich) gestures to his broken neck; what seems to be left deliberately unclear is whether his neck was broken as the result of a bad fall in the course of one of his acrobatic performances or because he has been hanged for his crimes against literary culture. Fielding satirizes pantomime perhaps most comprehensively in *Tumble-Down Dick,* a 1736 satire on the now-lost *Harlequin Phaeton* that pits an author-figure named Fustian (a proxy for Fielding) against the theater manager "Machine" (another proxy for Rich), who insists that Fustian make deep cuts in the Shakespearian mainpiece in order to allow more time for the ridiculous pantomime entertainment that follows. Fielding would continue to target pantomime in fiction as well, offering a famous definition of the form at the beginning of Book V of *Tom Jones,* one that is significant for the way that it silently recognizes even its own creator to be implicated in the confusing effects of modern entertainment. Fielding's narrator describes Rich's "most exquisite Entertainment" as follows:

> This Entertainment consisted of two Parts, which the Inventor distinguished by the Names of *the Serious* and *the Comic.* The *Serious* exhibited a certain Number of heathen Gods and Heroes, who were certainly the worst and dullest Company into which an Audience was ever introduced; and (which was a Secret known to few) were actually intended to be so, in order to contrast the *Comic* Part of the Entertainment, and to display the Tricks of Harlequin to better Advantage.
>
> This was, perhaps, no very civil Use of such Personages; but the contrivance was nevertheless ingenious enough, and had its Effect. And this will now plainly appear, if instead of *Serious* and *Comic,* we apply the Words *Duller* and *Dullest;* for the *Comic* was certainly duller than any thing before shewn on the Stage, and could only be set off by that superlative Degree of Dulness, which composed the *Serious.* So intolerably serious, indeed, were these Gods and Heroes, that Harlequin (tho' the *English* Gentleman of that Name is not at all related to the *French* Family, for he is of a much more serious Disposition) was always welcome on the Stage, as he relieved the Audience from worse Company.[18]

What the sarcastic tone of the narrator's joke obscures is that he intends this description to serve as an explanation of his own practice in providing "serious" and "comic" sections in *Tom Jones* itself; the same principle of "contrast" holds for both forms, making Fielding at least in some respects the functional equivalent of Rich. To that degree, at least, Fielding's mocking description of Rich's afterpieces has to be read as deeply self-ironizing, as if to admit the difficulty of distinguishing between one form of entertainment—pantomime—and the other—the "comic-epic in prose"—once the inventor of each has made up his mind to attempt to please an audience in the public sphere.[19]

Fielding's irony is disarming, but his analysis is not completely original, and might in fact be understood as the shrewd co-optation of an association that had for some years been made by others. In comparing himself to Rich, Fielding follows a line of argument that journalists had begun to outline in the early 1730s, when his first plays were sometimes equated with the lesser entertainments such as pantomime that had come to dominate the London theater.[20] Thus at the top of the left-hand cornice in "The Stage's Glory" the small "Genius" holds a copy of Fielding's *Tom Thumb*, which is here marked as one of the pieces that has benefited from pantomime's popularity (the other genius reads a copy of *Hurlothrumbo*, the peculiar 1729 play that was an improbable hit for its author, Samuel Johnson of Cheshire). Similarly, *The Universal Spectator* for April 10, 1731, decries the current "want of Taste" exercised by London theatergoers, lamenting how "our Stages are polluted with the Conjurations of an *Harlequin Faustus,* or render'd yet more ridiculous, from the Feats of a *Tom Thumb,*" referring of course in the last example to Fielding's *The Tragedy of Tragedies.*[21] Fielding's frequent mockery of pantomime separates his own plays from it in a critical context that, he was surely aware, was inclined at first to consider them as similar forms of entertainment.

The element of truth in this comparison is that Fielding *was* to some extent indebted to the success of pantomime in the 1720s, as it established the afterpiece as potentially a more popular and noteworthy part of the evening's performance schedule than the five-act mainpiece that had to that point been the primary object of critical attention and the central attraction for audiences. Fielding himself, as critics have frequently remarked, consistently attempted to succeed with traditional, five-act comedies and consistently failed, both with audiences and with critics, then and now. By contrast, Fielding's afterpieces were frequently enormous hits and critical successes. Fielding's short afterpieces undertake a spirited reconceptualization of the afterpiece "entertainment" itself, one that, I argue, was enabled by the success of pantomime, and was designed to co-opt its audience for the purposes of profit and instruction. Fielding moved into a marketplace defined and opened up by pantomime's great success in the 1720s, taking advantage of the acceptance and prominence of such performances to reclaim the afterpiece as a vehicle for more serious content.

This, in fact, is the burden of Aaron Hill's endorsement of Fielding's *Pasquin* in his journal *The Prompter* in April 1736, which is also significant for the way that it points us to the relationship to the visual that Fielding embraces in his afterpieces. Citing *Pasquin's* success as a sign that "the stage may (and as it may, ought to) be supported without pantomime," Hill observes that

> While our theatric sovereigns, with the best actors the age can afford, are forced to call in the assistance of wonderful scenery, surprising transformations, beautiful landscapes, dancers (the very best, both in the graceful and humorous manner) and in short all the attendant powers of inexplicable dumb shew, at very great expense, a gentleman under the disadvantage of a very bad house, with scarce an actor, and at very little expense, by the single power of satire, wit, and common sense, has been able to run a play on for 24 nights, which is now but beginning to rise in the opinion of the Town.[22]

As he endorses Fielding's attempt to replace pantomime as the favored entertainments for fashionable audiences, Hill argues that Fielding's afterpieces have a strong relationship to the visual arts, bringing over into performed satire such painterly elements as "the Stile of *Corregio*" (to display "common sense"), the "bold, daring Pencil of *Michael Angelo*" (to convey the force of tragedy), and even at times "a *Flemish* Touch, for the sake of the *Vulgar*."[23]

Hill's claim for the visuality of Fielding's afterpieces might seem surprising given the comparative lack of visual spectacle that Hill also praises as one of their distinguishing features, the sign of their seriousness and claim to literary excellence. Comparative, that is, to pantomime, and I take this to be the point: Fielding deliberately avoids the more objectionable components of pantomimic spectacles à la John Rich, eschewing dance, special effects, and elaborate scenery at every turn. In this way he signals not only his contempt for Rich, but his fealty to a conception of literature that he identifies with the word, a conception that is threatened by the modern theater's reliance on spectacle. That Fielding's resistance is particularly focused on pantomime in these works is perhaps most obvious at the end of *The Author's Farce*. As four poets try to cobble together an epilogue for the performance just past, Luckless brings on a cat that he proposes will "act the epilogue in dumb shew"—that is, pantomime. The cat, an obvious corollary to the

famous dog performed by Rich's Harlequin in *Perseus and Andromeda*—
which was, by no casual coincidence, the afterpiece against which *The
Author's Farce* was competing on its opening night in 1730—goes offstage
and returns as a woman.[24] She speaks an epilogue on the similarity between
women and cats, and ends by suggesting that women would be happy to see
their husbands transformed as well, in which case

> Many a Lord, who now his Fellows scorns
> Would then exceed a Cat by nothing—but his Horns. (63)

Jill Campbell has demonstrated that it is characteristic of Fielding to consider gender as a kind of "theatrical" construction, a conception that he views
with considerable ambivalence and suspicion.[25] For Fielding, the theatricality of gender threatens the stability of the social order, invoking the specter
of "petticoat government," a regime where women rule over men. The cat-
woman's speech might serve as confirmation of Campbell's insights about
Fielding's gender politics, and the manner in which this particular instance
of the threatened leveling of the sexes is staged confirms my argument about
what we might think of as the politics of spectatorship as well. Shunting the
crucial change of cat to woman offstage, Fielding deliberately refuses to gratify his era's desire to witness the spectacular transformations of pantomime,
demanding rather that we listen to his words and attend to the implications
of "transformation" in its broadest senses. There is a very real sense, then, in
which we can think of Fielding as a profoundly *antitheatrical* playwright, as
he systematically refuses to deploy the full range of the theater's apparatus.

Still, Hill's argument has merit if we think of Fielding's visuality in
metaphorical rather than literal terms. Fielding's afterpiece entertainments
appeal to the visual register of his audience in an abstract as much as a sensual dimension, offering their spectators a "view" into the inner workings of
the entertainment and political cultures that had come, by the 1730s, to be
taking cues from each other. Placing both the stage and the state in our critical "gaze" at once, Fielding's afterpieces urge us to *see* how their similarity is
the basis of their mutual corruption. Much as Jeremy Collier had composed
a "Short View" of the English stage in 1698 that was neither short nor, more
to the point here, particularly interested in visuality except as a metaphor for
the act of criticism, Fielding engages sight, not as an aspect of the performances he stages, but rather as a figure that enables him to pull aside the veils
of obfuscation and reification that the government and the theater had come
to rely upon to secure their authority.

Much the same logic shapes Fielding's political essays of the same period, which consistently aim to construct a proper "view" of whatever subject— the criminal class, the indigent—that forms the object of his and his readers' attention at that moment. The applicability of stage practice and theatrical metaphors is obvious in these cases, and it is worth noting that it is possible to identify this same desire to construct a quasi-visual relation to the socius in some of Fielding's political journalism from the 1730s, when he was simultaneously writing for the stage. In *The Craftsman* for March 23, 1734, for example, Fielding offers a sustained attack on the Walpole government's well-known penchant for concealing "the *Mysteries of State* from vulgar Eyes" by erecting "Screens" that serve to hide the workings (and particularly the transgressions) of government ministers.[26] As was commonly known, Walpole became famous as the "Screenmaster-General" of the nation for the way in which he covered up the involvement of the king, the king's mistress, and other high-ranking members of the government in the South Sea scheme in 1720, and Walpole continued to keep most of the operations of what Fielding calls "the whole Machine of Government" out of the public view through most of his career. Fielding claims a discursive vantage point that gives him critical leverage on both the state and the stage, as each becomes the object of a rational view that permits us to see behind surface appearances to the true causes of social and cultural problems. It is this vantage point that ultimately keeps the citizen from being, as Fielding says in *The Champion* in April 1740, "like the spectators of one of Mr. Rich's entertainments," so bamboozled by the spectacle that we fail to see beneath of the surface of either the entertainment or the examples of "political pantomime" that similarly aim to hide the "springs of the political motion."[27] In what follows, I want to specify how this dual critique frames the relationship between entertainment and the state, suggesting both what it opens to *our* critical view and what it screens off.

Fielding's first major success, *The Author's Farce,* situates itself in the broader milieu of performed entertainments in London, what the title of its own afterpiece, a "puppet-show" designed to be performed by human actors, calls the "Pleasures of the Town." Here Monsieur Pantomime (Rich) is joined by the bookseller Curry (Edmund Curll), Signior Opera (the castrato Senesino), Dr. Orator (John Henley), Mrs. Novel (Eliza Haywood), Don Tragedio (Lewis Theobald), and Sir Farcical Comic (Colley Cibber), constituting a full set of the entertainments available to contemporary Londoners.[28] Fielding's point of entry into this milieu is the figure of the individual author, embodied in the lead character, Luckless, an impoverished writer (and surely in part an avatar for Fielding himself) who is unable to get a play produced or a book published. We can read this orientation as already a gesture of resistance to contemporary entertainments such as pantomime and opera, which devalued the role of the author in favor of the power of the spectacle or the star performer. As one of Fielding's many other author-figures, Fustian of *Pasquin* complains, some of the "fine parts of their best authors" are cut from the evening's performance at contemporary theaters, to make room for "pantomimes, of which the master of the play-house, two or three painters, and half a score dancing-masters are the compilers."[29]

Acutely aware of the pressure on modern authors, Luckless's friend Witmore puts Luckless's situation into its broader context: "now, when Party and Prejudice carry all before them, when Learning is decried, Wit not understood, when the Theatres are Puppet-Shows, and the comedians Ballad-Singers: When Fools lead the Town, wou'd a Man think to thrive by his Wit? If you must write, write Nonsense, write Opera's, write Entertainments, write Hurlo-thrumbo's" (8). Fielding's object, then, is not so much Luckless's own plight as it is the relationship between the author who aspires to fulfill his aspirations to literary standards and status and the broader systems of publishing and play-production that mitigate against any such hopes. In Fielding's play, Marplay and Sparkish, figures for the actor-managers Robert Wilks and Colley Cibber, revel in their own cynicism as they turn away new plays, content to exploit the repertoire of stock plays by authors who demanded no compensation and the afterpieces that frequently had no single author to claim the proceeds of a benefit performance; as Marplay announces, showing his contempt for the audience, "any Man who loves hissing may have his three Shillings worth at me whenever he pleases" (18). Or, turning to the publishing industry, Fielding portrays the hacks at work in Mr. Bookweight's (Curll's) garret, churning out translations and pamphlets by the pound.

What is most important about Fielding's strategy in *The Author's Farce* is the way in which it brings the structural relationships that now determine what enters the public sphere as art into full view, displaying the true nature of the culture industry as it exploits author and audience alike. The rehearsal frame that Fielding adapts from the Restoration-era stalwart *The Rehearsal*, first produced in 1671 and frequently updated to reflect current theatrical trends ever since, brings the relationship between that constellation and the spectators onstage, presenting a case study in the phenomenology of spectatorship. The effect of this strategy, in which the institutions and material practices that mediate between the author and the spectator are made into an object of study in their own right, is to render our absorption in the spectacle impossible, to force the viewer of *The Author's Farce* to adopt a critical relation to the performance in front of him.[30] In Fielding's rehearsal plays, spectators who lose sight of the distinction between the entertainment onstage and the real world they inhabit are subject to mockery. An example is Lord Dapper of *The Historical Register,* a character from the rehearsal frame who starts to bid during the auction scene being staged in Medley's play within the play. Fielding's entertainment is fashioned to resist the absorption of the viewer in the spectacle placed before him; its ideal viewer is prompted to keep the several layers of performative satire separate in order to analyze their relationship critically and in so doing to keep the entire entertainment at arm's length.

The Historical Register for the Year 1736 extends virtually all of the strategies of *The Author's Farce,* erecting a virtual hall of mirrors of spectatorship where the relationship between spectator and performance is staged and then immediately outdone by being contained within yet another spectatorial frame. But more so than the earlier play, *The Historical Register* brings such relationships explicitly into the orbit of political critique. Fielding's author-figure, Medley, asserts the seamlessness of the analogy between the state and the theater, the degree to which "the political" is "connected with your theatrical": "When my politics come to a farce, they very naturally lead to the playhouse where, let me tell you, there are some politicians too, where there is lying, flattering, dissembling, promising, deceiving, and undermining, as well as in any court in Christendom" (16). As we have seen, *The Historical Register* has sometimes been taken as the prime cause of the Licensing Act's passage, a simplification of a much more complicated situation that nonetheless contains at least one element of truth: *The Historical Register* represents, as many critics have noted, a more explicit attack on contemporary politics than Fielding had mounted before.

In an anonymously published pamphlet supporting *The Historical Register* and intended to fend off any government plan to censor the playhouses, Fielding argues that any restraint on the theater on the part of the state would "intirely destroy the old Comedy, which seems at present greatly to flourish" because "we have an Author who is an acknowledged Proficient": that is, Fielding himself. The implicit claim is that his own practice of offering direct satire of individual persons—in *The Historical Register,* Colley and Theophilus Cibber, the auctioneer Christopher Cock, and of course Walpole—returns to the manner of Greek Old Comedians such as Aristophanes.[31] Fielding's invocation of old comedy recalls Ralph's argument in *The*

Touch-Stone from a few years earlier, where he had taken the form's decline to mark the depoliticization of the Greek theater, a move that, I argued, Ralph saw as being paralleled by the English theater's retreat from explicit satire in the 1720s. Here Fielding announces that he is in effect attempting to reverse the course of this narrative, that he intends to return public discourse to the direct, highly politicized character of the period before the South Sea Bubble and the advent of the entertainments that had avoided explicit political reference.[32]

But to understand the logic of Fielding's title and the frame it constructs for this, the next-to-last of his afterpiece entertainments, we need to expand *our* frame beyond literary-critical categories such as Aristophanic satire to include the discourse of governmentality, the attempt to deploy critical reason in matters of the state and its people. For Fielding's announced return to the historical real with *The Historical Register* is a programmatic aspect, not just of the play's satirical content, but of its form as well. Fielding's gloss on his own play points us to the ways in which *The Historical Register* appropriates the assumptions of the nonfiction work to which its title refers, which represents an attempt to deploy reason in the service of producing knowledge about the state. The actual *Historical Register,* published since 1716, was a volume that reviewed the events of the past year in Britain and, where they impacted on British concerns, Europe, and the colonies. In most cases, this was achieved by putting together excerpts from a variety of already printed sources, but even a pastiche is guided by principles of selection. In the case of *The Historical Register,* these principles constructed a particular kind of frame, defining what counts as "history" as those events that occur in a defined space within the span of a calendar year. The space is that of the nation-state, now understood to be the organizing principle for history itself; foreign events were included insofar as they impacted significant interests within Great Britain. What is more, the genre of the annual account rationalizes experience in terms of time, subjecting it to a modern, routinized mode of temporality, one organized by the calendar rather than, say, the life-span of a monarch.[33]

The significance of such a rationalized approach gains a new dimension once we realize that *The Historical Register* was originally a house publication of the Sun Fire Office, a London insurance company founded in 1710. The logic by which an insurance company would sponsor such a publication is not hard to discern. The annualized account gathered and published the very kinds of information about the public sphere that helped manage and contain risk, an effort in which policy-holders in insurance schemes could be expected to have a stake. In the case of *The Historical Register*, this information was presented as a kind of truth that had a particular force because of the way in which it was abstracted from either the biases of party politics or the unreliability of weekly journals that must publish in the maelstrom of events; as its first issue declared, the *Register* "shall not, like the common News-Papers, be cramm'd with the Hopes, or Fears, or Surmises of Parties or Factions," and, by not being bound to the pace of journals, it will also print only "such Things" as "Time . . . has already stamp'd with the undeniable Mark of Truth."[34] Such claims work to differentiate *The Historical Register* from other kinds of representation in the contentious public sphere of the 1710s, specifying the nature of its appeal to general and abstract norms rather than partial or particular ones. The annualized account, of which *The Historical Register* was an early example, might be understood as one of the public-sphere genres of popular governmentality; it brought the activities of the entire state into representation in an explicitly rational way, frequently supporting its claims with chronicles and statistics, as if to dramatize the objectivity of the facts it contained.

The Historical Register had severed its financial connection to the Sun Fire Office long before the first performances of Fielding's play in 1737, but its program of rationalization and abstraction still has bearing on the shaping and significance of his farce. Fielding appropriates the name of the well-known annual account as a way of giving his most partisan and critical work to date the pretense to objectivity, an objectivity founded in the annual's appeals to the impersonal span of the calendar and the nonpartisan site of the nation-state. He thereby motivates and claims the value of truth for the critical viewpoint that, as I have argued, his afterpieces offer as their salient contribution to the analysis of the states political and theatrical. They are, in effect, works of governmentality in the mode of entertainment, works that long precede Fielding's writings in the more conventional genres of the discourse in the form of his remarkable essays of the early 1750s on subjects like poor relief and urban criminality (works that, in a reversal of perspective that is nonetheless entirely consistent with Fielding's stance in his afterpieces, identify public "diversion" as one of the most important objects of the state's regulatory capacity). *The Historical Register*'s appropriation of the annual account's objective frame suggests that Fielding's sympathy with, if not perhaps his intimate knowledge of, governmentality began much earlier than his formal assimilation into the government itself.

But Fielding's allusion to *The Historical Register* also proposes a kind of challenge, daring us to compare the representation of the state of the nation in 1736 that he presents onstage, not so much with the historical real, the never completely knowable state of things as they "really" happened, but with the account of the year as compiled in the competing version of 1736 published under the very same name. Fielding's analysis of "history" in these afterpieces consistently frames it as the mutually constitutive relationship between the state and the products of culture, rather than, say, the actions of the monarch or the daily experience of the people. These are just two of the other frames through which history has been constructed at different times and in different places, and they remind us that there are other ways to conceptualize history than that assumed by Fielding's comparison between the political and theatrical states. Indeed, that comparison, I would argue, has the effect, and perhaps the intent, of seeming to provide a complete and fully adequate account of the state of things at any moment, to appear to be mapping the entirety of British culture by identifying how two of its most salient domains seem to be operating according to the same logic.

We need look no farther than the annual *Historical Register* for 1736, however, to see a very different understanding of what history might entail and comprehend. Comparing Fielding's farce with the account of 1736 in *The Historical Register*, what is striking is not only the (obvious) complete difference in tone, but the fact that Fielding's play fails to take any notice of the most urgent public crisis of that year, the widespread unrest and rioting throughout the country. In the course of the year, riots broke out in the west of England, in Spitalfields, and most seriously in Edinburgh (the "Porteus" riots). There were also a number of public protests in London over the passage of the Gin Act of 1736, which was designed to reduce the consumption of gin by the working class by greatly raising its price.[35] It is a testimony to the continuing power of Fielding's beloved world-as-stage metaphor that such uprisings have frequently been described in terms of theater, as, for example, in the work of E. P. Thompson, who saw in such uprisings a "counter-theater" of the people opposing the "theater" of patrician power.[36] Thompson understands such protests to constitute a collective response to the incursion of capitalist logic into traditional culture, such that "customary" rights and practices—the right to common land, the right to buy bread at an affordable price—were being overruled by the claims of the market.

Whether or not we comprehend these acts of resistance through the figure of the theater, what is clear is that they greatly alarmed the government and prompted debate in Parliament in search of a "general Cause" that would explain why so much unrest could have sprung up in so many different places at roughly the same time. To one unnamed member of the House of Lords, that "Cause" could be identified as "oppression and the neglect in the civil magistrate," a formulation that seems at first glance to be contradictory, as if it is blaming the government both for being too overbearing and inattentive at once.[37] The contradiction resolves itself, however, if we understand the peer's argument to be directed against the Walpole regime's attempts to impose the central government's power (read: "oppression") over domains of the society that had customarily been the object of what he takes to be the comparatively benign supervision of more locally based sources of authority ("the civil magistrate"). For Thompson, this diagnosis needs to be read as itself a symptom of an even more fundamental cause: the rearticulation of time and space that constitutes modern capitalist society, and for which the events of 1736 recorded in *The Historical Register* mark a particularly acute flashpoint. Fielding's *Historical Register* does not refer to or analyze these events, nor does it describe the government's attempts to understand what had prompted the disturbances.

Fielding's reticence is all the more remarkable when we consider that the London playhouses contained their own scenes of unrest in 1736, scenes performed in the pit and the gallery rather than behind the proscenium arch. These uprisings took the form of a series of riots over the right of footmen sent in advance in order to hold seats for their employers to occupy a gallery of their own, from which they were known to participate aggressively in praising or mocking the production onstage. These were not, however, riots incited by the footmen, but rather middle-class riots, in which members of the pit rose up to put a stop to the footmen's obstreperous behavior. The most notorious incident occurred on February 19, 1737, when the "theater" *within* the Drury Lane playhouse had the effect of negating the performance onstage, which happened to be the first performance of Fielding's afterpiece *Eurydice.* In chapter 3, I argued that, from the point of view of middle-class theatergoers, what had become intolerable was that the footmen's rowdiness was now understood to be usurping their betters' claim to have a monopoly on critical judgment. From the point of view of the footmen, however, the gallery and the ability to launch judgments from it had attained the status of a "customary" right, a tradition that they claimed was so long-standing as to have practically the force of constitutional law. In truth, this custom was not particularly ancient, but neither was the middle class's "right" to a monopoly on taste, either. These conflicting claims were both the products of modern shifts in, among other things, the constitution of the audience, the relationship between social classes, and the rules of public conduct. While there is no direct causal linkage between this riot and the widespread disturbances of the previous year, it seems clear that the swiftness and intensity of the government's reaction to the footmen's riots—calling out troops to restore order, having the Riot Act read to the audience in the theater—was probably owing to the fear that it might spill over and reignite tensions in the streets. All of these events, and, more important, the reasons for the social discontent that prompted them, occupy a significant place in the journalistic *Historical Register,* but are gestured to only very obliquely in Fielding's version. (We will discuss *Eurydice Hiss'd,* his response to the debacle of *Eurydice,* its first and only performance overwhelmed by the riot in the theater, shortly.)

To be sure, it is not as though Fielding never alludes to the public unrest of the decade in his afterpieces. In 1736's *Pasquin,* for example, a "Mob" appears onstage, according to the stage direction, "*crying out promiscuously, Down with the Rump, No Courtiers! No Jacobites! Down with the Pope! No Excise! a Place and a Promise! a Fox chase and a Tankard! At last they fall together by the ears, and cudgel one another off the stage*" (147). And in *Tumble-Down Dick,* produced the same year, Fielding alludes to the Gin Act and parodies pantomime at once when, in a satire on the conventional scene whereby a magician or spirit gives Harlequin the magic wand that carries his transformative powers, he casts the spirit as the "Genius of Gin" (20). The closest thing to a referent to the popular upheaval of the last year in *The Historical Register* itself occurs in the auction scene, when in the course of auctioning off a bottle of courage, the auctioneer Christopher Hen assures the bidders that it is without a crack even though "it has been in many engagements in Tothill Fields" and "has served a campaign or two in Hyde Park," both the sites of riots in August 1736 (31). So oblique a reference downplays the significance of the public unrest in the year that the play purports to "register," but even the more direct references in *Pasquin* and *Tumble-Down Dick* are fairly dismissive, depicting the rioters as a disorderly and incoherent mob. What Fielding's satires offer, then, is less the "historical register" of their moment that they advertise and will eventually identify themselves with, but a particular interpretation, one that conceptualizes the events of the mid-1730s very much through the filter of Fielding's dual critique, whereby the government and current entertainments seem fully to represent the state of the culture.

It is perhaps only in Fielding's very last afterpiece, *Eurydice Hiss'd, or a Word to the Wise,* which opened on April 13, 1737, just a few weeks before the Licensing Act was passed, that we can recognize his awareness that this critique actually has the effect of positioning him, not in some transcendent critical position outside both the state and the debased elements of the culture industry, but very much inside both. In particular, it collapses any distinction that Fielding had been trying to construct between the figure of the individual author and the broader systems of state and theatrical management that, from *The Author's Farce* on, had been its nemesis. *Eurydice Hiss'd* stages the failure of Fielding's *Eurydice* the previous year. In yet another play-within-the-play, the author figure Pillage attempts to pack the house with pliant friends and clients who will cheer his new play, *Eurydice,* in order to ensure its success. Pillage is perhaps the least attractive of all of Fielding's author-figures, as he is not only hapless but brazenly contemptuous of his actors and his audience, attesting that he is willing to "let after-ages damn me if they please" so long as he is able to "fill my loaded pockets with their pence."[38] The locus of moral virtue in *Eurydice Hiss'd* is neither Spatter (the author figure in the frame play) nor Pillage, but the character of Honestus, who urges his friend Pillage to

> give us a good tragedy for our money,
> And let not Harlequin still pick our pockets,
> With his low paltry tricks and juggling cheats,
> Which any school-boy, was he on the stage,
> Could do as well as he—In former times,
> When better actors acted better plays,
> The town paid less. (10:265)

Honestus's nostalgia marks him as a model civic humanist, the incorruptible citizen much featured in oppositional fantasies of the 1730s. His identification of Harlequin with the debased theater of the present that Pillage has all too readily agreed to serve helps make clear that Fielding/Pillage's mercenary turn in *Eurydice*—whose raw material of classical myth it, of course, shared with pantomime productions of the same story in the decade—conforms to rather than resists the typical practices of the decade. Pillage's effort fails, of course, as the audience turns against *Eurydice,* and even the friends he has planted in the house join in the hissing or slink away. Characteristically, Fielding resists representing the riot in *Eurydice Hiss'd,* preferring once again to describe rather than display spectacle. We only hear of the riots in the theater at second hand. Where Fielding had earlier pushed the spectacular scenes and special effects of Rich's vulgar entertainments outside the frame of representation, now he takes care that the "theater" of the masses remains offstage, contained wholly within language rather than offered directly to the eyes and ears of his audiences.

The most remarkable fact about *Eurydice Hiss'd,* however, is the way that Pillage functions as a figure for Walpole as well as for Fielding. The equation between the two is established from the very start of the play, when Spatter describes Pillage as "a very great man," (10:261), the sobriquet by which Walpole was widely known. The play repeatedly underscores the parallels between Fielding, the manager of the playhouse, and Walpole, the manager of the House of Commons, so much so that contemporary theatergoers like the Earl of Egmont took the play to be "a Satire on Sir Robert Walpole," and in particular, "an allegory on the loss of the Excise Bill," the failed venture that Walpole had in effect attempted to "stage" four years earlier.[39] This move, by which Fielding seems to identify himself with his nemesis, has often surprised scholars, who have viewed it as, for example, "a puzzling act of self-ridicule."[40] For his part, Spatter acknowledges the oddness of making such a "great man" not only an author, but "a master of a playhouse," calling it "a small violence to history" (10:261). As it turns out, however, this small act of violence whereby the author is yoked to the government that he has opposed identifies how the play points to the violence *of* history, the riots of the previous year and before, when the theater and the state had been the objects of popular revolt. The homology between author and minister that Spatter establishes pays off at the moment when the gentleman describing the audience's reaction to *Eurydice* describes the tipping point that turned a restless crowd into a riotous one. It came at the moment when

> At length, from some ill-fated actor's mouth,
> Sudden there issued forth a horrid dram,
> And from another rushed two gallons forth:
> The audience, as it were contagious air,
> All caught it, hallooed, catcalled, hissed, and groaned. (269)

The image of drams and gallons vomited forth from the actors' mouths alludes to the Gin Act, the most recent of Walpole's "productions" in the theater of the state. The allusion puts the final degrading touch on the analogy that *Eurydice Hiss'd* has constructed between Fielding's and Walpole's schemes, linking their dual failures in the most corporeal fashion. What is more, it suggests that this analogy might itself be seen as a kind of screen memory for the public violence of the mid-1730s, the disturbances and riots that responded to Walpole's schemes and Fielding's *Eurydice* alike. The allusion here, not just to the failure of the Excise Bill and Walpole's other legislative initiatives but to the disturbances they summoned forth, suggests how the comparison between Walpole and Fielding is not only an act of self-laceration on the latter's part, but a signal of the degree to which they shared the same perspective with respect to the people, the restive mass of persons whose reactions could not be fully predicted or controlled. In that sense, bringing the similarity between the first minister of government and the playwright to the fore of the audience's attention has the effect of directing spectatorial and critical attention away from the causes of popular discontent, and toward the theatrical and political institutions that seek to contain it.

Fielding's equation of himself and Walpole marks the point at which the comparison between the theater and the state both reaches its climax and breaks down. As we have seen, Walpole was early and often taken to be a performer in the political public sphere, a characterization most frequently in the 1730s accomplished by equating him with Harlequin. In *Eurydice Hiss'd*, Fielding also reverses the polarity of that equation, pointing to how closely the modern author and theater manager can come to obeying the logic of the state. It brings his own position into the purview of the critical gaze that he had once cast on stage and state alike. There may, then, be some truth in Martin Battestin's suggestion that Fielding's seeming identification with Walpole could mark his "brief flirtation" with the man who had been his enemy, and indeed any such gesture would be a forecast of their eventual rapprochement, whereby Fielding seems to have accepted his silencing in return for Walpole's subsidizing his move to a new career in the law.[41] Casting a broader view, we cannot help but observe how eagerly the licensed playhouses of Drury Lane and Covent Garden welcomed the passage of the Stage Licensing Act in June 1737, because the act called for the closure of all of the unlicensed theaters that had sprung up in the previous decade and therefore assured that the power of the state would be deployed to reinforce their cartel. If at the start of the 1730s it was fair to ask how different politics was from entertainment, by the end it would be equally fair to wonder how the theater distinguished itself from the government.

In the aftermath of the Licensing Act, as the unlicensed theaters either curtailed their operations or simply closed, as Fielding shifted his energies to law and, ultimately, fiction, and as the patent houses made things harder than ever for potential authors, it might seem that new and serious works for the stage were no longer possible. The failed provincial schoolmaster Samuel Johnson set out for London with the draft of a play, a verse tragedy called *Irene,* in his luggage in May 1737, perhaps the worst possible moment in the century to start a career as a playwright; it took more than a decade for *Irene* to be staged. But the public sphere abhors a vacuum. The legitimate theater in London would need to reestablish its credibility without, however, a significant infusion of new dramatic material, given the strictures that the Licensing Act imposed and the discouragement that the theater managers now felt more free than ever to dispense. It would be an actor, David Garrick—who, as it happens, accompanied his former teacher Samuel Johnson on the journey from Litchfield to London in May 1737—who would reinvigorate the London theater by infusing it with what was taken to be a new and more energetic style of performance. We shall see in the following chapter that Garrick's innovation may actually have consisted of a subtle co-optation of pantomime technique. More broadly, Garrick's complicated relationship to pantomime as performer, manager, and playwright will help us understand how these entertainments, which at the moment of their emergence to popularity seemed to threaten the legitimate theater, were eventually assimilated into it.

CHAPTER SEVEN

David Garrick and the Institutionalization of English Pantomime

*D*avid Garrick's debut on the London stage as Richard III in the fall of 1741 was perceived by some to herald a new style of acting, one that, as Joseph Roach has put it, "reputedly substituted speed, agility, and variety for the apparent heaviness and monotony of the reigning oratorical style" that had dominated mainpiece performance since at least the time of Thomas Betterton in the late Restoration period.[1] Like the Faustus entertainments of 1723, Garrick's arrival was understood to be an *event*, a public-sphere phenomenon that changed everything people thought they knew about the theater. His ascent to fame and authority was astonishingly swift, and he quickly became the vehicle of hopes of reformers who saw his virtuosity and his professed desire to promote the English repertoire of serious mainpiece drama as creating a long-awaited opportunity to restore the theater to its position as a central institution of culture rather than the site of mere entertainment that they believed it to have become. Yet Garrick's debut performance as Richard was shadowed by rumors that he had performed the role of Harlequin in March of the same year, when he seems to have stepped in to perform in Goodman's Fields's production of Henry Giffard's *Harlequin Student* when the regular Harlequin was too ill to go on.

In a letter to his brother in December 1741, Garrick tried to downplay the experience, and responds to the rumor with a mixture of firm denial and studied equivocation: "As to playing a Harlequin 'tis quite false—Yates last season was taken very ill & was not able to begin the Entertainment so I put on the Dress & did 2 or three Scenes for him, but Nobody knew it but him & Giffard: I know it has been Said I play'd Harlequin at Covent Garden but it is quite false."[2] Whether or not Garrick's direct association with the role of Harlequin was as false as he wished others to believe, we shall see that *Harlequin Student,* in which the figure of Harlequin is contrasted and opposed to that of Shakespeare as false and true icons of British theatrical and cultural history, would remain active in his memory and imagination, serving as a model for his own pantomime entertainment, *Harlequin's Invasion* (1759). And the way in which both entertainments exploit, yet then disavow, pantomime's popularity serves as a kind of allegory of Garrick's career, which, I will argue, assimilated some of pantomime's key features while proclaiming its loyalties to Shakespeare at every opportunity.

In this chapter, I want to use Garrick's relationship to English pantomime as a way of bringing provisional closure to the story of the form's emergence to prominence in 1720s. Garrick maintained a position of public hostility toward pantomime throughout his career. As manager at Drury Lane from 1747 to 1776, he programmed it regularly—and, as we shall see, composed one of the century's most popular pantomimes himself—but claimed that he did so only to satisfy the audience's depraved taste, a taste that he otherwise worked to reform and elevate. In Garrick's late work *The Theatrical Candidates* (1775), for example, Harlequin canvasses for votes among the audience against the more established "candidates" Comedy and Tragedy in a mock-election that will determine the future course of the stage. Harlequin's platform boils down to his argument that "Empty houses" would be the result if he were to lose the election and were to be banished by his opponents, neither of whom can sustain the public's interest on their own any longer.[3] Historians and critics have generally accepted Garrick's claims at face value and taken his continued programming of pantomime entertainments in the face of his consistent mockery of the form to be a sop to audience taste, or, more optimistically, a means of subsidizing his more serious ventures. My argument in this chapter will be that Garrick's relationship to pantomime is more complicated and interesting than this, that he exploited pantomime's popularity and its techniques in ways more fundamental than his own testimony would admit. In his performance style (to the extent that we can reconstruct it), and in his calendrical recalibration of pantomime as a seasonal entertainment, Garrick appropriated key features of the form as it had been developed in performance and positioned in the culture in the first half of the century. Most important, Garrick's very public career, as realized in his much-discussed acting style as well as in his practice while a theatrical manager, marks what I want to call the *institutionalization* of English pantomime, its assimilation into the mainstream of the theater. It identifies perhaps the final stage through which pantomime defines the transformation of older, traditional pastimes into modern entertainment. Garrick succeeded in making pantomime banal enough that it no longer seemed to threaten literary culture. But his intervention also shows how fully such diversions had been co-opted, their physicality and, just as important, their willingness to perform no purpose more important than their audience's sensual gratification, now accepted as itself a socially useful end.

Garrick's Rise and the Assimilation of Entertainment

No doubt part of the reason that Garrick's debut became such a sensation in late 1741 and early 1742 was that it occurred in the midst of upheaval in that other "state," the government, specifically the ministry of Robert Walpole, which had been in office since 1721. The temporal coincidence between Garrick's emergence to stardom and the fall of the Walpole government in early 1742 did not go without notice. The anonymous author of *The Case Between the Managers of the Two Theatres, and their Principal Actors* (1743) claimed that the return of "*Shakspeare, Congreve, Dryden,* and *Otway*" from "their long Banishment," an event facilitated by Garrick's first appearances in "the Year Forty-two," constituted a "happy Revolution" in the theater that paralleled the political changes of the same year, when Walpole was finally pushed out of office.[4] To observers accustomed to drawing analogies between the state of the theater and the state of the state, the parallel was striking; much as pantomime emerged as a dominant form in the vacuum created by Walpole's ascent, now his fall seemed to open an opportunity to restore the English theatrical tradition as well as the balance of the ancient political constitution. Garrick became—quite willingly—the symbolic crown prince of this theatrical restoration, and Harlequin the usurper to be banished. Like most such transfers of authority, Garrick's rise involved something other than a simple restoration of the past; rather, Garrick *assimilated* many of pantomime's practices into the mainstream of the theater, exploiting its materiality, spectacle, and emphasis on movement, all the while professing his distaste for pantomime in its pure form.

This process of stylistic assimilation took place in the context of institutional change in the relationship between the state and the licensed theaters, a change that constituted, I will argue, the full assimilation of diversion itself to the government's oversight. Garrick emerged to fame and then authority at a moment of institutional crisis in the London theater in the wake of the 1737 Licensing Act. This was a crisis that the patent theaters had aided and abetted by in effect siding with the government, seeing the Walpole regime's attempt to regulate the stage as a way of enforcing the virtual cartel rights it possessed over staged performance in London, rights that had been challenged by the proliferation of other playhouses in the 1730s. From the point of view of the patent theaters' managers, the government's imposition of prior censorship—from 1737 on, all new plays had to be submitted for approval in advance of their production—was a small price to pay for the administration's newfound zeal in enforcing their exclusive patent rights. In the wake of the act, such unlicensed theaters as the Haymarket, Goodman's Fields, Sadler's Wells, and the New Wells at Clerkenwell survived by deploying various kinds of clever subterfuge to get around the restrictions; for example, they might claim to be offering their performances gratis, and to be charging patrons merely for the tea or chocolate that was required for admission. What is more, the unlicensed houses now found themselves forced to rely even more heavily on spectacle and pantomime than they had before, as the government was prepared to move more aggressively not only against works that satirized its policies, but also against attempts to encroach on the monopoly over the mainpiece repertory of spoken drama held by the two patent theaters. The institutional distinction between the patent theaters and the unlicensed houses would eventually be given a kind of codification in 25 II George c. 36, "An Act for better preventing Thefts and Robberies; and for regulating Places of publick Entertainment; and punishing Persons keeping disorderly Houses" (1752), which ordered that the unlicensed theaters be issued licenses by local magistrates. Since these licenses, unlike the seemingly perpetual patents, were to be renewed annually, they put the managers of the newer theaters on notice that their ability to stay in business was contingent on good behavior and the government's continuing approval.

Government interventions such as the Licensing Act and the act of 1752 marked and to some degree prompted a legitimation crisis in the patent houses themselves. The installation of prior censorship after 1737 not only dampened political critique but drove vital voices, most famously Henry Fielding's, away from the theater, and reinforced the instinctual conservatism of theatrical managers, who now had another excuse beyond their usual caution for failing to mount new plays. On the one hand, the diversion of attention and energies away from the patent theaters led almost directly to the conflict between Samuel Richardson and Fielding over the nature and scope of that other domain of entertainment, fiction, a conflict that forms a crucial chapter in the story of the rise of the novel, however else that story might be told. But it also created the need for new means by which the standard repertory might be energized. Garrick represented that energizing force. But his innovation did not consist of an abstraction away from physicality. Rather, Garrick signals the subsumption and relegitimation of physical action within the framework of the patent theater system that was desperately in need of new approaches. With Garrick, the state-licensed patent theater revitalized itself by importing key elements of the entertainments that, less than a generation earlier, had seemed to threaten its existence.

To his first admirers of the early 1740s, Garrick's physicality seemed fresh and exciting, because it represented the new priority of (in Garrick's own formulation) "Action, Action, Action" over "Oratory."[5] The field of reference here is consciously limited to the actors of the previous two generations—Thomas Betterton, Barton Booth, James Quin—who had played the roles to which Garrick aspired, and to whom he wished to be compared. But to his critics, Garrick's actions seemed to represent a kind of excess, a hyper-kineticism that seemed to overwhelm language with a busy physicality. By this time, the obvious frame of reference for such activity was pantomime, and critics frequently associated Garrick with the form throughout his career. For example, Theophilus Cibber criticized Garrick's "studied tricks, his Overfondness for extravagant Attitudes, frequent affected Starts, convulsive Twitchings, Jerkings of the Body, sprawling of the Fingers, slapping the Breast and Pockets:—A Set of mechanical motions in constant use, the caricatures of Gesture suggested by pert vivacity,—his pantomimical Manner of acting every Word in a Sentence."[6] Thomas Morris, an army officer who saw Garrick perform in the 1760s or 1770s, objected to his "pantomime-gesture; and all trick, calculated to produce what is called stage-effect: miserable expedients fit only for a booth in a fair, not for the royal theatres of the metropolis."[7] Morris laments Garrick's substitution of gesture, action, "mute play," and "silent language" for the elocutionary standards of the previous generation, and though his critique is probably tinged with unmerited nostalgia, the opposition he depicts between reciters like Quin and actors like Garrick is clear, as is his claim that Garrick's style has become so widely imitated as to become the dominant mode in the English theater.[8] In very much the same terms, a correspondent to the theatrical journal *The Monitor* in 1767 observed that Garrick made up for the fact that "he had not the best natural perfections" (he was short and had a thin speaking voice) by introducing "stage tricks and gestures, as *scientific;* which were originally the motions of mountebanks, merry-andrews, and harlequins at Bartholomew-fair, to make them laugh."[9]

None of these accounts seem informed by rumor or speculation that Garrick had performed in the role of Harlequin, but they collectively recognize the way in which Garrick's much-heralded novelty and modernity derived in no small measure from his aggressive co-optation of the physicality that had been most prominently deployed on the eighteenth-century stage in pantomime. In this, Garrick was not so much doing something radically novel as realizing more fully than anyone had before an assimilation of pantomimic technique that had long been anticipated in eighteenth-century writings on acting. Referring, for example, to Charles Gildon's *The Life of Thomas Betterton* (1710), the most influential acting manual in the first half of the century, John Weaver argued that Gildon's portrait of Betterton could better be read as "a Draught of the Virtues and Qualifications of a *Pantomime.*"[10] In the 1730s, Aaron Hill figured the "*plastic imagination*" that he believed was required of the actor as a "Faustus for the theatres" that by itself "conjures up all changes in a moment."[11] That is to say that Hill imagines how the power of transformation that had been thematized as an external force in the Faustus pantomimes of the 1720s could be internalized, recast literally as a *motivation,* a mental impulse that shapes and drives the motions of the body. In his own *Essay on Acting* (1744), Garrick (here adopting the voice of a critic attacking a certain "little fashionable actor," namely himself) describes the "puppet hero" of his treatise by focusing on silent moments in his performance. Like Hill, he stresses that the performer's ability to be a "moving statue" depends upon the degree to which he is "mentally absorbed" in his role.[12]

Neither Weaver nor Hill could be described as an advocate for the pantomime entertainments that dominated the London theater in the 1720s and 1730s, and their arguments were not intended to provide theoretical support for pantomime. Hill was an open and vocal opponent of English pantomime in those decades, and Weaver's term *pantomime* refers in this context much more to the theater of ancient Rome that he wished to re-create on the London stage than to the entertainments that would appropriate that name beginning a few years later. But both men's invocation of pantomime in the context of more general descriptions of the art of performance underscore how eighteenth-century English pantomime drew upon and reflected the period's most widely accepted theories of acting, and the degree to which it represented a logical extension of theatrical practice rather than a violation of it. Garrick's emergence, which seemed to represent the incursion of pantomime style into mainpiece performance, marks the point at which the reverse became intelligible to observers and critics. In the 1720s, critics like Hogarth, Pope, and Fielding had attacked the patent houses for profiting from pantomime and other afterpiece entertainments, but they still took these performances to be excrescences to the mainstream tradition, a kind of tumor on the theater that might be excised. But by the 1740s, the patent theaters appeared to be assimilating pantomime into the internal logic of their performance style, a process that crystallized around the figure of Garrick, at once the most talented and the most aggressively self-promoting of the first generation of performers to come to prominence after the passage of the Licensing Act. Such an association would call forth new strategies for distinction and authorization, an effort that, as we shall see, would attempt to disguise the apparent overlap between pantomime and other modes of performance, and one in which Garrick plays a central role.

The process by which Garrick co-opted pantomime technique with his performance style was paralleled by the assimilation at mid-century of what were once upstart performance modes and venues into the legal and institutional mainstream of state-supervised diversions. This claim might at first glance seem surprising, since statutes such as the 1737 Stage Licensing Act and the 1752 act for regulating the theaters made a point of specifying the distinction between the patent theaters and other sites of performance, and a recent study of the London theater in the aftermath of 25 George II c. 36 argues that this statute in particular had the effect of demarcating the boundary between serious, "legitimate" performance and lowbrow, "illegitimate" modes more sharply than ever before. In her book *Illegitimate Theatre in London, 1770–1840,* Jane Moody argues that the act of 1752 "unwittingly established an enduring division in the regulation of London theatre," one in which the "non-dramatic sphere of bodily performance utterly distinct from the drama staged at Drury Lane and Covent Garden" became marked as an "illegitimate" entertainment in contrast to the "legitimate" drama offered at the patent theaters.[13] But it is not as though the drama began to distinguish itself in these years by eschewing or even downplaying the human body;

quite the opposite was true, as Garrick and the public fascination with, acclaim for, and occasional disparagement of his performance style indicates. More important, I would also argue that both pieces of legislation had the effect rather of *legitimating* the previously unlicensed performances at the other playhouses, not in the sense of giving them critical stature, but by conferring on them *legal* standing, which had the effect of bringing them more directly under the purview of the state than ever before. To that extent, we can consider 25 II George c. 36 in particular as yet another aspect of *police* as I have used the term in this book, in the sense of the government's active supervision and rationalization of the population, a responsibility that obliged it to extend its reach into previously ignored domains of the culture.

Thus the act addresses itself in the first instance, not to the playhouses and other sites of entertainment, nor to the kinds of actions that took place in them, but rather to classes of *people*—criminals, theatergoers, and keepers of brothels. What was taken to distinguish the unlicensed theaters was not so much their modes of performance as their clientele, which was typically understood to be what Henry Fielding in his *An Enquiry in the Causes of the late Increase of Robbers* (1751) defined as "the thoughtless and tasteless Rabble."[14] If, then, at the level of expressed statute, the state demarcated "serious" from "frivolous" diversions, at the less fully articulated level that we can identify as that of ideology or even the unconscious, its actions were aimed at comprehending both "legitimate" and "illegitimate" forms of entertainment within a much broader framework, one that deployed those definitions in the service of the much more important work of *social* classification. In that respect, we might best understand laws like the Stage Licensing Act and the act of 1752 as being designed in part to set the terms under which the middle class could reassure themselves that the serious drama at the patent houses was not to be confused with the entertainments staged at alternative performance sites. And the state's interest in diversions ostensibly designed for the lower classes had much less to do with delegitimizing them than with reimagining the relationship between diversions and the common people in the interests of claiming authority over the former in order better to reform and manage the latter.

Fielding's *Enquiry* in fact provides a useful gloss on how "illegitimate" modes of diversion were actually assimilated into the state's purview, given a kind of legitimacy by being apprehended through the frame constructed by the discourse of police. In a manner similar to that of Fielding's afterpieces of the 1730s, Fielding's writings on social issues of the early 1750s attempt to bring their object of study into critical "view," as, for example, when in his

Proposal for Making an Effectual Provision for the Poor he observes that the "Sufferings of the Poor" are less "observed" than their "Misdeeds" only because the "Pictures of human Misery" that they present are rarely if ever seen by the middle classes.[15] Thus the *Enquiry into the Causes of the late Increase of Robbers* takes its mission to be the need to identify, not the names of criminals or the nature of their exploits, which together constituted an enormous body of writing in the period, but the root "causes" of crime itself. And as he brings these causes into the light of day, Fielding finds himself attempting to define the relationship between entertainment and the state from his newly gained position within the latter. For when the "Present Reigning Vices" of 1751 are "impartially exposed" (61) in Fielding's *Enquiry*, the most prominent cause of the crime wave besetting London is the outbreak of "Diversion" from its customary times and places into the domains frequented by "the lower Order of People" (83). Fielding's argument reiterates the claim that, as we saw in chapter 5, the physical spread of entertainment venues across the topography of London that was apparent by the mid-1730s corresponded to a more abstract, and much more dangerous, spread of diversion across other boundaries, notably those of class, but also the conceptual boundaries that separated entertainment from other areas of culture.

In addition to this, however, Fielding specifies another area in which this breakdown of distinctions has occurred, that of temporality. Much as Joseph Addison had a generation earlier, Fielding offers a myth of origin for the invention of diversion. As we saw in chapter 3, Addison had cited and then silently recast the Stuart ideology that cast the supervision of diversions as one of the essential components of statecraft; what had, under the Stuart monarchs, been a claim that the monarch's individual supervision of pastimes and other diversions signified his fatherly care for his people and thereby supported his legitimacy, became, under Addison's Whig revision, the claim that the government's interest in public "sports and shews" derived from their ability to divert the people from affairs of state, and helped establish "entertainment" as a domain separate from politics, one that could be assessed by its own norms. Fielding's genealogy of diversion bypasses both of these claims to find the origin of public entertainments in the ancient world, specifically, on the one hand, the Old Testament's reservation of one day in seven for rest and, on the other, the Greek and Roman customs of putting "Seasons of Idleness" into the calendar (80).[16] The point of such periods of diversion, idleness, and pastimes, Fielding argues, is to provide a respite from work in order that the laboring classes might be more efficient upon their return to it. Diversion was thus rare, occurring only on the Sabbath and a few times of the year, a situation that, Fielding observes, has completely changed in contemporary London. Now "the Places of Pleasure are almost become numberless": spread out across the city (Fielding seems to be thinking most specifically of masquerades and the pleasure gardens of Ranelegh and Vaux Hall as well as theaters and fairs, but his rhetoric is designed to comprehend as many kinds of diversion as possible), and available on virtually every day of the year, diversion has been "perverted" from its origins and now constitutes a threat to the social order.

The problem is one of social mimetic desire; as they see the middle and upper classes enjoying their pleasures year-round, members of the working classes will naturally want to emulate them, a desire spurred by the sensual "Voluptuousness" of modern pleasures, "where the Eyes are feasted with Show, and the Ears with Music, and where Gluttony and Drunkenness are allured by every Kind of Dainty" (79). Fielding takes the universal availability of sensual pleasure to be not only a cause of crime, as workers are tempted to steal in order to pursue pleasures that rightly belong to other classes, but a threat to the economic and social order, as indulgence in diversions on the part of the working classes represents a "loss of Time" that the nation cannot afford. Here, Fielding echoes Richardson and Lillo, who, as we saw in chapter 5, identified the sacrifice of time to diversion as one of the greatest threats that the spread of entertainment posed to the working class, and to young men in particular.

The virtue of Fielding's critical analysis, as opposed to Richardson's and Lillo's expressions of their shared concern, is that it clarifies significant changes in the understanding of the relationship between entertainment and the state by mid-century. Now, it is not (as it was for Addison) so much a question of how pastimes might gain a useful purpose by keeping the people's attention diverted from politics. Rather, Fielding wants to know how diversions contribute to, or detract from, the state conceived as a rationalized entity, its prosperity measurable and quantifiable. Fielding's inquiry registers and consolidates the shift from partisan politics to the nation as the frame within which entertainment was defined and located. And for Fielding the magistrate, whose career as a writer of afterpiece entertainments had been abruptly halted by the government a decade and a half earlier, the *Enquiry's* discussion of diversion's negative effects seems ironically to confirm the state's power in restricting diversions that it deems to be incursions on its own vital interests. Fielding is careful to state that he is calling not for the "Extirpation" of such forms of entertainment, but rather for their "Retrenchment" (83), by which he means not so much their reduction as their further regulation. Rather than driving them out of legitimacy, such a move would assimilate them *into* the purview of the law, from which they could be supervised as legitimate, if déclassé entertainments, a grudging concession to the working class's need for some diversion from work.[17]

Garrick never left a body of theoretical or political writings, so we do not have so direct a path of access to his conscious understanding of the changing relationship between the state and public entertainment in the middle of the eighteenth century as we have with Fielding. Rather, besides the accounts of witnesses who described his performances, what we have is the record of his tenure as manager of Drury Lane from 1747 to 1776, as well as the plays he wrote to be staged there. In the following section, I will try to show how Garrick's conception of the common people and of the proper diversions for them come into intelligibility in his complex relationship to pantomime. Garrick is responsible for a significant innovation in the scheduling of pantomime entertainments, as he more than anyone else defined pantomime as a specifically Christmas diversion during his tenure as manager. This innovation, and Garrick's approach to pantomime more generally, had the effect of domesticating pantomime, bringing it more fully under the institutional control of the more legitimate of the patent houses. It also reflects, I argue, a broader reconceptualization of the place, temporality, and significance, not only of pantomime, but of diversion itself. And by reading closely the Christmas entertainment that Garrick wrote under his own name—*Harlequin's Invasion,* first produced in 1759—we will see how this reconceptualization incorporated an understanding of social class that resembles Fielding's. Much as mid-century observers of the theater condensed their hopes and concerns about the institution in the person of Garrick, he in turn condensed his program in embodied figures. In particular, Garrick appropriated an already extant discursive opposition between the contemporary star of the London stage, Harlequin, and the "timeless" Bard of the English national theater, William Shakespeare. Such an opposition put names and faces on the popular and canonical, transient and permanent modes of performance that Garrick's program worked to distinguish—and assimilate.

Garrick's Shakespeare, Harlequin's Invasion

It is a probably a measure of the depth of Garrick's indebtedness to pantomime that his absorption of its style entailed an equally aggressive disavowal, a public distancing of himself from pantomime that began with his attempts to obscure his own experience in the role of Harlequin. This was most fully expressed during his career as manager of Drury Lane from 1747 until his retirement in 1776. As manager, Garrick continued to program pantomime regularly, introducing new works as well as recycling proven favorites. In fact, the evidence suggests that one of his goals upon becoming manager was to improve Drury Lane's pantomime offerings, enhancing their quality so as to take audiences and critical attention away from John Rich's Covent Garden. By no later than 1752, newspaper critics were attesting to his program's success. Reviewing Drury Lane's new pantomime of that year, *The Genii,* a writer in *The Scourge* claimed that "this new entertainment, I think, hath fully decided the controversy, and fix'd the superiority of pantomime to Drury-lane theatre, as it had before had of almost everything else."[18] But Garrick frequently and publicly begrudged pantomime's popularity, casting it as merely a necessary concession to audience taste, and attempting to associate his tenure with loftier goals than mere entertainment or profit. His supporters publicized and amplified the point. As his early biographer Arthur Murphy put it, Garrick's primary aim as manager was to "reform" the British stage by ensuring that "*Lun* and his favourite harlequin" would give "way to a just representation of nature."[19] But what, exactly, is "nature," and how can we identify a "just representation" of it?

So abstract a goal demanded a concrete figure that could concentrate and personalize it, an emblem around which the associations that eighteenth-century culture was attributing to the natural—beauty, spontaneity, sublimity—could condense. To a great extent, that figure would be equated with William Shakespeare, who had frequently been described as the poet of nature since the late seventeenth century. In the Restoration period, this was not necessarily an unequivocal compliment; as Michael Dobson, for example, has demonstrated, as the offspring of the "poet of nature," Shakespeare's plays were also understood to be rough, irregular, and untamed, much less polished than the works of the "poet of art," Ben Jonson, and less clever than those written by the "poet of wit," John Fletcher.[20] But by the 1730s, Shakespeare's fulfillment of the ideals of nature was understood to make him the most important of all figures in the national literary tradition. How this happened is a story that goes well beyond the scope of this book. What is important here is to recognize how fully Garrick linked his own professional image and success with his claim to be restoring Shakespeare to his rightful place in a theatrical institution that had for at least two decades been dominated by pantomime, opera, ballad opera, and other kinds of lesser entertainment. To be sure, Garrick shares responsibility for Shakespeare's elevation to being what Dobson succinctly describes as "the paradigmatic figure of literary authority" with many others, and he capitalizes and builds on a movement that, as Dobson and others have documented, had been ongoing for more than half a century.[21] But few public figures of the period were more assertive in aligning their own persona with that of Shakespeare than was Garrick, and a crucial component of that program was Garrick's strategic appropriation of pantomime to serve as the other against which Shakespeare's transcendence could be defined.

For in Garrick's public rhetoric about himself and the theatrical company that he headed, Shakespeare was frequently deployed as Harlequin's opposite and antithesis. In his prologue composed for the opening of the 1750 season, Garrick makes it clear that Drury Lane would be doing something other than pantomime if only the audience would let them:

> Sacred to Shakespeare was this spot design'd,
> To pierce the heart, and humanize the mind.
> But if an empty House, the Actor's curse,
> Show us our Lears and Hamlet lose their force;
> Unwilling we must change the nobler scene,
> And in our turn present you Harlequin.[22]

Garrick's indefatigable efforts to promote Shakespeare as the singular figure who simultaneously represents and transcends the British stage and, by extension, British culture itself rely to a great extent on his positioning of the figure of Harlequin as Shakespeare's demonic other, the rival whose illegitimate usurpation of the stage must be exposed and repulsed.[23] In this, too, Garrick was following ample precedent.

As early as the 1720s, critics were opposing Shakespeare to Harlequin as representative figures of different aspects of the theatrical tradition, the drama of the spoken word versus performances whose meanings were conveyed through the body. In the dedication to *Shakespeare Restored* (1726), Lewis Theobald, probably already collaborating with John Rich on pantomimes at Lincoln's Inn Fields, used Rich's Harlequin as a foil for his own "classic" and "restored" version of Shakespeare.[24] Garrick's one-time employer Henry Giffard, as we shall see shortly, built *Harlequin Student,* the 1740 pantomime in which Garrick performed as Harlequin, around the same opposition. But even if this opposition was not original to Garrick, no one worked harder than him to identify his own person and professional fortunes with Shakespeare. Garrick's opposition of Shakespeare to Harlequin was a shrewd and decisive tactical move, a local appropriation of pantomime's popularity from the 1720s through the 1750s that enabled him to offer Shakespeare as an emblem around whom a broad range of literary, historical, and nationalistic associations could condense. Garrick's career, as actor and particularly as theatrical manager, marks a crucial stage in the elevation of Shakespeare to a position that was in effect beyond criticism or temporality, the timeless "Bard" whose writings occupy a never-to-be-surpassed pinnacle of British culture. In what follows, I want to return to his sole pantomime, *Harlequin's Invasion* (1759), which I discussed briefly in the entr'acte to this book, better to specify how the relationship between Harlequin and Shakespeare that Garrick sets up in that afterpiece provides clues for understanding how he articulates both national identity and modern entertainment.

Time and temporality are key to understanding the way that Garrick, like other eighteenth-century critics, made Shakespeare into a symbol of Britishness. In the entr'acte, I argued that *Harlequin's Invasion* exploits what Homi Bhabha has described as the "double-time" through which the modern nation is constituted, the simultaneous "pedagogical" and "performative" axes of articulating imaginative constructs like the nation and its people, entities that must at once be imagined as never-changing and ever-new.[25] There, I suggested that Harlequin's black mask was a sign of African identity that served to consolidate Britishness; described twice in *Harlequin's Invasion* as a "Blackamoor," Harlequin stands as a timeless Other to an emergent sense of British nationhood that had its own embodiment in the figure of Shakespeare. National pride is, in fact, never far from the surface of *Harlequin's Invasion,* and Shakespeare's ascendancy in the play needs to be understood as a sign of British cultural preeminence designed to rhyme with a military puissance that Britain demonstrated in the year of its first production. The year 1759 was hailed in Britain as a "year of victories" over France, as the British military defeated French forces at Quiberon Bay, Quebec, and Minden. Garrick's pantomime, which premiered on New Year's Eve, 1759, celebrates the year that marked a turning point in the Seven Years' War, casting Harlequin as the foreign invader who, at the start of the performance, has in effect *already* been repulsed.[26] It is not surprising, then, to discover that Garrick's song "Heart of Oak," a celebration of British naval power and one of the most popular patriotic songs of the century, was first performed at the 1759 premiere of *Harlequin's Invasion.*

But *Harlequin's Invasion* was performed for many years, which would indicate that its appeal exceeded the patriotic fervor of its moment, and that we can and should specify further how Garrick's entertainment exemplifies or even perhaps exploits the different axes of temporality that Bhabha describes. We might, for example, imagine Shakespeare as the degree zero of the pedagogical axis, as his works were in the course of the eighteenth century elevated to become objects of professional, critical inquiry in part by being their author's being classed as an antique, a figure with status equivalent to that of the classic writers of Greece and Rome. This is the logic by which Theobald justified his effort in the 1730s to be "restoring" Shakespeare's works to what they had meant to his original audience by claiming that Shakespeare lived on the other side of an historical break, a chasm between the last age and the present that rendered him something other than a contemporary writer. By implication, this identifies pantomime as a *modern* form, a genre corresponding to an age that, if not (to Theobald) particularly enlightened, is surely on this side of the historical breach that has rendered Shakespeare a "Classic Writer," as opposed to a modern.[27] His works were therefore in need of the kind of scholarly recovery that, as Theobald saw it, Alexander Pope was unable or unwilling to perform in order for their meaning to be fully available to a modern readership. Writing in 1765, Samuel Johnson, in the preface to his own edition of Shakespeare's *Works,* similarly observes that Shakespeare can be considered as an "ancient."[28] At the same time, Shakespeare's association with nature also contributes to his imagined timelessness, as it links him to an unchanging domain so self-identical as to defy any attempt to locate it in any particular time or even order of temporality. Garrick builds upon these formulations to define Shakespeare as somehow both ancient and modern at once, a figure who exists outside of normal time. Shakespeare and Britain each take advantage of the abstract and permanent qualities of the other in a mutually constitutive and powerful construct by which Shakespeare's naturalness becomes an aspect of British power and the nation-state's permanence is conferred upon the Bard.

Garrick secures the opposition between Shakespeare and Harlequin in part by changing the rules concerning the times of the year in which pantomime was featured, giving it a specificity that contrasted with the timeless generality of Shakespeare's works. Garrick is responsible for an innovation in the scheduling of new pantomimes that persists to the present day, namely the segregation of pantomime to the Christmas season. Starting in 1750, Garrick began introducing new pantomimes just after Christmas, generally on Boxing Day, an innovation in scheduling that became the norm and expectation: *Queen Mab* (1750), *Harlequin Ranger* (1751), *The Genii* (1752), *Fortunatus* (1753), *Harlequin in China* (1754), *Proteus* (1755), and *Mercury*

Harlequin (1756).[29] This was a change from previous practice; since their emergence to widespread popularity in the early 1720s, new pantomimes had appeared throughout the season, and although it is difficult to discover a hard-and-fast pattern, they had probably most frequently premiered between late January and early March.[30] To be sure, Drury Lane continued to perform pantomimes throughout the year after Garrick's innovation; moreover, the many secondary houses that relied on pantomime and other spectacles do not seem to have conformed to the pattern that he introduced. And indeed, part of Garrick's motivation may well have been to distinguish Drury Lane's pantomimes from those offered by the other theaters, to mark them as distinctive and special, a holiday treat rather than a routine entertainment. But by changing the performance schedule to associate pantomime with the Christmas season, Garrick in effect installed Harlequin in a different order of time than that inhabited by Shakespeare; he contained Harlequin by segregating him to a specific season that was now marked as a time of festivity *unlike* the normal, homogeneous time of the workaday world. Rendered the star of a diversion identified with a particular time, Harlequin is pointedly different from Shakespeare, whose generality makes him, literally, a man for all seasons.

In particularizing Harlequin by associating pantomime with a specific season of the year, Garrick was exploiting his institutional advantage as manager of the theater to intervene in a performance schedule with a traditional rhythm and punctuation that, even at mid-century, still had significance for London audiences. Nicholas Rowe's *Tamerlane,* a 1701 allegory of the reign of William III, was still performed every year on November 5, the anniversary of William's arrival in England (and also, providentially enough, Guy Fawkes's Day), to celebrate the Glorious Revolution and the Whig regime that it had ushered to power. And Garrick, we recall from chapter 5, was credited with one well-known alteration of the theater's schedule, as he was said to have substituted *The London Merchant* for *The London Cuckolds* as the annual Lord Mayor's Day production for London's apprentices. In a sense, Garrick's positioning of pantomime as a Christmas entertainment would seem to be merely returning to a tradition in which certain kinds of pastimes and entertainments were associated with particular periods of the year, with many of them (such as Stuart court masques on the one hand, and holiday mumming on the other) associated with the Christmas season. But there is a key difference. By the 1750s, such performances were clearly marked *as* such a return; tinged with a kind of nostalgia, they offered customary, festive time as a commodity to audiences who understood their experience of temporality to be considerably more homogeneous than that of their ancestors.

In its timing as a "Christmas gambol," for example, Garrick's 1759 Christmas pantomime *Harlequin's Invasion* identifies itself as an occasional entertainment, a special treat for a season that is different in kind from the ordinary time of the rest of the year. In a sense, the term "Christmas" is redundant, as "gambol," which since the sixteenth century had described the leap of a dance, was already strongly associated with the Christmas season; the *OED* cites Philipps's 1706 dictionary, which speaks of "*Gambols,* certain Sports or Tumbling Tricks in use about Christmas-time."[31] The redundancy of Garrick's subtitle calls attention to the term's anachronistic quality, the way it can be identified with a past that the audience now gets to visit as part of its annual holiday from the homogeneous workaday temporality of the present. As they constantly reinvoke, indeed revive, the traditional performance in the manner of a ritual act, such annual works constitute the audiences that they address—the British people, the apprentices—as (to pick up Bhabha's terms once more) both the objects of a pedagogical discourse that links the present to the past, and as the subjects in an ongoing performance. The group must be understood as the central actors in the drama of modern nation-building, their presence and participation at a regular and repeated event having a meaning of its own that far transcends the content of the work they have come to witness together.

Much of this may well have been unarticulated, at least at the conscious level, by the eighteenth-century spectators of *Harlequin's Invasion,* but what they could not have failed to notice immediately about *Harlequin's Invasion* was that Garrick's Harlequin spoke. This innovation was not widely adopted—English Harlequins most typically remained silent for years after this point, although there are exceptions—but it is nonetheless significant for the way that it goes against the grain of the form's conventions and its history. To be sure, it is not as if Harlequin was silent throughout the early part of the century in Britain. Harlequin frequently sang; moreover, Continental Harlequins performing as members of visiting troupes (such as the company that performed at the Haymarket in 1720) seem to have spoken, as that was the norm outside of England. And the Harlequin in Behn's *The Emperor of the Moon,* which was frequently revived through the first part of the eighteenth century, also spoke. But *Harlequin's Invasion* marks the first time that the character had spoken in a new, British entertainment since before the turn to speechless dance promoted by John Weaver and John Rich in the 1710s. What is the significance of *this* innovation?

Garrick's own explanation for giving his Harlequin the power of speech is not wholly convincing, but it provides useful hints. Garrick seems to have felt called upon to defend his "speaking Harlequin," and in his prologue for a 1762 revival of *Harlequin's Invasion,* he takes the opportunity offered by John Rich's recent death to claim that only Rich himself could get away with performing Harlequin without words:

> But why a speaking Harlequin?—'tis wrong,
> The wits will say, to give the fool a tongue:
> When Lun appear'd, with matchless art and whim,
> He gave the pow'r of speech to ev'ry limb;
> Tho' mask'd and mute, convey'd his quick intent,
> And told in frolic gestures all he meant.
> But now the motly coat, and sword of wood,
> Require a tongue to make them understood.[32]

Garrick's compliment in effect claims that Rich fulfilled the desires of pantomime's theorists such as Weaver to make dance into a kind of universal language of the body, an attempt to articulate gesture in such a way as to "speak," instantly, to all kinds of spectators. But if we consider the play that follows this dedication closely, Garrick's claim that Rich's passing now "requires" Harlequin to speak as a way of making up for the loss of the best English performer ever to play him rings hollow, and not only because many other speechless Harlequins had succeeded in the London theater. Rather, *Harlequin's Invasion* indicates that Garrick puts Harlequin's speech in the service of further *particularizing* him, identifying him, not as the universally intelligible performer epitomized by Rich, but as the denizen of a specific, and foreign, nation. In the context of Garrick's patriotic, even jingoistic piece, Harlequin's speech signifies his foreignness and particularly his Frenchness. An incident in the 1740s shows, in fact, how firmly a Harlequin's power of speech was taken to be a national trait identifying him as specifically French.

In the course of a dispute between the actors and the theater managers in 1743, a pamphlet on behalf of the Drury Lane performers attacked the patent-holders for employing "a speaking *French* Harlequin" and thereby depriving an English actor of a job; here, "speaking" and "*French*" go together as associated terms, each of which marks a violation of the customary rules of the theater as both national institution and workplace.[33] *Harlequin's Invasion* exploits the same association, but cuts deeper, attacking the very rationale of pantomime as a form; in many respects, Garrick's most important rearticulation of British pantomime is simply to undercut what theorists like Weaver would have understood to be its raison d'etre by giving Harlequin the capacity of speech.[34] To Garrick's innovation in scheduling, which implies that Harlequin is the representative of an older order of temporality, his innovation of speech underscores the alienness that almost three decades of Harlequin's extraordinary popularity on the London stage had gradually eroded.

By thus particularizing Harlequin in time and space, *Harlequin's Invasion* casts Harlequin as an alien presence in a theater whose Britishness is confirmed by its identification with Shakespeare. In *Harlequin's Invasion,* Garrick reproduces, as several critics have noted, the basic structure of *Harlequin Student,* the 1741 pantomime in which he had, however furtively, once appeared.[35] Like Giffard's pantomime, *Harlequin's Invasion* stages a harlequinade displaying a number of Harlequin's tricks, but then abruptly reverses course to conclude with a spectacular tableau in which the statue of Shakespeare rises to banish Harlequin from the stage. Both Giffard's and Garrick's final tableaux appropriate the typical conclusion of earlier pantomimes. These, too, had frequently closed with the arrival of the classical gods, which were on some occasions performed as or by statues, such as *Perseus and Andromeda*'s statue of Mercury, which transforms into Harlequin, establishing a structural isomorphism between classical and modern tricksters. But *Harlequin Student* and *Harlequin's Invasion* (where Mercury incites townspeople to repulse Harlequin and to celebrate Shakespeare) call upon the spectators' memories of such earlier pantomime climaxes for the purpose of delegitimating the form itself. In their concluding tableaux, the comic and serious plots are not reconciled, as in *Perseus and Andromeda,* but pushed apart, with harlequinade decisively routed and scapegoated, its emblematic figure, Harlequin, driven from the stage as Shakespeare takes his place, a polarization summed up in one of *Harlequin Invasion*'s final stage directions: "*Shakespear rises: Harlequin sinks*" (224). As Denise Sechelski describes this conclusion, "the obvious disjunctions between the two theatrical forms rest in the images of the real 'bodies' onstage: the harlequin's multivalent body opposes the statuesque 'body' of Shakespeare."[36] Sechelski shrewdly uses the thematics of the body to link the Harlequin/Shakespeare dichotomy to that between the carnivalesque, popular tradition and the elite culture that was posited by Mikhail Bakhtin and elaborated by Stallybrass and White. As she suggests, the conclusion of *Harlequin's Invasion* stages the contradictions in Garrick's practice, which explicitly attempted to promote the "classical body" of Shakespeare while it unconsciously absorbed the techniques of a "lower" form.

Given all the ways that it undercuts pantomime as it had established itself from the 1720s on, *Harlequin's Invasion* might better be dubbed an "antipantomime"—a work that undermines the genre to which it seems to declare its affiliation. This is true to a point, but a more specific reading of *Harlequin's Invasion* is possible and necessary, one that makes use of its topical and thematic referents to detail the cultural work that Garrick's popular afterpiece—it was frequently revived and had 167 performances in all—performed. Such a reading suggests that Garrick's relationship toward pantomime might best be described less as thoroughly antagonistic than as ambivalently opportunistic. For all that it advertises itself as a holiday entertainment that would seem to make little reference to the everyday world, *Harlequin's Invasion* stitches together class, national, legal, and professional themes as it rearticulates the classic commedia romance plot on which pantomimes of the 1720s through the 1750s had been constructed.

Garrick's Pantaloon figure is Snip, a London tailor whose shrewish wife sends him out to get the head of the invading Harlequin. Meanwhile, his daughter Dolly, performing the function of Colombine, has ditched her beau Abram, a young tailor apprenticed to her father, and fallen in love with Harlequin, whom she somehow recognizes to be a character in a play from the outset: "Wiser folks than you and I, Mama, prize him more than your tragedies or your comedies, aye, or your singing, either" (215). But Dolly joins her mother in wishing for Harlequin's death once she learns that it might be the means for her social advancement as well. Both women are motivated by their ambitions to ascend from the urban working class to the nobility, what Mrs. Snip calls being "Qualitified"; she believes that her husband might gain a noble title for his heroism if he kills Harlequin, while Dolly fantasizes about becoming "Lady Doll Snip." Significantly, for Dolly this means having access to the playhouses throughout the year rather than merely "at holiday time" (217)—that is, when *Harlequin's Invasion* was staged. Dolly of course wants to be able to afford to go to the theater more often, but her ironic gesture to the situation of the performance that she is in also shows how the distinction between ordinary and festive temporality has been cast as a distinction in social class as well, as the lower classes are here understood to inhabit a different, older order of time than that of their betters, for whom entertainment is normatively available year-round. Most important, as he offers women's social aspirations as a target for the audience's condescension, Garrick nonetheless severs the links between Harlequin and Colombine that had provided the plot engine of the "grotesque" or "comic" portions of earlier pantomimes.

In its place Garrick offers essentially a narrative of pursuit, as an alliance of national types joins together to catch and if possible kill Harlequin, a job that, as we have seen, Snip is prodded into taking on as his own heroic task. But his attempt to kill Harlequin backfires; Harlequin tricks Snip, cuts his head off, then sews it back on. That is, Garrick's Harlequin is a tailor himself, though one with no established master or home; as he announces, "I am nobody and came from nowhere" (207). By granting Harlequin the skill of the tailor's craft, Garrick may be making an association between the protean Harlequin and the tailoring trade based on a contemporary understanding of the latter as an art of transformation, the profession that was able to "make the man," permitting anyone to pass for the member of another social class. What is more, the equation between Snip and his nemesis replicates that between Garrick and Harlequin; in each case, the English craftsman and the Continental "invader" share a skill-set, one that, however, sets them in opposition to each other. We could read *Harlequin's Invasion,* then, as an allegory of Garrick's professional ambitions, a recasting of the narrative of assimilation and then repulsion that I have offered to describe Garrick's engagement with pantomime. More important, Garrick here assumes the kind of vantage point offered by the contemporary discourse of police to affiliate Harlequin with what Fielding terms the "lower order of people," a member of the class whose activities were increasingly an object of inquiry and specification on the part of the state.

For Garrick's choice of tailor as Snip's profession defines him as a plebeian from a cohort known for its volatility, frequent criminality, and occasional vagrancy. If we think of him as a rootless tailor, Harlequin can be understood to be a journeyman in a trade that was marked by notoriously contentious labor relations. Journeymen tailors were among the first tradesmen to form unions, and there were a series of conflicts in the eighteenth century between them and their masters, with major disputes over pay and working conditions flaring up in 1720–21, 1745, 1752, 1767–68, 1778, and 1800.[37] Tailors were frequently suspected of petty thievery; Snip articulates a long-standing belief (on the part of their clients) that tailors abused their access to valuable dry goods by remarking in fear that Harlequin might "make no more of killing me than I would of stealing a piece of cloth" (208).[38] Harlequin's professional criminalization fits *Harlequin Invasion's* frequent identification of him as a "Nobody," a man without a proper place or home, a characterization that, as one of three justices brought on to sentence him says, means that "he comes within the statute description of incorrigible rogue" (212). The statute in question is the Vagabond Act of 1744, 17 George II c. 5, which greatly specified the procedures and penalties relating to "Rogues, Vagabonds, Beggars and other idle and disorderly Persons."[39] Yet another expression of the eighteenth-century British state's interest in rationalizing, or, to quote the title of the act, making "more effectual" its authority over the population, the Vagabond Act also restated the persistent classification, going back to Elizabeth I, of unlicensed performers as vagrants as well, associating unauthorized players with gypsies, fortunetellers, men who abandon their wives and children, chapmen, peddlers, and, for good measure "all Persons wandring abroad, and lodging in Alehouses, Barns, Outhouses, or in the open Air, not giving a good Account of themselves." In truth, actors were rarely if ever prosecuted as vagrants, but the persistence and recent recodification of their status as such enables Garrick to associate Harlequin with the companies of performers against which Drury Lane wished to define and distinguish itself, the secondary houses that had themselves been brought more tightly under the purview of the law with the entertainment act of 1752. In sum, *Harlequin's Invasion* demonizes Harlequin as both a foreign and a domestic threat to bourgeois order, casting him not only as a French invader but also as an English plebeian who must be marginalized, neutralized, and ultimately expelled.

My reading of *Harlequin's Invasion* can only be understood as the play's *unconscious* rather than its manifest content, as a bourgeois fantasy about the power of British culture and the ease with which its enemies could be contained or repulsed. With Garrick, the affirmative and critical aspects that we observed to be coexisting in an entertainment like *Perseus and Andromeda* have been in effect split apart. As Garrick appropriated pantomimic technique in order to revolutionize performance style in mainpiece drama, he also exploited its parodic capacity in order to align it in opposition to a Shakespeare who now stood for the legitimate British stage as such. Pantomime was now understood as *mere* entertainment, a diversion defanged of its satirical content and thereby rendered safe, innocuous, an ally of bourgeois desires to reform the stage rather than the threat to them, as Pope, Fielding, and Hogarth had feared a generation earlier. In its turn, pantomime became part of the established order of the British stage, assimilated into the legitimate theater as a harmless diversion, its proper place carefully defined and demarcated. Attacks on pantomime diminish greatly after mid-century, which is as good an indicator as any that it no longer represented a threat.

After Garrick, pantomime of course continued to be produced in the London theaters, and even at times to thrive. Garrick's godson Thomas

Dibden, for example, was a popular and skilled Harlequin and creator of pantomime scenarios, writing and performing from the 1790s into the 1820s. Dibden's most successful works, such as *Harlequin and Mother Goose; or, The Golden Egg* (1806) and *Harlequin and Humpo; or, Columbine by Candlelight* (1812), were enormously popular and frequently revived for years.[40] Despite the presence of Harlequin in both of those titles, he was becoming a less central figure in English pantomime than he had been from the 1720s through the 1750s. In the early nineteenth century, the great performer Joseph Grimaldi elevated the Clown figure to become the focal point of the performance, and although Harlequin continued to be featured in nineteenth- and even twentieth-century pantomime, both he and the commedia dell'arte framework in which he figured was becoming increasingly less significant.[41]

Pantomime changed from decade to decade and even from year to year in the course of the Victorian period, and a full accounting of these changes is the subject of another book. In general, however, it seems that the commedia scenarios increasingly were pushed to the very end of an entertainment that more prominently featured various kinds of performances from the emerging music-hall tradition and fairy-tale stories intended largely for children.[42] By the early twentieth century, the harlequinade section was frequently omitted altogether from what was now frequently just called "panto." When it *was* staged, the harlequinade frequently functioned as a coda to the panto, offered as a kind of artifact, a sample of an old-fashioned, obsolete form of entertainment whose staging served now largely to connect theatergoers in the present moment to their ancestors, joining the current generation to those of the past in a common experience that affirmed their shared identity as Britons. Eighteenth-century pantomime may have its more influential if less obvious descendents in performances other than panto itself, in, for example, the American minstrelsy and British music hall traditions. The line of transmission through the music hall is intriguing, for it suggests that some of pantomime's characteristics may also have reemerged in silent movie comedy, as early silent movie stars like Charlie Chaplin came out of music halls. But in its reconceptualization of pantomime as a seasonal diversion, and its evacuation of the form's critical potential, Garrick's *Harlequin's Invasion* may be used to mark the moment when a particularly vital phase in this mode of entertainment had come to an end.

NOTES

Introduction

1. The critical literature on eighteenth-century British pantomime is not extensive. See, however, Emmett L. Avery, "Dancing and Pantomime on the English Stage, 1700–1737," *Studies in Philology* 31 (1934): 417–52, and "The Defense and Criticism of Pantomimic Entertainments in the Early Eighteenth Century," *ELH* 5 (1938): 127–45; Paul Sawyer, "John Rich's Contribution to the Eighteenth-Century London Stage," in *Essays on the Eighteenth Century English Stage,* ed. Kenneth Richards and Peter Thompson (London: Methuen, 1972), 85–104, "Smorgasbord on the Stage: John Rich and the Development of Eighteenth-Century English Pantomime," *The Theatre Annual* 34 (1979): 37–65, and "The Popularity of Pantomime on the London Stage, 1720–1760," *Restoration and Eighteenth-Century Theatre Research* series V (1990): 1–16; Michael S. Wilson, "Columbine's Picturesque Passage: The Demise of Dramatic Action in the Evolution of Sublime Spectacle on the London Stage," *The Eighteenth Century* 31 (1990): 191–210; and Antoni N. Zalewski Zadlak, "Harlequin Comes to England: The Early Evidence of the *Commedia dell'arte* in England and the Formulation of English Harlequinades and Pantomimes" (Ph.D. diss., Tufts University, 1999).

2. Henry Fielding, "Dedication" to *Tumble-Down Dick,* in *The Works of Henry Fielding,* ed. Leslie Stephen, 10 vols. (London: Smith, Elder, 1882), 10:273.

3. See Jürgen Habermas, *The Structural Transformation of the Public Sphere: An Inquiry into a Category of Bourgeois Society,* trans. Thomas Burger with the assistance of Frederick Lawrence (Cambridge, Mass.: MIT Press, 1991).

4. Jürgen Habermas, "The Public Sphere: An Encyclopedia Article," *New German Critique* 3 (1974): 49–55.

5. Here I am indebted to Jonathan Brody Kramnick's discussion of the public sphere in his book *Making the English Canon: Print-Capitalism and the Cultural Past, 1700–1770* (Cambridge: Cambridge University Press, 1998).

6. Mitchell Dean, *Governmentality: Power and Rule in Modern Society* (London: Sage, 1999), 10.

7. See Michel Foucault, "Governmentality," and "'Omnes Et Singulatim': Toward a Critique of Political Reason," in *Power,* ed. James D. Faubion, *Essential Works of Foucault, 1954–1984* (New York: The New Press, 2000), 201–21, 298–325.

8. Susan Stewart, *Crimes of Writing: Problems in the Containment of Representation* (New York: Oxford University Press, 1991), 1.

9. The fullest account of antitheatricalist arguments and ideology remains Jonas Barish, *The Antitheatrical Prejudice* (Berkeley: University of California Press, 1981).

10. See William B. Warner, *Licensing Entertainment: The Elevation of Novel Reading in Britain, 1684–1750* (Berkeley: University of California Press, 1998).

11. I adopt the term *liveness* from Philip Auslander, *Liveness: Performance in a Mediatized Culture* (London: Routledge, 1999).

12. Michael Warner, "The Mass Public and the Mass Subject," in *Publics and Counterpublics* (New York: Zone Books, 2002), 159–86.

13. See, among others, Jean-Cristophe Agnew, *Worlds Apart: The Market and the Theater in Anglo-American Thought 1550–1850* (Cambridge: Cambridge University Press, 1986); Judith Butler, *Gender Trouble: Feminism and the Subversion of Identity* (New York: Routledge, 1990); David Marshall, *The Figure of Theater: Shaftesbury, Defoe, Adam Smith, and George Eliot* (New York: Columbia University Press, 1985).

Chapter 1. Perseus and Andromeda *and the Meaning of Eighteenth-Century Pantomime*

1. David Mayer has discussed the application of some scenic techniques with reference to early nineteenth-century English pantomime in *Harlequin in His Element: The English Pantomime, 1806–1836* (Cambridge, Mass.: Harvard University Press, 1969), esp. 109–64. See also Richard Southern, *Changeable Scenery: Its Origin and Development in the British Theatre* (London: Faber and Faber, 1952).

2. *The Weekly Journal, or Saturday's Post,* April 6, 1723, 1363.

3. Cesar de Saussure, *A Foreign View of England in 1725–29: The Letters of Monsieur Cesar De Saussure to His Family,* trans. Madame van Muyden (New York: Caliban, 1995), 172.

4. Roger Fiske, *English Theatre Music in the Eighteenth Century,* 2nd ed. (Oxford: Oxford University Press, 1986), 86.

5. See Lewis Theobald, *Perseus and Andromeda* (London, 1730) and the anonymously published *The Tricks of Harlequin: or, the* Spaniard *Outwitted* (Darby, 1739). The latter prints a provincial company's version of "the Comic Part of the celebrated Entertainment of *Perseus and Andromeda*." *The Tricks of Harlequin* only indicates *where* the serious sections are located, but does not describe them in detail; nonetheless, it prints the same version of a wizard's song to Harlequin as the one printed in the 1730 libretto to *Perseus and Andromeda,* and matches up with the arrangement of the serious sections quite well. For another discussion of the Lincoln's Inn Fields *Perseus and Andromeda,* see Antoni N. Sadlak, "Harlequin Comes to England: The Early Evidence of the *Commedia dell'arte* in England and the Formulation of English Harlequinades and Pantomimes" (Ph.D. diss., Tufts University, 1999), 478–86.

6. On this performance history, see Sadlak, "Harlequin Comes to England," and also Mitchell Preston Wells, "Pantomime and Spectacle on the London Stage, 1741–1761" (Ph.D. diss., University of North Carolina, 1934).

7. Fredric Jameson, *The Political Unconscious: Narrative as a Socially Symbolic Act* (Ithaca, N.Y.: Cornell University Press, 1981); Bill Brown, *The Material Unconscious: American Amusement, Stephen Crane, and the Economies of Play* (Cambridge, Mass.: Harvard University Press, 1996); and Eric Lott, *Love and Theft: Blackface Minstrelsy and the American Working Class* (New York: Oxford University Press, 1993).

8. Sadlak, "Harlequin Comes to England," 394–96.

9. See Max Horkheimer and Theodor W. Adorno, *Dialectic of Enlightenment,* trans. John Cumming (New York: Continuum, 1944), esp. 120–67.

10. Northrop Frye, *The Anatomy of Criticism* (Princeton: Princeton University Press, 1957), 44.

11. John Rich, preface to Lewis Theobald, *The Rape of Proserpine* (London, 1727), A2, iv. Since one of the most frequently used attacks against Rich was that he was illiterate, there is some reason to be suspicious of his authorship of this preface, but whether it was written by him or not, it seems fair to take it as a piece of evidence that explains what Rich claimed he was doing.

12. James Miller, *Harlequin-Horace: Or, the Art of Modern Poetry,* ed. Antony Coleman (Los Angeles: William Andrews Clark Memorial Library, 1976), 24.

13. Theobald, *The Censor* #7 (April 25, 1715), in *The Censor,* 3 vols. (London, 1717), 1:46.

14. See F. Le Rousseau, *A Chacoon for a Harlequin* (London, 1730), reprinted in Cyril W. Beaumont, *The History of Harlequin* (1926; New York: Benjamin Blom, 1967), 121–32.

15. Several eighteenth-century pantomimes equate Harlequin with Mercury, and historians of the commedia dell'arte have made the connection frequently as well. Pierre Louis Duchartre, for example, gushes that Harlequin "remains intangible, for he is without doubt of divine essence, if not, indeed, the god Mercury

himself, patron of merchants, thieves, and panders"; *The Italian Comedy*, trans. Randolph T. Weaver (1929; New York: Dover, 1966), 124.

16. Stephen Greenblatt, "Invisible Bullets," in *Shakespearean Negotiations: The Circulation of Social Energy in Renaissance England* (Oxford: Clarendon, 1988), 44.

17. Laura Mulvey, "Visual Pleasure and Narrative Cinema," in *Feminism and Film Theory*, ed. Constance Penley (New York: Routledge, 1988), 57–68. For a recent application of Mulvey's work to the English theater of this period, see Jean Marsden, "Female Spectatorship, Jeremy Collier and the Anti-Theatrical Debate," *ELH* 65 (1998): 877–98.

18. Laura Mulvey, "Afterthoughts on 'Visual Pleasure and Narrative Cinema' Inspired by *Duel in the Sun*," in *Psychoanalysis and Cinema*, ed. E. Ann Kaplan (New York: Routledge, 1990), 24–35.

19. Neil Hertz, "Medusa's Head: Male Hysteria under Political Pressure," *Representations* 4 (Fall 1983): 27–54.

20. On "the Ladies" as a topos in discourse in and around the seventeenth- and eighteenth-century London theater, see John Harrington Smith, "Shadwell, the Ladies, and the Change in Comedy," *Modern Philology* 46 (August 1948): 22–33; and David Roberts, *The Ladies: Female Patronage of Restoration Drama, 1660–1700* (Oxford: Clarendon, 1989).

21. Kristina Straub, *Sexual Suspects: Eighteenth-Century Players and Sexual Ideology* (Princeton, N.J.: Princeton University Press, 1992), 19.

22. Examples of pantomimes where Harlequin is transformed into a woman include *Harlequin Doctor Faustus* (1723) and *Harlequin Incendiary* (1746).

23. I am indebted to Elizabeth Lewis's essay on Santlow's performance as Harlequine for directing my attention to the figure. See Elizabeth Miller Lewis, "Hester Santlow's Harlequine: Dance, Dress, Status, and Gender on the London Stage, 1706–1734," in *The Clothes That Wear Us: Essays on Dressing and Transgressing in Eighteenth-Century Culture*, ed. Jessica Munns and Penny Richards (Newark: University of Delaware Press, 1999), 80–101.

24. Zacharias von Uffenbach, *London in 1710*, trans. and ed. W. H. Quarrel and Margaret Mare (London, 1934), 31. Continental examples of Harlequine also appear in Gregorio Lambranzi's 1716 manual *New and Curious School of Theatrical Dancing*.

25. Douglas Hay, "Property, Authority, and the Criminal Law," in *Albion's Fatal Tree: Crime and Society in Eighteenth-Century England*, ed. Douglas Hay, Peter Linebaugh, John Rule, E. P. Thompson, and Cal Winslow (London: Allen Lane, 1975), 17–63.

26. Fredric Jameson, "Reification and Utopia in Mass Culture," in *Signatures of the Visible* (New York: Routledge, 1992), 25.

27. Jane Moody argues that this is one of the salient differences between eighteenth- and nineteenth-century versions of the form, as the latter more frequently

"dramatized the pleasures, fears, and absurdities of urban life"; Moody, *Illegitimate Theatre in London, 1770–1800* (Cambridge: Cambridge University Press, 2000), 210.

Chapter 2. Pantomime, Popular Culture, and the Invention of the English Stage

1. Antonin Artaud, *The Theater and Its Double*, trans. Mary Caroline Richards (New York: Grove, 1958), 85.

2. See, for example, Victor Turner, *From Ritual to Theatre: The Human Seriousness of Play* (New York: PAJ Publications, 1982); and Richard Schechner, *Between Theater and Anthropology* (Philadelphia: University of Pennsylvania Press, 1985), and *The Future of Ritual: Writings on Culture and Performance* (London: Routledge, 1989).

3. James Wright, *Historia Histrionica: An Historical Account of the English-Stage* (New York: Garland, 1974), 32. In his recent book, *Cities of the Dead,* Joseph Roach has rightly stressed the way that Wright gestures in this dialogue to the memorial, ritual function of the theater itself, its capacity to act as a form of collective memory, to embody the past in such a way as to recapture what might otherwise disappear into oblivion. See Joseph R. Roach, *Cities of the Dead: Circum-Atlantic Performance* (New York: Columbia University Press, 1996), 93.

4. On the fairs, see Henry Morley, *Memoirs of Bartholomew Fair* (London: Frederick Warne, 1874); and Sybil Rosenfeld, *The Theatre of the London Fairs in the 18th Century* (Cambridge: Cambridge University Press, 1960).

5. See, among many other works, Michael D. Bristol, *Carnival and Theater: Plebeian Culture and the Structure of Authority in Renaissance England* (New York: Methuen, 1985); Peter Burke, *Popular Culture in Early Modern Europe* (New York: Harper & Row, 1978); Stuart Hall, "Notes on Deconstructing 'the Popular,'" in *People's History and Social Theory,* ed. Raphael Samuels (London: Routledge, 1981), 227–40; Leah Marcus, *The Politics of Mirth: Jonson, Herrick, Milton, Marvell, and the Defense of Old Holiday Pastimes* (Chicago: University of Chicago Press, 1986); Barry Reay, *Popular Cultures in England 1550–1750* (London: Longman, 1998); Scott Cutler Shershow, *Puppets and "Popular" Culture* (Ithaca, N.Y.: Cornell University Press, 1995); E. P. Thompson, *The Making of the English Working Class* (New York: Vintage, 1963), and *Customs in Common: Studies in Traditional Popular Culture* (New York: The New Press, 1993).

6. Thompson, *Customs in Common,* 8, 12.

7. See Roger Chartier, "Culture as Appropriation: Popular Cultural Uses in Early Modern France," in *Understanding Popular Culture: Europe from the Middle Ages to the Nineteenth Century,* ed. Steven L. Kaplan (Berlin: Mouton, 1984), 229–53, and *The Cultural Uses of Print in Early Modern France,* trans. Lydia G. Cochrane (Princeton, N.J.: Princeton University Press, 1987).

8. Scott Shershow has recently applied Chartier's concept in reverse, focusing on the appropriation of the low, "popular" culture form of puppetry by bourgeois and elite groups as a foil against which to define their own high, literary culture. His own appropriation of Chartier's strategy is a particularly useful model for any study of eighteenth-century English pantomime, not only because of puppetry's links with the commedia dell'arte (most obviously in the form of its star performer Punch, drawn into the English puppet theater from commedia in the late seventeenth century as a diminutive version of the human character variously known on the Continent as Punchinello, Polinchinelle, Pulcinella, etc.) but because, by virtue of its inescapable materiality, puppetry shares some of the features of eighteenth-century pantomime, which was indeed frequently attacked on the grounds that it reduced humans to puppets or automatons. See Shershow, *Puppets and "Popular" Culture,* 5–7.

9. Reay, *Popular Culture in England 1550–1750,* 201.

10. Eric Lott's coupling of "love" and "theft" in his book of the same name usefully condenses the complexly affective character of appropriation and disavowal that characterizes the dynamic construction of culture. See Eric Lott, *Love and Theft: Blackface Minstrelsy and the American Working Class* (New York: Oxford University Press, 1993).

11. See *The British Stage: Or, the Exploits of Harlequin: A Farce* (London: T. Warner, 1724), 13.

12. *The English Stage Italianiz'd* (London: A. Moore, 1727), iv. This mock-afterpiece is credited on its title page to Thomas D'Urfey, who was, by 1727, long dead. As Michael Dobson points out, D'Urfey was by this time the byword for a licentious and incompetent poet, "the very personification of derivative smut," and for that reason a useful name to assign to a work spoofing the popularity of illegitimate entertainments. See Michael Dobson, *The Making of the National Poet: Shakespeare, Adaptation, and Authorship, 1660–1769* (Oxford: Clarendon, 1992), 102.

13. Peter Stallybrass and Allon White, *The Politics and Poetics of Transgression* (Ithaca, N.Y.: Cornell University Press, 1986), 103.

14. I have been educated here by Elaine Hadley's discussion of what she calls the "modern principle of classification," by which culture is organized into various horizontal strata, strata that include economic class but also systems of "public policy, economics (through accounting, for instance), social and natural sciences, and medicine"; *Melodramatic Tactics: Theatricalized Dissent in the English Marketplace, 1880–1885* (Stanford: Stanford University Press, 1995), 22. Hadley is interested in the operations of this principle in the early nineteenth century; in this chapter, I trace an earlier manifestation of a similar process.

15. Stallybrass and White, *The Politics and Poetics of Transgression,* 31.

16. Goldoni's is apparently the first traceable usage of the term *commedia dell'arte,* which gained circulation soon after he introduced it in his *Teatro Comico* in 1750. Roger Henke suggests that the term might have been in use before that date, but also confirms that it does not seem to appear in print before then, and only went into

wide circulation after mid-century. See Henke, *Performance and Literature in the Commedia Dell'Arte* (Cambridge: Cambridge University Press, 2002), 5, 217. The distinction between improvisatory and scripted performances that Goldoni relies on had been made by Luigi Riccoboni in his *Histoire du Théâtre Italien* (1728); see Kenneth Richards and Laura Richards, *The Commedia Dell'arte: A Documentary History* (Oxford: Basil Blackwell, 1990), 8–9. Goldoni is credited not just with the popularization of the term, but with having decisively changed the form itself, at least as it was performed in eighteenth-century Italy. Commissioned to write a commedia scenario for a troupe in 1745, Goldoni was angry at the liberties the performers took with his text, and demanded that they memorize a written script, an innovation credited with dealing a decisive blow to the tradition of improvised performances loosely based on a predetermined plot outline. See Lee Hall's introduction to Carlo Goldoni, *A Servant to Two Masters* (London: Methuen, 1999), xvii–xix.

17. On the Stuart court masque, the essential texts are Stephen Orgel, *The Illusion of Power: Political Theater in the English Renaissance* (Berkeley: University of California Press, 1975); and Stephen Orgel et al., *Inigo Jones: The Theatre of the Stuart Court* (London: University of California Press, 1973). For a more political reading of the Stuart masque as a form, see also Lawrence Venuti, *Our Halcyon Dayes: English Prerevolutionary Texts and Postmodern Culture* (Madison: University of Wisconsin Press, 1989).

18. In *Britannia Triumphans,* a late Carolean masque (1637) by Inigo Jones and William Davenant, for instance, "Harlekin" appears as one of many figures of disorder who interrupt the noble masquers. Leah Marcus observes that Ben Jonson's *The Vision of Delight,* a 1617 masque, includes several pantaloons; see *The Politics of Mirth,* 67.

19. See Peter Anthony Motteux and John Eccles, *The Rape of Europa by Jupiter and Acis and Galatea* (Los Angeles: William Andrews Clark Memorial Library, 1981). See also Leo Hughes, "Afterpieces: or, That's Entertainment," in *The Stage and the Page: London's "Whole Show" in the Eighteenth-Century Theatre,* ed. George Winchester Stone Jr. (Berkeley: University of California Press, 1981), 55–70; Virginia P. Scott, "The Infancy of English Pantomime: 1716–1723," *Educational Theatre Journal* 24 (1972): 125–38; and Lucyle Hook, "Motteux and the Classical Masque," in *British Theatre and the Other Arts, 1660–1800,* ed. Shirley Strum Kenny (Washington: Folger Shakespeare Library, 1984), 105–15.

20. See Edward Ravenscroft, *The Anatomist: Or, the Sham Doctor* (London: R. Baldwin, 1697). Ravenscroft's play is a loose translation of Hauteroche's *Crispin médecin,* and although it includes no commedia characters, its plot—in which a servant named Crispin first witnesses a dissection, and then, impersonating a pompous doctor, pretends to perform one on the living body of a blocking patriarch—strongly resembles a commedia scenario. On Ravenscroft, see Robert D. Hume, *The Development of English Drama in the Late Seventeenth Century* (Oxford: Clarendon, 1976), 416.

21. John Thurmond, *Harlequin Doctor Faustus: With the Masque of the Deities* (London: W. Chetwood, 1724), 13.

22. Another example is puppet shows, which continued to be performed through the Interregnum, particularly when they were based on religious subjects; the best study on puppetry in this period remains George Speight, *The History of the English Puppet Theatre,* 2nd ed. (Carbondale: Southern Illinois University Press, 1990). Part of the reason for puppetry's acceptance in the face of attacks on other kinds of theatrical performance may be that puppets, by virtue of their miniature size and obvious artificiality, never seduce the spectator into mistaking them for real persons.

23. Andrew Grewar has shown that Italian commedia troupes were performing in England by no later than the 1540s, and we know that visiting Continental companies remained a regular feature of the London theater into the eighteenth century, where they sometimes performed their own works in direct competition with the Anglicized versions being staged at Drury Lane and Lincoln's Inn Fields. See Andrew Grewar, "Shakespeare and the Actors of the *Commedia dell'arte,*" in *Studies in the Commedia Dell'Arte,* ed. David J. George and Christopher J. Gossip (Cardiff: University of Wales Press, 1993), 13–47. See also Ifan Kyrle Fletcher, "Italian Comedians in England," *Theatre Notebook* 8 (July 1954): 87.

24. See Richards and Richards, *The Commedia Dell'arte,* 275–77.

25. See K. M. Lea, *Italian Popular Comedy,* 2 vols. (New York: Russell & Russell, 1962); Allardyce Nicoll, *The World of Harlequin: A Critical Study of the Commedia Dell'arte* (Cambridge: Cambridge University Press, 1963); and Henry Salerno, ed., *Scenarios of the Commedia dell'Arte: Flaminio Scala's Il Teatro delle favole Rappresentative* (New York: Limelight, 1967).

26. Nashe, cited in Richards and Richards, *The Commedia Dell'arte,* 274–75.

27. On *A Duke and No Duke,* see Roger Fiske, *English Theatre Music in the Eighteenth Century,* 2nd ed. (Oxford: Oxford University Press, 1986), 68–69.

28. See James Stuart, *The King's Majesties Declaration to His Subjects, Concerning Lawful Sports to be Used,* in *Minor Prose Works of King James VI and I,* ed. James Craigie (Edinburgh: Scottish Text Society, 1982), 101–9.

29. Marcus, *The Politics of Mirth,* 3.

30. On Charles II's efforts to reestablish traditional pastimes, see David Underdown, *Revel, Riot, and Rebellion: Popular Politics and Culture in England 1603–1660* (Oxford: Clarendon, 1985), 275–91.

31. *Ideology and Politics on the Eve of Restoration: Newcastle's Advice to Charles II,* ed. Thomas P. Slaughter (Philadelphia: American Philosophical Society, 1984), 64.

32. See Michel Foucault, "Governmentality," in *Power,* ed. James D. Faubion, *Essential Works of Foucault, 1954–1984* (New York: The New Press, 2000), 201–22.

33. Behn, *The Emperor of the Moon,* in *The Works of Aphra Behn,* ed. Janet Todd, 7 vols. (Columbus: Ohio State University Press, 1996), 7:157.

34. E. S. de Beer, ed., *The Diary of John Evelyn,* 6 vols. (Oxford: Clarendon, 1955), 4:75.

35. Richards and Richards, *The Commedia Dell'arte,* 278.

36. For a good recent discussion of Langbaine, see Paulina Kewes, *Authorship and Appropriation: Writing for the Stage in England, 1660–1710* (Oxford: Clarendon, 1998), 97–129, 207–19.

37. Langbaine, *Account of the English Dramatic Poets* (London, 1691), A3r.

38. Prompters seem to have enjoyed a kind of customary right over the playhouse's texts—the playtexts and various parts, of course, but also the account books and records of performances. William Chetwood, the prompter at Drury Lane for much of the 1720s and 1730s, also published a number of plays, as well as novels, under his own imprint, and wrote *A General History of the Stage* (1750), based on the playhouse records. Downes's epigraph refers to the prompter's function as a record keeper, attesting that his book is "Non audita, sed comperta," that is, he reports, not on what he has heard, but what has been recorded, presumably in the account books and other playhouse records for which he was responsible.

39. *Comparison,* 46, 34, 46.

40. Simon Shepherd and Peter Womack, *English Drama: A Cultural History* (Oxford: Basil Blackwell, 1996), 147.

41. My attention was first prompted to this echo by Jonas Barish, who cites William Spingairn as his source. See Jonas Barish, *The Antitheatrical Prejudice* (Berkeley: University of California Press, 1981), 226. For an interesting recent account of Rymer's *A Short View of Tragedy,* see Paul D. Cannon, "*A Short View of Tragedy* and Rymer's Proposals for Regulating the English Stage," *Review of English Studies* 52, no. 206 (2001): 207–26.

42. My understanding of the "case" as a category of knowledge has been greatly enriched by James Chandler, *England in 1819: The Politics of Literary Culture and the Case of Romantic Historicism* (Chicago: University of Chicago Press, 1998), esp. 39–40.

43. Collier, *A Second Defense of the Short View of the Prophaneness and Immorality of the English Stage* (1700; New York: Garland, 1972), 3, 37.

44. Ibid., 91.

45. John Weaver, *An Essay towards an History of Dancing* (London: J. Tonson, 1712), 118.

46. See Antoni N. Sadlak, "Harlequin Comes to England: The Early Evidence of the *Commedia dell'arte* in England and the Formulation of English Harlequinades and Pantomimes" (Ph.D. diss., Tufts University, 1999), 394–95.

47. Henry Bourne, *Antiquitates Vulgares; or, the Antiquities of the Common People* (Newcastle, 1725), 115. Bourne is a foundational figure in the historiography of English folklore, as *Antiquitates Vulgares* was the basis for many of the histories of rural pastimes that would follow by the late eighteenth and early nineteenth centuries. Bourne's book was in effect subsumed into John Brand's *Observations on*

Popular Antiquities (1777), which was itself frequently reprinted and expanded well into the nineteenth century, and then became an essential source book for students of English folklore in the twentieth century.

48. Mel Gordon, *Lazzi: The Comic Routines of the Commedia Dell'arte* (New York: PAJ Publications, 1983), 23.

49. Erika Fischer-Lichte, "Theatre and the Civilizing Process: An Approach to the History of Acting," in *The Show and the Gaze of Theatre: A European Perspective* (Iowa City: University of Iowa Press, 1997), 33–34.

Chapter 3. Wit Corporeal

1. Richard Kroll, *The Material Word: Literate Culture in the Restoration and Early Eighteenth Century* (Baltimore: Johns Hopkins University Press, 1991), 19.

2. The performance records can be found in *The London Stage, 1660–1800,* ed. Emmett L. Avery (Carbondale: Southern Illinois University Press, 1965).

3. There are a number of secondary accounts of the eighteenth-century theater audience. See Harry William Pedicord, *The Theatrical Public in the Time of Garrick* (Carbondale: Southern Illinois University Press, 1966); Leo Hughes, *The Drama's Patrons: A Study of the Eighteenth-Century London Audience* (Austin: University of Texas Press, 1971); John Loftis, "The Audience," in *The Revels History of Drama in English:* vol. V, *1660–1750,* ed. John Loftis, Richard Southern, Marion Jones, and A. H. Scouten (London: Methuen, 1976), 13–25; and David Roberts, *The Ladies: Female Patronage of Restoration Drama, 1660–1700* (Oxford: Clarendon, 1989).

4. *Oxford English Dictionary,* 3rd ed. online, definition 3. Here I am persuaded as well by Michael McKeon's argument about the invention of the concept of "aristocracy" in the seventeenth century as part of a new logic of social categorization: "'aristocracy' is itself the new term, the 'antithetical' simple abstraction, needed to announce the emergence of a new social organization, an announcement which is reciprocal to that accomplished two centuries later by the 'thetical' language of class"; Michael McKeon, *The Origins of the English Novel, 1600–1740* (Baltimore: Johns Hopkins University Press, 1987), 169.

5. On the middling sort, see, among other texts, Peter Earle, *The Making of the English Middle Class: Business, Society and Family Life, 1660–1700* (London: Methuen, 1989).

6. Samuel Pepys, Robert Latham, and William Matthews, *The Diary of Samuel Pepys,* 11 vols. (Berkeley: University of California Press, 1970), December 27, 1662, 3:295–96; January 1, 1668, 8:2.

7. Dennis, "The Decay and Defects of Dramatick Poetry," in *The Critical Works of John Dennis,* ed. Edward Niles Hooker, 2 vols. (Baltimore: Johns Hopkins University Press, 1939–43), 2:276.

8. Ibid., 2:278.

9. Dennis, "A Large Account of the Taste in Poetry," in *Works,* 1:293.

10. On the footmen's claim that the upper gallery was "our property," see the *Gentleman's Magazine,* March 7, 1737; other accounts of the incident appear in Hughes, *The Drama's Patrons,* 15–20; and Martin Battestin and Ruthe R. Battestin, *Henry Fielding: A Life* (London: Routledge, 1993), 213.

11. *The Daily Journal,* February 22, 1737.

12. Elaine Hadley's discussion of the 1809 Old Price riots exaggerates the uniqueness and novelty of that event, leaving the reader with the impression that eighteenth-century audiences were comparatively complaisant; see her *Melodramatic Tactics: Theatricalized Dissent in the English Marketplace, 1800–1885* (Stanford, Calif.: Stanford University Press, 1995), 34–76. But that is not the case. Playhouse disturbances were frequent, with major riots occurring roughly once a decade. There were disturbances over attempts to change members of the cast of *Cato* in 1718 and *The Beggar's Opera* in 1733; there were riots responding to increases in ticket prices in 1743 and 1763; and riots occurred over the presence of French dancers in David Garrick's *Chinese Festival* in 1755, and in 1776 over fears of miscegenation raised by a performance of *The Blackamoor Wash'd White.* For a recent discussion of eighteenth-century playhouse disturbances in London, see Heather McPherson, "Theatrical Riots and Cultural Politics in Eighteenth-Century London," *The Eighteenth Century: Theory and Interpretation* (Fall 2003): 236–52.

13. The most dramatic change occurred at Drury Lane in 1765, when David Garrick replaced the chandeliers over the stage and auditorium with a more sophisticated lighting system, in emulation of those he had seen on a long tour of theaters on the Continent, which made it possible to dim the illumination in the audience and to throw more concentrated light onto the playing area. See C. B. Hogan, *The London Stage,* V, vol. 1, lxv.

14. John Macky, *A Journey through England. In Familiar Letters,* 2nd ed. (London: J. Hooke, 1722), 1:170–71. My thanks to Cynthia Wall for directing me to Macky's book.

15. Centlivre, "Epilogue" to *The Basset Table,* in *The Plays of Susanna Centlivre,* 3 vols. ed. Richard C. Frushell (New York: Garland, 1982), 1: unpaginated.

16. The phrase is from *The Country-Gentleman's Vade Mecum* (London, 1699), 39. As Elaine Hadley has shown, the decline of this ideal was met with great resistance in the early nineteenth century, when rebuilt and remodeled houses permitted wealthy members of the audience to conceal themselves from view. See Hadley, *Melodramatic Tactics,* esp. 34–76.

17. For Betterton's description of the theater as a "mimic state," see Charles Gildon, *The Life of Mr. Thomas Betterton* (London, 1710), 10. My attention was directed to the phrase by Joseph R. Roach, *Cities of the Dead: Circum-Atlantic Performance* (New York: Columbia University Press, 1996), 92.

18. Theophilus Cibber, *Theophilus Cibber, to David Garrick, Esq., with Dissertations on Theatrical Subjects* (London, 1759), 6.

19. Julie Stone Peters, *Theatre of the Book, 1480–1800: Print, Text, and Performance in Europe* (Oxford: Oxford University Press, 2000), 191.

20. On seventeenth-century perspective scenery, the best text remains Richard Southern, *Changeable Scenery: Its Origin and Development in the British Theatre* (London: Faber and Faber, 1952).

21. See Cibber, *An Apology for the Life of Colley Cibber*, ed. B.R.S. Fone (1740; Ann Arbor: University of Michigan Press, 1968), 255–56. As Shepherd and Womack observe, Cibber "mourns the extra ten feet of downstage space" because "he had lost some of the ambivalent zone between the scenery and the crowd which was the spatial and social medium of the fops that made him famous" (124).

22. Here my thinking is indebted to discourse about spectatorship in early twentieth-century film, an institution that faced some of the same problems addressed by the eighteenth-century theater. See, for example, Miriam Hansen, *Babel and Babylon: Spectatorship in American Silent Film* (Cambridge, Mass.: Harvard University Press, 1991).

23. Michael Warner, *Publics and Counterpublics* (New York: Zone Books, 2002), 164.

24. Steele, *The School of Action*, in *Richard Steele*, ed. G. A. Aitken (London, 1893), 368–69.

25. Joseph Addison, "The Play-House," in *Anthology of Poems on Affairs of State*, ed. George deLord (New Haven: Yale University Press, 1982), 578–81.

26. Addison, *Spectators* #39 and 40 (April 14 and 15, 1711), in the Donald F. Bond edition of *The Spectator*, 5 vols. (Oxford: Clarendon, 1965), 1:167, 171; hereafter, references will be cited in the text.

27. *The Drummer*, in *The Miscellaneous Works of Joseph Addison*, ed. Adolph Charles Louis Guthkelch, 2 vols. (1913; Claire Shores, Mich.: Scholarly Press, 1978), 1:478.

28. In understanding Addison's "pleasures of the imagination" series, I have been educated by Neil Saccamano's essay "The Sublime Force of Words in Addison's 'Pleasures,'" *ELH* 58 (1991): 83–106.

29. Jonathan Crary, *Techniques of the Observer: On Vision and Modernity in the Nineteenth Century* (Cambridge, Mass.: MIT Press, 1991), 60.

30. This part of my discussion is indebted to Joseph R. Roach, *The Player's Passion: Studies in the Science of Acting* (Newark: University of Delaware Press, 1985), 62.

31. René Descartes, "Treatise on Man," in *The Philosophical Writings of Descartes*, ed. John Cottingham, Robert Stoothoff, and Dugald Murdoch, 2 vols. (Cambridge: Cambridge University Press, 1984), 2:102.

32. Addison's original manuscript is reproduced in *Some Portions of Essays Contributed to the Spectator by Mr. Joseph Addison, Now first Printed from his MS. Note Book*, ed. J. D. Campbell (Glasgow, 1854).

33. Roach, *The Player's Passion*, 62–66.

34. Steele clearly has the Cartesian system in mind when, in his notes to *The School of Action,* he proposes that Booth, projected to take the role of Orestes in a play-within-the-play, should be instructed to move "from passion to passion in a Hurry" as he contemplates killing his mother Clytemnestra; Steele, *The School of Action,* in Aitken, *Richard Steele,* 305.

35. John Weaver, *An Essay Towards an History of Dancing* (London: Jacob Tonson, 1712), 16; hereafter, cited in the text.

36. Weaver, *The Loves of Mars and Venus: A Dramatick Entertainment of Dancing, Attempted in Imitation of the Pantomimes of the Ancient Greeks and Romans* (London: W. Mears, J. Browne, 1717), 23.

37. See, for example, R. J. Broadbent, *A History of Pantomime* (1901; New York: Benjamin Blom, 1964), 188.

38. Steele, *The Tatler,* January 3, 1710, in the Donald F. Bond edition of *The Tatler,* 3 vols. (Oxford: Clarendon, 1987), 2:186. On Nicolini's appeal, see Joseph Roach, "Cavaliere Nicolini: London's First Opera Star," *Educational Theatre Journal* 28 (May 1976): 189–205.

39. Steele, preface to *The Conscious Lovers,* in *The Plays of Richard Steele,* ed. Shirley Strum Kenny (Oxford: Clarendon, 1971), 299.

40. Steele, *Tatler* #8 (April 28, 1709), 1:72.

41. Cibber, *Apology,* 60, 57.

42. William Warner, *Licensing Entertainment: The Elevation of Novel Reading in Britain, 1684–1750* (Berkeley: University of California Press, 1998), 232–34.

43. Benedict Anderson offers an eloquent account of the nation-building effects of this simultaneity in his *Imagined Communities: Reflections on the Origin and Spread of Nationalism* (London: Verso, 1983), 37–38.

44. In a note left with his papers at the time of his death, Steele records his intention "to ridicule ye whole Mechanick of Dr. Faustus, &c., and all things of that kind for ye Theatre—make persons to play tricks, break necks, and the like"; Aitken, *Richard Steele,* 304.

45. *Grub-Street Journal* 384 (May 4, 1737), 1.

46. John Weaver, *Anatomical and Mechanical Lectures Upon Dancing* (London, 1721), 4. Weaver was credited by Charles Burney with three contributions to *The Spectator* (numbers 67, 334, and 370); Richard Ralph, pointing out that Burney's recollection came many years after the fact, suggests plausibly on the basis of internal evidence that Weaver can be credited with having written the letter from a dancing-master that forms part of *Spectator* 366 and that he probably at least influenced the others. See Richard Ralph, *The Life and Works of John Weaver* (New York: Dance Horizons, 1985), 110–15.

47. *Anatomical and Mechanical Lectures,* vii.

48. See, for example, Norbert Elias, *Power and Civility: The Civilizing Process,* vol. II, trans. Edmund Jephcott (New York: Pantheon, 1982); and Joseph R. Roach, "Power's Body: The Inscription of Morality as Style," in *Interpreting the*

Theatrical Past: The Historiography of Performance, ed. Thomas Postlewait and Bruce McConachie (Iowa City: University of Iowa Press, 1989), 99–118.

49. See Gildon, *The Life of Mr. Thomas Betterton,* 49–50.

50. James Ralph, *The Touch-Stone* (1728; New York: Garland, 1972), 111.

51. John Weaver, *The Fable of Orpheus and Eurydice,* title page, reproduced in Richard Ralph, *The Life and Works of John Weaver* (New York: Dance Horizons, 1985), 767.

52. *The Weekly Journal,* April 6, 1723, 1363.

53. *British Journal,* March 18, 1727.

54. Weaver, *The History of the Mimes and Pantomimes* (London: J. Roberts, 1728), 1.

55. Ralph, *The Life and Works of John Weaver,* 84.

56. Theophilus Cibber, *The Harlot's Progress, or, the Ridotto Al'Fresco,* reprinted in *The Harlot's Progress and The Rake's Progress* (Los Angeles: William Andrews Clark Memorial Library, 1977), 12.

Chapter 4. Magic and Mimesis

1. John Thurmond, *Harlequin Doctor Faustus: With the Masque of the Deities* (London: W. Chetwood, 1724), 13.

2. The fullest description available of both Faustus performances is in Antoni Sadlak's 1999 dissertation, "Harlequin Comes to England: The Early Evidence of the *Commedia dell'arte* in England and the Formulation of English Harlequinades and Pantomimes" (Ph.D. diss., Tufts University, 1999), 425–47.

3. In his introduction to *The London Stage,* for instance, Emmett Avery states that the success of these two productions "established the vogue of elaborate spectacles" that followed; see Emmett L. Avery, ed., *The London Stage, 1660–1800,* vol. II (Carbondale: Southern Illinois University Press, 1965), cxviii.

4. See William Mountfort, *The Life and Death of Doctor Faustus, Made into a Farce,* introd. Anthony Kaufman (1697; Los Angeles: William Andrews Clark Memorial Library, 1973). Mountfort's farce was not published until 1697 (several years after his death), but Kaufman presents credible evidence that its first performances occurred sometime between 1684 and 1688.

5. Marshall Sahlins, "The Return of the Event, Again: With Reflections on the Beginnings of the Great Fijian War of 1843 to 1855 between the Kingdoms of Bau and Rewa," in *Clio in Oceania: Towards a Historical Anthropology,* ed. Aletta Biersack (Washington: Smithsonian Institution Press, 1991), 37–99.

6. See Raymond Williams, *Marxism and Literature* (Oxford: Oxford University Press, 1977).

7. See Michael Cordner, "Playwright Versus Priest: Profanity and the Wit of Restoration Comedy," in *The Cambridge Companion to English Restoration Theatre,* ed. Deborah Payne Fisk (Cambridge: Cambridge University Press, 2000), 209–25.

8. Susanna Centlivre, "To the Reader," preface to *The Perjur'd Husband* (1701), in *The Dramatic Works of the Celebrated Mrs. Centlivre*, ed. Richard Frushell, 3 vols. (New York: AMS, 1968), 1: unpaginated.

9. See Richard Steele, "Mr. Steele's Apology for Himself and his Writings," in *Tracts and Pamphlets*, ed. Rae Blanchard (Baltimore: Johns Hopkins University Press, 1944), 277–346, esp. 311–12.

10. James Leheny, ed., *The Freeholder* (Oxford: Clarendon, 1979), 193; hereafter, cited in the text. The first collected edition of the journal, published in 1716 by the Whig publisher Jacob Tonson, tellingly subtitles the series "Political Essays" as if to distinguish it from the ostensibly apolitical *Spectator*.

11. For a good recent discussion of the affective relations generated by partisan conflict in this period, with particular reference to Addison, see Julie Ellison, *Cato's Tears and the Making of Anglo-American Emotion* (Chicago: University of Chicago Press, 1999).

12. Leah Marcus, *The Politics of Mirth: Jonson, Herrick, Milton, Marvell, and the Defense of Old Holiday Pastimes* (Chicago: University of Chicago Press, 1986), 3–4.

13. James Ralph, *The Fashionable Lady, or, Harlequin's Opera* (London: J. Watts, 1730), 30.

14. I take the latter phrase from the title of an anonymous 1745 verse satire on pantomime, *British Frenzy, or the Mock-Apollo* (London: J. Robinson, 1745). On the relationship of the Walpole government to the imaginative literature of the 1730s, see Bernard Goldgar, *Walpole and the Wits: The Relation of Politics to Literature, 1722–1742* (Lincoln: University of Nebraska Press, 1976); Christine Gerrard, *The Patriot Opposition to Walpole: Politics, Poetry, and National Myth, 1725–1742* (Oxford: Clarendon, 1994); and Tone Sundt Urstad, *Sir Robert Walpole's Poets: The Use of Literature as Pro-Government Propaganda, 1721– 1742* (Newark: University of Delaware Press, 1999).

15. See William B. Warner, *Licensing Entertainment: The Elevation of Novel Reading in Britain, 1684–1750* (Berkeley: University of California Press, 1998), 176–230. Warner's term *media event* seems to be drawn from twentieth-century cultural criticism about the mass media, most notably Daniel Dayan and Elihu Katz's *Media Events: The Live Broadcasting of History* (Cambridge, Mass.: Harvard University Press, 1992). Warner uses the term not to refer, as Dayan and Katz generally do, to the construction of the "news," but to describe the effect of the systems of media on cultural forms and the way they are brought into public discourse.

16. See John Henry Jones, *The English Faust Book: A Critical Edition, Based on the Text of 1592* (Cambridge: Cambridge University Press, 1994).

17. *A Dramatick Entertainment, Call'd the Necromancer: Or, Harlequin, Doctor Faustus*, (London: T. Wood, 1724), vi, iv; hereafter, cited in the text.

18. I was introduced to the connection between the two Faust stories by Adrian Johns's recent history of the printing press. See Adrian Johns, *The Nature of the*

Book: Print and Knowledge in the Making (Chicago: University of Chicago Press, 1998), 351ff.

19. On Fust, see Albert Kapr, *Johann Gutenberg: The Man and His Invention*, trans. Douglas Martin (Aldershot: Scolar, 1996), esp. 156–59.

20. [Daniel Defoe], *The History of the Principal Discoveries and Improvements, in the Several Arts and Sciences* (London: W. Mears, F. Clay, and D. Browne, 1727). This is an anonymous work, but the odds seem to be in its favor of its being Defoe's; it has survived even the recent purge of the Defoe canon conducted by P. N. Furbank and W. R. Owen in their *Defoe De-Attributions: A Critique of J. R. Moore's Checklist* (London: Hambledon, 1994).

21. Johns, *The Nature of the Book*, 374.

22. *Round about our Coal-Fire; Or, Christmas Entertainments* (London: J. Roberts, c. 1730), 1; hereafter, cited in the text.

23. *The Weekly Journal*, December 11, 1723.

24. Thomas Brown, *Amusements Serious and Comical*, ed. Arthur L. Hayward (London: Routledge, 1927), 35.

25. Thurmond, *Harlequin Doctor Faustus*, 10.

26. Julie Stone Peters, *Theatre of the Book, 1480–1880: Print, Text, and Performance in Europe* (Oxford: Oxford University Press, 2000), 1.

27. See *Orchesography, or, the Art of Dancing, by Characters and Demonstrative Figures*, reprinted in facsimile in Richard Ralph, *The Life and Works of John Weaver* (New York: Dance Horizons, 1985). Weaver's treatise is essentially a translation of Raoul Feuillet's *Choreographie* (1700). Richard Ralph records Richard Steele's letter of praise to Weaver on the publication of the translation, which sums up what I take to be Weaver's own intentions in promoting this system of recording dance steps in the manner that words record language and paintings or engravings record images: "I am mightily pleased to observe, that the Art of Dancing, is, of late, come to take Rank in the Learned World, by being communicated in Letters and Characters, as all other parts of Knowledge have for some Ages been"; quoted in Ralph, *The Life and Works of John Weaver* (New York: Dance Horizons, 1985), 108.

28. Peters, *Theatre of the Book*, 35. She describes "masque books" printed for the King's company in the early seventeenth century, as well as pamphlets sold to the audience of the Dryden/Davenent version of *The Tempest* (which emphasized spectacle) in 1674, and at performances of Peter Motteux's *The Novelty* (1697).

29. One sign that the presence of such texts had become an expectation is that it was able to be mocked; in *The English Stage Italianiz'd* (1727), a satire on pantomime entertainments in the form of a closet entertainment in its own right, the author states that the libretto to his play (that is, the text we hold in our hands) will "be sold by the Orange-Women and Door-Keepers, at Six Pence each, during the Time of its Performance"; quoted in Peters, *Theatre of the Book*, 49.

30. *The Dunciad* (1728), in *The Poems of Alexander Pope*, ed. John Butt (New Haven: Yale University Press, 1963), 416, ll. 228–36.

31. Johnson, "Prologue Spoken at the Opening of the Theater in Drury-Lane, 1747," in *Samuel Johnson: Poems*, vol. VI of *The Yale Edition of the Works of Samuel Johnson*, ed. E. L. McAdam Jr. and George Milne (New Haven: Yale University Press, 1964), 87–90, 89.

32. I'm influenced here by Maureen N. McLane's recent work on eighteenth-century British balladeering and minstrelsy, work that underscores the significance of the media—oral, written, performed, textualized—through which cultural and historical phenomena are conceptualized. See, for example, her essay "The Figure Minstrelsy Makes: Poetry and Historicity," *Critical Inquiry* 29 (Spring 2003): 429–52.

Entr'acte

1. Samuel Richardson, *Familiar Letters on Important Occasions* (New York: Dodd, Mead, 1928), 215.

2. Henry Fielding, *The Champion* (May 3, 1740), in *The Works of Henry Fielding*, ed. Leslie Steven, 10 vols. (London: Smith, Elder, 1882), 5:430.

3. *The Dunciad* (1728) in Alexander Pope, *The Poems of Alexander Pope*, ed. John Butt (New Haven: Yale University Press, 1963), 416.

4. *British Frenzy: Or, the Mock-Apollo* (London: J. Robinson, 1745), 4.

5. Ronald Hutton, *The Stations of the Sun: A History of the Ritual Year in Britain* (Oxford: Oxford University Press, 1996), 126–27.

6. E. K. Chambers, *The English Folk-Play* (Oxford: Clarendon, 1933), 164. Here Chambers actually cites his own 1903 study *Medieval Drama*, but see also *The English Folk-Play*, 85, where Chambers describes black-faced characters in Mummer's Plays.

7. Otto Driesen, *Der Ursprung des Harlekin* (Berlin, 1904), cited in Antoni N. Sadlak, "Harlequin Comes to England: The Early Evidence of the *Commedia Dell'arte* in England and the Formulation of English Harlequinades and Pantomimes" (Ph.D. diss., Tufts University, 1999), 103.

8. Ibid., 103–4.

9. Colley Cibber, *An Apology for the Life of Colley Cibber*, ed. B.R.S. Fone (Ann Arbor: University of Michigan Press, 1968), 87–88.

10. Ibid., 87.

11. Roxann Wheeler, *The Complexion of Race: Categories of Difference in Eighteenth-Century British Culture* (Philadelphia: University of Pennsylvania Press, 2000).

12. Sir Thomas Browne, *Pseudodoxia Epidemica*, ed. Robin Robbins, 2 vols. (Oxford: Clarendon, 1981), 1:507–30.

13. Wheeler, *The Complexion of Race*, 54.

14. *Daily Journal*, April 5, 1723, cited in David Dabydeen, *Hogarth's Blacks: Images of Blacks in Eighteenth Century British Art* (Athens: University of Georgia Press, 1987), 17.

15. "Proclamation by the Lord Mayor of London, September 14, 1731," cited in James Walvin, *The Black Presence: A Documentary History of the Negro in England, 1555–1860* (New York: Schocken, 1972), 65. See also Folarin Shyllon, *Black People in Britain 1555–1833* (London: Oxford University Press, 1977).

16. Dabydeen, *Hogarth's Blacks*, 17.

17. Anthony Gerard Barthelemy, *Black Face, Maligned Race: The Representation of Blacks in English Drama from Shakespeare to Southerne* (Baton Rouge: Louisiana State University Press, 1987).

18. Julie Ellison, *Cato's Tears and the Making of Anglo-American Emotion* (Chicago: University of Chicago Press, 1999), 49.

19. On *Cato*, see also Srinivas Aravamudan, *Tropicopolitans: Colonialism and Agency, 1688–1804* (Durham, N.C.: Duke University Press, 1999). Aravamudan usefully stresses, more so than Ellison, that the point is not necessarily the blackness of Addison's African characters as their "transitivity," the way that their alterity permitted them to serve as vehicles through which British identity could be "virtualized": imagined anew by projected outward onto the colonial Other.

20. See ibid., 59–70.

21. See Barthelemy, *Black Face, Maligned Race*, 18–41. My account in this paragraph of black performers in court masques in this period is indebted to his study.

22. Jonson, *The Masque of Blackness*, in *Court Masques: Jacobean and Caroline Entertainments 1605–1640*, ed. David Lindley (Oxford: Oxford University Press, 1995), 6.

23. Barthelemy, *Black Face, Maligned Race*, 42. See also Elliot H. Tokson, *The Popular Image of the Black Man in English Drama, 1550–1688* (Boston, Mass.: G. K. Hall, 1982).

24. For examples, see Barthelemy, *Black Face, Maligned Race*, 42–71; and Peter Fryer, *Staying Power: The History of Black People in Britain* (London: Pluto, 1984).

25. E. P. Thompson, *Whigs and Hunters: The Origin of the Black Act* (Harmondsworth: Penguin, 1975). See also Pat Rogers, "The Waltham Blacks and the Black Act," *Historical Journal* 17 (1974): 465–86. Thompson and Rogers describe the same historical phenomenon, but from widely divergent points of view. For Rogers, the Blacks constituted a criminal conspiracy of "extortionists and protection-racketeers," and were thus a great enough threat to public order that the government's campaign against them was fully justified (466). Thompson's account portrays the Whig government as in effect the criminals who provoked residents of rural districts into violence by having violated customary relations about the use of common land. As will become clear, my sympathies are largely with Thompson's version of events.

26. *The History of the Blacks of Waltham in Hampshire; and Those under the Like Denomination in Berkshire* (London: A. Moore, 1723), 9.

27. *The Lives of the Most Remarkable Criminals, Who have been Condemn'd and Executed; For Murder, Highway, House-Breakers, Street-Robberies, Coining, or other Offences,* 2 vols. (London, 1735), 1:353.

28. See *The Usefulness of the Stage* (London, 1738), 17.

29. Winifred Smith, *The Commedia Dell'arte* (New York: Benjamin Blom, 1964), 22.

30. Luigi Riccoboni, *Histoire du Theatre Italien Depuis la Decadence de la Comedie Latine* (Paris, 1728), 4.

31. Even Cibber seems to have been aware of such theories. In his description of Penkethman's performance as Harlequin, he notes that the character has most typically been masked in order to follow "the Practice of the ancient Comedy"; Cibber, *Apology,* 87.

32. Cited in Adam Lively, *Masks, Blackness, Race, and the Literary Imagination* (New York: Oxford University Press, 2000), 16–17.

33. Maurice Sand, *The History of the Harlequinade,* 2 vols. (New York: Benjamin Blom, 1968), 1:10–11.

34. See *The Memoirs of Count Carlo Gozzi,* trans. John Addington Symonds, 2 vols. (New York: Scribner & Welford, 1890), 1:32.

35. Pierre Louis Duchartre, *The Italian Comedy,* trans. Randolph T. Weaver (1929; New York: Dover, 1966), 124.

36. The split between the classical and regional explanations for the origins of Harlequin register on the level of language, specifically the derivation of the term *Zanni,* the class of characters to which Harlequin and Brighella (also frequently traced to Bergamo) belong. Writers arguing for the classical origins of the character such as Riccoboni and Pierre Duchartre believe the word to be a corruption of "sanniones," a type of performer in Roman Atellanean farce; writers arguing for the character's association with a region of Italy such as Winifred Smith take it to be the characteristic way of pronouncing Giovanni in the Bergamese dialect.

37. Carlo Goldoni, *Memoirs of Carlo Goldini, Written by Himself,* trans. John Black (New York: Knopf, 1926), 300.

38. Richardson, *Familiar Letters,* 215.

39. Homi K. Bhabha, "Dissemination: Time, Narrative, and the Margins of the Modern Nation," in *The Location of Culture* (New York: Routledge, 1994), 139–70, 145.

40. Ibid.

41. David Garrick, *Harlequin's Invasion,* in *The Plays of David Garrick,* ed. Harry William Pedicord and Fredrick Louis Bergmann, 2 vols. (Carbondale: Southern Illinois University Press, 1980), 1:213, 223.

42. See David Mayer, *Harlequin in His Element: The English Pantomime, 1806–1836* (Cambridge, Mass.: Harvard University Press, 1969), 94–95. See also

George F. Rehin, "Harlequin Jim Crow: Continuity and Convergence in Black-face Clowning," *Journal of Popular Culture* 9 (1975): 682–701.

43. A. E. Wilson, *King Panto: The Story of Pantomime* (New York: Dutton, 1935), 17.

Chapter 5. "Infamous Harlequin Mimicry"

1. Samuel Richardson, *The Apprentice's Vade Mecum (1734)* (Los Angeles: William Andrews Clark Memorial Library, 1975), 12.

2. Edmund Burke, *A Philosophical Enquiry into the Origin of Our Ideas of the Sublime and the Beautiful,* ed. James T. Boulton (Notre Dame, Ind.: Notre Dame University Press, 1968), 49–50.

3. Here I am influenced by Bill Brown's argument about the epistemological spread of the concept of "play" in the 1890s United States, as exemplified by the case of Stephen Crane's writings of that period. See Bill Brown, *The Material Unconscious: American Amusement, Stephen Crane, and the Economies of Play* (Cambridge, Mass.: Harvard University Press, 1996).

4. I take the term *mass subject* from Michael Warner, *Publics and Counterpublics* (New York: Zone Books, 2002), esp. 159–86.

5. Lucinda Cole, "*The London Merchant* and the Institution of Apprenticeship," *Criticism* 37 (Winter 1995): 57–84, 58.

6. Paul Griffiths, *Youth and Authority: Formative Experiences in England, 1560–1640* (Oxford: Clarendon, 1996), 160–69.

7. See Peter Burke, "Popular Culture in Seventeenth-Century London," in *Popular Culture in Seventeenth-Century England,* ed. Barry Reay (New York: St. Martin's, 1985), 31–58.

8. Moxon, *Mechanick Exercises* (1684), cited in Ellic Howe, ed., *The London Compositor: Documents Relating to Wages, Working Conditions and Customs of the London Printing Trade 1785–1900* (London: The Bibliographical Society, 1947), 23.

9. See Burke, "Popular Culture in Seventeenth-Century London," 34. But Griffiths expresses caution about calling apprentices a culture or subculture, pointing out that there were many different groups within that "amorphous body," which was frequently divided by profession, location, and status. See Griffiths, *Youth and Authority,* 161. His observation is important, not just as a spur to further research, but because it points to the habit of genericization, of assembling a disparate collective of individuals into an intelligible body for the purposes of address and discourse, which is one of the objects of inquiry for this chapter.

10. *The Craftsman,* May 24, 1740, cited in Howe, *The London Compositor,* 29. Howe also reprints an account of an identical ceremony from Thomas Gent's diary, dated 1746, which describes the "Alphabetical anthem, tuned literally to the vowels" (27). On Richardson as apprentice and master, see also T. C. Duncan

Eaves and Ben D. Kimpel, *Samuel Richardson: A Biography* (Oxford: Clarendon, 1971), 42.

11. J. A. Leo Lemay and P. M. Zall, eds., *Benjamin Franklin's Autobiography* (New York: Norton, 1986), 37.

12. These attacks were frequently violent; in the early seventeenth century, the Venetian ambassador wrote that the London apprentices on these occasions "display such unbridled will and are so licentious, that in a body three or four thousand strong they go committing outrages in every direction"; cited in Griffiths, *Youth and Authority*, 149.

13. Ben Jonson, *Bartholemew Fair*, in *The Complete Plays of Ben Jonson*, ed. G. A. Wilkes, based on the edition edited by C. H. Herford and Percy and Evelyn Simpson, 4 vols. (Oxford: Clarendon, 1982), 4:98; Griffiths, *Youth and Authority*, 155. See also Ronald Hutton, *The Stations of the Sun: A History of the Ritual Year in Britain* (Oxford: Oxford University Press, 1996); and Barry Reay, *Popular Cultures in England 1550–1750* (London: Longman, 1998).

14. Griffiths, *Youth and Authority*, 154.

15. Robert D. Hume, *The Development of English Drama in the Late Seventeenth Century* (Oxford: Clarendon, 1976), 302.

16. Ibid., 355.

17. Robert Campbell, *London Tradesman*, cited in John Rule, *The Experience of Labour in Eighteenth-Century Industry* (London: Croom Helm, 1981), 103.

18. Edward Ravenscroft, *The London Cuckolds* (London, 1682), 6.

19. Ibid., 1.

20. Ibid., 40.

21. See E. P. Thompson, "Time, Work-Discipline, and Industrial Capitalism," in *Customs in Common: Studies in Traditional Popular Culture* (New York: The New Press, 1993), 352–403.

22. Christopher Brooks, "Apprenticeship, Social Mobility and the Middling Sort, 1550–1800," in *The Middling Sort of People: Culture, Society, and Politics in England, 1550–1800,* ed. Jonathan Barry and Christopher Brooks (London: Macmillan, 1994), 52–83, 54.

23. O. Jocelyn Dunlop, *English Apprenticeship and Child Labour: A History* (New York: Macmillan, 1912), 196. Peter Linebaugh offers a less sentimental account, one that stresses how the "recomposition of the London proletariat" with the decline of the protections offered by the guild system and the rise of new professions unimagined in the era when the system had been developed and codified as well as new systems of the division of labor changed the traditional systems of rank, work, and personhood in which apprentices had gained public intelligibility. Peter Linebaugh, *The London Hanged: Crime and Civil Society in the Eighteenth Century* (Cambridge: Cambridge University Press, 1992), 15.

24. *Harlequin Hydaspes: or, The Greshamite. A Mock-Opera* (London, 1719), 36.

25. *The Tricks of Harlequin* (Darby, 1739), 19.

26. Fielding, *Tumble-Down Dick*, in *The Works of Henry Fielding, Esq*, ed. Leslie Stephen (London: Smith Elder, 1882), 10:287.

27. I am indebted here to the account of Sheppard's career in Linebaugh, *The London Hanged*, 7–41.

28. The rhetoric here is very close to Richardson's language in his *Seasonable Examination . . . of the Play-Houses* (1735), about which more in the following section: "Because of the shameful Depravity of the *British* Stage, which frequently fetches its Heroes and Heroines from *Newgate* and *Bridewell;* and as every Rogue that has made a Noise for his Enormities in the World, has of late made a prime Character for the Stage; and that not for the Sake of Poetical Justice in his Punishment; but to divert the Audience by his Tricks and Escapes from Justice; to which, if he has been brought at last, it has been in such a Manner, as to move the Pity of the Audience for him;" Samuel Richardson, *A Seasonable Examination of the Pleas and Pretensions of the Proprietors of, and Subscribers to, Play-Houses, Erected in Defiance of the Royal Licence* (London: T. Cooper, 1735), 18.

29. *Authentic Memoirs of the Life and Surprising Adventures of John Sheppard* (London: Joseph Marshall, 1724), 70–71. For more contemporary texts on Jack Sheppard, see John Mullan and Christopher Reid, eds., *Eighteenth-Century Popular Culture: A Selection* (Oxford: Oxford University Press, 2000), 185–201.

30. *Authentic Memoirs*, 53.

31. Theophilus Cibber (or, more probably, someone writing under his name) claimed in 1753 that *The London Merchant* "was often acted in the Christmas and Easter holidays, and judged a proper entertainment for the apprentices &c. as being a more instructive, moral, and cautionary drama, than many pieces that had usually been exhibited on those days, with little but farce and ribaldry to recommend them"; Sir John Hawkins identified the most popular of the earlier "pieces" as *The London Cuckolds*. See Theophilus Cibber, *The Lives of the Poets of Great Britain and Ireland to the Time of Dean Swift*, 5 vols. (London: R. Griffiths, 1753), 5:340. *The Gentleman's Magazine* observed that Garrick had that year "omitted to exhibit that scandalous piece the *London Cuckolds*, on the evening of the lord mayor's day, contrary to immemorial custom"; *The Gentleman's Magazine*, November 1742, 535. *The London Merchant* remained the stock offering for such holidays until 1819, when it was retired, in part as a result of the change in the laws relating to apprenticeship; see Cole, "*The London Merchant* and the Institution of Apprenticeship," 77–79.

32. See Robert D. Hume, *Henry Fielding and the London Theatre 1728–1737* (Oxford: Clarendon, 1988). As Hume describes it, "the 1730s are comparable to the 1660s—a time in which young playwrights learnt their trade and opened up new possibilities in both subject and form. The boom triggered by the unprecedented success of *The Beggar's Opera* in 1728 (just at the start of Fielding's theatrical career) gave rise to heated competition, with up to six companies operating simultaneously, conditions unprecedented since before 1642" (viii).

33. *Seasonable Examination*, 17.

NOTES TO PAGES 155–158   255

34. The most detailed account of the events around both Barnard's bill and the Licensing Act itself is offered in Vincent J. Liesenfeld, *The Licensing Act of 1737* (Madison: University of Wisconsin Press, 1984). I diverge from Liesenfeld's account in having less sympathy than he does for the businessmen who were calling for restrictions on the theater. Liesenfeld takes their testimony at more or less face value, trusting that their complaints about the bad effects of the expansion of the theaters were valid.

35. Barnard was himself a former Lord Mayor of London who is in some library catalogues credited with the most popular of all eighteenth-century manuals for apprentices, *A Present for an Apprentice,* which warns its readers, among other things, against going to the theater "until they have undergone a very thorough Purgation, and appear what they ought to be, the schools of refined Manners, and unblemished Virtue"; *A Present for an Apprentice: Or, a Sure Guide to Gain both Esteem and Estate* (London, 1738), 34. But Barnard is the dedicatee of the book, and thus probably not its author. The sentiment, however, is almost a commonplace, and the fact that Barnard has been taken to be the author is a sign of how well the book seems to represent the ideology of his class.

36. Richardson explains that his interest in the topic is in part propelled by memories of his own experience as an apprentice and the way that his master controlled all the times that might be free for diversion; see *Vade Mecum,* v.

37. *Serious Examination,* 10.

38. Michel Foucault, "'Omnes Et Singulatim': Toward a Critique of Political Reason," in *Power,* ed. James D. Faubion, *Essential Works of Foucault, 1954–1984* (New York: The New Press, 2000), 317.

39. Tobias George Smollett, *The Expedition of Humphry Clinker,* ed. Thomas R. Preston and O. M. Brack (Athens: University of Georgia Press, 1990), 121.

40. John Fielding, *An Account of the Origin and Effects of a Police* (London: A. Millar, 1758), viii.

41. Harry William Pedicord, "George Lillo and 'Speculative Masonry,'" *Philological Quarterly* 53, no. 3 (1974): 401–12, 403.

42. What is more, the Drury Lane prompter, occasional playwright, part-time bookseller, and loyal Mason William Chetwood wrote *The Generous Freemason, or, the Constant Lady,* produced in 1731. In what can only be described as a Masonic-Orientalist fantasy, English lovers escaping from patriarchal proscription at home are saved by the Moorish pirate who initially turned them over to the king of Tunis when he shanghaied their vessel. It turns out that the pirate, Mirza, was born the son of the British consul in Tunis and was forced by the king to convert to Islam. He became a Mason through the good offices of other Englishmen in Tunis, and once he recognizes that Sebastian, one of the fleeing lovers, is a Mason too, he enables Sebastian and his lover Maria to escape. As Sebastian puts it, finding a fellow-Mason in such a place is not all that extraordinary, since "the Brotherhood['s]. . . lustre spreads from Pole to Pole."

43. George Lillo, *The London Merchant,* ed. William H. McBurney (Lincoln: University of Nebraska Press, 1965), 12; hereafter, citations will be given in the text.

44. For more on the indenture, see Cole, "*The London Merchant* and the Institution of Apprenticeship," 59–60.

45. Richardson's sentiments remained an active part of the annual practices of the Stationers' Company for two centuries. The company gave a version of his advice to apprentices as they were bound into the organization, along with a Bible and a book of common prayer, until at least the 1930s. The history of the text is this: in 1732, Richardson wrote a letter to his apprentice and his own nephew Thomas Verren Richardson outlining the duties and expectations—practical and moral—of the role. This letter became the basis for *The Apprentice's Vade Mecum,* which Richardson published two years later. But a revised version of the original letter was printed separately, and was given to incoming apprentices in the Stationers' Company for generations. It was published for a general readership for the first time in *The Imperial Review* of August 1804. Richardson's biographer William Sale records that the Stationers' Company version of the letter was still being distributed to apprentices in the 1930s; see William M. Sale, *Samuel Richardson: Master Printer* (Westport, Conn.: Greenwood, 1977). At some point between then and now, this tradition came to an end, but it is impossible to say at this writing when that occurred. Robin Myers, the archivist of the Stationers' Company, reports that she cannot track down precisely when it was that apprentices stopped being given a copy of Richardson's letter. Apprenticeship itself was abolished in the early 1960s, though some members of the company, she reports, still bind their children "for sentiment's sake" and these incoming members of the company are to this day given a bible and book of common prayer at that point. Personal communication, January 30, 2001.

46. See Robert Darnton, *The Great Cat Massacre and Other Episodes in French Cultural History* (New York: Basic Books, 1984), 88. Darnton's description of the daily life of an eighteenth-century Parisian print shop demonstrates a good deal of overlap between the terminology and practices of workplaces in the two cities.

47. Albert O. Hirschman, *The Passions and the Interests: Political Arguments for Capitalism before Its Triumph* (Princeton, N.J.: Princeton University Press, 1977), 60–63. Lillo is particularly close to Montesquieu's rhetoric in these passages.

48. See Tejumola Olaniyan, "The Ethics and Poetics of a 'Civilizing Mission': Some Notes on Lillo's *The London Merchant*," *English Language Notes* 29 (June 1992): 33–47.

49. For a good recent discussion of Millwood, see Lisa A. Freeman, "Tragic Flaws: Genre and Ideology in Lillo's *London Merchant*," *South Atlantic Quarterly* 98 (1999): 539–61.

50. Diedre Shauna Lynch, *The Economy of Character: Novels, Market Culture, and the Business of Inner Meaning* (Chicago: University of Chicago Press, 1998), 30.

51. See the title page to *The Prison Breaker* (London, 1725), which observes that the play was "intended to be Acted at the Theatre-Royal in Lincoln's-Inn Fields."

52. [Thomas Walker], *The Quaker's Opera, As it is Perform'd at Lee's and Harper's Great Theatrical Booth in Bartholomew Fair* (London, 1728), A3.

53. Steele, *The Spectator* #65 (May 15, 1711), in the Donald F. Bond edition, 1:278.

54. John Dennis, "A Defense of Sir Fopling Flutter," in *The Critical Works of John Dennis*, ed. Edward Niles Hooker, 2 vols. (Baltimore: Johns Hopkins University Press, 1939–43), 2:245.

55. Here I am indebted to James K. Chandler's reading of *The Conscious Lovers* as an example of a new conception of "sentimental probability." See his "Moving Accidents: The Emergence of Sentimental Probability," in *The Age of Cultural Revolutions: Britain and France, 1750–1820*, ed. Colin Jones and Dror Wahrman (Berkeley: University of California Press, 2002), 137–70.

56. Steele, *The Theatre* #3 (January 9, 1720), *Richard Steele's The Theatre 1720*, ed. John Loftis (Oxford: Clarendon, 1962), 9, 10.

57. As Hannah Pitkin puts it, such a representative "does not act for others; he 'stands for' them, by virtue of a correspondence or connection between them, a resemblance or reflection"; Hanna Fenichel Pitkin, *The Concept of Representation* (Berkeley: University of California Press, 1967), 61.

58. Helen Burke, "*The London Merchant* and Eighteenth-Century British Law," *Philological Quarterly* 19 (1993): 347–66.

59. Ibid., 362.

60. Linebaugh, *The London Hanged*, 20. See also John Bender, *Imagining the Penitentiary: Fiction and the Architecture of Mind in Eighteenth-Century England* (Chicago: University of Chicago Press, 1987).

61. *The Weekly Journal*, December 5, 1724, cited in Ronald Paulson, *Hogarth's Graphic Works* (New Haven: Yale University Press, 1970), 1:110.

62. *A Foreign View of England in 1725–29: The Letters of Monsieur Cesar de Saussure to his Family*, trans. and ed. Madame van Muyden (London: Caliban, 1995), 72.

63. Bernard Mandeville, *An Enquiry in the Causes of the Frequent Executions at Tyburn (1725)*, ed. Malvin R. Zirker Jr. (Los Angeles: William Andrews Clark Memorial Library, 1964), A4v; hereafter, cited in the text.

64. Timothy Murray, "Introduction," in *Mimesis, Masochism, and Mime: The Politics of Theatricality in Contemporary French Thought* (Ann Arbor: University of Michigan Press, 1997), 14.

65. Richardson, *Familiar Letters on Important Occasions* (1741; New York: Dodd, Mead, 1928), 220.

66. *British Frenzy, or, the Mock-Apollo* (London: J. Roberts, 1745), 6.

67. Henry Fielding, *Joseph Andrews* and *Shamela*, ed. Douglas Brooks-Davies (Oxford: Oxford University Press 1980), 71.

68. Thomas Cooke, *The Mournful Nuptials* (London, 1739), 72.

69. C. Harold King, "God's Dramatist," in *Studies in Speech and Drama* (Ithaca, N.Y.: Cornell University Press, 1944), 369–92; 369, 386.

70. Ibid., 371.

71. John Rich's wife wrote to John Wesley in 1746 to observe that her husband was adding a song to one of his older pantomimes to the effect that he was not in fact a Methodist. See Albert M. Lyles, *Methodism Mocked: The Satiric Reaction to Methodism in the Eighteenth Century* (London: Epworth, 1960), 17.

72. John Wesley, *The Works of John Wesley: Journal and Diaries III (1743–54),* ed. W. Reginald Ward and Richard P. Heitzenrater (Nashville: Abingdon, 1991), 3.

73. Henry Abelove, *The Evangelist of Desire: John Wesley and the Methodists* (Stanford: Stanford University Press, 1990). Abelove states that Methodists rented unused theaters "at Rochdale, at London, at New Bury, at Wigan, at Sheerness, and at Birmingham" (106).

74. Charles Wesley, *The Journal of the Rev, Charles Wesley, M. A.,* ed. Thomas Jackson, 2 vols. (London: John Mason, 1849), 1:261.

75. L. Tyerman, *Life of the Reverend George Whitfield* (London, 1877), 2:356.

Chapter 6. Harlequin Walpole

1. Henry Fielding, *The Historical Register for the Year 1736,* ed. William W. Appleton (Lincoln: University of Nebraska Press, 1967), 49.

2. See Robert D. Hume, *Henry Fielding and the London Theatre 1728–1737* (Oxford: Clarendon, 1988), 236–37; and J. Paul Hunter, *Occasional Form: Henry Fielding and the Chains of Circumstance* (Baltimore: Johns Hopkins University Press, 1975), 61–67.

3. *The Weekly Journal,* April 6, 1723, 1364.

4. Ibid.

5. Angelica Goodden, *Actio and Persuasion: Dramatic Performance in Eighteenth-Century France* (Oxford: Clarendon, 1986), 100–101.

6. Steele's complaint appears in *The Theatre* #21, March 12, 1720: "These [theatergoers] who did not understand the Language, were, it seems, inform'd by the Gesture of the Actor, the main Drift of the Play, which was no more nor no less than to promote (as one of our own Prologues of King *Charles's* Reign has it) the hopeful Work of *Propagation*"; Steele, reprinted in John Loftis, ed., *Richard Steele's* The Theatre *1720* (Oxford: Clarendon, 1962), 90.

7. *The Grub-Street Journal,* April 8, 1731, 66.

8. *The Weekly Journal,* March 31, 1733, cited in John Loftis, *The Politics of Drama in Augustan England* (Oxford: Clarendon, 1963), 114.

9. Vincent J. Liesenfeld, *The Licensing Act of 1737* (Madison: University of Wisconsin Press, 1984), 67.

10. *The Usefulness of the Stage to Religion and Government* (London, 1738), 25, 11.

11. *The Weekly Journal,* June 15, 1723, 1425.

12. On the *London Journal*'s switch in loyalties, see Laurence Hanson, *Government and the Press 1695–1763* (Oxford: Oxford University Press, 1936), 107–8.

13. *The Touch-Stone* (London, 1728), 94; hereafter, page numbers will be cited in the text.

14. On *The Craftsman,* see Isaac Kramnick, *Bolingbroke and his Circle* (Ithaca, N.Y.: Cornell University Press, 1968).

15. The most recent critic to describe Fielding's complicated relationship to the act is Matthew J. Kinservik, *Disciplining Satire: The Censorship of Satiric Comedy on the Eighteenth-Century London Stage* (Lewisburg: Bucknell University Press, 2002), esp. 55–94.

16. See Paul Langford, *The Excise Crisis: Society and Politics in the Age of Walpole* (Oxford: Clarendon, 1975), George Rudé, "'Mother Gin' and the London Riots of 1736," in *Paris and London in the Eighteenth Century* (New York: Viking, 1971).

17. Thomas Lockwood, "John Kelley's 'Lost' Play *The Fall of Bob* (1736)," *English Language Notes* 22 (1984): 27–32.

18. Henry Fielding, *The History of Tom Jones, a Foundling,* with an introduction by Martin C. Battestin, text edited by Fredson Bowers (Middletown, Conn.: Wesleyan University Press, 1975), 213–14.

19. Here I am indebted to William Warner's description of Fielding's ironizing tendencies, as well as his pointing to other places where Fielding can be compared to Rich. See, for example, his discussion of the similar "predicament" faced by the reader of *Joseph Andrews* and the spectator of a pantomime as Fielding describes it in *The Champion* for April 22, 1740: *Licensing Entertainment,* 273–74. Where I part company slightly is assuming that this only has to do with the phenomenon of novel-reading, and is not a problem for entertainment in a sense that pertains equally well in the theater.

20. William J. Burling, "Fielding, His Publishers, and John Rich in 1730," *Theatre Survey* 26, no. 1 (1985): 39–46.

21. Cited in *Essays on the Theatre from Eighteenth-Century Periodicals,* ed. John Loftis (Los Angeles: Clark Memorial Library Publications, 1960), 17.

22. Aaron Hill and William Popple, *The Prompter: A Theatrical Paper (1734–1736),* ed. William W. Appleton and Kalman A. Burnim (New York: Benjamin Blom, 1966), 166.

23. Ibid., 168.

24. Fielding, *The Author's Farce* (London, 1730), 55; hereafter, cited in the text.

25. Jill Campbell, *Natural Masques: Gender and Identity in Fielding's Plays and Novels* (Stanford, Calif.: Stanford University Press, 1995), 20.

26. Fielding, *The Craftsman* #403 (March 23, 1734), in Martin C. Battestin, *New Essays by Henry Fielding: His Contributions to the Craftsman, 1734–1739 and Other Early Journalism* (Charlottesville: University Press of Virginia, 1989), 24.

27. *The Champion* (April 22, 1740), in the Leslie Stephen edition of *The Works of Henry Fielding,* 5:417.

28. Such a taxonomy is deeply indebted, as Martin Battestin has argued, to Fielding's intimacy with James Ralph in the late 1720s, a friendship that surely led Fielding to do a close reading of Ralph's *The Touch-Stone,* which also takes up each of these types of entertainment in turn. There is a sense in which Ralph and *The Touch-Stone,* which seems not to have been successful as a book—its "second edition," retitled *The Taste of the Town* and issued in 1731, consists largely of unsold sheets from the first press run, repackaged with a new title page—were influential in setting a program for the London theater of the 1730s. Noting that one of the "*True Britons,* and stanch *Protestants*" have often opposed Italian opera on nationalistic grounds, Ralph proposes that English theater managers adapt native plot material to modern operatic entertainment, and cites (among others) the stories of Tom Thumb, the "London 'prentice," and the dragon of "Wantcliff" as likely candidates for such a program. Each of these would in fact become an enormously popular work of the 1730s London stage, in the forms of Fielding's *The Tragedy of Tragedies,* George Lillo's *The London Merchant* (1731), and Henry Carey's *The Dragon of Wantley* (1737), one of the most popular afterpieces of the period, which in part turns the ballad story into an allegory of Walpole's Excise scheme. There is no way of proving Ralph's direct influence in any of these specific cases, but it is especially hard not to think that Fielding in particular took Ralph's tongue-in-cheek proposal as a prompt, given what we know about how closely they were working and playing in these years.

29. Fielding, *Pasquin,* in *Works,* 10:184.

30. Here I agree with William Warner's analysis of the antiabsorptive narrative strategy that Fielding adopts in his fiction, which I see as part and parcel of his practice in the theater as well.

31. *Some Thoughts on the Present State of the Theatres, and the Consequences of an Act to destroy the Liberty of the Stage,* reprinted in *The Daily Journal,* March 25, 1737.

32. See Kinservik, *Disciplining Satire,* 55–94.

33. On the annualized account, see James Chandler, *England in 1819: The Politics of Literary Culture and the Case of Romantic Historicism* (Chicago: University of Chicago Press, 1998), esp. 122–25.

34. "Introduction" to *The Historical Register* (London, 1717), ii.

35. On these events, see, for instance Rudé, "Mother Gin and the London Riots of 1736"; and Jessica Warner and Frank Ivis, "'Damn You, You Informing Bitch,' *Vox Populi* and the Unmaking of the Gin Act of 1736," *Journal of Social History* (Winter 1999): 299–330.

36. See E. P. Thompson, "Patricians and Plebs," in *Customs in Common: Studies in Traditional Popular Culture* (New York: The New Press, 1993), 16–96, esp. 45–83.

37. *The Historical Register for the Year 1737* (London, 1738), 379.

38. Fielding, *Eurydice Hiss'd,* in Stephen ed., 10:263; hereafter, cited in the text.

39. Historical Mss. Commission, Egmont's *Diary,* II. 390, cited in Martin Battestin and Ruthe R. Battestin, *Henry Fielding, A Life* (London: Routledge, 1993), 221.

40. Ibid.

41. On the likelihood that Fielding's silence was bought by Walpole, see Battestin, *Henry Fielding,* 221; and Hume, *Henry Fielding and the London Theatre 1728–1737,* 252–53.

Chapter 7. David Garrick and the Institutionalization of English Pantomime

1. Joseph R. Roach, *The Player's Passion: Studies in the Science of Acting* (Newark: University of Delaware Press, 1985), 56.

2. David Garrick to Peter Garrick, in *The Letters of David Garrick,* ed. David M. Little and George M. Kahrl, 3 vols. (Cambridge, Mass.: Belknap, 1963), 1:34.

3. Garrick, *The Theatrical Candidates,* in *The Plays of David Garrick,* ed. Harry William Pedicord and Fredrick Louis Bergmann, 2 vols. (Carbondale: Southern Illinois University Press, 1980), 2:314.

4. *The Case Between the Managers of the Two Theatres, and their Principal Actors, Fairly Stated, and Submitted to the Town* (London: J. Roberts, 1743), 3.

5. Garrick to Lieutenant Edward Thompson (September 12, 1766), *Letters,* 2:542.

6. Theophilus Cibber, *Theophilus Cibber, To David Garrick, Esq., With Dissertations on Theatrical Subjects* (London, 1759), 56.

7. Thomas Morris, *Miscellanies in Prose and Verse* (London, 1791), 45.

8. Ibid., 44.

9. Letter from "Phillippus," in *The Monitor,* October 24, 1767, 5.

10. John Weaver, *The History of the Mimes and Pantomimes* (London: J. Roberts, 1728), 28.

11. Aaron Hill, *The Prompter* 66 (June 27, 1735), in *The Prompter: A Theatrical Paper (1734–1736),* ed. William W. Appleton and Kalman A. Burnim (New York: Benjamin Blom, 1966), 85.

12. David Garrick, *An Essay on Acting,* in *Actors on Acting,* ed. Toby Cole and Helen Krich Chinoy, rev. ed. (New York: Crown, 1970), 133–35.

13. Jane Moody, *Illegitimate Theatre in London, 1770–1840* (Cambridge: Cambridge University Press, 2000), 17–18.

14. Henry Fielding, "An Enquiry into the Causes of the Late Increase of Robbers," in *An Enquiry into the Causes of the Late Increase of Robbers and Related Writings,* ed. Malvin R. Zirker, 81; hereafter, citations will appear in the text.

15. Henry Fielding, "A Proposal for Making an Effectual Provision for the Poor," in *An Enquiry into the Causes of the Late Increase of Robbers and Related Writings,* ed. Zirker, 230.

16. Fielding also notes that English law has made provision for diversions and pastimes at certain times, but the frame of reference he constructs is conspicuously broader than one comprehending English customs alone.

17. Fielding also attacked the "Fury after licentious and luxurious Pleasures" in his *Charge Delivered to the Grand Jury at the Sessions of the Peace Held for the City and Liberty of Westminster* (1749), printed in Zirker's edition of *An Enquiry into the Causes of the Late Increase of Robbers and Related Writings*, 24.

18. *The Scourge* 14, reprinted in the *Gentleman's Magazine* 23, December 1752, 582.

19. Arthur Murphy, *The Life of David Garrick, Esq.*, 2 vols. (1801; New York: Benjamin Blom, 1969), 2:164, 161.

20. See Michael Dobson, *The Making of the National Poet: Shakespeare, Adaptation, and Authorship, 1660–1789* (Oxford: Clarendon, 1992).

21. Ibid., 2.

22. Garrick, "Occasional Prologue, Spoken by Mr. Garrick at the Opening of Drury-Lane Theatre, 8 Sept. 1750," in *The Poetical Works of David Garrick,* 2 vols. (1785; New York: Benjamin Blom, 1968), 1:103.

23. See Dobson, *The Making of the National Past*, 176–84; and Denise Sechelski, "Garrick's Body and the Labor of Art in Eighteenth-Century Theater," *Eighteenth-Century Studies* 29 (Summer 1996): 369–89.

24. See the dedication to Lewis Theobald, *Shakespeare Restored: Or, a Specimen of the Many Errors, as Well Committed, as Unamended by Mr. Pope in His Late Edition of This Poet* (London, 1726).

25. Homi K. Bhabha, "Dissemination: Time, Narrative, and the Margins of the Modern Nation," in *The Location of Culture* (London: Routledge, 1994), 139–70, 145.

26. Jonathan Bate, *Shakespearean Constitutions: Politics, Theatre, Criticism 1730–1830* (Oxford: Clarendon, 1989), 28.

27. Ibid., v.

28. For a much fuller discussion of the period's canonization of Shakespeare, see Jonathan Brody Kramnick, *Making the English Canon: Print-Capitalism and the Cultural Past, 1700–1775* (Cambridge: Cambridge University Press, 1998), 107–36.

29. All of these pantomimes had been composed by Henry Woodward, who was also Drury Lane's Harlequin. Woodward took over the management of a theater in Dublin in 1758, leaving it to Garrick to craft a new pantomime for the 1759 Christmas season, which became *Harlequin's Invasion*. It as not as though pantomimes stopped being performed at other times of the year; even during the mid-Victorian period, they were staged in other seasons. But with Garrick, it became customary to expect the theater companies to put forth their best new efforts for the Christmas pantomime, enforcing a strong association between pantomime and the Christmas holidays.

30. I base this figure on the performance record in Mitchell Preston Wells's 1934 dissertation, "Pantomime and Spectacle on the London Stage, 1714–1761" (Ph.D. diss., University of North Carolina, 1934), 222–448.

31. *OED*, s.v. "gambol." Similarly, Addison's Sir Roger de Coverley, the most archaic figure in the club, expresses his satisfaction with the "*Christmas* Gambols" that cheer up his rural tenants; Addison, *Spectator* #269 (January 8, 1712), in the Donald F. Bond edition, 2:550.

32. George Winchester Stone Jr. and George M. Kahrl, *David Garrick: A Critical Biography* (Carbondale: Southern Illinois University Press, 1979), 221.

33. *Queries to be Answered by the Manager of the Drury-Lane Theatre* (London, 1743), 10.

34. See Stone and Kahrl, *David Garrick,* 221.

35. The similarity between *Harlequin Student* and *Harlequin's Invasion* was first noticed by Elizabeth Stein, who edited the first published edition of Garrick's play; see her edition of *Three Plays by David Garrick* (New York: William Edwin Rudge, 1926). I will be using Harry Pedicord and Fredrick Bergmann's edition of *Harlequin's Invasion,* printed in *The Plays of David Garrick,* 1:199–225. Page references will appear in the text.

36. Sechelski, "Garrick's Body and the Labor of Art in Eighteenth-Century Theatre," 376.

37. On eighteenth-century tailors, see *Select Documents Illustrating the History of Trade Unionism, I. The Tailoring Trade,* ed. F. W. Galton (London: Longmans, Green, 1896).

38. Peter Linebaugh notes that tailoring was frequently associated with thievery; its mythical origins lay in the theft of the arts by Prometheus, and modern tailors were frequently suspected of using their shears liberally in order to produce large amounts of "cabbage," the excess cloth that was considered theirs by customary right. See Linebaugh, *The London Hanged,* 241–48.

39. 17 George II, c. 5 in *Statutes at Large,* 40.

40. The text of *Harlequin and Humpo* has recently been reconstituted in *The Broadview Anthology of Romantic Drama,* ed. Jeffrey N. Cox and Michael Gamer (Peterborough, Ont.: Broadview, 2003), 205–20.

41. See David Mayer, *Harlequin in his Element: The English Pantomime, 1806–1836* (Cambridge, Mass.: Harvard University Press, 1969).

42. On the history of nineteenth- and early twentieth-century pantomime in England, see A. E. Wilson, *King Panto: The Story of Pantomime* (New York: Dutton, 1935).

Bartholomew Fair, 35, 165, 214

Battestin, Martin, 207

Behn, Aphra, 46–47. Works: *The Emperor of the Moon*, 43, 45–46, 119, 122, 225; *Oroonoko*, 124–25, 128

Bender, John, 172

Betterton, Thomas, 80, 83, 209, 213–14

Bhabha, Homi, 134–36, 222

"Blacks, The," 127–29, 133, 250n. 25

Booth, Barton: as Cato, 80; compared to Garrick, 213; and Charles Le Brun, 80; and Hester Santlow, 24; and Steele, 245n. 34

Bourne, Henry, 57, 241n. 47

British Frenzy: Or, the Mock-Apollo, 118, 176

Brooks, Christopher, 149

Brown, Bill, 5

Brown, Thomas, 108

Browne, Sir Thomas, 122

Burbage, Richard, 42

Burke, Edmund, 139

Burke, Helen, 171

Burke, Peter, 36–37

Campbell, Jill, 196

Carey, Henry, 260n. 28

casuistry, 40, 47, 51, 54, 99, 241n. 42

Centlivre, Susanna, 98. Works: *The Basset Table*, 68; *The Perjur'd Husband*, 98; *The Wonder: A Woman Keeps a Secret*, 10

Chambers, E. K., 118

Chandler, James, 241n. 42

Chapman, George, 5

Chartier, Roger, 37

Chetwood, William, 127, 255n. 42; *A General History of the Stage*, 241n. 38

Cibber, Colley: and Fielding, 199; on Harlequin's mask, 120, 122, 251n. 31; on theater buildings, 244n. 21; and Whiggism, 98. Works: *Apology for the Life of Colley Cibber*, 72, 83, 119, 244n. 21; *Love's Last Shift*, 127

Cibber, Theophilus: and Fielding, 199; and Garrick, 213; as Harlequin, 58; and Masonry, 158; on theater audiences, 69

classification, 38, 129, 132; and apprentices, 142, 158, 252n. 9; and "The Blacks," 129; and entertainment, 216; and Hadley 238n. 14; and McKeon, 242n. 4; and pantomime, 88; and Stage Licensing Act, 216

Cole, Lucinda, 141

Collier, Jeremy, xv–xvi, 28, 31, 33, 48–57, 88, 98–99, 129–30, 196

commedia dell'arte: and Goldoni, 39; Harlequin within, 119, 150; and monarchy, 46; Renaissance adaptations of, 42, 95; Restoration adaptations of, 43, 95; and Shakespeare, 42–43, 130; and Steele, 185; traced to ancient Rome, 129

Comparison Between the Two Stages, A, 33, 49

Congreve, William: *The Judgment of Paris*, 91; and Whiggism, 98

Cooke, Thomas, *The Mournful Nuptials*, 176, 178

Craftsman, The: and Fielding, 197; and print shops, 143; and Walpole, 103, 191

Crary, Jonathan, 77

criminal justice system: and entertainment, xxiii, 149–54, 171–75; and Fielding, 216–19

Crowne, John, *Sir Courtly Nice*, 100–101

Fielding, Henry (*continued*)
  Andrews, 176; *Pasquin*, 195, 198, 204; *A Proposal for Making an Effectual Provision for the Poor*, 217; *Tom Jones*, 193–94; *Tragedy of Tragedies*, 194, 260n. 28; *Tumble-Down Dick*, 151, 193, 204
Fielding, John, 157–58
Fiorelli, Tiberio, 43, 144
Fischer-Lichte, Erika, 58
Fletcher, John, 74, 93
Foote, Samuel, 179–80
footmen: riots over, 203–4; in theater audiences, 64, 67
Foucault, Michel, xvii, 45, 88, 157. *See also* governmentality; police
Franklin, Benjamin, 143
Freud, Sigmund, 22
Frye, Northrup, 10

Galliard, Thomas, 3
Garrick, David: and Cibber, 119; and Harlequin, 209–10, 214; and *Harlequin Student*, 209–10, 263n. 35; and Johnson, 115, 208; and *The London Cuckolds*, 155, 254n. 31; and pantomime, xxiv, 115, 136, 209–31; and public sphere, 207, 209; and Quin, 214; and Rich, 227; and Shakespeare, xxiv, 209, 222–28; and theatrical lighting, 243n. 13; and Whitefield, 179. Works: *Chinese Festival*, 243n. 12; *Essay on Acting*, 214; *Harlequin's Invasion*, xxiv, 135, 151, 210, 219, 222, 225–31, 262n. 29, 263n. 35; "Heart of Oak," 222; *The Theatrical Candidates*, 210
Gay, John: *The Beggar's Opera*, 11, 12, 103, 139, 151, 155, 158, 165, 192, 243n. 12, 254n. 32; *Polly*, 192

Giffard, Henry, 155–58. Works: *Harlequin Shipwreck*, 185; *Harlequin Student*, 209–10, 221, 227, 263n. 35
Gildon, Charles, *The Life of Thomas Betterton*, 80, 88, 214
Gin Act, 185, 192, 202, 204, 206
Goldoni, Carlo: and commedia dell'arte, 39, 238n. 16; and Harlequin, 131–33
Goodden, Angela, 184
governmentality: and absolutist monarchy, 45; defined by Foucault, xvii; and entertainment, 201; and Fielding, 200–205, 216–19; and Garrick, 229–30; and *The Historical Register* (journal), 201; and theaters, 212–13, 215–16. *See also* police
Gozzi, Carlo, 131
Gutenberg, Johann, and John Faustus, 106, 108

Habermas, Jürgen, xv–xvi, 47–48, 72, 102. *See also* public sphere
Hadley, Elaine, 238n. 14, 243nn. 12, 16
Hansen, Miriam, 244n. 22
Harlequin: and apprentices, 150; and blackface, 118–37; compared to Shakespeare, 135–36, 210, 219–28; as criminal, 138, 150–54, 229–30; as dangerous example, xxiii, 138–40; embodiment of, 58, 227; and Methodism, 175, 177–78; and nationalism, 226–27; and "the people," 58; performed as "Harlequine," 24; and politics, 96, 104, 181–208; performed by John Rich, 3, 60, 94; traced to ancient Rome, 130–31; traced to Renaissance Italy, 131; and Walpole, xxiii, 186. *See also* pantomime

Harley, Robert, 99
Harrington, James, 144
Hay, Douglas, 25
Haywood, Eliza, 72
Hertz, Neil, 22
Hill, Aaron: and Fielding, 195–96;
  and pantomime, 214
Historical Register, The (journal),
  200–203
History of the Blacks, The, 128
Hogarth, William: and Methodism,
  176; and pantomime, 12–13, 91, 115,
  176–78, 215, 230 Works: *Credulity,
  Superstition, and Fanaticism*,
  176–78; *The Harlot's Progress*, 91;
  Industry and Idleness, 149; illustra-
  tions to *Perseus and Andromeda*,
  12–13
Horkheimer, Max, 7, 28
Hume, Robert: and 1730s, 155, 254n.
  32; and Tiberio Fiorilli, 144; and
  The London Cuckolds, 145

James I, *Book of Sportes*, 44, 46, 101
Jameson, Fredric: and mass culture,
  27–28; and political unconscious, 5
Johns, Adrian, 106
Johnson, Samuel: and theater, xviii,
  115. Works: *Irene*, 207; *Preface to
  Shakespeare*, 15, 223
Jonson, Ben: and commedia
  dell'arte, 42; and Shakespeare, 220.
  Works: *Bartholomew Fair*, 143–44;
  The Masque of Blackness, 125;
  Workes, 43

Kramnick, Jonathan Brody, 234n. 5
Kroll, Richard, 62

Langbaine, Gerard: *Account of the
  English Dramatick Poets*, 48;

Momus Triumphans, 33
language: material aspects of,
  xvii–xviii, 49, 62, 74–75; pan-
  tomime as universal, 62, 88
Lea, Kathleen, 42
LeBrun, Charles: and Dennis, 167;
  and the passions, 79–81, 167; and
  Steele, 81
Lewis, Elizabeth, 24
Liesenfeld, Vincent, 185
Lillo, George, *The London Mer-
  chant*, xv–xviii, 140–41, 148,
  154–64, 167–72, 218, 224, 254n. 31,
  260n. 28
Linebaugh, Peter, 153–54, 172, 263n.
  38
Lockwood, Thomas, 192
London Cuckolds, The. See Ravens-
  croft, Edward
London Merchant, The. See Lillo,
  George
Lott, Eric, 5
Lynch, Diedre, 163

Macky, John, 68
Mandeville, Bernard, *An Enquiry
  into the Causes of the Frequent
  Executions at Tyburn*, 173–75
Marcus, Leah, 44
Marlowe, Christopher, *Doctor Faustus*, xxii, 95, 105
Marmontel, Jean-François, 130, 133
Marvell, Andrew, 46
Masonry, 158–59, 255n. 42
masque, Stuart court: as antecedent
  for pantomime, 15, 40–41; and "the
  people," 41; reconceived by Motteux, 41
mass culture: as aspect of modernity,
  xiii; complexity of, 271; and politics, 188